RENEWALS 458-4574
DATE DUE

WITHDRAWN
UTSA LIBRARIES

INTERNATIONAL COMPARATIVE SOCIAL STUDIES

EDITORIAL BOARD

DUANE ALWIN, Ann Arbor, USA - WIL ARTS, Tilburg, The Netherlands
MATTEI DOGAN, Paris, France - S.N. EISENSTADT, Jerusalem, Israel
JOHAN GALTUNG, Versonnex, France - LINDA HANTRAIS, Loughborough, UK
JIM KLUEGEL, Urbana-Champaign, USA
CHAN KWOK BUN, Hongkong, China - FRANK LECHNER, Atlanta, USA
RON LESTHAEGHE, Brussels, Belgium - OLA LISTHAUG, Trondheim, Norway
RUBIN PATTERSON, Toledo, USA - EUGENE ROOSENS, Leuven, Belgium
MASAMICHI SASAKI, Tokyo, Japan - SASKIA SASSEN, New York, USA
JOHN RUNDELL, Melbourne, Australia - LIVY VISANO, Toronto, Canada
BERND WEGENER, Berlin, Germany - JOCK YOUNG, London, UK

VOLUME VI

YOUTH AND WORK IN THE POST-INDUSTRIAL CITY OF NORTH AMERICA AND EUROPE

With an Epilogue by Saskia Sassen

EDITED BY

LAURENCE ROULLEAU-BERGER

BRILL
LEIDEN · BOSTON
2003

This book is printed on acid-free paper.

Die Deutsche Bibliothek – CIP-Einheitsaufnahme

Bibliographic information published by Die Deutsche Bibliothek
Die Deutsche Bibliothek lists this publication in the Deutsche
Nationalbibliografie ; detailed bibliographic data are
available in the Internet at http://dnb.ddb.de.

Library of Congress Cataloging-in-Publication Data

The Library of Congress Cataloging-in-Publication Data is also available

Library
University of Texas
at San Antonio

ISSN 1568-4474
ISBN 90 04 12533 7

© Copyright 2003 by Koninklijke Brill NV, Leiden, The Netherlands
Cover design by Thorsten's Celine Ostendorf

All rights reserved. No part of this publication may be reproduced, translated, stored in
a retrieval system, or transmitted in any form or by any means, electronic,
mechanical, photocopying, recording or otherwise, without prior written
permission from the publisher.

Authorization to photocopy items for internal or personal
use is granted by Brill provided that
the appropriate fees are paid directly to The Copyright
Clearance Center, 222 Rosewood Drive, Suite 910
Danvers MA 01923, USA.
Fees are subject to change.

PRINTED IN THE NETHERLANDS

CONTENTS

Introduction
by Laurence Roulleau-Berger 1

1. INEQUALITIES AND DISCRIMINATIONS AT SCHOOL

François Dubet
Youth experience, socialization and inequalities in France 11

Pedro A. Noguera
Racial isolation, poverty and the limits of local control as a
means for holding public schools accountable 43

Jean-Paul Payet
The paradox of ethnicity in French secondary schools 59

Madeleine Gauthier
Qui s'instruit s'enrichit? Re-examining standards and
barriers in education in Quebec 72

2. INCERTITUDES AND REVERSIBILITIES IN BIOGRAPHIES

Paul Anisef and Paul Axelrod
Baby boomers in transition: Life-course experiences of the
'class of '73' [in Canada] 91

Claude Trottier, Mircea Vultur and Madeleine Gauthier
Vocational integration and relationship to work among
Quebec youths without high-school diplomas 106

Juan A. Santos Ortega
'Long term youth': Discontinuity in labor profiles of young
Spanish people in the age of informational flexibility 122

Andy Furlong and Fred Cartmel
Explaining transitions through individualised rationality
(in the UK) 136

3. YOUTH, EMPLOYMENT POLICIES AND SOCIAL PRACTICES

Eric Verdier
The negotiation of vocational education qualifications: an efficient alternative to the deregulation of the youth labour market? 155

Diane-Gabrielle Tremblay
Juggling youth unemployment and employment precariousness in Canada and in Quebec: from a social to a more liberal approach to employment policies? 175

Constanza Tobío
The younger generation of Spanish mothers in the family and in the workplace 190

Frank Braun
Labour market policies and youth in Germany from the early 50s until today 204

4. WORK, YOUTH AND IMMIGRATION

Myriam Simard
Regional youth of immigrant origin in Quebec: Innovative relationship to work 217

Claire Schiff
Work, youth and immigration in France 232

Julio J. Cammarota
Channeling Latino youth into the low-wage trap: Race and class polarization in California 247

Min Zhou
Making it in urban America: Challenges and prospects for the children of contemporary immigrants 265

5. YOUTH AS SECOND-CLASS WORKPLACE CITIZENS

Stuart Tannock
Why do working youth work where they do? 285

Robert Castel
Do young people have a specific relationship to work (in France)? 304

Jacques Hamel
Young people and work in Quebec: taking stock 319

Laurence Roulleau-Berger
Economic disqualification and social differenciation in the post-industrial city: youth, work and marginalization in France 336

6. YOUTH AND MARGINALIZATION IN THE POST-INDUSTRIAL CITY

Michel Peraldi
The law of networks: case histories of second-generation immigrants in the worlds of trade 357

Vladimir I. Chuprov, Julia A. Zubok
Russian Youth and Work: Social Integration and Exclusion Under Conditions of Risk 378

Roch Hurtubise, Shirley Roy and Céline Bellot
Youth homelessness: the street and work, from exclusion to integration 395

Loïc Wacquant
Labour market insecurity and the criminalization of poverty 408

Saskia Sassen
Epilogue: Transversal anchorings among youth today 420

Notes on contributors 427

INTRODUCTION

Laurence Roulleau-Berger

We live in a global society characterized by reticular social structures and processes of individualization, rationalization and social differentiation. In this society shaped by the information technology revolution and the restructuring of capitalism, which has made work more flexible and unstable, the individualization of labour raises, most vitally, the question of the globalization of economic activities. Work is becoming increasingly individualized and taking place in a multiplicity of different locations, thereby creating a sort of faceless collective capitalism structured around a network of financial flows that is very much alive in the global cities that are the centres of globalized processes ranging from international finance to immigration (Sassen, 1991; Castells, 1996). These structural trends have given rise to employment systems that reinforce social inequalities and in which the least skilled are regularly excluded and relegated to deskilling and deskilled jobs and ethnic segmentation seems to be becoming ever more pronounced, giving rise to a new social narrative in the process.

These changes in the organization of an economic space of variable geometry have conspired in recent years to blur or even uproot identities, particularly among the most vulnerable populations, such as the young, women and migrants. Amid this confusion, new, cross-cutting anchoring points for economic activity and individual identities are being mapped out (Sassen, 2001), linked by more or less visible lines along which the impoverished populations move. Paradoxically, informal, non-monetary, non-market economies have once again taken on an obvious importance; at the same time, the wholesale restructuring of the global economy has caused 'black holes' of poverty and discrimination to proliferate in the global cities of Europe and North America. Risk is certainly an inherent part of globalisation. Indeed, the global risk society renders impracticable any attempt to predict or control the future consequences of human actions or the unintentional effects of radical modernization (Beck, 1999).

Young people and the insecurity of wage work

In 'risk societies' the conditions under which young people enter the labour market have changed radically in the last thirty years. The slowdown in economic growth has affected the social groups in different and unequal ways. It is the younger generations of the working classes that have been most affected; they have been hit by the rise of services and exploding unemployment, which has squeezed them out of the labour market and created a completely deskilled population. Young working-class people of foreign origin have felt the effects of this exclusion from the social structure particularly badly; consequently, it has been particularly difficult for them, in some cases impossible, even to gain a toehold on the established pathways of upward or downward social mobility. Many of them, having no access to the labour market, develop forms of *horizontal mobility*, moving from one precarious work situation to another and the forms taken by this mobility vary depending on the societal context. Whereas the forms of upward or downward social mobility associated with changes of social status in the wage society shed light on the evolution of social structures, the various forms of horizontal mobility reflect what happens in the darker recesses of society. Fewer and fewer young people, particularly the academically least well endowed, are obtaining access to wage work. Consequently, they are finding it increasingly difficult to acquire a status in society, a place in the social space; they see themselves being socially disqualified. These young people are the victims of the stalling of the processes of upward social mobility that characterized the three decades of economic growth following the Second World War, a period that saw radical changes in the employment structure and the expansion of the service sector in liberal societies. Age, a factor that used not to be very discriminatory, has become a factor in intergenerational inequalities. The economic slowdown has created a crisis of transmission that spares nobody but hits the working classes harder because the handing on of status from father to son has been hindered by the devalorization of the working classes, by work intensification, by the increasing precariousness of employment relationships and by the multiple downgrading processes arising out of the ferocious competition between academic qualifications (Baudelot, Establet, 2000; Beaud, Pialoux, 1999).

Inequalities and discriminations in school

The education system continues to function as if young people's trajectories were predictable. In doing so, it contributes actively both to the proliferation of hierarchies of social inequalities (cf. Dubet in Part 1) that manifest themselves in the phenomenon of school dropout (cf. Gauthier in Part 1) and to the production or indeed the reproduction of the inequalities linked to ethnic origin (cf. Payet in Part 1; Noguera in Part 1) that precede the processes of discrimination that determine access to employment. Given the increasingly precarious nature of wage work, young people are exposed to very considerable social risks: the academically least able may well not gain access to a 'position' at all, while the more able are often able only to gain access to segments of the labour market reserved for young people that offer very little in the way of occupational socialization. Forty years ago in various wage societies, a good half of young people aged between 15 and 25 were in employment; today, young workers in this age group are disappearing. Moreover, those young people between 15 and 25 who are active in the labour market appear to be increasingly less skilled than the average young entrant (Nicole-Drancourt, Rouleau-Berger, 2001). Indeed, the relationships between the education market and the labour market are continuously being distorted and this distortion is reflected in a widening gap between the nominal value of qualifications and their value as measured in terms of transactions in the labour market. And the dual phenomenon of mass higher education and the increased length of time spent in the education system has done nothing to reduce social differentiation, since inflation in qualifications has helped to reinforce social inequalities.

Uncertainties and reversibilities in young people's life course

The life course of young people today seems to be increasingly less linear and increasingly more fragmented, diversified and complex (Ortega in Part 2). Entry into the world of work seems to be an increasingly complex and uncertain process. The relationship between young people and work in an environment in which wage work is becoming more and more precarious reveals the complexity of a modernity characterized by insecurities, uncertainties and reversibilities in employment situations that make it difficult for individuals to map out their paths and hasten the fragmentation of identities (Taylor, 1998). Uncertainty is a fact of life for all of them but they do not all have at their disposal the same resources for managing that uncertainty in societies increasingly shaped by a heightened process of 'structured individualization' (Furlong, Cartmel and Anisef and Axelrod in Part 2). The cleavages caused by social differences seem to be less clearly visible when the inequalities between those who can and those who cannot find employment in the wage society are not weakened but strengthened. In increasingly polarized societies, access to the labour market for populations of foreign origin seems really to be hierarchized: access and treatment differ with regard not only to sector of activity but also to employment status, pay, work schedules and career trajectories. This gives rise to what might be called 'segmented assimilation' (Portes and Zhou, 1993; Zhou, 1997), with entry into the labour market differentiated and hierarchized on the basis of ethnic origin and gender (cf. Tobio in Part 3), generational position, linguistic skills, urban morphologies, family relationships and networks, and educational and qualificational levels (cf. Schiff and Simard in Part 4). Although it has remained little investigated in Quebec and is in its early stages in Europe, ethnic origin very quickly emerged in American research as a key factor in determining access to employment, with standard theories on assimilation initially showing how the children and grandchildren of immigrants gradually acceded to the social statuses of the host society and that this process had an element of irreversibility about it. Today, however, other studies show that the process whereby young people of the new second generations enter the labour market is reversible. Intergenerational mobility seems to be increasingly less linear and may give rise to a 'segmented assimilation' that reflects the irregular, non-mechanistic, unexpected, multidimensional and differentiated aspects of the process of labour market integration (cf. Min Zhou in Part 4).

Public disqualification and fragmentation of the employment relationship

As they are forced to move from one uncertain situation to another, young people experience a loss of both resources and a sense of self (Roulleau-Berger in Part 4) that manifests itself in the management or government of the self, which Foucault (1984) terms 'the culture of self'. The more contrasted and disjointed the situations that have to be managed seem to be, the more retrospective losses individuals suffer (Sennett, 2000), with those losses in turn playing an active part in fragmenting social identities and putting individuals at risk of disqualification and social contempt. The risk of being socially despised, of being relegated to the ranks of the least competitive in the name of the principles governing the global economy has become increasingly great for all those who seem to be socially invisible, particularly those without jobs or status, who very quickly come to feel that they are socially useless. The experience of being despised in this way diminishes young people, making them incapable of demonstrating their true qualities anywhere; they become so small that they render themselves invisible.

Thus young people living with precariousness have a complex relationship to work that is characterized by the emergence of 'double binds' among individuals caught between the injunction to work and the impossibility of gaining access to the standard forms of employment; and it depends on the nature and the quality of social and familial ressources (cf. Castel in Part 5). Young people's aspirations have become gradually blurred, restricted and hardened, while work has increasingly given rise to a fear of never achieving a stable position in the labour market, of never being able to obtain a job that is both skilled and skilling (cf. Trottier, Vultur Gauthier in Part 2). Deprived, exploited and forced to work in the places where they are also consumers (cf. Tannock in Part 5), these young people's experiences confirm them in the belief that work is a cause of suffering and a reason for revolt against their relegation to the lowest rungs of the social structure. The process of social disqualification produces disillusion and then plays an active part in blurring young people's aspirations and in creating double binds, which do not necessarily give rise to more distanced relationships to work but rather reveal that wage work remains a basic vector in the construction of social identities (cf. Hamel in Part 5).

The increasing precariousness of wage work and public action

Depending on the historical, political and economic context, capitalist societies developed various forms of welfare state through public policies linking economic development, the acquisition of social rights and the market. Each society then constructed its own particular forms of public action depending on the nature of the link between the public reference points and the basic societal territorialized agreements (cf. Verdier in Part 3). As a result, the mechanisms of labour market integration are now becoming increasingly territorialized (cf. Braun in Part 3). France seems to constitute a specific case compared with the other European countries, particularly Germany and the United Kingdom, where young people have only limited choices. In France, as in Spain, there is a diversity of entry mechanisms that generate positive discrimination and increasingly bring into play actors linked to the labour market and the public authorities. Despite the development of policies on labour market entry and initial vocational training, competition among young people for access to jobs has become more intense as non-graduates have come to be regarded as underqualified. In the United Kingdom, young people try to stay as long as possible in the education system, while there is only one programme for the young unemployed (the New Deal); those refusing to join the scheme run the risk of losing benefits.

In Canada in general and Quebec in particular, which also suffer from chronic unemployment, a liberal and individualistic concept of responsibilities in respect of unemployment seems to be at work in the employment policies aimed at young people. However, these policies also have a social and collectivist aspect. Indeed, community-based organizations and other associations are playing an increasingly important role in the development of training and access to employment (see Tremblay in Part 3). In the USA, the Workfare State policies (Morel, 1998) are conceived as a patchwork of social programmes and institutions whose principal effect is to produce discrimination. There seems to be no equivalent of the labour market entry programmes aimed at young people. Young people excluded from the labour market are subjected to a state policy criminalizing poverty, a policy consistent, incidentally, with the generalisation of wage and social insecurity (cf. Wacquant in Part 6).

The war on the poor

The 'war on poverty' has been replaced by a war on the poor (Gans, 1995), the primary targets of which are young people of foreign extraction in various cities in the world who are often forced to live in 'ethnic enclaves' (cf. Péraldi in Part 6 in Part 5). We can speak of the development of a subservient class, unable to gain access to better resources or opportunities and relegated to the status of cheap labour serving the economic interests of those in power (cf. Cammarota in Part 5). Cultural forms emerge that may in turn produce modes of social affiliation and labour market integration or of exclusion from the mainstream (cf. Chuprov, Zubok in Part 6). Sanchez-Jankowski (1991), following on from Thrasher, sees gangs, for example, as an alternative social order that produces 'risk cultures' for young people in poor districts. Conversely, while it is difficult to speak of gangs in France and in Quebec, informal structures can be identified that develop into networks; these structures have a local base and links to a particular, and in turn produce cultures of uncertainty based on various ways of managing urgent and uncertain situations through the production of collective competences that play an active role in structuring individual identities (Roulleau-Berger, 1999). Finally, itinerancy seems to be a growing social phenomenon in various societies, it appears to have developed considerably over the last ten years (cf. Hurtubise, Roy and Bellot in Part 6) and may give rise to 'street cultures' characterized by a rejection of social marginalization and a form of resistance, or at least opposition, to economic exploitation and cultural segregation (Bourgois, 1995).

And at the same time, with the return of various forms of cosmopolitanism, defined as 'the synergies produced by vast flows and conjunctions of differences which, nevertheless, have a cohesion that appears to be paradoxical because it is never achieved by the order of nation states' (Tarrius, 2000), new, multi-polar spatial, social and economic configurations are emerging and producing new cross-fertilizations that generate networks of exchanges, mobility and otherness. And international migrations are increasing, leading to the development of diasporas, the organizational form that best matches the globalization of the migratory spaces (Ma Mung, 2000) within which the figure of the young migrant clearly emerges, as S. Sassen's final contribution shows.

BIBLIOGRAPHY

Baudelot, C., Establet, R. (2000), *Avoir trente ans en 1968 et en 1998*, Paris, Seuil.
Beaud, S., Pialoux, M. (1999), *Retour sur la condition ouvrière*, Fayard, Paris.
Beck, U. (1999), *World Risk Society. Toward a new modernity*, Cambridge, Polity Press.

Bourgois, P. (1995), *In Search of respect: selling crack in el barrio*, Cambridge University Press, New York.
Castells, M. (1996), *The rise of the network society*, Blackwell Publishers Ltd, Oxford.
Foucault, M. (1984), *Histoire de la sexualité III: le souci de soi*, Gallimard, Paris.
Gans, H. J. (1995), *The war against the poor*, Basicbooks, HarperCollins Publishers, Inc.
Ma Mung, E. (2000), *La diaspora chinoise, géographie d'une migration*, Paris, Orphys.
Morel, S. (1998), Emploi et pauvreté aux Etats-Unis: les politiques de Workfare in Barbier, J. C., Gautie, J.: *Les politiques de l'emploi en Europe et aux Etats-Unis*, Paris, PUF.
Nicole-Drancourt, C., Roulleau-Berger, L. (2001), *Les jeunes et le travail: 1950–2000*, Paris, PUF.
Portes, A., Zhou, M. (1993), "The new second generation: segmented assimilation and its variants among Post-1965 Immigrant youth", *Annals of The American Academy of Political and Social Science*, n° 530, pp. 74–98.
Roulleau-Berger, L. (1999), *Le travail en friche. Les mondes de la petite production urbaine*, Editions de l'Aube, La Tour d'Aigues.
Sanchez-Jankowski, M. (1991), *Islands in the street: gangs and American urban society*, Berkeley, University of California Press.
Sassen, S. (1991), *The global city: New York, London, Tokyo*, Princeton, N.J.: Princeton University Press.
―――― (2001), Ancrages transversaux: les jeunes et le monde du travail, in Roulleau-Berger, L., Gauthier, M. (eds) (2001), *Les jeunes et l'emploi dans les villes d'Amérique du Nord et d'Europe*, Editions de l'Aube, La Tour d'Aigues.
Sennett, R. (2000), *Le travail sans qualités*, Albin Michel, Paris.
Taylor, C. (1998), *Les sources du moi*, Seuil, Paris.
Tarrius, A. en collaboration avec Missaqui, L. (2000), Les nouveaux cosmopolitismes. mobilités, identités, territoires, Editions de l'Aube, La Tour d'Aigues.
Zhou, M. (1997), Segmented assimilation: issues, controversies and recent research, on the new second generation, International Migration Review 31(4).

Note: I would like to thank the translators who have contributed to this book, more especially Ian Lamb and Andrew Wilson.

PART ONE

INEQUALITIES AND DISCRIMINATIONS AT SCHOOL

YOUTH EXPERIENCE, SOCIALIZATION AND INEQUALITIES IN FRANCE

François Dubet

The term "youth" maybe easily understood as the meeting point between two great social mechanisms. The first is the specificity of a moment of socialization which is dominated by the shift from the status of the child to that of the adult. The second is the hold exerted by the ways in which the opportunities of gaining access to such and such a position in the adult world are distributed. Usually it is the school on which this process of social distribution falls. Nowadays, these two dimensions underpinning youth experience are characterized by a detectable evolution which, far from being a simple response to the moment, is playing a role in the construction of modernity.

The processes of youth socialization are marked by a continuous disinstitutionalization, not only because of the weakening of the initiatic rites, but especially because school can no longer be considered as an institution in the classical sense of the term. For this reason, we will define the ways of being young in terms of the way school experiences occur. The shift from the notion of role to that of experience is testimony to the nature of this change. We are reasoning here only in terms of the school context but it is clear that many other spaces of socialization could be examined in the same way.

Regarding the distribution of actors according to the various social positions, this is dominated by an ever-increasing tension between the affirmation of the equality between subjects and the development of social inequalities. This is not new, but this form of tension is particularly strong during youth because the call for autonomy, which is engendered by disinstitutionalization, confronts young people more than the other types of actors with the characteristic trials of modernity. In this sense, the sociology of youth must be a general sociology.

I. *Transformation of youth*

Without giving in to the fascination of the always new, we must recall, at the risk of sounding banal, the three characteristics of young people today in France.

1. The first is *the extension of youth* to a whole age group.[1] If one takes adult age as being that of settling down to a stable professional and family life, then the notion of age groups has considerably shifted in all categories of the population. People are leaving school later, settling down to a relatively stable professional life later, having children later, and buying household equipment later. The duration of youth could be said to have doubled in the last thirty years. This extension may be explained by factors that may be considered as positive, such as the lengthening of the period of study and training with the standard recognition of youth autonomy and a strong optimization of the notion of youth.[2] On the other hand, this lengthening of the period of youth may also be explained in negative terms, due to the difficulty of obtaining adult status: unemployment, precariousness of employment, difficulty of seeing oneself in the future. In simplistic terms, it could be said that the youth of the middle classes is more sensitive to the positive factors of the lengthening of the youth period, whereas the working class youth perceive this lengthening as being a constraint and as an objective difficulty to becoming an adult. In all cases, these moments when one moves up from one age group to another are nowadays less fixed and more indeterminate than in traditional societies, in which the stages of life were heavily marked by rites or quasi-rites.

2. The second characteristic of youth today is *the composite dimension of this moratorium*. This is obviously because today there are different types of youth, a notion we have understood for a long time. But above all, the various dimensions of the youth experience are now being divided, and it is nowadays a random experience to wish to construct regular stages in this period of life. Family cohabitation, residential independence, obtaining employment, gaining access to a sexual life, becoming a political citizen, and becoming a consumer are not stages which can be set out according to a regular coher-

---

[1] Galland O., *L'allongement de la jeunesse*, Arles, Actes Sud, 1993.
[2] Dubet F., Filâtre D., Merrien F-X., Sauvage A., Vince A., *Université et ville*, Paris, l'Harmattan, 1994.

ent schedule. Not only is there a marginalized youth today, but this period in life functions on a trial and error basis. Young people are now living together as couples before forming a new family. Despite the rigidity of the French school system, school trajectories are becoming more and more composite. Leaving or coming back to the family household are becoming more and more frequent. While the amount of precarious employment and the number of little jobs is increasing, entry into political life now operates more on a trial and error basis.[3] In other words, the youth experience can be defined more than ever before as being a period of crisis. Yet we are all aware of the inadequacy of this representation which is the central player in much of the fiction and more or less sociological literature. Indeed, a period of crisis which lasts this long is not a crisis and the actors do not always live this situation as being a crisis, a period of anguish and unhappiness. Moreover, because the period of youth is becoming longer, it is largely disconnected from adolescence as a psycho-physiologic process of maturing. Finally, the statutory and moral norm of the position of the adult is itself becoming more and more uncertain to the point where we may wonder, without indulging ourselves in fictional sociology, whether "normality" is not this youth moratorium and the statutory uncertainty which characterizes it. It is for this reason that the notion of youth forces us to rethink the notion of socialization.

3. The transformations of youth are mainly due, particularly in France, to *the lengthening of the period of studies*, in which almost 80% of an age group is still pursuing some form of study at the age of 20. And if we add to this figure the hundreds of thousands of youngsters who are following some form of professional training or courses, we may conclude that youth is at school in some way or other. It is of little importance whether the development of schooling is to be considered as a social and cultural progress, as an economic necessity to increase human capital or as a way of delaying the arrival of young people on the work market; youth today is inextricably linked with school and training systems. This has two major consequences on the production of youth. The first comes from the fact that school is the great distributor of positions and social aspirations. For example, although social careers are determined by the social origins of individuals, in a mass form of democratic schooling, it is

---

[3] Muxel A., *Les jeunes et la politique*, Paris, Hachette, 1996.

the educational system itself which distributes individuals into its professional categories. The child of a worker who is in a professional training school is more likely to feel closer to one of his friends who is from the middle classes than another child from the working class who has managed to get into one of the top *lycées*. The second consequence concerns the process of socialization itself. In my opinion, the school experience is central in the process of forming this youth moratorium and identity. Just as the classical sociology of work has considered that the experience of working is at the center of all social experience, it may be that the school experience is the most structuring aspect of this youth experience. This hypothesis is strengthened by the fact that many young people are defined by their failure, exclusion and marginality in school.

II. *Changes in school socialization: disinstitutionalization*

1. The system of *the French republican school* until the end of the 1960s had a certain number of characteristics allowing us to conceive of school as being *an institution*.

The republican school was characterised by the *direct* control of social inequalities on school careers. In other words, the republican school system had constructed a school for each social category, thereby allowing a strong adjustment of supply and demand. Until the 1950s 'working class children' went to elementary school and then, after their compulsory schooling, most went into professional activity, succeeding their parents in the agricultural world or entering the craft industries or heavy industry early, where they were able to acquire professional qualifications as they worked. Some passed through company training centers or through some of the professional institutions, which were not numerous. It is to be remembered that in 1965, half of young people left school at the end of compulsory schooling. The most deserving or the most talented of the 'children of the people' could obtain grants to go to high school or in certain cases to the *lycée* and university. But alongside these few recipients of grants, there were the *héritiers* (heirs), pupils socially programmed for long studies and who went to the *little lycée* instead of elementary school. School organization directly reproduced the social divisions and the school models corresponded to the demands of the publics. It was widely accepted that the source of inequalities was inherent in society or in the natural gifts of individuals, much more than in the school. Therefore, each type of youth had its type of school education.

The republican school system was relatively Malthusian. It was both a way of maintaining the social equilibrium and of guaranteeing the social efficacy of qualifications. In other words, only part of the youth of France entered professional life through their qualifications; the others were caught up in their social destinies and individual adventures. From the age of 12, 14 and then 16, many youngsters no longer had any reason to be at school, and the latter did not have to take these youngsters into account.

This situation enabled school to function as an institution according to a Durkheimian model. Republican socialization could be considered as access to the universal, that of the Republic and the nation for the people, that of the great culture and the humanities for the *héritiers*, by way of a stable pedagogic relationship. In all cases, the teacher embodied values to which the pupil identified by identifying with the teacher, and then by becoming more and more autonomous. The child therefore moved from the particular culture of his family, social class and religion, to the culture of the "great society" which made him an adult citizen.[4] The others went directly into the great society by their work and by a series of more or less formal initiatory rites. The "crisis of adolescence" therefore remained bound by a process of socialization conceived of as an increase in autonomy by the interiorization of more or less complex and abstract norms and models.[5]

2. This type of institution which we have described too simplistically no longer corresponds to the situation of *democratic mass schooling* and to the conception of the subject on which it is based.

The process of mass schooling induces a change in the nature of the selection processes. In the sense that all the pupils begin the competition in exactly the same conditions, even if their chances of success are in relation to their social position, the school no longer selects youngsters on the basis of a process performed upstream. School conducts the selection on the basis of school criteria. The fact that school criteria produce socially determined performances

---

[4] Durkheim E., *Education et sociologie* (1922), Paris, PUF, 1993; *L'éducation morale* (1925), Paris, PUF, 1992.
[5] Piaget J., *Le jugement moral chez l'enfant*, Paris, PUF, 1969.

does not stop the school itself from doing the dirty work. We have now moved from the system of republican elitism to the requirement for all to succeed. And paradoxically, since school is less and less unfair,[6] it is seen as being more and more unfair. This is because for its actors, school produces inequalities and cannot place all the responsibility for this on the shoulders of society. This fundamental change has led to several types of consequences.

The most spectacular of these consequences is the deregulation of pedagogical relationships, since the adjustment of supply and demand has progressively ceased to function. Many teachers now think that they are not teaching the pupils they have a right to teach.[7] The cultural connivance which linked the *héritiers* and the grant-holders to their teachers have now been broken, and this explains to some extent the level of school violence. Although sheltered for a long time from the difficulties of social life, school today seems to be invaded by social problems. It is invaded by a youth and various youth cultures which it does not know how to handle, and it feels that it may give in to this "youthism", or rather that it may shut itself in behind its academic walls. Moreover, it is invaded by social difficulties because it can no longer get rid of the difficult pupils produced by unemployment, immigration, and various mechanisms of social, ethnic and urban segregation.

3. Mass schooling is also increasing the production of diplomas and school qualifications. The result is an *inflation in qualifications*. This does not mean that they are losing their value but does mean that the value itself is shifted to another point in the school trajectory.[8] Above all, in a system where most pupils have a qualification, then not having a qualification or having a qualification which is too low represents an almost redhibitory handicap for obtaining work. In other words, nobody can escape the control of school and the function of filter that it plays. Even though many of the qualifications are hardly of any use, the fact of not having a diploma becomes a

---

[6] Duru-Bellat M., Kieffers A., *La démocratisation de l'enseignement "revisitée"*, Dijon, Les Cahiers de l'IREDU, 1999; Joutard Ph., Thélot C., *Réussir l'école. Pour une politique éducative*, Paris, Seuil, 1999.

[7] Dubet F., Bergounioux A., Duru-Bellat M., Gauthier R. F., *Le collège de l'an 2000*, Paris, La documentation française, 1999.

[8] Baudelot C., Glaude M., "Les diplômes se dévaluent-ils en se multipliant?", *Economie et statistique*, 225, Octobre 1989; Passeron J-C., "L'inflation des diplômes. Remarques à l'usage de quelques concepts sociologiques", *Revue française de sociologie*, XXIII, 1984.

real stigma. This situation increases the utilitarianism of school and weakens the purely cultural dimension of study. The legitimacy of teachers and of the subjects they teach are becoming more and more indexed to their efficacy. A training program which is considered as being good is that which opens up perspectives or which does not shut them off, at least. As for the "good" teacher, he is first and foremost efficient.

Moreover, the very widening of the notion of youth is associated with the development of youth culture and the control of the mass media. School culture is no longer the one great culture which is capable of opening up to the world, so it is losing its monopoly hold. For this reason, many youngsters are tempted to grow up in a universe which is entirely juvenile, separated from or opposed to the world of school. The cultural meaning of studying is no longer self-evident to such youngsters, so there occurs a clash, a tension between their tastes and interests, between the cultural representation they have of themselves as identified in the media and their interest in school training.

4. In this context, *school is no longer an institution*. It is no longer possible to conceive of school as being a body centred on transmitting values and knowledge by way of strongly regulated practices. School has now entered the reign of the rule of the gods. It has to pursue several relatively contradictory objectives. 1) It has to transmit common culture and ensure a minimum of social integration. 2) It must produce useful and efficient training. 3) In a society dominated by moral individualism, it must allow individuals to attain a certain authenticity. These divergent objectives are now leading to a general crisis of motivation that the individuals must arbitrate.

The declining cultural and pedagogical connivance for many pupils, and the obligation to obtain diplomas and to follow the various school finalities have created a situation where, from lower high-school onwards, pupils have difficulty in motivating themselves.[9] Why go to school? Why work? There are three major types of motivation which structure the school experience of pupils.

The first concerns the area of social integration, relationships and tensions between the social world of pupils and that of school. This relationship is no longer self-evident for pupils from the lower social categories, and it is also made unstable by the distance and tensions

---

[9] Dubet F., Martuccelli D., *A l'école*, Paris, Seuil, 1996.

between youth life and culture, on the one hand, and school culture, on the other. In certain cases, this tension becomes a real conflict because those who are small or weak in the school order are big or powerful in the youth order. Pupils must learn how to combine these two normative and identifying registers, and sometimes this conflict seems insurmountable because they have the choice of either being rebels, on the one hand, or clowns and collaborators, on the other.

The second type of motivation is usefulness. A pupil will work if he perceives the usefulness of his studies and if he considers them as a rational investment. This supposes that there is a link between his efforts and his results. But this is far from being guaranteed, contrary to what the pedagogical dogma postulates. If the perception of usefulness it to continue, this supposes that the pupils are engaged in training programs which are useful for their future professional and social insertion. Yet, in many cases, the foreseeable usefulness is low or even negative. Training is seen as being hardly beneficial and all that the pupils knows is that if there is no training, this will pose you considerable problems. In this situation, the pupil does not know what he can win; but he knows what he can lose.

Finally, motivation is underpinned by the meaning of learning itself, the content of knowledge and skills that the pupil may perceive as participating in the development of his personality and autonomy or, on the other hand, as being totally foreign to what he is or what he believes he is. School work is not only an objective form of work, it is working on oneself. Yet when this notion is not supported by the cultural reality surrounding the pupil, he must overcome the distance which separates school culture and social culture; he must overcome the tension existing between school usefulness and subjective interests.

With time, the pupil and therefore the young person is subjected to a test of his motivation. Since he may no longer base his conduct on definitions of stable roles and clear anticipated goals, he is obliged to motivate himself, to give meaning to his own experience. In other words, the pupil is no longer defined by his social role but by his experience, which obliges him to combine and integrate several rationalities of action. As soon as pupils enter youth, the institutional socialization through roles is replaced by trials of social experience. Socialization no longer consists in learning a role but in playing with various cards and constructing oneself in this game. Of course, this game is not purely subjective since the cards are very objectively distributed in relation to the positions of the actors. However, it remains the case that the player is a subject who is constructing himself within this game by his capacity to play. This capacity to play and construct one's own school experience are at the very basis of the constitution of the various ways of being a young person today.

III. *Young people at school*

The variety of situations and experiences is infinite, even more so since our society is now mobile. But mobility does not mean fairness simply because what school has to offer has diversified, because the principles of stratification have become more numerous between the classes, the sexes and the cultures. The increase in the number of ways action may be understood has led many researchers to study interactionism, not by taking interactions at the level of social practice but as being the very essence of a society which is no longer organized by a number of central principles. To overcome this risk of dispersion, we must take the risk of establishing analytical typologies.

To define the modes of youth experience in the school framework, we may choose, perhaps not arbitrarily, to differentiate school experiences in terms of the resources that the actors have at their disposal and which induce four major types of relationship at school, all of which are forms of socialization.[10]

1. Many young people manage easily to construct their experience at school where they are able to affirm their identities, tastes and interests. Youth culture and school culture go together, the usefulness of studying is not questioned and young people feel that school helps them grow up. Of course, this type of *integrated experience* may come about when the pupils have many cultural, social and school resources at their disposal. They control the selection process and do not undergo it. They acquire the spirit of their training, as we have observed in medical students, political science students and in the *grandes écoles*, where the price of prior selection is rewarded by very strong youth and school integration, where studies have both a vocational and useful dimension at the same time.[11] However, this type of experience is not limited only to excellence at school.

---

[10] Ibid.
[11] The notion of vocation is taken here according to the meaning given to it by Weber in *The Protestant Ethic and the Spirit of Capitalism*: the ethic of self-realization in one's professional activity.

Even if the critical discourse is very largely dominant in school matters, we must not forget that the school system has undergone a considerable move to mass education without splitting apart. The number of *bacheliers* (graduating 12th graders) has doubled in twenty years while the level of education has not undergone the drop that was announced by some. Not all new pupils in *lycées* are losers. For example, although children from immigrant families often experience a more difficult period at school than their comrades of French origin, this does not stop many from succeeding at school and gaining access to qualified jobs.[12] We must underline here that the notion of success at school is relative and that the young girl from a working class North African family who has a baccalaureate has achieved something considerable in relation to her mother who has no job or qualification, even if some people might consider that this is only a mediocre achievement. The statistics show that girls in general have much better school qualifications than before.[13] The fact that the norms of excellence are not always met by youngsters should not be thought of by teachers as being testimony to the overall failure of mass education. Rather, this is the price of successful mass education.

2. The relationship that the *new lycéens* and the new students have with their studies is no longer constructed on the model of intellectual vocation or total commitment to a project of social mobility. In other words, these new publics are no longer fulltime *lycéens* or students. These youngsters now have a *double life*. Whenever study time concerns courses which are perceived as giving a low yield, whenever families no longer manage to fully ensure the expected living conditions, whenever the distance between the cultural universe of school and that of the juvenile world is not filled, these new publics no longer place all their hope in school training. There are basically two tendencies to this double life.

The *lycéens* of the technical and general training programs and the first and second year students of the mass university training programs try to reconcile their youth autonomy with an academic life. Many of them consider that time spent studying is the time of youth and its many experimentations. Study time has to be prolonged in order to construct a period of youth composed of little jobs, the

---

[12] Tribalat M., *Faire France*, Paris, La découverte, 1995.
[13] Baudelot C., Establet R., *Allez les filles*, Paris, Seuil, 1992; Duru-Bellat M., *L'école des filles*, Paris, l'Harmattan, 1990.

premises of living as a couple, phases of family cohabitation and decohabitation. In this view, the period spent studying is thought of less as a period for training oneself than as a period for really growing up and constructing one's personal resources, which will perhaps one day be convertible in terms of employment. These publics invest in a limited way in their studies, from which they expect little benefit, and they make sure that they gain their own life experiences. They indulge in cultural passions, learn how to be group leaders, get music groups together, do sport and do a whole range of little jobs. They construct their own autonomous life curriculum in which qualifications are only one of many components. These are not full-time students but are rather ritual students aiming at minimal success in their exams in order to be able to put off the moment at which they enter the professional world, which is perceived as being chaotic and unsure. In this way, some long training courses have now changed their meaning. Rather than being the pursuit of intellectual and scientific excellence, they are seen as being hesitations in the move towards adult life.[14]

The least privileged *lycéens* and students sometimes undertake a dual training. Realizing that their qualifications will not be sufficient to open up work opportunities, some *lycéens* begin to work in the professional world, and in this way become working *lycéens* or students. This part-time employment which is often harsh, unstable and poorly paid, not only aims at providing some income; it is also a way of entering active life, of testing oneself for the real world at a time when working at school does not seem to be worthwhile, and has no perspective or any real training content. Alongside this superficial life at school which provides little motivation, these *lycéens* and students are now choosing a form of *ad hoc* self-training. In fact, they are only playing the school game in name.[15]

3. There is another form of youth and school experience which is relatively difficult to grasp because it is not a spectacular one, nor is it assumed by the individuals themselves. However, it is important: *interior exile*. This is an exit-and-retreat strategy adopted within the school system itself. Pupils spend their energy in maintaining a situation in which they are setting up in youth, friendship, consumption, school survival, in order to put off the moment of the real trials.

---

[14] Dubet F., "L'étudiant en université de masse", *Revue française de sociologie*, 4, 1994.
[15] Ballion R., *Les lycéens et leurs petits boulots*, Paris, Hachette, 1994.

Frequently, school and training courses are adapted for this type of experience in which the youngster expects only a sort of social status. Youngsters in this context are no longer really playing within the school, nor are they playing alongside it or against it. We could describe at length these survival strategies which aim at getting the average mark, not being noticed, having a minimum of leisure activities, and maintaining only a few chosen friends. This is the most negative and most alienated of youth experience, particularly because it is the least noticeable and the one which fits in the most easily with situations in which schooling or training are simply the pretence of schooling or training. In this respect, the hypothesis of a training policy as a way of putting off entry into active life would seem to have considerable content. Such a youth experience aims at putting off for a certain time the trials of preparing for a professional life. Youngsters shut themselves in with the present and with the youth culture itself.

4. Mass education has not reduced the process of selection but has made it an ongoing process by way of successive orientations and reroutings. While some of the losers prefer to no longer participate actively and prefer to retreat, others adopt a *conflict* strategy. This is one of the meanings of youth violence. In fact, school violence cannot be reduced only to the effects of the social violence of the difficult residential quarters. It is also the refusal of a type of school which stigmatizes failure, which makes pupils responsible for that failure, and which keeps these new publics in school, where they are made to feel their inability daily. Therefore, such pupils, particularly in the underprivileged lower high-schools and professional *lycées*, adopt a strategy of opposition to school. They oppose the juvenile world to that of the school, and defend their honor against a system which invalidates them and makes them lose their own self-esteem.

It is here that the process of selective mass education reaches its limitations. Schooling is perceived as a form of violence against which pupils exert their own violence. Of course, not all youth violence can be understood in these terms, but we cannot ignore the fact that many of these new school publics feel trapped in a system which encourages them to commit themselves, while refusing them access to useful gratifying forms of study. In the past, when obligatory schooling was brief and at a time when the job market offered opportunities for unqualified youngsters, these publics left school early.

Today, they have to stay there a long time and are unable to establish themselves either intellectually, socially or in professional terms.

To summarize this typology, it may be said that school produces four types of youth experience. 1) A group *socialized in* school. 2) A group *socialized in and alongside* school. 3) A group *protected by* school without being socialized in it. 4) A group *socialized against* school.

IV. *Beyond school*

Not only do these four groups that we have just defined globally represent a school and social hierarchy, they also define the modalities of entering life in which the individuals must navigate during their youth. The first group is very likely to be able to continue school training and therefore gain professional insertion, if only because they often gain access to the protected training courses which themselves lead to the relatively protected work markets. The second group seem relatively well equipped to face the problems of professional insertion because they can act at several levels. The last two groups are defenceless and may move either towards processes of marginalization or towards being taken charge of by the socio-professional insertion policies. In this respect, school can be seen to be playing the role of filter and signal in the process of entering the work market.[16]

1. Even if we should not dramatize the situation, attention must be drawn to marginal integration. I have taken the view that the "rough times", known in French as *galère*, are caused by the destruction of three elements which can structure the experience of the youngsters who come from the most underprivileged milieu.[17] Integration into a social class constituted as a cultural community is no longer possible. Youngsters no longer have the ability to integrate and the fact that they no longer have any class consciousness leaves them feeling hate and rage, which frequently leads them to self-destruction. This may have two consequences.

The first is the shift towards a marginal delinquent economy. One's residential quarter may become the place where one finds one's

---

[16] White M., "Information et chômage des jeunes", *Sociologie du travail*, 4, 1990.
[17] Dubet F., *La galère*, Paris, Fayard, 1987.

economic income in ways ranging from the underground economy to the delinquent economy. This is a network economy which is more controlled than repressed by the police but which defines totally only a minority of youngsters who have one foot in and one foot out, who shift from little official jobs and training periods to illegal activities. There is little data about the way youngsters come out of this experience but we do know that some never do.

The second aspect of the way youngsters come out of this experience is constituted by the retreat to local identities, to those of the residential quarter, to ethnic identities, to a sense of ethnicity; i.e. the affirmation of an identity as a response to the impossible integration rather than as a return to cultural traditions which have already been destroyed. Youngsters waver between cultural activity and more or less legal networks of assistance, which may be more or less based on social and municipal policies.[18]

While it is true that we cannot define these behaviors only in terms of delinquency and marginality, it seems excessive to my mind to present the question in too favorable a light, i.e. in terms of a free, expressive and creative moratorium. To do so would be to underestimate the cultural conformism of these youngsters, who may be defined by their frustrated desire to participate and consume. It would seem that our society has more or less accepted the idea of this "cursed portion" of society, and these youngsters are probably the most visible part of this portion. They are not a new popular class but rather a "destitute middle class", so great is the distance between the power of the consumer models that the middle class have and the lack of cultural and social resources that the youngsters have to attain them.

2. The gap between school training and the professional world, and the persistence of a reservoir of young unemployed have led the state to develop insertion policies. This is a curious notion which tends to imply a sort of social integration, whereas it really means a range of public policies. Considered as a modality of social integration, insertion can only give a sort of legitimacy and recognition to the intermediary positions between autonomous salaried employment and marginality.[19] While the modes of insertion and to a lesser

---

[18] For these two different perspectives, see: Lepoutre D., *Coeur de banlieue. Codes, rites et langages*, Paris, O. Jacob, 1997; Roulleau-Berger L., *La ville intervalle*, Paris, Méridiens-Klinksieck, 1991.

[19] Guérin-Plantin C., *Genèse de l'insertion*, Paris, Dunod, 1999.

extent their efficacy are well known, much less is known about the educative processes implemented.[20] However, there are a sufficient number of reports about these public policies for the limitations to appear clearly.[21]

There is a real risk that youngsters may end up permanently in a state of precariousness. Because the work market is segmented, youngsters do not really enter into competition with adults. The end of a training course, the end of a limited duration contract or part-time training does not always place the youngster within the work market. This type of organized precariousness is also accentuated by the fact that youth labor is used as a tool to counter the rigidities of the professional market and labor law. Many companies, associations and the French administration itself have learned how to function with this ever-changing labor force. Therefore, this force is useful because it is transitory. Such is the case with the assistant educators employed in the French national education system; they are useful because they are young and because they lighten the load of the socialization tasks that teachers see as being too heavy or too debasing. But what will happen to those who do not manage to get out of this framework? In cynical terms, the relative marginality of these youngsters may be seen as a professional quality which is useful for certain social functions situated at the very borders of social marginality and a formal economy.

Another problem with these insertion procedures is the fact that they themselves create stratifications within the publics that they are aiming at, and that for the least qualified of these youngsters, their own personal networks appear more efficient than the organizations that these policies are trying to form. It also happens that the organizations whose role it is to train these youngsters are themselves composed of workers in a precarious position. And finally, it was thought for a long time that these insertion policies would induce a revolution in the school system. Yet it has to be admitted that this is hardly the case and that the part-time courses are reserved for the weakest pupils, those with the least resources, and that the socio-

---

[20] Dubar C. (ed.), *L'autre jeunesse, stagiaires sans diplôme*, Lille, PUL, 1987.

[21] Nicole-Drancourt C., *Le labyrinthe de l'insertion*, Paris, La documentation française, 1990; Nicole-Drancourt C., Roulleau-Berger L., *L'insertion des jeunes en France*, Paris, PUF, 1995; Wuhl S., *Insertion. Les politiques en crise*, paris, PUF, 1996. In general, the policies have been studied more than the educative processes. See the excellent synthesis in *Les jeunes et l'emploi*, *Cahiers travail et emploi*, Paris, La documentation française, 1996.

cultural distance between the world of school and the world of work remains one of the French national specificities.[22]

So may it be said that these insertion policies constitute a multi-faceted device making socialization to precariousness the norm? Such a view is without doubt too negative because many youngsters do get out of the *galère*, even if they are not able to find a relatively stable job. However, this viewpoint should be attenuated by the fact that professional precariousness does not necessarily mean social precariousness. Chantal Nicole-Drancourt and Laurence Roulleau-Berger have shown that the actors learn how to live in this situation, to accumulate various resources, and to use the institutional and informal networks, and also to mobilize generational and inter-generational forms of solidarity. The actors are also able to shed the stigma which is imposed on them, and to be able to construct moments of freedom and expression. Such studies show that precariousness is not necessarily tragic in a society where the welfare state remains present. But it is precisely this which is perhaps tragic: the capacity to organize the unacceptable.

V. *The tensions of inequalities*

The sociology of youth can easily be considered as a cultural and social anthropology which aims at collating and describing a thousand and one ways of being young. On the other hand, it can be thought of as a general sociology in which youth experience is considered as the product of social mechanisms which are much wider than youth alone. Youth experience is dominated by tensions between on the one hand, a principal of equality which is identified with the right to hope for relative equality of opportunities, which themselves are reinforced by egalitarian themes of youth culture, and on the other, *de facto* social inequalities. However different these two dimensions may be, they almost come together in the experience of individuals where their interface exacerbates the sensitivity to inequalities. The development of the new social movements is testimony to this: feminist struggles, community movements, the struggle to defend minorities or the dispossessed, people who have no official papers, no accommodation and no work. French sociology, which is often

---

[22] Askouni N., Van-Zanten A., "L'école et la transmission des savoirs et des attitudes face au travail et aux entreprises", in *Les jeunes et l'emploi*, ibid.

linked to these movements and is sometimes influenced by Anglo-Saxon sociology, has devoted a number of studies to the question of the new inequalities. Of course, most of these inequalities are not new and are even less strong than they were before, as is the case of sexual inequalities. Yet they constitute a new object of research and analysis because the actors now have a much greater consciousness than in contexts where these inequalities were part of the natural order of things.

1. *New types of inequality*. The dominant form of analysis in terms of classes has now been shattered by the introduction of new definitions of what constitutes inequality; these criteria were hardly considered before. In the space of 30 years, the working population has become much more feminized and women represented 44.7% of the work force in 1994. However, all the studies show that this rise in the number of working women, which supposed an increase in equality, has not in fact rid us of most of the inequalities, and in fact has led to new ones. Beyond the question of salary differences, differentiation in the workplace has been maintained and has even been increased. Women dominate the service sector, are the majority in the education and health sectors, while they are no longer hardly present in the manufacturing industries, except as unskilled workers, in politics and in other sectors which still remain largely male-dominated. We could in fact talk of segregative emancipation or controlled emancipation.[23] Worse still is the fact that the autonomy of salaried women has often led to a reinforcement of work and private constraints, since the sharing of domestic tasks has not really been affected by this emancipation at work. Moreover, this autonomy has increased the vulnerability of women who are head of the family, since they are less protected by tradition and more affected by poverty if ever they meet with economic difficulties and divorce. Single-parent families, women living alone with their children, are over-represented among the recipients of the *RMI* (minimum insertion payment). Generally speaking, the private and public sectors still remain extremely distant and specific and are sexually marked.[24] The finer the sociological studies, the more they demonstrate the maintenance or reinforcement of these micro-inequalities.

---

[23] Lagrave R.-M., 1992, "Une émancipation sous tutelle. Education et travail des femmes au XXe siècle", in Duby G., Perrot M., (eds), *Histoire des femmes en Occident. Le XXe siècle*, Paris, Plon.

[24] Héritier F., 1996, *Masculin, féminin, la pensée de la différence*, Paris, Odile Jacob.

Girls have been the great beneficiaries of mass school education. However, although they succeed better than boys, they hardly move toward the more economically viable training programs such as the scientific programs.[25] All the studies seem to demonstrate that women have not been in a winning situation in any respect, and that their irrefutable equality has been paid for by new inequalities which are even more intolerable because they stand in the way of an objective progression of equality.

Ethnic inequalities have undergone the same type of mechanism. In France in general, immigrants and especially their children progressively integrate French society.[26] But this integration, which can be evaluated with very global indicators, has not stopped the formation of a very strong segregation and of ethnic dead-ends in the poorest quarters. Above all, there is now segregation and racism in the sectors of accommodation and employment.[27] In this respect, the realization of these inequalities is much greater today than before, because while the immigrants are more integrated and therefore more equal, they are assigned to certain quarters, certain types of employment, and must confront all the aspects of racism everyday of their lives. This paradox subtends a mechanism which is new in France: the transformation of immigrants into minority groups.[28] While the migrants were involved in a specific process of economic integration associated with the aspiration linked to returning home, their children are now very widely assimilated with the culture of their host country, but feel excluded from its economic and social fruits. While their fathers were integrated into the economy and not assimilated into the culture, the sons and daughters are assimilated and even super-assimilated in terms of consumer models, and do not feel integrated and even feel that they are an excluded, rejected minority. While the immigrants are the inferior fringe of the proletariat, minorities may be defined only in terms of their identities and ethnic and cultural stigmas; in this respect, minorities end up existing only in the critical eye that stigmatizes them and engenders their inequality.

The distribution of inequalities between the age classes has undergone profound transformation during the last thirty years in relation

---

[25] Duru-Bellat M., 1990, *L'école des filles*, Paris, L'Harmattan.
[26] Tribalat M., 1996, *De l'immigration à l'assimilation*, Paris, La Découverte.
[27] Bataille P., 1997, *Le racisme au travail*, Paris, La Découverte.
[28] Dubet F., 1989, *Immigration, qu'en savons-nous?*, Paris, La Documentation Française.

to employment policies and modalities of social redistribution. While the youngsters of the Glorious Thirties who were born just after the war benefited from extremely favorable conditions in relation to their elders, the tendency is now the opposite and age has now become an important factor of inequality. Youngsters in the working population are more affected by unemployment than adults and above all, they must undergo a long period of uncertainty and precariousness before finding a stable job.[29] Demography, the economic situation and social policies all come together to explain these new inequalities, and everything points to France having chosen to make youngsters pay. Of course, this is not really a choice but is rather a more or less anticipated consequence of the many choices which have led in particular to the devaluation of qualifications and to the increased cost of entering the adult world, defined as the moment at which life projects may be embarked upon. Whereas in the sixties, youngsters were taken on at salaries relatively close to those of adults, the gap has considerably widened today.[30] Of course, these global inequalities between the various age groups do not exclude the formation or maintenance of other inequalities within each age group in terms of sex, type of training, type of employment, and so on. The sociology of inequalities is an inexhaustible subject and youngsters are caught up in all of them.

2. *Multiple causes.* This list of new inequalities is limitless, with a multiplicity of groups which could be considered victims of specific inequalities. We will not discuss the latter here. However, the analysis of all these inequalities has really transformed the way sociologists consider the problem, because most of them are neither the result of one's birth nor one's class position; they result from the association of a whole set of complex factors and often seem to be the more or less perverse product of practises and social policies which precisely aim at limiting them. Although criticism of the perverse effect of the welfare state has always had secondary motives, some of these perverse effects simply cannot be ignored, particularly the effects of dependency and stigmatization, and especially the fact that these policies are often favorable to those who are the least

---

[29] Chauvel L., 1998, *Le destin des générations. Structure sociale et cohortes en France au XXe siècle*, Paris, PUF.
[30] Baudelot C., Establet R., 2000, *Avoir trente ans en 1968 et en 1998*, Paris, Ed. du Seuil.

under-privileged. Analysis of the mechanisms of social transfer demonstrates that it is not rare for the middle classes to be the principle beneficiaries in the area of education or health, since the most privileged pay the most and are therefore the most active users.[31] Such classes are looked after better and often their children undertake longer and better studies. Their life expectancy and retirement period are longer, and they go to the opera; yet everybody pays for the opera through their taxes.

The sociology of education illustrates this change very well. In France for a long time, the paradigm of reproduction has dominated the sociology of education by attributing the responsibility for school inequalities only to social inequalities. The paradigm of methodological individualism proposed a theoretical alternative which did not fundamentally change the reasoning on this point. In both cases, school was considered as a neutral black box simply recording social inequalities in the form of cultural handicaps in one case, and a set of socially situated rational calculations in the other. By reaction to these theories leading to a certain political fatalism and under the influence of the new English sociology of education, a number of authors attempted to demonstrate that school plays its own role in the production of inequalities.[32] First, it became apparent that what school has to offer is far from being equal, including in a republican system which is reputed to be homogeneous. The offer tends to be of better quality when it is destined for the most privileged, despite efforts of affirmative action.[33] Then, a whole macro-sociology of education demonstrated that school interactions and the reciprocal expectations of teachers and pupils had a favorable impact on pupils coming from the middle and upper classes. Various inegalitarian effects have been demonstrated until now: class effect, particular school effect, teacher effect. In this way, school adds its own inequalities to the social inequalities. While for a long time in France it was thought that making the offer equal was tantamount to producing equality,

---

[31] Cf. Gaullier X, 1996, « La machine à exclure » in *L'Etat-providence. Arguments pour une réforme*, Paris, Le Débat/Gallimard; préface de F. X. Merrien à Esping-Andersen G., 1999, *Les trois mondes de l'Etat-providence*, Paris, PUF.

[32] Duru-Bellat M., Van-Zanten, A., 1999, *Sociologie de l'école*, Paris, Armand Colin.

[33] Despite the policy of the ZEP (Education Priority Zones), the school offer remains of better quality when it concerns the most privileged pupils. The case of the *grandes écoles* and the *classes préparatoires* is the most evident and perhaps the most shocking: Dubet F., Duru-Bellat M., 2000, *L'hypocrisie scolaire*, Paris, Ed. du Seuil.

we now realize that not only was it not really equal but that this equality could even produce inegalitarian effects added to those that it aimed at reducing. Thus, we are moving imperceptibly here from a political philosophy less centered on equality than on equity.

The desire for equity cannot be separated from the complexity of tools in the social sciences and statistics which demonstrate the diversity of the levels of inequality and manage, at least theoretically, to distinguish the various social causes and those which concern the individual. Therefore, in the area of success at school, it appears that the role of one's birth diminishes as the pupil advances in his studies, while his own school history becomes more and more decisive: his performances, his age and the courses he chooses. Theoretically nothing stops us (not the insurance companies at least) from distinguishing the genetic causes of diseases, the random causes, and those which may be attributed to the environment or to the individual's lifestyle. From the point of view of equity, we must therefore consider a whole set of opportunities and risk factors which in the long term lead us to consider inequalities as being an extremely complex system of causes and decisions in which the individual is considered in the light of a multiplicity of registers and perspectives. The question that Sen asks can no longer be avoided: do we know whether an individual who has a physical handicap is more privileged than another in good health simply because he has higher income?[34]

3. *The multiple individual.* Let us now consider the social actors and individuals. We will disregard the richest 10% and the poorest 10% of a society because the risk is too great that the former will accumulate all the advantages and the latter all the handicaps. With respect to the registers chosen, the former will be rich, powerful, cultivated and in good health, while the latter will be poor, invisible, ignorant and ill. If we rule out those groups placed at the two extremities of the social spectrum and of the relationships of domination, then statutory incongruence becomes the rule.[35] Weber distinguished class, status and power as being analytically independent dimensions of the individual's position. Weber's intuition has now come true.[36] The organization of inequalities only in terms of social classes appears to

---

[34] Sen A., *Repenser l'inégalité*, Paris, Seuil, 2000.
[35] Lenski G. E., 1954, « Status crystallization: a non vertical dimension of social status », *American Sociological Review*, XIX, 4.
[36] Crompton R., 1993, *Class and Stratification*, London, Polity Press.

be a historically fortuitous phenomenon due to the domination of industrial society, the maintenance of barriers and aristocratic distances, and to the organization of political life in terms of more or less crude representations of class interests. Once these various dimensions are no longer valid, then they affect each group and each individual. Positions on the various social ladders are no longer necessarily congruent.

Individuals are more or less equal in terms of the various spheres constituting their position: sex, age, employment, work, training and origins. In many registers of his existence, a black executive will be less equal than a white worker. If we accept that this diversity supposes the affirmation of the equal dignity of everyone as a central postulate in democratic societies, then it is easy to understand why identity appears to be less a given fact of life than something which is constructed and demanded by individuals. According to their projects and areas of action, individuals choose to mobilize and to put forward such and such a dimension of their identity and experience. While workers used to be able to act as workers because they had no other available identities, today one can choose to act and put forward one's identity as a woman, a worker, as a Black, as a believer, as a qualified person and as a music lover, for example. It is also for this reason that the themes of stigma and self-image have acquired such a wide dimension. Putting oneself on the scene and caring for one's look cannot be explained only by the power of mass consumption but also by the need to constantly exhibit the identity one has chosen to show other people. Individuals construct their identity and therefore their claim for equality by selecting items from a whole set of identities which are imposed on them in their multiple roles and affiliations.[37] By increasing social differentiation, modernity has also multiplied the number of registers of these inequalities and the individual is able to construct his own identity only by establishing himself as a subject, as the equal of others. This implies that he is a player on various scenes and in various registers of equality, which may accentuate his reflexivity and sensitivity to the more subtle inequalities.[38] The link between identity and inequalities is not only one of relative frustration or the envy caused by the shock occurring between the equality of principles and real inequalities. It

---

[37] Dubar C., 2000, *La crise des identités. L'interprétation d'une mutation*, Paris, PUF, 2000.
[38] Elster J., 1985, *The Multiple Self*, Cambridge, Cambridge University Press.

is also a matter of the very definition of the subject himself who is not always equal or unequal according to the various dimensions of his own experience.

Each individual or group is less defined by his role than by his experience which is pervaded by a set of logics which are not at first sight necessarily coherent and harmonious.[39] Each one of us has several statuses and several identities which are more or less recognized and given value by others, and this engenders several forms of inequality. A youngster from an immigrant family is very likely to be "equal" in the sports world but to be less so in a police station. Each one of us acts at the level of several "markets" where he has available resources and "capital". And even if power is not defined by a game which has no real value, it still remains that power is acquired by one's own strategic capacity and that it is not only imposed by the structure of positions. The heterogeneity of the registers of human action determines the nature of this game of inequalities without fixing the stakes totally, and the actors are also supposed to construct part of their equality, or what they consider to be their equality, by defending themselves, their dignity and their honor.

VI. *The social experience of inequalities*

Never has the contradiction between the two sides of equality (or inequalities) been so acute. *Never has the interface between the affirmation of the equality of individuals with the multiple inequalities that subtend the situations and the social relations been so violent and so menacing for the subject.* Conservative liberal thought often denounces this passion for equality by promoting the theme of relative frustration: envy becomes the basic social feeling whenever the slightest inequality becomes intolerable, whenever the individual wishes to claim that he is equal or "more equal". This therefore denies all the natural or social differences, thereby threatening freedom and leading to considerable economic inefficiency.[40] Although this analysis is valid for the Terror or bolshevism, in general it disregards the fact that egalitarian societies are also the most democratic and the least poor. Above all, conservative liberalism likes to play at frightening itself by pretending to

---

[39] Dubet F., 1994, *Sociologie de l'expérience*, Paris, Ed. du Seuil.
[40] For a detailed defence of this hypothesis, see Nozick R., 1988, *Anarchie, Etat et Utopie*, Paris, PUF.

ignore the fact that the societies which establish the primacy of the principle of equality are, despite everything else, pervaded by tolerated and often legitimate inequalities. The problem posed therefore is that of the fair inequalities or at least those which may be considered as tolerable, because the aspiration for equality is not, in the experience of the actors of such societies, equivalent to the aspiration for egalitarianism. Such actors would like the diversity of individuals to be recognized and inequalities to be fair at the same time.

1. *The obligation to be free*, to be a subject, to be the author of one's life subtends the very project of modernity and cannot be dissociated from the claim that everybody should be equal. If the empirical equality of everybody is probably the enemy of freedom, then the claim for equality supposes freedom. In democratic societies, individuals cannot hope to be equal unless they are free, unless every man is born free and is his own master, as Rousseau stated. This mastery of oneself, one's capacity to be the only master, is not the guarantee of real equality, but is the prerequisite for the equality of opportunities and therefore of fair inequalities, because it is the result of competition between equals. It is in this respect that freedom and equality may so often be opposed or linked in part. Equality supposes the obligation of being free and of being oneself. The only thing that can be opposed to false hierarchies is fair hierarchies, hierarchies founded on merit and on individual responsibility and freedom.

From the Reform to the Enlightenment, the modern notion of the individual has never stated anything other than the fact that there is a necessary link between equality and freedom. This has led to the heroic definition of the individual who constructs himself, who becomes the author of his own life, successes and failures. The fact that this ideal has never been realized perfectly, and even far from it, does not stop it from being the only real norm of equality likely to produce acceptable inequalities. No doubt it is because sport is the dramatic spectacle of this confrontation between equal competitors and for the fair hierarchy of performances that it is taken to be the central theater in which the gods of democracy (equality) and those of capitalism (merit and work) confront each other. To be able to function, sports competition is based on two necessary fictions. The first postulates that whatever the conditions prior to the competition, both teams or both individuals are equal as soon as the competition starts, and that the team in the second division is able to beat the first division team, just like an underrated tennis player can beat a world star.[41] Without the belief in this fiction, any match is a masquerade. The second fiction is that of the clarity of the rules and their reciprocity: the rules are always the same, the referees are impartial, the stopwatches are objective and the teams change sides at half time in order to neutralize the effects of the wind or the sun. Inequalities arising in a sport's competition are therefore of the same type as the fair inequalities because they are based only on merit, virtue, work or the courage of the players. Of course, sport mobilizes other passions and nobody is naïve enough to believe in its "purity"; however nobody would participate in sport if they did not believe somewhat in this fiction, in this combination of freedom, equality and merit. The same alchemy and fiction are at work in other spheres such as school competition and economic competition. Like the naïve amateurs in sport, sociologists the least naïve to the mechanisms of school reproduction are also civil servants granting qualifications and necessarily believing somewhat in their own form of justice, while the workers who are the most critical of exploitation know how to distinguish he who becomes rich through his own work and he who is simply content to be born in the right place.

Yet the obligation of being free as a prerequisite for equality exposes individuals to a series of subjective trials which are the trials of equality or more exactly the trials that are generated by the desire for equality and the existence of real inequalities. The freer and more autonomous the subject wishes to be, the more this trial exposes the individual, who may experience it as destructive.

2. *Trials of equality* may be declined in a series of specific scenarios.

Unhappy consciousness
Because equality demands self-responsibility, it progressively deprives individuals of the consolations which are part of legitimately inegalitarian and undemocratic societies. The great systems of religious and political consolation which explain and justify inequalities independently of the action of individuals are no longer in a position to explain as efficiently the social inequalities and failures of individuals.

---

[41] This can happen just in one event, but is less frequent when the events take place regularly over a season or a career. In amateur sport, it is therefore not absurd to believe in equality between competitors. Besides, who would watch a match if he did not think that David could beat Goliath?

Once this happens, the individual perceives himself as being responsible for his own unhappiness and begins to be filled with unhappy consciousness. The triumph of the principle of equality desocializes the experience of inequalities in a society which remains fundamentally inegalitarian, but which tends to produce inequalities through a series of individual trials and no longer through collective trials, or more exactly which tends to hide the collective trials behind the personal trials.

Let us take the case of school inequalities.[42] For a long time, the French school system was structured in an inegalitarian way, access to the various forms of training being directly determined by birth, with each social category being offered a certain type of school and therefore a certain type of opportunity for success. In this way, children from the people went to the school for the people, whereas children from the bourgeoisie went to the *lycée*, and a few particularly gifted and hard-working individuals managed to escape this social channelling of school careers. The latter were the heroes but not all were obliged to be heroic in this socially cleaved system. Since individuals from birth were not considered as equal in terms of education, failure at school could easily be explained by social causes, by the injustice of the system and sometimes by natural injustice, since the children of the people were less gifted and less ambitious than those of the bourgeoisie. The advantage of this system was not to call into question the self-esteem of those pupils who did not have brilliant careers and who were not destined for them. Anybody could explain his failures through social causes and through a set of causes exterior to himself and to his own value. An adolescent who became a worker and a young girl who became a housewife at the end of their schooling could blame social injustice whenever their destiny did not seem fair, without feeling that they personally were the cause of their life trajectory. They simply had not been offered the chance to be anything else.

The whole situation is different in the democratic mass education school which tries, and not only formally, to establish the conditions of equal opportunities in a competition open to everyone. Pupils are no longer selected upstream of the system, but are selected during

---

[42] Dubet F., Martuccelli D., 1996, *A l'école. Sociologie de l'expérience scolaire*, Paris, Ed. du Seuil; Dubet F., 1999, « Sentiments de justice dans l'expérience scolaire », in Meuret D. (ed.), *La justice du système éducatif*, Bruxelles, De Boeck.

their studies in relation only to their performance. Of course, sociologists are not unaware that this competition is socially determined by social inequalities, but from the point of view of the individuals, their failures and successes mainly depend on their performances and qualities. An individual may see his failure as not being due to the fact that he is the child of a worker who is forbidden to go to the *lycée* and condemned to earn his living early, but because his school performances are low. If we accept this, then how can we reconcile the claim for equality for everyone and the inequality of everybody's merit; how can we make the two sides of equality compatible?

In a republican system strongly claiming its democratic vocation, as in the French case, it is work which serves as mediator between these two opposing principles. Work is the currency linking the notion of equality for everybody and everyone's merit, because inequalities are fair and do not call into question the equality of individuals, providing that it is accepted that the performance of pupils results from the quantity of work that they freely put into their schooling.[43] All the time that the individuals consider that their school inequalities are the result of the amount of work they do, their fundamental equality is maintained because they are supposed to be free to work or to play around. But when they discover that they are unequal despite the quantity of work that they do (and this regularly happens), they can only doubt their own value and their own equality. They can only blame themselves and they can only feel inferior. And the only way they can act is either to leave a game where they are losing or to destroy the game itself through violence.

It is because the ways in which inequalities are established serve to highlight these inequalities that the latter lead to the loss of self-esteem and to this unhappy consciousness. School meritocracy can act as a liberating principle; nevertheless, it legitimizes inequalities because it attributes the responsibility for these inequalities to the victims themselves. Even if this reasoning concerning the situation at school is not a complex one, its logic can, in my opinion, be extended to other areas. Professional life is not totally closed on the first position held, and the individualization of careers, skills and retributions accentuates this phenomenon. Should we then only see in

---

[43] Dominique Meda insists on this role of work as the principle of justice in a classical political economy, particularly in Adam Smith, in *Le travail, une valeur en voie de disparition*, Paris, Aubier, 1995.

this a simple strategy of management and manipulation, not because this is absent from what policymakers intend to do but because the actors are often torn between a desire for security and a collective career, and a desire that their own personal merits should be recognized? The workers criticize the liberal form of management which imposes overwhelming responsibilities on them, and also criticize the bureaucracy which ignores these responsibilities. In the same way, today's discourse on the body, love and the education of one's children is now tending to replace destiny by responsibility. One is responsible for one's body, it is sufficient to practise sport, diets and not to smoke; one is the master of one's love life and one must master the subjective and erotic skills, according to the magazines for women. As regards the education of children, it is as if parents are exercising a profession. Here again, these tendencies cannot be reduced to a form of control and manipulation, which of course they are, but they are part of the very project of modernity, responsibility, reflexivity and therefore guilt.

Scorn
The call for the heroic notion of the equal subject widens the dimension of scorn because the individual is deprived of the inegalitarian social and cultural structures which stop him being free and responsible. But when anyone is responsible for his life, he then becomes subject to the scorn which accompanies the fact that he cannot be worthy of this freedom, and that he cannot assume this equality.[44] At the same time as calling upon the principles of equality, the intellectuals of modernity have demonstrated a pronounced aristocratic taste for the avant-garde, and a scorn which is just as pronounced for the masses and petit-bourgeois tastes. Indeed, if an individual is to be sovereign, he must first be recognized as a particular original person who is capable of constructing his life without giving in to principles other than his own. Whereas shame comes from the feeling of being laid bare, scorn is generated by the desire to recognize oneself, one's uniqueness. Shame is felt when the individual can no longer play his role, and his scorn comes from being reduced to this role, and from the fact that he is not recognized.

Because it is inevitably part of the notion of self-responsibility, the desire for equality generates a never-ending need for recognition. In

[44] Honneth A., 2000, *La lutte pour la reconnaissance*, Paris, Cerf. *on*, Paris, Aubier, 1995.

this way, the trial of domination and unjust inequalities is first and foremost experienced as a manifestation of scorn, or the way in which the individual is reduced to his status in full view of everybody. Those who believe that the triumph of democratic individualism removes all conflict from work by weakening communities are very clearly mistaken. Beyond the wage claims and call for better treatment, there is always a fight against scorn, against the ignorance of the specific value of individuals. And it is often the heart of the protests and groups which cannot be controlled by the traditional trade-union frameworks. The poor do not accept to be reduced to this status of social cases, of being ignored and above all being forced to claim that they have projects for the future, whereas they have been dispossessed of this capacity. Adolescents in *lycées* perceive school hierarchies as networks of scorn in which the actors pour scorn on the others in order to feel less subject to scorn themselves. You only need to look at the obsession with face values and challenges which underpin the sociability of suburban youngsters to see how much scorn is perceived as the elementary social feeling of those who come up against the most acute contradiction between their fundamental equality and their social inequalities.[45] But while shame socializes social experience, scorn desocializes it, so it becomes a case of looking at oneself. Scorn degrades the class experience into a series of narcissistic or harmful interactions, as in the analyses of Goffman, whose sociology is more interesting when it is considered as an anthropology of modernity than as a sociological paradigm. Goffman's individuals wish to be considered as equals and to "calm down the sucker" by preserving the face of he who dominates and manipulates. Essentially, Goffman's individuals are both cynical and interested in equality, both capitalistic by being their own capital and democratic by trying to preserve a form of equality.[46]

Retreat and violence
In situations dominated by unhappy consciousness and by scorn, particularly in youngsters and when individual values are put to the test, several strategies may be distinguished according to the Hirschman model. Many of the actors preserve their self-esteem by refusing to

---

[45] Dubet F., 1987, *La galère*, Paris, Fayard.
[46] This way of reading Goffman is certainly not the only one: cf. Martuccelli D., 1999, *Sociologies de la modernité*, Paris, Gallimard.

play a game in which they have the feeling that they will always lose. In this way, pupils decide not to work in order that their performance should not call into question their value and fundamental equality. Such pupils have chosen to fail at school, which avoids their being affected by failure. Whereas a bad mark for homework is difficult to take, it pales into insignificance once the individual has decided not to do his work. Beyond this radical form of retreat, we are now seeing at school, as in the underprivileged quarters, a whole set of strategies consisting in pretending to play. Pupils will exchange a limited form of conformism at school for average marks which ensure their peaceful survival within the system. By threatening their teachers with total withdrawal from the system or with violence, they finish up by obtaining a sort of low level equilibrium which guarantees them a certain equivalence between the goodwill that they show and average marks. In the same way, the users of the social services are prepared to exchange a certain form of goodwill for a system of welfare which is indexed on their desire to make it through their problems. In this case and as at school, nobody is really taken in by a game whose form is maintained but whose content is emptied, while saving the face of all the protagonists.

Other pupils break the rules of the game with violence which to them is the only way of refusing the negative image of oneself drawn down by failure and one's freedom. Pupils may invalidate the school game by attacking their teachers and by making enemies of them. Not only does violence allow one to save one's dignity; it also makes its perpetrator bigger in the eyes of his peer group. However, we may wonder why such violence does not transform into conflict and why it does not call into question the structural mechanisms of school inequalities. In fact, the recourse to violence may be explained by this impossibility and by the fact that the trials of equality can only ever be individual trials in a society which is both democratic and competitive. Basically, violent pupils break the rules of the game because they believe in the game as much as others, if not more so. With violence, they are destroying the game which destroys them, but they have nothing else to replace it with, as is clear in the culture of defiance which structures their life and consumer behavior. And even if this explanation does not account for all violence and everywhere, it demonstrates one of its dimensions, i.e. the wish for recognition. But while in most cases recognition calls upon a principle of justice and the need for social identity, this type of violence is the expression of a pure claim to be a subject, like the violence of the *Bonnes* in Jean Genet, with the subject disappearing within his own violence.

Just as Parsons considered that American youth in the 1950s was a concentration of the most characteristic traits of society of that time, contemporary juvenile experience in France today may be analyzed as the expression of the most fundamental tensions in our society. On the one hand and continuously, juvenile socialization escapes the control of institutions despite the increasing role of school, because school can no longer be considered as an institution encompassing stable and legitimate values and role models. School is an internal market, subjected to the calculations of usefulness that its actors make and to the competition of mass culture. In this space, youngsters are subjected to the obligation to construct their school experiences through which they are supposed to become motivated and to socialize. The social control thus implemented is based less on a search for moral conformism than on the well understood sense of school interests. In such a situation, those who feel that school is useless escape its control and refuse the forms of authority that no longer seem legitimate to them. It is therefore utilitarian individualism which performs the essential task of regulating behaviors.

On the other hand, the more youngsters are invited to conquer their position as an adult in a society where acquisition is stronger than inheritance, the more they are forced to consider themselves as equal and responsible. But in a society whose mode of functioning supposes a continuous competition and permanent inequalities, the principle of equality between subjects and that of the inequality of merits induces a strong subjectivation of youth trials, which leads to unhappy consciousness. The latter leads in turn to violence. Therefore, youth experience is dominated both by the anomy due to former institutions and by the continuous game of competition and the equality of individuals. (The fact that competition and equality are not perfect does not invalidate this analysis.)

When one looks closely, youth experiences may be seen as the products of what our societies have the most fundamentally to offer under the dual aspect of cultural liberalism and economic liberalism. In this sense, youngsters are well socialized for the society in which they will live. This analysis, which has a critical undertone, therefore raises two political and moral problems. How may we construct democratic institutions in the knowledge that the return to tradition is a lost cause, and how can we reduce inequalities? Or rather, what can we do so that these "fair" inequalities do not destroy the individuals themselves?

RACIAL ISOLATION, POVERTY AND THE LIMITS OF LOCAL CONTROL AS A MEANS FOR HOLDING PUBLIC SCHOOLS ACCOUNTABLE

Pedro Antonio Noguera

There is perhaps no other sector that reflects the fractured nature of civil society in the United States more than public education. Despite a Supreme Court decision calling for schools to be racially integrated, public schools across the United States remain largely segregated with respect to the race and class make-up of their student populations (Orfield and Eaton 1996). Public schools are not only segregated, but in most American cities, poor children have been consigned to schools that show very little evidence of serving their educational needs. On every known measure of academic performance, the vast majority of students attending urban public schools in the United States (especially those who are African American and Latino), are deficient with respect to basic literacy and math skills (Miller 1995; James, Jurich and Estes 2001).

In California, the state's Academic Performance Index (API) rankings reveal that poor academic performance is most common in school districts serving low-income populations, particularly in racially isolated urban areas where poverty tends to be concentrated (Ed-data 2002). This is true in large cities such as Los Angeles, Fresno and Oakland, and it is also true in smaller cities such as Compton, Marin City and East Palo Alto. The State of California holds local school districts accountable for the academic performance of students, but it does relatively little to ensure that schools meet the conditions that are necessary to provide adequate educational opportunities for all students. Although numerous studies have shown that poverty and racial isolation contribute significantly to school failure (Coleman 1966; Jencks 1972; Kozol 1991), the state does very little to mitigate the effects of these external conditions. Instead, responsibility for monitoring educational quality is delegated to educational leaders in school districts and elected school boards in keeping with the longstanding practice of allowing local communities to manage and operate public schools (Blasi 2001).

There is a vast body of research and evidence that shows such an approach does not work. In most cases, poor communities lack the resources necessary to monitor the quality of education provided to students. Concentrated poverty and racial isolation limit the ability of parents to exert control over the schools that serve their children, and educational leaders in such communities often lack the resources to take the task on themselves. For a variety of reasons that shall be presented, conditions external to schools such as poverty, crime, housing affordability and health care access, exert considerable influence over conditions within schools (Coleman, et al. 1966; Noguera 1996). Unless the state intervenes decisively to support schools in low-income communities, it is unlikely that such schools will ever improve.

Drawing on research and work carried out in schools and community organizations in Oakland, California over a twenty-year period, this paper presents an analysis of the ways in which poverty and racial isolation have contributed to the problems that have plagued schools in the district. The analysis presented draws upon the concept of social capital, a concept that has been used by social scientists to study how social relationships and networks are related to the quality of civic life. Social capital has also been employed to understand a variety of issues and problems facing inner-city communities (Sampson 2000; Waquant 1998). Through an analysis of the factors that hinder the development of social capital in low-income communities, I will show why local control is inadequate as a mechanism for holding schools accountable in high poverty areas. I also hope to use such an approach to draw attention to what it might take to transform inner city schools into genuine assets for the communities that they serve.

Poverty, racial isolation and Oakland's failing schools

As is true for most other school districts in the United States that cater to poor children and their families, on most measures of academic performance the Oakland Unified School District demonstrates little evidence of success in educating its students. For example, recent data from the California Department of Education shows that 43 of Oakland's 56 elementary schools received a ranking of 5 or less on the Academic Performance Index (API).[1] This means that according

---

[1] The academic performance index is a rating system which assesses the performance

to the state's performance measure, two thirds of Oakland's elementary schools are considered "low performing". Under the 1999 Public School Accountability Act "low performing" schools are to be subject to various sanctions and possible state takeover if they show no improvement over three years.

The challenge confronting the district as a result of the new policy is daunting. More than half of Oakland's elementary schools received an API rating of 1 or 2 (the lowest possible score) from the state. Prospects for change appear even more remote among secondary schools. All but one of the 16 middle schools and all seven of the district's high schools received API ratings below 5. The API ratings for Oakland's schools are consistent with a broader set of academic indicators such as the drop-out rate (25.2%),[2] the suspension and expulsion rate, student grade point averages, and college eligibility rates (19.6%).[3] All of these indicators serve to reinforce the widespread impression that Oakland public schools are failing and that enrollment in them should be avoided by those who can.

Oakland has received more than its share of ridicule and blame for the failure of its schools. In 1996 national attention was focused on the district as a result of the controversy created by the district's adoption of a policy that called for Ebonics (also known as Black vernacular English) to be treated as a legitimate second language. As news and confusion spread about the School Board's new language policy, Oakland was immediately subjected to ridicule and scorn for promoting what critics referred to as "bad English" and "slang" in the media (Perry and Delpitt 1997). Within a few weeks of the Board's resolution, the California State Legislature and US Congress moved quickly to prohibit the use of state or Federal funds to support implementation of the policy. The District even came under attack from several prominent African American leaders who charged the District with damaging the education of Black children through its poorly conceived policy.[4]

---

of schools based upon the average scores received by its students on the Stanford 9 achievement tests. For information on PSAA see http://www.cde.ca.gov/iiusp/.

[2] Most researchers regard official dropout rates as inaccurate because it fails to capture students who dropout before entering high school. See Civil Rights project.

[3] College eligibility rates are determined by the number of high school graduates who have successfully taken the courses and obtained the test scores necessary for admission to either the University of California or the California State University system.

[4] In addition to the attacks from the media and politicians, critics of Oakland's language policy included individuals such as the Reverend Jesse Jackson and poet

Responding to the non-academic needs of students and the "captured market" problem

Interestingly, even as Oakland's schools were castigated over the Ebonics resolution, few of those who engaged in the attack offered any recommendations for actions the district might take to solve the problem it was attempting to address. The widely misunderstood policy had been adopted by the School Board in response to a recommendation from a task force on African American student achievement. The task force had been formed for the purpose of devising a strategy to address widespread academic failure among African American students. (The grade point average for Black students in Oakland in 1996 was 1.8) While it might be fair to question the District's emphasis on Ebonics as a strategy for raising student achievement, the absence of alternative suggestions served as the strongest indication that the critics had no idea themselves of what should be done to respond the problem.

Yet, as disturbing as the outlook for schools in Oakland might appear, a closer look at the characteristics of the students it serves reveals that the situation is more complex than it seems. According to the state's data, nearly two thirds of students in the district qualify for free or reduced lunch based upon household income (Education Data Partnership 2001), and over 40% of its students come from families served by the CalWORKS program (formerly AFDC). The concentration of poverty is even more intense when one considers that all of the schools that received an API rating of 1 or 2, and have been designated "low performing", serve student populations where over 90% of the children qualify for free or reduced lunch. Additionally, more than a third of the district's students are from families that recently migrated to the United States whose first language is not English (Education Data Partnership 2001). The school district is also responsible for providing adequate educational opportunities for these students who together speak over seventy different languages.

Oakland students also come to school with a wide array of unmet social, material and emotional needs that affect their ability to learn.

Maya Angelou. However, once these individuals learned that the district had not intention of teaching children Ebonics as had been reported in the press, but rather sought to train teachers on how to work with students who speak Ebonics so that they can be taught standard English, their positions were reversed.

For example, because their families are often uninsured, many poor children lack access to adequate health and dental care (Alameda County Health Department 1998). This means that they are less likely to receive preventative treatment and more likely to rely upon hospital emergency rooms when they become ill. As is true for poor children elsewhere in the country, Oakland students are more likely to suffer from asthma and tooth decay and less likely to receive eye glasses when they need them (Alameda County Health Department 1998). As a result of poverty and the high cost of housing in the Bay Area, many Oakland students experience a high level of transience and are forced to change schools frequently when their families move into new housing. Finally, although data on these issues is less reliable, anecdotal evidence from teachers suggests that large numbers of Oakland's students come to school hungry, without adequate clothing, and suffering from stress as a result of domestic conflict in their families (Noguera 1996).

At Lowell Middle School in West Oakland where I conducted rescarch in the early 1990s, over 40% of the students suffered from some form of chronic respiratory condition, and two thirds of all students lived in a household with someone other than a biological parent (Noguera 1996). District officials applied considerable pressure on the school's leadership to raise test scores (which were among the lowest for middle schools in the District), but they did little to address the health and welfare needs of students at Lowell even though they were well aware of the obstacles these created. District administrators adopt a narrow focus on raising student achievement, not because they do not understand that a broad array of social and economic factors influence academic outcomes, but because they lack the resources to address the external conditions that impact student learning.

Despite the severity of the problems facing children in school districts like Oakland, such matters have generally not resulted in state or national intervention. Rather, under the pretense of local control Oakland's educational problems are treated as local matters to be addressed by locally elected officials and the community itself. The state and federal government allocates a variety of supplemental funds to serve the special needs of particular populations of students (e.g. special education, bilingual education, compensatory education, etc.), authority for managing the affairs of schools in Oakland is delegated to the locally elected school board. With seven elected and three appointed members,[5] the Board of Education has responsibility for managing a district comprised of 55,000 students with an annual operating budget of approximately 370 million dollars. Although the per pupil expenditure in Oakland is greater than the state average ($7,120 in Oakland, $6,334 is the state average), the funds available are largely insufficient to meet the health and welfare needs of Oakland's impoverished students.

Yet, lack of financial resources is only one of the reasons why so many of the needs of Oakland's children are unaddressed. Despite the severity of the education and welfare challenges facing Oakland's schools, matters related to financial management have often taken precedent over these issues. The Oakland Unified School District (OUSD) is the largest employer in the city, and in a city with high levels of poverty and unemployment, economic considerations, such as the letting of contracts for construction, maintenance and educational consulting, and collective bargaining issues generally, often take on greater importance and receive more attention than educational issues. Conflicts over how to allocate the resources controlled by the school district is of such great importance to the economy of the city that providing quality education to all students has often not been treated as a priority issue.

Finally, there is another important reason why educational issues have often been neglected in Oakland, and in many school districts that are located in impoverished communities throughout the country. Public schools in Oakland serve a captured market. The student population, which as I've pointed out is largely poor, immigrant, and non-white, is completely dependent upon the school system. Private schools are not accessible to most poor families due to cost, and leaving the system is typically not possible even if one is dissatisfied with the quality of school services provided. With a majority of the students served by Oakland's schools trapped by economic circumstances, dependent and unable to leave, affairs of the district can be managed with little concern for whether or not those served are

---

[5] As a result of a charter amendment proposed by Oakland Mayor Jerry Brown (Former Governor of California), the Mayor has the power to appoint three members to the School Board. The Mayor called for this measure to be instituted so that "genuine" reforms could be made in the system.

Most observers agree that while this additional support will be helpful, that it will not be sufficient to address the wide disparities in funding among school districts. For an analysis of the new education bill see New York Times, January 8, 2002.

satisfied with the quality of education provided. With the exception of the superintendent and principals who are removed easily and frequently, employees in the district can be confident that their positions are secure even though the system they work for largely fails to fulfill the mission for which it was created. Like other school districts in California, state funding to Oakland's public schools is determined by the average daily attendance of its students. As long as parents continue to enroll their children in the district's failing schools, the miserable status quo can be sustained indefinitely.

The role of social capital in improving the quality of public schools

Several researchers have suggested that the quality of education children receive is directly related to the ability of parents to generate social capital (Coleman 1988, Laraeu 1996; Noguera 2001). Social capital is a concept that has been used by social scientists to describe benefits individuals derive from their association with and participation within social networks and organizations (Sampson 1998; Woolcock 1998, Putnam 1995). Like economic capital, social capital can provide concrete benefits to those who have access to it, such as jobs, loans, educational opportunities and a variety of services. The more connected one is to groups or individuals that have access to resources, the greater the possibility that one can obtain concrete material and social benefits.

However, becoming connected to influential social networks is not easy. Access to some networks may be based upon family ties, income, religious affiliations or association with powerful groups that have been cultivated over time. It is generally not possible to simply join an exclusive social network. In addition to having less economic capital, the poor often have less social capital than the affluent because the connections they have tend to be limited to other poor people or to organizations with fewer resources (Saegert, et al. 2001).

In cities such as Oakland, poverty and racial isolation constitute significant barriers to acquiring social capital, particularly "bridging" and "bonding" forms of social capital that have been identified as most important for community development (Woolcock 1998). Bridging social capital refers to the connections that link poor people to institutions and individuals that have access to money and power. In Oakland, poor people of color generally lack bridging social capital because they are often excluded from influential social networks as a result of race and class barriers, and social isolation. For example, although Oakland has several powerful and influential Black churches, their membership is more likely to be drawn from middle class residents who reside in more affluent neighborhoods and the suburbs than from the lower class communities in which the churches are located (Commission for Positive Change 1990). The same is true of many African American political clubs in Oakland such as the NAACP, the Niagra Democratic Club, and the East Oakland Democratic Club. Influential churches and civic associations play important roles in the political life of the City and often provide important services to the poor. But most poor people in Oakland do not participate in these organizations and their absence further exacerbates their marginalization and social isolation.

Bonding social capital, which provides connections among and between poor people (Woolcock 1998), and that serves as a basis for solidarity and collective action, is also in short supply in Oakland. Over the last fifteen years, Oakland has attracted large numbers of Mexican and Asian immigrants who have moved into neighborhoods in East and West Oakland that have been traditionally African American (Clark 1998). This demographic shift has had the effect of diminishing community cohesion as language and cultural differences have contributed to fragmentation and distrust between new and older residents (League of Cities 2000). Aside from the fact that they reside on the same streets and even live in the same apartment buildings, these rapidly changing communities are made up of strangers who perceive themselves as having little if anything in common.[6] Rather than working together in pursuit of common community interests, growing diversity has increased the level of competition over community resources, which in turn has heightened tensions and fueled inter-group conflict. Tensions and occasionally violent outbursts related to demographic change have most frequently been manifest in Oakland's public schools, one of the few sites where

---

[6] Efforts to address the lack of community organization in Oakland have recently been supported by the Koshland Committee of the San Francisco Foundation. For the last five years, the committee has developed an initiative in the San Antonio district, an area comprised of Latinos, Southeast Asians, older African Americans, Native Americans and white small business owners.

different groups come into direct contact with each other (Noguera and Bliss 2001).

Finally, poor people in Oakland tend to be concentrated in neighborhoods that lack strong social institutions, public services and businesses. The census tracts where poor people reside in greatest numbers also have the highest rates of crime and are therefore regarded as less desirable places to live by the middle class (City of Oakland 1994). In east and west Oakland, the poorest sections of the city, there are few banks, pharmacies or grocery stores. Libraries, parks and recreational centers are present in these neighborhoods, but residents frequently complain that drug trafficking and crime have rendered these potential community assets unusable (Office of Economic development 1994). Sociologist, Loic Waquant, has argued that public institutions in inner city neighborhoods may actually generate negative social capital (i.e. undermine social cohesion) because their unresponsiveness to the needs of residents undermines and erodes the social well being of the community (Waquant 1998). Furthermore, in addition to possessing few social assets, the poorer neighborhoods of east and west Oakland have a disproportionate number of vacant, abandoned and derelict sites. Undesirable land use facilities such as solid waste transfer stations, drug treatment centers and industrial plants that emit toxic pollutants are also plentiful in these areas (Office of Economic Development 1994).

Social capital and institutional responsiveness

The prevalence of race and class isolation often has direct bearing upon the quality of schools children attend. In Oakland, children tend to enroll in schools located in neighborhoods where they live. As a result of this practice, the poorest children generally enroll in the lowest performing schools, while middle class children from more affluent neighborhoods attend better schools. As the chart below reveals, differences between schools in different neighborhoods is striking. Though the District does not prevent low-income parents from enrolling their children in higher performing schools, lack of transportation and limited space make this an option that few can exercise.

Selection of Oakland schools by neighborhood and API rating

School	Neighborhood	API rating
	(Poor)	
Golden Gate	West Oakland	1
ML King	West Oakland	2
Sobrante	ParkEast Oakland	1
Brookfield	East Oakland	1
	(Affluent)	
Chabot	Claremont	9
Hillcrest	Montclair	10
Joaquin	MillerHills	10

The relationship between poverty and school quality requires further elaboration. Research shows that poor children are generally less prepared than middle class children with respect to their academic skills at the time they enroll in school (Jencks and Phillips 1998). Rather than adopting measures that might reduce the effects of differences in prior academic preparation, schools often exacerbate pre-existing differences in ability by providing poor children with an inferior education.

In this respect, Oakland is no exception. The schools where a majority of poor children are enrolled not only have lower test scores, they also tend to have inferior facilities, and are generally more disorganized. They also have fewer certified teachers and higher turnover among principals (District Profile 2001). Some of the schools, such as Lowell Middle and McClymonds High School in West Oakland, tend to have lower enrollment because they have difficulty attracting students, while several of the schools in the San Antonio and Fruitvale sections of East Oakland are overcrowded and literally bursting at the seams.

Despite the consistency of this pattern, there is no evidence that shows that the condition of schools in low-income neighborhoods in Oakland is a product of intentional policy or a conspiracy aimed at depriving poor children quality of education. At least part of the problem lies with the lack of social capital in Oakland's low-income communities created by poverty and social isolation, and the disproportionate social capital possessed by others. The leadership of Oakland's public schools is more likely to be pressured with demands from its unions and the small but influential number of middle class parents it serves, than by advocates and parents of poor children.

The first two constituencies are well organized, politically savvy, and have access to financial and legal resources. Occasionally, poor parents also organize themselves to apply pressure on the school district, but their efforts are rarely sustained. Even when they are, the demands of poor parents can be more easily ignored because they typically lack the ability to exert leverage upon school officials.

*A dream deferred:
racial politics and the unfulfilled promise of black power in Oakland*

With academic failure so persistent and widespread one might wonder why a community with a reputation and history for political activism would not have acted long ago to radically reform its schools. Oakland was after all the birthplace of the Black Panther Party, an organization that took on another public institution that was perceived as failing to serve community needs, namely the police department, which it accused of engaging in rampant harassment and brutality. Oakland's history of Black leadership and political activism goes back to the 1930s when it served as the national headquarters of the powerful Sleeping Car Porters Union (Franklin and Moss 1988). In the 1920s Oakland had one of the most active chapters of UNIA (Universal Negro Improvement Association—the largest Black political organization in US history headed by Marcus Garvey) on the west coast (Martin). In the 1970s, Oakland voters transformed the city from a company town dominated by Kaiser Aluminum and controlled by white Republicans, into a city where all of the major public officials (Mayor, City Manager, Superintendent of Schools, Police Chief, State Assemblyman and Congressman) were African American (Bush 1984).

However, political activism and racial succession in politics have not made it possible for those served by the Oakland public schools to exert influence and control over them. Unlike unions and political organizations that have typically been comprised of individuals from middle and stable working class backgrounds, since the advent of school desegregation, public schools in Oakland have catered primarily to children from lower class families. Poor parents and community activists have organized at various times to call for reform and improvement in the City's schools. For the most part, such efforts have not resulted in significant or sustained improvements. Moreover, the fact that Black middle class administrators have held important positions throughout the district for over thirty years has done little to bring about greater accountability and responsiveness to the needs and aspirations of those who rely upon the public schools.

For the last ten years attempts there have been renewed attempts to mobilize grassroots pressure for school improvement. The Oakland Citizens Organizations (OCO), a broad multi-racial, faith-based coalition, has mounted considerable pressure upon the district for meaningful improvement and reform. At large public gatherings it has organized, OCO has pressured public officials to pledge their support for changes in the operation and management of the schools. Yet, while their efforts have led to the adoption of significant policy changes such as site-based decision making and an initiative to create several new, smaller schools (Thompson 2001), general academic improvement remains unattained.

Dennis Chaconas, the new superintendent of Oakland's public schools, has made concerted efforts over the last two years to address the problems plaguing the school district. He has shaken up the central administration by replacing several long-term managers with younger professionals recruited from outside the district. He has also applied greater pressure on the principals of low performing schools and removed several principals from schools where there was little evidence of progress in raising achievement. It is undoubtedly too early to know whether the Superintendent's efforts will produce meaningful improvements in Oakland's schools. However, past experience suggests that placing greater demands upon the District Administration, the School Board, or the schools themselves is unlikely to lead change. Unless increased pressure is accompanied by systemic changes in the way schools respond to the needs of students and parents, and genuine assistance is provided to the schools serving the neediest children, it is unlikely that lasting, significant change will be made.

Conclusion

Conditions in school districts that serve largely impoverished student populations cannot be improved without external assistance. To ask local communities to assume responsibility for this task is not unlike asking the sick to heal themselves. Poor communities lack the resources and social capital to exert control over their schools and move them to improve. This does not mean that parents and community residents should not be encouraged to be actively involved in their schools, but it does mean that they cannot be expected to fix their schools on their own.

The state's emphasis on raising student achievement has significantly increased awareness of racial disparities in academic performance. The so-called "achievement gap" is evident in every publication of test scores that identifies the racial make-up, socio-economic status and location of a school. The question confronting political leaders in the state of California is whether they will go beyond publicly humiliating schools and districts where performance is low and actually find ways to provide tangible assistance. As the state with the largest population and the fastest growing number of immigrants (Clark 1998), California will undoubtedly be a trend-setter for the nation. How we respond to the needs of failing schools in low-income areas may very well be an indication of how we will respond to other challenges affecting the health and welfare of the state.

Rather than presuming that all schools can be treated the same, state officials must recognize that socioeconomic conditions within the local context act as significant constraints limiting possibilities for local control of schools. Put more simply, without the power and resources to exert control over schools, low-income communities cannot be expected to hold their schools accountable. Nor is it reasonable to expect that schools in such communities will be able to solve the vast array of problems confronting students and their families on their own. Unless measures are adopted to mitigate against the effects of poverty and racial isolation, local control will remain little more than a guise through which the State can shirk its responsibility for insuring that all students have access to quality education.

The Federal government's recently approved education reform measure called "Leave No Child Behind Act", will significantly increase the Federal government's role in failing local school districts, however it is unlikely to provide the help that is needed. Although more money is to be set aside for low performing schools, the measure does nothing to address the horrid conditions present in those schools, and it does not even begin to attempt to ameliorate the social inequities that impact schooling.

Public education has historically occupied a special place within American society. It has often been the birthplace of democratic reforms and expansions in civil rights (Tyack 1980). Education is also the only social entitlement available to all children in the United States regardless of race, class or national origin (Carnoy and Levin 1986). In the last ten years, support for improving public education has also been the only domestic issue that has generated broad bipartisan consensus among policymakers. Given its unique status it makes sense for those interested in finding ways to reduce poverty and racial inequality to focus at least some of their energies on efforts to improve the quality and character of public education in the United States.

References

Ada, A. F. (1988), "The Pajaro Valley Experience: Working with Spanish speaking parents to develop children's reading and writing skills through the use of children's literature" in *Minority Education* edited by Tove Skutnabb-Kangas and Jim Cummins. London: Multilingual Matters, Ltd.

Alameda County Health Department (1998), "By the numbers: A public health dataview of Oakland" Arnold Perkins, Director.

Anderson, J. (1988), *The Education of Blacks in the South, 1860–1935*. Chapel Hill, NC: University of North Carolina Press.

Blasi, G. (2001), "Reforming Educational Accountability". Unpublished conference paper.

Brown, P. (2001), "Oakland's schools military bearing rankles some" in *The New York Times*, August 24.

Bush, R. (1984), *The New Black Vote*. San Francisco: Synthesis Publications.

Carnoy, M. and H. Levin (1986), *School and Work in a Democratic State*. Palo Alto, CA: Stanford University Press.

Cibulka, J. (2001), "Old Wine, New Bottles" *Education Next*, Winter www.educationnext.org.

Chubb, J. and T. Moe (1990), *Politics, Markets and America's Schools*. Washington, D.C.: Brookings Institute.

City of Oakland (1994), West Oakland Community-Existing Conditions. Office of Economic Development.

Clark, W. (1998), *The California Cauldron*. New York: The Guilford Press.

Clinchy, E. editor (2000), *The New Small Schools*. New York: teachers College Press.

College Board (1999), *Reaching the Top: Report of the national Task Force on Minority High Achievement*. New York: The College Board.

Coleman, J. (1988), "Social capital in the creation of human capital" *American Journal of Sociology* 94 (supp): S 95–120.

Comer, J. (1980), *School Power*. New York: Free Press.

Commission for Positive Change (1990), Good Education in Oakland. Oakland, CA.

Conchas, G. (2001), "Structuring success and failure: understanding variability in Latino school engagement." *Harvard Educational Review*, 70 (3), 475–504.

Dryfoos, J. (2001), "Evaluation of community schools: an early look" http://www.communityschools.org/evaluation/evalbrieffinal.html.

Education Data Partnership (2001), http://www.ed-data.k12.ca.us.

Ed Data (2002), District Financial Statements. http://www.ed-data.k12.ca.us/fiscal/fundingsummary.asp.

Elmore, R. (1996), "The new accountability in state educational policy" in H. Ladd, ed., *Performance Based Strategies for Improving Schools.*
Epstein, J. (1993), "A Response". *Teachers College Record*, 94 (4), 710–717.
Fantini, M., M. Gittell, R. Magat (1970), *Community Control and the Urban School.* New York: Praeger.
Fine, M. (1993), "(Ap)parent involvement: reflections on parents, power and urban schools". *Teachers College Record*, 94 (4): 26–43.
Franklin, J. and A. Moss (1988), *From Slavery to Freedom.* New York: Knopf.
Friere, P. (1970), *Education for Critical Consciousness.* New York: Continuum Press.
Gold, E. (2001), "Clients, consumers or collaborators? Parents and their roles in school reform" August, *Consortium for Policy Research in Education.*
Gormley, W. editor (1991), *Privatization and its Alternatives.* Madison, WI: University of Wisconsin Press.
Hernstein R. and C. Murray (1994), *The Bell Curve: Intelligence and class structure in American life.* New York: Free Press.
Hess, G. A. (1999), "Community participation or control? From New York to Chicago". *Theory Into Practice*, 38 (4), 217–224.
Horton, M. and P. Freire (1990), We make the Road by Walking. Philadelphia, PA: Temple University Press.
James, Donna W., Sonia Jurich and Steve Estes *Raising Minority Academic Achievement.* (2001), Washington, D.C.: American Youth Policy Forum.
Jencks, C. (1972), *Inequality.* New York: Harper Books.
Katznelson, I. and M. Weir (1994), *Schooling for All.* Berkeley, CA: University of California Press.
Kozol, J. (1991), *Savage Inequalities.* New York: Crown Books. The importance of cultural capital". Sociology of Education, 60, 73–85.
Lareau, A. (1989), *Home Advantage: Social class and parental intervention in elementary education.* New York: Falmer Press.
Linn, R. (2000), "Assessments and Accountability" 29 *Educational Researcher* 4.
Maeroff, G. (1989), "Whithered Hopes and Stillborn Dreams: The Dismal Panorama of Inner-City Schools" in *Phi Delta Kappan*, 69:632–638.
Martin, A. Marcus Garvey
Massey, D. and N. Denton (1993), *American Apartheid.* Cambridge, MA: Harvard University Press.
Mc Whorter, J. (2000), *Losing the Race.* New York: New Press.
Miller, Scott L. *An American Imperative.* New Haven, CT: Yale University Press, 1995
Noguera, P. (1996), Confronting the Urban in Urban School Reform" in *Urban Review*, Vol. 28. No. 1, pp. 1–19.
Noguera, P. and A. Akom (2000), "Disparities Demystified" *The Nation*, June 5.
Noguera, P. and M. Bliss (2001), "A Four Year Evaluation Study of Youth Together" Oakland, CA: Arts, Resources and Curriculum.
Office of Economic Development (1994), Creating a Community Vision: Community Goal Statements and Proposal Implementation Strategies. Report published by the City of Oakland.
Perry, T. and L. Delpitt (1997), The Real Ebonics Debate. *Rethinking Schools*, Vol. 12, No. 1.
Portes, A. and R. Rumbaut (2001), *Legacies: The Story of the Immigrant Second Generation.* Berkeley, CA: UC Press.
Putnam, R, (1995), "Bowling Alone: America's Declining Social Capital." *Journal of Democracy* 6 (1): 65–78.
Rouce, C. (199?), *Rhetoric Versus Reality.* Washington, D.C. Rand Corporation.
Saegert, S., P. Thompson and M. Warren (2001), *Social Capital in Low-Income Communities.* New York: Russell Sage.
Sampson, R. (1998), "What Community Supplies" in *Urban Problems and Community*

Development by R. Ferguson and W. Dickens. Washington, D.C.: Brookings Institute.

Steele, S. (1996), *The Content of Our Character*. New York: St. Martin's Press.

Stone, C. (2001), Building Civic Capacity. Lawrence, KA: University of Kansas Press.

Thompson, C. (2001), "Class Struggle" *East Bay Express*, Vol. 23, No. 27.

Tyack, (1980), *The One Best System*. Cambridge, MA: Harvard University Press.

Wacquant, L. (1998), "Negative Social Capital: State Breakdown and Social Destitution in America's Urban Core" in *Netherlands Journal of Housing and the Built Environment*, Vol. 13, No. 1.

Wilgoren, J. (1997), "Young Blacks Turn to School Vouchers as Civil Rights Issue" in *The New York Times*, April 27.

Woolcock, M. (1998), "Social Capital and Economic Development: Toward a Theoretical Synthesis and Policy Framework" in *Theory and Society*, 27:151–208.

THE PARADOX OF ETHNICITY IN FRENCH SECONDARY SCHOOLS

Jean-Paul Payet

Unlike statistical studies, which seek to demonstrate the fairness of the French educational system in its dealings with immigrant populations, a socio-anthropological approach to educational establishments—junior high schools and vocational *lycées*—located in working-class or socially mixed districts reveals a more contradictory reality, one in which integration and exclusion intertwine. This reality is a conflictual one made up of a tissue of misunderstandings and dilemmas. The treatment of immigrants in a "post-republican" education system is best described in terms of a paradox characterised by a permanent and unstable oscillation between the spotlighting and concealment of pupils' national origins. Ethnicity in this education system is sometimes prominent and significative, sometimes hidden and censored; it might equally well be said to be constantly present and constantly rendered invisible. Its full import is revealed when the veil of appearances is torn away, when the pretence required to sustain the paradox falls apart. In view of the treatment of ethnicity within the school system, the first task in a socio-anthropological approach is to elucidate observations made in the field that suggest that the school careers of pupils from immigrant backgrounds are characterised by a tension between institutional discrimination and resistance from the actors concerned. The relationship between education and immigration then has to be relocated within a dynamic perspective, in which the history of that relationship helps to shed light on current conflicts and the issues likely to be contested in the future. Finally, the search for a response to the issues identified requires a debate around democracy in the French education system and its openness to pluralism.

Fabricating classes

Observations made in the field (Payet, 1992, 1995; Debarbieux, 1997) show that pupils' origins constitute an important strategic criterion for school administrators. Over and above any views that might prevail in individual schools, the task of allocating pupils to the various classes within the same section does not take on its full significance until it is located within a broader context that includes other schools in the vicinity and the wider urban environment. In a context characterised by competition and segregation, it has to be regarded as one of the tasks that helps to shape the supply of education. It has an organisational dimension as well, since it is also part of the division of labour within schools and as such interacts with the process of establishing teachers' duties and the management of workplace relations, both vertical and horizontal. The distribution of pupils among the various classes, a process which justifies our description of it as the "fabrication of classes", is a strategic activity that is shrouded in secrecy and gives rise to deliberate dissimulation. All head teachers, without exception, routinely declare that classes are put together either in accordance with explicit criteria (such as choice of language) or entirely randomly (random allocation) and that in any event the allocation of pupils to classes is an ordinary, everyday task to which no special significance or motive should be imputed.

Nevertheless, closer scrutiny contradicts the official view of a unified high school made up of undifferentiated classes. Contrary to this received wisdom, a whole range of techniques is used in order to put together classes differentiated both by attainment level and attitudes, as attested in judgments on pupils' school careers to date or as reflected in "common-sense" judgments based on prejudices, stereotypes or experience (i.e. "subjective evidence"). The notion of "classes based on attainment level" (Duru-Bellat and Mingat, 1997) cannot adequately describe groupings produced by a series of procedures and in accordance with a multiplicity of criteria that cannot be adequately captured by the notion of attainment level because of the vital role played by judgments of pupils' character and conduct. This differentiation is in fact based on several variables, including attainment level, social origin, gender and "ethnic" origin. Social origin and ethnic origin are of course very closely linked, since children from immigrant families generally come from the same social background. However, when class profiles are reconstituted, it becomes apparent that classes differ by attainment level, socio-ethnic background and gender. Those classes that have few if any low-achievers or slow-earners are also those in which girls and pupils born to French parents are overrepresented; conversely, those classes in which low-achievers and slow-earners are concentrated are those in which boys and pupils born to non-French parents are overrepresented. Far from their being any causal relationship between origin, gender and attainment level, the differential make-up of school classes is in reality a fabrication. As soon as the effect of attainment level is neutralised by applying the "all things being equal" principle, that is taking each age cohort as a whole, the socio-ethnic differentiations in the allocation of pupils to "good" or "bad" classes remain. It is as if the whole process of allocating pupils to classes results in the separating out of two categories of pupils, girls born to French parents and boys born to non-French parents.

This objective discrimination within a republican system can only be understood by looking at the system "from the bottom up", that is by attempting to recreate and understand the point of view of the heads of schools that are segregated or at risk of segregation. While the possible existence of cynical actors cannot be excluded, it is important to stress that the vast majority of head teachers subscribe to democratic values and that the establishment of a proper "social mix" is one of their most cherished objectives, a "higher good" (to borrow the expression used by Charles Taylor, 1998) that they seek to achieve. In the current educational context, however, considerable obstacles stand in their way. This context can be characterised by increasing tension between a powerful state supervisory apparatus inherited from the past and more liberal forces tending towards greater individual freedom. These latter are reflected in the value that strategically-minded families attach to the school their children attend. Such families wish to choose their children's school for themselves and sometimes take steps to reconfigure the local educational provision to their own advantage. These liberal dynamics also find expression in the competition between the private and public sectors, as well as within the public sector, for access to the distinctive institutional and human resources that determine the quality of educational provision and, consequently, demand for that provision (which, once captured, in turn becomes a distinctive resource specific to a particular school).

The search for the higher good of a proper "social mix" takes place within a framework characterised by opacity and conflict between state control and liberalism. In this form of "educational market" unique to France, the search for a proper "social mix" proves to be all the easier the more favourable the position occupied in that market, and vice versa. The heads of segregated or mixed-origin schools take a variety of measures to reduce or halt the flight of good pupils and pupils from French families (Payet, 1995; Broccolochi and van Zanten, 1997; Ball and van Zanten, 1998; Laforgue, 1999). In reality, these attempts to recruit pupils from families that are already actively seeking the best school for their children, and are therefore prepared to be mobile, work against the interests of those families unable to move. In this way, a school's overall heterogeneity, whether relative or real, is maintained or even increased by putting together classes that are homogeneous in terms of attainment level and attitude and thereby help to retain or attract pupils from middle-class French families. Thus the socio-ethnic mix at the level of the individual school is obtained through an internal process of segmentation between "good", "less good" and "bad" classes that are differentiated from each other on the basis of social background, gender and ethnicity.

This segmentation calls for an analysis of the varying extents to which social mix and segregation are produced within the school system and of the complex processes involved. The production of social mix and segregation interacts with the production in the wider urban environment of socio-ethnic divisions and with the political and institutional management of the housing and education markets. In the absence of a voluntarist segregation policy, individual schools tend to retreat to safer ground, with the absence of central regulation accentuating the search for local solutions, which end up competing with each other (Laforgue, 1999). However, there is also a need to be wary of the effects of voluntarist policies that fail to move beyond the bureaucratic position of reinforcing segmentation. In the light of the unequal resources on which the various social strata are able to draw, it is certainly to be feared that a policy of this kind will lead only to a widening of the gap between aspirations and strategies.

Day-to-day relations within the school system

The second type of phenomena revealed by a socio-anthropological approach relates to the interpersonal relationships between school staff and pupils and between staff and parents during formalised meetings in which civil roles come into play (i.e. situations in which the social dimension is combined with the exercising of rights). These public "stages" are linked to behind-the-scenes areas in the "wings", as it were, in which the actors become increasingly distanced from their roles, thereby revealing their unease with the interactions in which they are engaged. Thus the republican principle of indifference to differences can be seen to operate very variably: it is generally applied in those areas in which there is contact with the general public and, conversely, ignored or even contradicted in those areas in which school staff are shielded from the public gaze. The day-to-day discourse of school staff tends increasingly to put forward pupils' ethnic/cultural origins as a relevant factor in explaining behaviour and transgressions and, more generally, in attributing responsibility for the current worsening of the conditions under which staff have to work (Payet, 1995; Favre-Perroton, 1999). It goes without saying that knowledge of foreign cultures is seldom based on any theoretical knowledge, such as that derived from anthropology, but rather on informal knowledge derived from presuppositions and prejudices rooted in the national consciousness. The dynamic and complex nature of the culture of immigrant families is not understood.

The argument that ethical awareness among the actors is declining is usually adduced in order to explain the new ethnicisation of the day-to-day discourse of school staff. Certainly, it is difficult to imagine how the world of education, as it has been affected by processes of social exclusion over the past two decades, could have been completely impervious to the ideology of rejection and xenophobia. However, ideas in themselves are not sufficient to explain and understand the current legitimacy of essentialist arguments. It is because these arguments seem to be plausible when tested against everyday reality that opinions are formed despite widespread support for general values opposed to such arguments. They are rooted in the direct, "common-sense" perception of phenomena in the daily life of schools. With reference to the previous point, mention could be made here of the effects on staff attitudes of the ethnicisation of class composition when it is not perceived as a construct. A class's low attainment and recalcitrance are attributed to the characteristics of the majority of its pupils and not to the deviancy-inspiring effects of a process whereby, intentionally or unintentionally, disadvantaged or "difficult" pupils are grouped together in the same class. The logic of the self-fulfilling prophecy comes into its own with a vengeance here.

More generally, differences emerge in the ways in which pupils and parents of different ethnic origins experience school; what is more, the agents perceive these differences as such, that is as specific or *natural* differences, even though they participate in constructing them (i.e. in *naturalising* them). (We should emphasise here the importance we attach, in defining ethnicity, to the processes whereby it is constructed and given prominence, in contradistinction to essentialist approaches (Douglass and Lyman, 1976).) Examination of lists of pupils punished for various misdemeanours shows that pupils of foreign extraction are overrepresented; this applies to both boys and girls, but more particularly to boys. A survey of more than 1000 junior high school pupils confirms this finding, since pupils from immigrant backgrounds claimed to be punished more frequently than those born to French parents. The same questionnaire also shows that foreign origin is a variable correlated with a strong feeling of injustice towards the education system. Finally, other counts show that pupils of foreign origin are overrepresented among class representatives (Payet, 1985, 1995; Payet and Sicot, 1996).

The ethnography of non-teaching spaces within schools—the offices of teachers, secretaries or head teachers, parent-teacher meetings etc.—reveals a pattern that is characteristic of the direct relationship between staff and immigrant populations or those from an immigrant background. This relationship can be defined by drawing on Goffmann's notion of a "stigmatised" encounter, that is one fraught with a fundamental uncertainty (Goffmann, 1975). It has been shown that more pupils from foreign backgrounds seek to engineer meetings which they then try to redefine along more informal lines. Similarly, more meetings with these pupils or their parents are characterised by familiar or informal attitudes on the part of certain members of staff. However, they may also have the effect of distancing school staff from immigrant pupils and their parents when staff adopt bureaucratic attitudes. Such meetings are in fact characterised by a permanent hesitation between familiarity and excessive formality, between closeness and remoteness. These "unsettled, anxious interactions" usually produce misunderstandings and conflicts. They take place with less civility on both sides and fuel a suspicion that pre-exists them and which is, as it were, self-reproducing.

Thus the relationship between schools and immigrant populations or those from immigrant backgrounds unfolds in conditions of high visibility animated by two interdependent principles, namely commitment and stigmatisation. The stigmatisation motivates pupils from immigrant backgrounds to commit themselves to redefining their status and image more favourably. In turn, this commitment gives rise to stigmatisation when the forms of commitment seem to be unacceptable or when they do not allow the other to be given a positive construction, for example when they are based on the discrediting or humiliation of the agents, whether direct or indirect, i.e. when it is intentional or perceived as such by them. The commitment displayed by pupils of foreign origin and their parents does not take a single form; rather, it oscillates between the two poles of cooperation and opposition, combining the two styles in various ways as the interaction proceeds. They are more dependent than other relationships on the effects of the immediate situation and on modes of communication. As a result, they are more risky, in that they require a combination of attack (fighting stigmatisation) and defence (remaining on guard) that leaves the behaviour of such pupils and their parents open to being interpreted as transgressions of the school's codes of behaviour.

The relationship between schools and immigrant populations in a dynamic perspective

In the academic literature, the relationship between immigrant families and the education system is invariably described as a relationship in which much has been invested, at least on the symbolic if not always on the practical level. Such arguments are an attempt to counteract the widespread view of families whose attitude towards the school system is one of resignation and disinterest. From this perspective, the school becomes a major emblematic and strategic arena for immigrants seeking to "integrate" themselves into French society. The education system is of great strategic importance in determining access to qualifications and socio-economic advancement, and schools are emblematic in the sense that they seem to be the *last republican space* in a world characterised by banishment, whether from housing or public spaces, or from public services or leisure facilities. However, the republican pretensions of the school system are undermined by discriminatory processes and practices. In the case of failure at school, the level of disappointment is commensurate with the high hopes vested in the education system. This disappointment may be reflected in violence. However, what an ethnography of school life reveals is that the readiness of immigrant pupils and their families to take action is not simply an attitude that emerges at key moments in a pupil's school career (notably when courses of study are being chosen) but one that informs the entire experience of immigrant populations in their dealings with the education system, even on a day-to-day basis. It manifests itself in a practical attitude towards education that lasts throughout a pupil's school career and is applied to all areas of the educational process.

The standard references to the "expectations" immigrant populations have of the school system have an advantage as well as a drawback. On the one hand, they raise the status of the relationship of these populations to the education system. On the other hand, however, they do not make it clear that this relationship may be informed by distance or conflict. The risk is that these expectations may be conceived of in terms of a normative, school-centred schema (i.e. the mental model that underpins the relationship of the middle classes to the education system), which may give rise to doubts about the validity of a positive view of the relationship to the education system when that relationship acquires conflictual elements. The use of the term expectations cannot be sustained unless the relationship of families to the school system can be redefined in political terms as part of the relationship between the nation and its immigrant populations.

To state that education is the last republican space for immigrant populations is to underline the fact that the school system has been invested with the dual task of making reparations and providing compensation. Thus the educational system is required to make amends for past indignities and to provide compensation for the current effects of those indignities, which are aggravated by segregation, discrimination and racism. When the education system fails in these tasks, it becomes an object of "discontent" for immigrant families (to use the expression adopted by Hirschmann, 1995; Bajoit, 1988). The constraining world in which they are confined causes their reactions to take the form of protest rather than loyalty, defection or apathy. Defection is not an easy option for them, since they enjoy less freedom to move within the educational market than French families with comparable expectations. They are less likely to withdraw their children from segregated schools, despite the strategies they deploy, which prove to be ineffective (Vissac, 1998). Nevertheless, the incidence of withdrawal seems to be increasing among immigrant families, as suggested by locally gathered evidence of their use of the private sector (Mazzela, 1997). The rejection of apathy (which we have designated in another vocabulary by the term "need for commitment") is an aspect of the families' behaviour that is both private and public. Apathy could represent the attitude of the first generation, and particularly that of the father, the "immigrant", to his experience of emigrating in search of work. For him, apathy was commingled with withdrawal, in the sense that his capacity for planning was usually directed toward the ever diminishing hope of a return to the native country (Boubeker, 1999). The rejection of apathy by the younger generations of immigrants, particularly boys, is most clearly reflected in their refusal to follow their fathers into manual jobs by opting for the shorter vocational training courses.

Thus the notion of immigrant populations' expectations of the education system must be given an historical dimension and be seen to contain elements of protest. Implicit in these expectations is a demand for reparation of an inherited, lasting and continuous situation of discrimination (particularly from the post-colonial minorities). However, the ways in which this demand is expressed mean that it does not come across as a structured, collective claim. When it does, as in the affair of the Islamic shawl or *chador*, the education system reacts by falling back into intransigeance. The demand is then expressed in minor interactions which, if badly handled, can flare into violence. In the conflict between the education system and immigrant populations, what policy could transform "inchoate demands into reasoned argument" (Rancière, 1995; Anselme, 2000)?

Pluralism and democracy in schools

What escape can there be from this spiral of mobilisation-stigmatisation? We could content ourselves with the republican response, in its individualist/statist version, that advocates and puts into effect genuine indifference to differences. However, that would be to continue to identify equality with justice, whereas equal treatment for populations that have been discriminated against cannot produce equality. It would also be to disregard the question of the cultural and religious pluralism that is characteristic of contemporary societies and the essential role assigned to schools (Bourgeault et al., 1995; Touraine, 1997). Above all, it would be to ignore the fact that the notion of "indifference to difference" no longer constitutes the sole philosophy underlying institutional action within the education system. In official documents and institutional discourses, references to adaptation to local contexts and regard for the specificity of "difficult" (i.e. working-class *and* immigrant) localities are to be found alongside the more traditional references to uniform and standardised measures (Payet, 1994). In this confused framework, and in the absence of any attempts to refashion the reference philosophy, the rhetoric of adaptation to the populations living in the suburbs and to immigrant populations seems to produce the most essentialist excesses. At a time when different sets of beliefs or doctrines coexist alongside each other, the adapted "gaze" operates without a reference point of view. Thus young trainee teachers may, in all naivety, be tempted to apply a culturalist interpretation to all the behaviour of young people from immigrant backgrounds and a particular social milieu—boys, girls and adolescents alike—that displays a subjective element (Varro, 1999).

Does this point to a current confusion of doctrines or to an original confusion in the republican doctrine? The coexistence of the republican doctrine and of the differentialist doctrine (adaptation to local contexts) does indeed raise questions. It may be that such coexistence is possible in reality because it lies at the heart of a republican doctrine that has never abandoned its essentialist connotations and has never really broken with a colonial ideology. The whiff of communitarianism that "true republicans" brought with them by way of an offering to "false republicans" would then be a form of barrier erected to defend the doctrine from scrutiny from within. A third route, which might offer a way out of the debate, which in France has been formulated in the wrong terms, between "individualistic statism" and communitarianism, would seek to link democracy and pluralism, giving priority to the latter. It would seek justice not by ignoring the condition and demands of minority groups but by recognising their legitimate dignity. How might this dignity be produced without going to the opposite extreme of a communitarianism that would take us away from the notion of a common good and further strengthen inequalities? Three areas for action can be identified.

The first is democracy in schools and concerns the relations between staff and pupils and between staff and parents. The negative ethnicisation of assessments made in schools arises out of the democratic deficit within the school system. The use of ethnicity as a reference point in making assessments is lost in the gaping chasm of the democratic deficit. It is the failure to raise the level of generality in universal categories that provides a justification for an increase in the level of generality in ethnic categories. The untenable separation of individuals and roles in the education system (school staff whose judgments are disputed or who are the victims of violence react by launching a full-frontal attack, in the same way as their pupils, while professional errors are attributed to the personalities of individual teachers, just as failure at school is attributed to pupils' personal shortcomings) leads to the individualisation and privatisation of conflict resolution. The views of parents and pupils can be represented only through argument, since in the eyes of the school and its staff they represent a threat. Ethnicity is ultimately a practical resource that can be drawn on all the more readily since it is sometimes used defensively by pupils and parents seeking to make accusations of provocation or racism. Conversely, it has to be recognised that, in reality, pupils and parents from immigrant backgrounds provide a different model of the relationship between schools and users of education services (over and above the specific meaning this model has for them). The democratisation of the relationships between educational professionals and users of educational services provides an answer to the question of the conflict between the education system and immigrant populations without specifying it; such democratisation would encompass that conflict and go beyond it as part of a wide ranging exercise in renewal throughout the public service as a whole. This renewal would cover all aspects of the representation of pupils and parents, the expression of their views, the management of incidents and disputes, punishments and the defence of pupils and appeals against judgments and punishments. It cannot be confined to the periphery of the classroom since the question of reciprocity and co-operation lies at the heart of the question of knowledge and the means by which it is transmitted.

The second area for action is pluralism in the education system. This can be conceived of only as the establishment of a pluralist culture throughout the education system, and not as its introduction into specific areas for specific target populations, as happened in the period of cross-culturalism. This was based on the assumption that "cultures" existed only in schools educating immigrant children. This assumption gave legitimacy to the notion that French culture was synonymous with a universal culture. To put it another way, it was only foreigners who had any kind of ethnicity. It has since been shown that the culture of the educational system and its pedagogy had experienced some difficulties in divesting itself, at worst, of a form of nationalism or, at best, of a sense of unease about cultural and religious pluralism (Lorcerie, 1994). Apart from a secular education in the anthropology of cultures and religions, knowledge of immigration, its history, is current reality and the points at issue inside and outside the immigrant populations would contribute to the spread of tolerance (Baccaïni, Gani, 1999).

The third area for action is the treatment of inequalities in schools. This is the only one of the three areas for action that deserves differential treatment. Segregation is on the increase in the education system, and most of its victims are children and young people from immigrant backgrounds, although they rub shoulders with the most excluded groups of children from working-class French families. In the light of this situation, it is essential to put in place—finally—a policy of positive discrimination. Such a policy would not ignore the fundamental question of the composition of school staff rooms which, in schools in disadvantaged areas, is generally governed by a law that dictates that teachers move towards more favoured schools over the course of their careers. It would help to improve staff commitment by putting in place high-quality management structures and improving working conditions. It would be uncompromising in its commitment to the shared objectives and mission of the education system, while at the same time having regard for parents and the area in which they live. It would not wait for the unlikely return of the French middle classes to upgrade neglected schools. Finally, it would not allow the terms of the debate and the measures to be taken to be dictated by the moral necessity of combating violence in schools.

Bibliography

Anselme, M. (2000), *Du bruit à la parole. La scène politique des cités*, L'Aube, La Tour d'Aigues.

Baccaïni, B., Gani, L. (1999), "L'immigration en France: connaissances et opinions des lycéens de terminale", *Sociétés Contemporaines*, n° 35, pp. 131–161.

Bajoit, G. (1988), "Exit, voice, loyalty... and apathy. Les réactions individuelles au mécontentement", *Revue française de sociologie*, XXIX, pp. 325–345.

Ball, S., van Zanten, A. (1998), "Logiques de marché et éthiques contextualisées dans les systèmes scolaires français et britannique", *Education et sociétés*, n° 1, pp. 47–71.

Boubeker, A. (1999) *Familles de l'intégration. Les ritournelles de l'ethnicité en pays jacobin*, Stock, Paris.

Bourgeault, G., Gagnon, F., Mc Andrew, M., Page, M. (1995), "L'espace de la diversité culturelle et religieuse à l'école dans une démocratie de tradition libérale", *Revue Européenne des Migrations Internationales*, vol. 11, n° 3, pp. 79–102.

Broccolichi, S., van Zanten, A. (1997), "Espaces de concurrence et circuits de scolarisation. L'évitement des collèges publics d'un district de la banlieue parisienne", *Les Annales de la Recherche Urbaine*, n° 75, pp. 5–31.

Debarbieux, E. (1997), "Ethnicité, effet-classe et punition: une étude de cas", *Migrants-Formation*, n° 109, pp. 138–154.

Douglass, W. A., Lyman, S. M. (1976), "L'ethnie: structure, processus, saillance", *Cahiers internationaux de sociologie*, pp. 197–220.

Duru-Bellat, M., Mingat, A. (1997), "La constitution de classes de niveau dans les collèges: les effets pervers d'une pratique à visée égalisatrice", *Revue française de sociologie*, XXXVIII, pp. 759–790.

Favre-Perroton, J. (1999), Ecole et ethnicité. Une relation à double face, thèse de doctorat de sociologie, université Bordeaux 2.

Goffman, E. (1975), *Stigmate. Les usages sociaux du handicap*, Minuit, Paris.

Hirschman, A. O. (1995), *Défection et prise de parole*, Fayard, Paris.

Laforgue, D. (1999), Ségrégation scolaire et expériences professionnelles de chefs d'établissement de collège: trois études de cas, DEA de sociologie, université Lumière Lyon 2.

Lorcerie, F. (1994), "L'islam dans les cours de Langue et Culture d'Origine: le procès", *Revue Européenne Migrations Internationales*, 10–2, pp. 5–43.

——— (à paraître), "Ecole et minorités issues de l'immigration".

Mazella, S. (1997), "Belsunce: des élèves musulmans à l'abri de l'école catholique. L'école publique en butte aux stigmates et aux procédures", *Les Annales de la Recherche Urbaine*, n° 75, pp. 79–87.

Payet, J.-P. (1985), "L'insolence", *Les Annales de la recherche urbaine*, n° 27, pp. 49–55.

——— (1992), "Civilités et ethnicité dans les collèges de banlieue: enjeux, résistances et dérives d'une action scolaire territorialisée", *Revue Française de Pédagogie*, n° 101, pp. 59–70.

——— (1995), *Collèges de banlieue. Ethnographie d'un monde scolaire*, A. Colin, Paris.

——— (1997), "Le "sale boulot". Division morale du travail dans un collège en banlieue", *Les Annales de la recherche urbaine*, n° 75, pp. 19–31.

Payet, J.-P., Sicot, F. (1996), "Expérience collégienne et origine 'ethnique'. La civilité et la justice scolaire du point de vue des élèves étrangers ou issus de l'immigration", *Migrants-Formation*, n° 109, pp. 155–167.

Ranciere, J. (1995), *La mésentente*, Galilée, Paris.

Taylor, C. (1998), *Les sources du moi. La formation de l'identité moderne*, Seuil, Paris.

Touraine, A. (1997), *Pourrons-nous vivre ensemble ? Egaux et différents*, Fayard, Paris.

Varro, G. (1999), "Les futurs maîtres face à l'immigration. Le piège d'un 'habitus discursif'", *Mots*, n° 60, pp. 30–42.

Vissac, G. (1998), La dimension spatiale de la scolarisation des enfants d'origine immigrée dans les collèges du Rhône: un exemple de ségrégation scolaire, DEA de sociologie, université Lumière Lyon 2.

QUI S'INSTRUIT S'ENRICHIT?
RE-EXAMINING STANDARDS AND BARRIERS
IN EDUCATION IN QUEBEC

Madeleine Gauthier

During the democratization of schooling in the province of Quebec[1] that took place during the 1960s and 1970s, the advocates of universal education made great use of the catch phrase *Qui s'instruit s'enrichit*, "Education brings prosperity." This slogan was based on the idea that schooling would allow its possessors of knowledge to gain access to a higher standard of living—the proof of this being that individuals prospered more, both economically and socially, in those societies where higher standards of education were in evidence. Every society which advocated prosperity through schooling based this goal on a fairly damning reading of the socioeconomic effects of poor schooling. In the case of Quebec, a comparison with France—and, to a greater degree, with English-speaking countries, especially anglophone regions of Canada—demonstrated "the inferiority of French Canadians" in this area and the effects of this inferiority on their standard of living and their status among the developed nations of the world.

As a fact, the Royal Commission of Inquiry on Education in the Province of Quebec (1963), known as the Parent Commission, proclaimed that

> It is universally understood that the society of today—and even more that of tomorrow—make unprecedented demands on education. For modern civilization to progress, and progress is a condition of its survival, every citizen without exception must have adequate schooling, and a very considerable number must receive advanced education (1963: 57).

---

[1] In Canada, the education system is determined by the provinces and varies so greatly from one province to the other that comparisons are sometimes problematic. The province of Quebec, with a francophone majority, uses a cycle of study that one does not find in the other provinces, the *collège d'enseignement général et professionnel* (CEGEP). This cycle involves two years of general studies in preparation for university, or three years of technical study, which are usually final but can also lead to university.

The idea of education as the driving force for both individual and societal advancement was hitting its stride. International organizations were its chief advocates (UNESCO, OECD). Even though a wider access to schooling had come about over time, every recession, economic setback, and individual struggle with employment became an additional argument for the overhaul of the education system; in the most affected personal cases, it was considered proof of the need to seek extra training or new specializations. At the start of the 1980s, during the most dire unemployment crisis which young adults in the most of the West had known since the Great Depression, better education was the first remedy that came to mind. Terms of discourse change with time: advocacy of schooling as the essential cure is now expressed in terms of the "knowledge society," with scientific and technological knowledge regarded as the favoured tool for competitiveness in the "world society". The Conseil supérieur de l'éducation du Quebec summarizes this connection between knowledge and economics as follows:

> The increasing salience of the interrelated concepts of "knowledge society" and "knowledge economy" is a trend that deserves particular attention. It is a major concern of nations in terms of the goals of their education systems. It is becoming more and more urgent that we train a labour force to be qualified in the high-technology sectors in order to maintain our international competitiveness (2001: 6).

The present study will focus on the effects of scholastic and professional training on individuals and the social categories under construction, rather than the effects of such training on society itself. The democratization of schooling has not reached one of its basic goals: namely, universal access to a diploma or high-quality professional training. Social origins, in the forms characteristic of our age, still play a significant role in the promotion of a student from one educational rank to the other. But the same pattern of privileged or disadvantaged social groups does not apply. A diploma is not the cure—which its holders were promised. It contributes to the reconfiguration of new social categories. The successful paths to integration vary according to these categories and the structural factors linked to changes in the labour market, but also to geography and the new employment sectors which favour certain groups and leave others who choose more traditional or risk-laden avenues at a disadvantage.

1. *The recipients of education: who are they?*

Before "testing" the relative importance of academic qualifications in the professional integration of modern youths,[2] we should form an image of the young people who gain or do not gain access to the various educational ranks. Out of a desire to level the playing field, secondary schools have created new inequities; the modern situation can in fact be usefully re-examined in light of the time-worn studies in Edmond Goblot's *La barrière et le niveau* ["Barriers and Standards"] (1925). Curiously enough, the well-known work by Bourdieu and Passeron on *La reproduction* (1970) was in vogue in Quebec at the time the majority of the population was upwardly mobile; this trend was especially pronounced during the economically prosperous period from the 1950s through to the end of the 1970s (Langlois et al., 1990: 237). Social origins are now rarely taken into account in studies that deal with the difficulties faced by young adults with regards to professional integration. It seems that "social heritage" is not in fact the sole criterion for social advancement. But this dimension is not always given due consideration. As we shall see, professional integration is already an issue during high-school years—in the relationship between studies and lifestyle, geographic distance from the major urban centres, and socioeconomic origins.

It would be improper to deny the gains made by Quebec and Canadian society through the democratization of schooling. One need only view the results obtained in a historical light to recognize these gains. The full-time school attendance rate among youths aged 15–19 in Quebec rose from 68.8% in 1971 to 82.6% in 1996, and, among those aged 20–24, from 16.5% to 41.6%, an increase that exceeds the Canadian average (Statistics Canada, *Recensements du Canada*). In 1995, nearly 87% of Quebec residents, including both adults and young people, held a high-school diploma, as compared with the OECD-nations average of 80% (Ministère de l'éducation du Québec, Web site, April 2002).

The rub, however, lies in the fact that the elevated graduation rate comes partly by way of adult education. The high-school dropout

---

[2] When we speak of *youths*, age determination is always fraught with problems. When are we young and when do we stop being young? The prolongation of studies, and its effects on professional integration, have led to the tendency to consider those under 30 as "young"—the Government of Quebec defines the term in these terms. See Gauthier (2000) on the social construction of age.

rate[3] has, in fact, been a challenge for those in charge of the education system over the last decade. How can these young people be kept in the regular school system until they obtain this first diploma, which, rightly or wrongly,[4] is held to be the passport for entry into the labour market?

Why do young people abandon a system where everything is designed to accommodate them? To begin with, consider the following: the dropout rate is much higher among boys than girls (41.3% versus 26.0% in 1997–98 according to a 1999 report from the Conseil supérieur de l'éducation). After consulting researchers and studies of the problem, the council highlighted the significance of the "social influences" which applied differently according to gender and appeared in the form of behaviour and social roles related to masculinity and femininity. These influences held sway over student attitudes to school. Reading, for example, was associated with feminine qualities. Different cognitive styles operated such that schools, as represented by their programs and teachers, did not provide boys with the same opportunities as girls.

But dropout factors are not governed solely by gender differences. So-called "social" influences could well have other origins. A team of researchers,[5] without wiping the slate clean of all these explanations, is attempting to see—not at the point of leaving school, but over the course of the five subsequent years—what social representation dropouts make of school and, just as importantly, of the labour market which they are trying to penetrate. Despite the on-going status of this research, the results are surprising and may well show strategies of recovery and alternative or parallel training which could explain why graduation rates among thirty-year-olds are so high despite the alarming overall statistics for dropout. Could the attraction of employment, autonomy and consumer power not explain the pre-graduation abandonment of studies among boys just as well

---

[3] Mandatory schooling extends until the age of 16, which may explain how a student, without breaking the education law, can leave the regular education system at this age but not have obtained a diploma.

[4] On the matter of professional integration without a diploma, see the article co-authored by Claude Trottier, Mircea Vultur and Madeleine Gauthier in this volume.

[5] I am directing this team composed of Jacques Hamel of the Université de Montréal, Marc Molgat of the Université d'Ottawa, Claude Trottier of the Université Laval, and Mircea Vultur of the INRS-Urbanisation, Culture et Société. The research plan covers professional integration and the employment situation of young people without a diploma five years after leaving secondary or collegiate studies.

as the factors listed above? This problem also involves factors related to geography and location. The lowest educated populations, where attendance rates fall off after the ninth year of schooling, are those located in resource regions, where the economy is based more on extraction and secondary industry than on the service sector and the knowledge economy. In the cities, such populations are found in the districts most removed from employment related to the knowledge economy (Statistics Canada, 1996). Specialized knowledge or a diploma may not necessarily be required for securing the jobs that are available. Why should girls from the same regions or city districts be more motivated to persevere in their studies? An inquiry into the migratory ambitions of youths during their high-school years demonstrates how the girls cannot find jobs in their communities with requirements as low as those applicable to their male counterparts (Roy, 1992). The types of work still favoured by young women require a minimum of training and technical skills—the sales and service sectors, for example.

One problematic factor is the costs posed by the access-distance of secondary schools and, to a greater degree, of collegiate and university institutions. Although tuition fees may be non-existent or minimal before university, separation from family can represent a high cost. The student-loan system is one solution, but it also involves a long-term debt to which a growing percentage of students are committed (CNCS-FEUQ, 2001: 69–73 and 149–151). Some students try to minimize their debt-burden through a combination of work and study. But if exaggerated, this combination inevitably leads to the abandonment or prolongation of schoolwork; the graduation rate, for example, is higher for those who undertake a bachelor's degree full-time and at a young age (Pageau and Bujold, 2000: 18–19).

The dropout rate during post-secondary studies also poses a problem for those in charge of education. Not only does it have consequences for the individual (we shall weigh these later on), but it leads to economic and social costs that represent a real burden for society as a whole. One explanation provided by the author of a study on school processes recalls how the education system had to abandon its pre-democratization strictness in order to accommodate new varieties of student groups. Hence it is necessary to consider the combination of work and study, the possibility of family commitments and so on; these factors are not without consequence.

> Thus, part-time studies, evening courses, short programs, the possibility of leaving courses and resuming them later, the freedom to spread things out over an indefinite number of school terms— these have all not merely allowed a more flexible journey through the system, but have 'decentralized' education, such that coursework becomes just one among various activities. If the academic environment is now more flexible, it has also permitted a certain lack of commitment (Pageau, 2000: 41).

This lack of commitment represents a primary influence on the dropout rate. Part-time studies, for example, retain fewer students than full-time programs. Thus, students enrolled in the bachelor's degree programs at the various campuses of the Université du Québec[6] (a total of 76,000 students) have a dropout rate of 41.8% if enrolled part-time and a rate of 18.8% if enrolled full-time. The same pattern holds true for the graduation rate: 40.8% for part-time students and 75.1% for full-time students (Pageau and Bujold, 2000: 12).

In addition to the geographic factors and the issues related to modern-student lifestyles which explain either the low level of schooling or the abandonment of studies before graduation, there are the social origins to consider. Certain studies have allowed us to follow student cohorts during post-secondary studies. These show that the economic status of the family of origin influences access to collegiate or university studies (Table 1). Selection occurs during secondary studies, which partly explains a certain homogeneity evident in the higher educational ranks. One of these studies (Veillette et al., 1993) sheds light on both the geographical and the social characteristics of scholastic success in the Saguenay–Lac-Saint-Jean region. Another concludes that "the access-rate to bachelor's degree programs increases in proportion to the original socioeconomic status" (Pageau and Bujold, 2000: 17).

Although an already significant selection has occurred prior to university entry, a percentage of youths still succeed in hoisting themselves up despite their "low" socioeconomic origin, to use the above category. However, the authors bring certain nuances to bear on this judgement that involve the education level of the parents. This level influences the path which their children will take through the

---

[6] The Université du Québec, the state university, is located in four separate regions removed from the major urban centres of Montreal and Québec: namely, Chicoutimi, Hull, Rimouski and Rouyn-Noranda. It is also present in Montreal, Québec and Trois-Rivières.

Table 1. Enrolment in full-time bachelor's degree programs as a function of original socioeconomic status

	N	%
Low status	627	30.0
Average status	718	34.4
High status	745	35.6
Total	2,090	100.0

Source: Pageau Danielle and Johanne Bujold, *Dis-moi ce que tu veux et je te dirai jusqu'où tu iras. Les caractéristiques des étudiantes et des étudiants à la rescousse de la compréhension de la persévérance aux études*. Université du Québec, October 2000, Table 6, p. 17. Calculations by the author.

school system. "Among full-time students, the graduation rate is lower for those whose parents did not advance beyond the primary school level (67%), compared to those (76%) whose parents reached the secondary level at least" (Id.: 19).

If the issue of differences according to gender is a relevant factor with regards to high-school dropout, it constitutes a determining factor on admission and graduation rates at post-secondary institutions. In 1999, for example, the access-rate[7] to collegiate studies was 51.1% for men and 68.8% for women. At university, the rate for those seeking bachelor's degree (the first university diploma) was 29.6% among the men and 42.3% among the women. It will come as no surprise that we find a higher percentage of women in programs leading to a master's degree: 9.8% as compared to 9.2% for men. Only in doctoral programs do we find the men better represented: 2.1% as compared to 1.8% for the women (Ministère de l'Éducation, 2001: 67 and 69). The graduation rate is even more revealing of the success of women at the collegiate and university levels: 49.4% for women at the collegiate level, versus 29.7% for the men, and 33% versus 21.7% at the bachelor's level (Id.: 111 and 113).

If all Quebec residents have access to secondary schooling and have the possibility of enrolling in collegiate and university studies, not all take advantage of these openings or make use of them when it is most opportune, both for them and the education system itself. A variety of explanatory elements arises equally from the lifestyles

---

[7] These rates are calculated over one generation.

of youths who combine studies and employment as from their socio-economic origin and their geographic distance from post-secondary school premises. Lack of interest in school is one of the unexpected effects of educational democratization, and has a negative influence on the professional integration of young adults. In contrast, the strong presence of young women in all schooling ranks and their success in obtaining diplomas represents one of the positive effects of this democratization. These two considerations merit special attention in future research on school success and professional integration.

2. *Extensive schooling: the advantages*

During the 1980s, Tanguy offered a stern rebuke to the current state of France through the title of his work *L'introuvable relation formation/emploi* (1986), or "Training, employment, and their imaginary connection." This harsh criticism still applies partly to modern Quebec, and should be considered above and beyond the basic picture provided by employment statistics. Pageau and Chenard, in analyzing the measurement tools used by the Ministère de l'Éducation in its follow-up studies of graduates, find that these tools provide an understanding of the viewpoint of the individuals under study, but do not provide an objective picture of the phenomenon itself. They conclude that "the evaluation made by the subjects of the training-employment relationship is highly relative and discretionary" (1991: 233). A subject questioned at different times over the course of his or her professional integration may supply contradictory answers, which, in the absence of contrary indicators, fail to provide a true understanding of the dynamics of professional integration.

Trottier, after Vincens in France (1997: 33), recently noted in this context that the concept of professional integration, in the same way as that of activity and joblessness, is fundamental to any understanding of the youth employment situation. These researchers insist on a better definition of this period, one that includes both a starting-point and an end-point which delimits the chance factors (more or less prolonged and more or less difficult, depending on the individual) involved in the search for work and a more definite entry into the labour market. Such a definition should contribute to a determination of objective criteria that allow a truer evaluation of the integration level and, at the same time, provide a satisfactory picture of the subjects' perceptions.

As the conditions for professional integration increase in variety, it becomes more and more necessary to establish such objective criteria. The statistics do not always bring out this variety: they have a tendency to smooth over differences through generalization. But it remains clear that the answers provided by graduates to inquiries made ten or twenty months after school-leaving demonstrate a significant disparity, especially for those having done career training at the secondary level, between the training received and the employment obtained (Figure 1). Would objective indicators provide a different picture? If the studies demonstrate a fairly elevated satisfaction rate among post-secondary graduates—as far as the relationship between ambitions held and jobs occupied is concerned—this could be ascribed, according to certain authors already cited, to satisfaction at having found a job of one's own (Pageau and Chouinard, 1991: 194).

The lack of precision in the integration and satisfaction measurements is an indication of changes that have occurred in the relationship of youths to labour—a relationship about which we know little, except for the tendency to define all the vague desires of young people to branch out or to find satisfaction outside of work itself as "a loss of central work value." The perception that graduates have of their jobs could serve to contradict this judgement.[8] The concept of work transfers (or "deployments") has gained ground since the unemployment crisis at the start of the 1980s, which came as a particular surprise to young people at the time. The instrumental nature of work has gradually taken root again and job satisfaction come to lie not simply in the fact of having employment but in the type of position and the gains it could afford.

A study carried out by Statistics Canada (Finnie, 2001: 36–44) confirms the hypothesis that the situation of post-secondary graduates has not declined since the 1980s crisis. Unemployment rates have dropped, incomes have risen, the wage gap between men and women has diminished. The author of this study goes so far as to claim that "as well as benefiting from unemployment rates generally lower than those of the population as a whole, graduates of post-secondary schools do not seem to have suffered any significant overall decline in job possibilities from the start of the 1980s until the middle of the 1990s" (Id.: 40). Furthermore, women with a post-

---

[8] See in this work the text of Jacques Hamel, who refutes the idea that work has lost its central importance for the young people of today.

Figure 1. Rate of full-time employment related to training as a function of education level, Quebec, 1997, 1999 and 2001

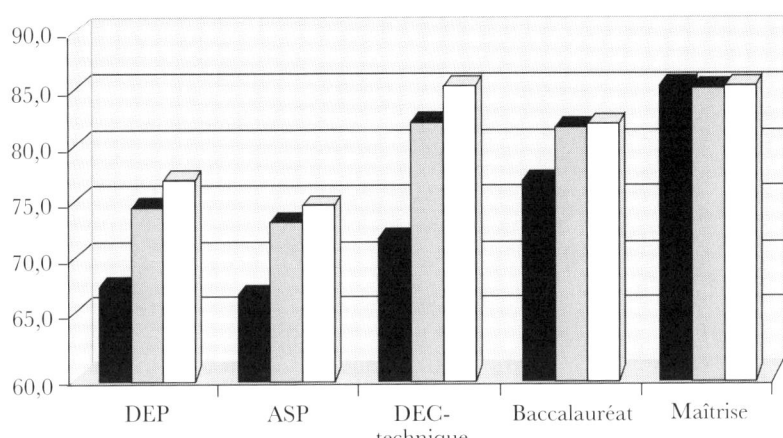

Definitions:
1. Rate of full-time employment related to training: percentage of graduates who hold a position related to the their field of study, in ratio to all job-holders, 10 months after receipt of a DEP, ASP or DEC (see below) and 20 months after receipt of a bachelor's or master's degree.
2. DEP: *diplôme d'études professionnelles* (vocational diploma).
3. ASP: *attestation de spécialisation professionnelle* (Attestation of Vocational specialization, AVS).
4. DEC-technique: *diplôme d'études collégiales de la formation technique* (Diploma of College Studies, DCS).
5. Baccalauréat: Bachelor's degree (first-cycle university diploma).
6. Maîtrise: Master's degree (second-cycle university diploma).

Source: Ministère de l'éducation du Québec, Enquêtes Relance, MÉQ Web site; data provided by Guy Baillargeon.

secondary diploma have made significant gains towards achieving equity with men in employment and wages. According to Finnie, "the differences generally vary in inverse proportion to the educational level, with the gains made by women being greatest at the doctoral level, then less close to men at the master's and bachelor's levels, and lowest at the level of collegiate education" (Id.: 42).

The preceding analysis applies to the whole of Canada. But geographic disparities in this huge, sparsely-populated nation suggest that one should not conclude too hastily that this analysis can remain unqualified for all provinces and regions, or for urban, suburban and rural environments. In Quebec, for example, the least educated proportion of the population is found in the four regions which are most removed from the major urban centres and include a high percentage of rural dwellers (Statistics Canada, 1999). The most educated proportion is found in Montreal, Québec and the Ottawa River Valley, three regions with a high urban density and a strong attraction for migrant populations, including those originally from rural communities (Gauthier, dir., 1997).

The most educated are also those who correspond most directly to the "knowledge society," according to the current characteristics. Figure 2 illustrates the fact that, in terms of the major professional categories, it is young adults who presently hold the new positions in the natural and applied sciences sector and its associated professions. If we consider professionals in the knowledge society as a whole, two cohorts can be distinguished as separated by an age gap of fifteen years: the 35-and-under cohort described above, and the 45-and-over cohort which is found in professions related to social sciences, teaching, public administration and religion. Here we find an illustration of a cohort effect that is especially pronounced in terms of academic history. When the most educated complain that they cannot find profitable work in public administration,[9] it is because others have got there first. At the same time, the average age of those who hold these positions leads one to predict the necessity of their eventual replacement.

The catch phrase *Qui s'instruit s'enrichit* was surely imagined with the following chart in view. Regardless of whether they are graduates or not, those under 25 have on average the same income. Entry into the labour market is achieved slowly, for the most part. But above this age, the curve flattens out for the less educated, while for those with university diplomas it shoots up impressively. Even though some progress is made in the other categories of graduates, it never attains the level of the university graduates, whose income keeps increasing until the end of their professional lives.

The preceding charts demonstrate both the hypersensitivity of young people to fluctuations in the economy and the labour market, and the advantage of those who find themselves on the right side of the new economy. While this sensitivity involves the incon-

---

[9] A forum for youths in public service departments in Quebec was established by young members of the public administration. Following consultation, some deplored the fact that many jobs in the public service were offered or filled on an insecure basis. Half the personnel in certain departments have only casual-employee status (2000: 17).

Figure 2. Distribution of certain professions as a function of age, Quebec, 1996

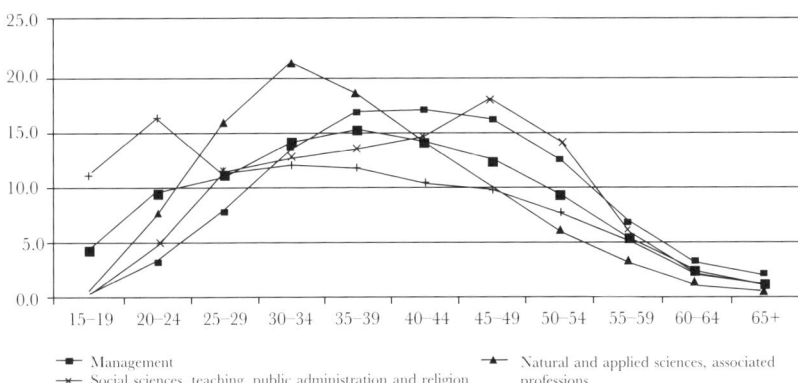

Source: Institut de la statistique du Québec, data taken from the Canada census of 1996, calculations at the Observatoire Jeunes et Société.

Figure 3. Average job income as a function of age and the highest education level obtained, Quebec, 1995

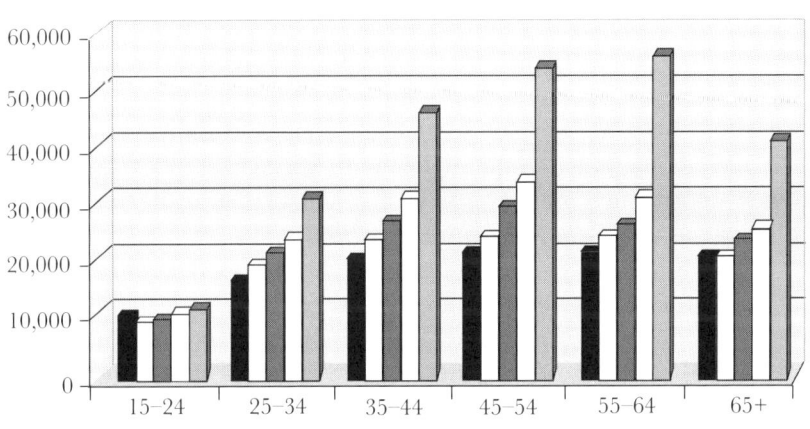

- Level below the 9th year
- Between 9th and 13th year with secondary leaving certificate
- University grade
- Between 9th and 13th year without secondary leaving certificate
- Level below university grade

Source: Institut de la statistique du Québec, data taken from the Canada census of 1996.

venience of exposing the youngest applicants to the chance factors of a chaotic entry into the labour market, not all of them suffer to the same degree. For the most educated, the coincidence of their entry into the labour market and the rise of the "knowledge society" puts them in a privileged position. The classification of professions and studies into cohorts is highly revealing in this respect.

3. *The vulnerability of the uneducated*

Over the last two decades, many studies have demonstrated the complicated nature of what José Rose terms *transitions professionnelles* (Rose, 2000; other scholars describe it as a process). The entry into the labour market is made in stages. The first job is not necessarily long-lasting—a job characterized by stability, which the individual does not foresee leaving or losing in the short or medium term (Trottier, 2000: 100). This process can turn out to be fairly short for some, particularly in sectors with jobs that normally make use of a young labour force or those which correspond to the new employment fields in which they received their training (Figure 2), despite the assertion by recent pillars of the high-tech community (Nortel, for example) that they are not entirely safe from the ups and downs of the market economy. For others, however, the entry process to a stable job can represent a long and difficult path, one that includes periods of unemployment, social assistance, and continued dependence on the family of origin. Roulleau-Berger defines this path as *socialisation professionnelle* (1999: 203).

While the process corresponds quite directly to the experience of the uneducated, it also holds true for those who have only a basic training, without specializations, and who did not continue their studies beyond this stage. They may find themselves in jobs which do not require any special qualifications. Others will acquire these skills through work experience itself, with companies having an obligation to devote part of their capital to the training of employees. In contrast to other cohorts that have managed to integrate the industrial sector, and, until recently, would have become life-time employees (assuming the company remained in business), uneducated young people spend more time in finding a job that will guarantee them some measure of stability.

Figure 4 demonstrates once again the significant gap which exists between graduates (those with 11 years of education or more) and

Figure 4. Unemployment rate as a function of education, youths aged 15–24, Quebec, 1990–2001

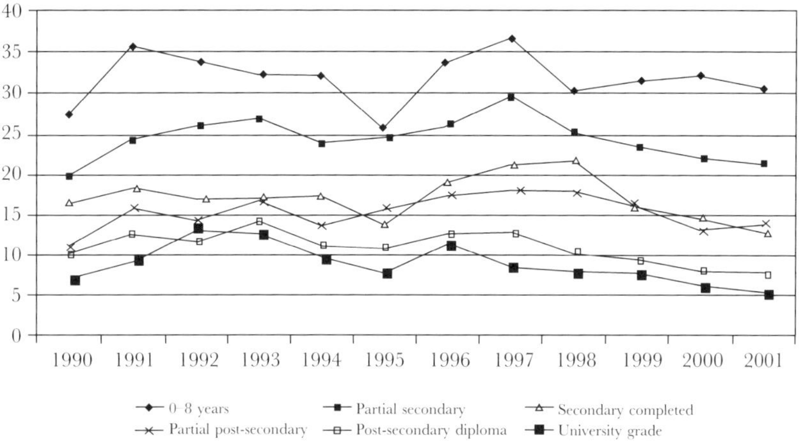

Chart showing unemployment rates from 1990 to 2001 for six education levels: 0–8 years, Partial secondary, Secondary completed, Partial post-secondary, Post-secondary diploma, University grade.

Source: Statistique Canada, *Revue chronologique de la population active*, CD-ROM 2002.

non-graduates (0–8 years and partial secondary education) with regards to the unemployment rate in the 15–24 age group of the active population. It should be noted, however, that the unemployment rate of those with 9 or 10 years of schooling (partial secondary) tended to diminish after 1996, as was the case at the start of the 1990s. The risk of being unemployed is especially clear for non-graduates and high-school graduates, while those with at least some post-secondary instruction suffered many fewer fluctuations. The hypersensitivity of young people to the vagaries of the labour market thus proved much more pronounced among those with weaker academic credentials.

Among those aged 30 and younger, the rate of enrolment for social assistance has fluctuated greatly in the last 25 years, changing from 3.8% of the 18–29 age group in 1975 to 7.9% in 2000. Much higher rates, however, were recorded in 1983 and 1994: 11.5% and 13.4%, respectively (Lemieux and Lanctôt, 1995 and 2001: 33), reflecting periods when the unemployment rate was significantly higher. The great majority of those under 30 who sought social assistance belonged to the non-graduate category (83.4%), although it is true that the presence of graduates increases in proportion to the age group (Lemieux and Lanctôt, 1995: 47). Thus, 90.2% of youths under 21 who benefit from social assistance do not hold a diploma. The majority of them are single; some are migrants, or searching for autonomy, or exiles from their family homes for various reasons (Gauthier, Molgat and Saint-Laurent, 1999: 33–53).

Beyond these statistics, inquiry by way of interviews brings into relief certain dimensions of schooling that would otherwise escape notice. Academic perseverance, although it represents an "ordeal" for many young people and has somewhat lost its usefulness in terms of labour-market appeal, still remains the best way of gaining access to a job that is stable and profitable. But that is not its only virtue. The interviews show us, in a negative sense in the case of those who left the system very early, that the school environment represents a preparation for the various pathways of integration into adult society. In other words, an educational institution is not merely a place for learning intellectual or technical skills, but a place for learning the nature of community life. Difficulties with integration into the world of work do not exist in a vacuum; they follow upon difficulties experienced in the school environment, and have the same symptoms: lack of discipline, inability to adapt to rules and authority, problems with mental or physical well-being, absence of interpersonal relationships, significant geographic mobility (i.e. a change of school following each change of address).

Furthermore, uneducated youths do not benefit from the support-structure that teaching institutions provide until students reach their twenties. This structure includes financial aid for housing (student accommodation), family support, and student loans and grants programs. Differences in the trajectory of an individual's drive towards autonomy—the separation between successful and troubled lives—are often decided by the absence of one or more of these elements (Gauthier, Molgat and St-Laurent, 1999: 206–207).

The preceding examples are sufficient proof of an unavoidable fact. In an advanced economy such as the one found in Canada and Quebec, the uneducated do not normally hold the best positions, despite the willingness of some portions of the labour market to make use of a non-specialized work force.

Conclusion

Generalizing too hastily on the concept of precariousness, and defining professional integration on the basis of the first employment found following graduation, can obscure the varied nature of the labour-market experiences of young adults; a clear view of the effects of training on their future and the construction of new social categories is also prevented. Special attention must be paid to the relationship that young men have with institutions of learning, and to the investment which young women make in their training. What kind of society and what social categories will arise from this differentiated relationship with education?

An unforeseen consequence of the democratization of education is that we find ourselves faced with the need to reach a certain standard vis-à-vis the complicated link between scholastic environments and the world of employment. It creates problems of access for those who have trouble conforming to it, and allows others to surpass it with greater ease. It is constantly being upgraded. This standard is constantly being upgraded even if some youths are succeeding in bypassing it. We do not yet have a firm understanding of the new barriers which the most uneducated of our youths run into. Are these barriers governed more by the characteristics and choices of the individual than by faults in the system? To what extent has the academic "origin" of the parents come to represent the new determinant of the success of their children at school and at work? Gender differences increase even more the complicated nature of these issues, beyond the factors of geography and socioeconomic origin.

Bibliography

Bourdieu, Pierre and Jean-Claude Passeron, (1970), *La reproduction. Éléments pour une théorie du système d'enseignement*, Paris, Les Éditions de Minuit.
Royal Commission of Inquiry on Education in the Province of Quebec, (1965), *Report*, Québec, Government of Quebec, 1963, Pt. 1.
Conseil national des cycles supérieurs, (2001), *Les sources et modes de financement des étudiants aux cycles supérieurs. Étude*, Montreal, Fédération étudiante universitaire du Québec (research report).
Conseil supérieur de l'éducation, (2001), *La gouverne de l'éducation. Logique marchande ou processus politique, Rapport annuel sur l'état et les besoins de l'éducation 2000–2001*, Government of Quebec.
Conseil supérieur de l'éducation, (1999), *Pour une meilleure réussite scolaire des garçons et des filles, Rapport annuel 1998–1999*, Government of Quebec.
Finnie, Ross, (2001), "Emploi et gains des diplômés de l'enseignement postsecondaire" in STATISTIQUE Canada, *Perspective*, No. 75-001-XPF in the catalogue, pp. 36–46.
Forum des jeunes de la fonction publique québécoise, (2000), *Les 109 se prononcent, Cataraqui 1999*, Québec (consultation report).
Fournier, Geneviève and Bruno Bourassa, (2000), "Le travail des 18 à 30 ans: vers une nouvelle norme" in G. Fournier and B. Bourassa, *Les 18 à 30 ans et le marché du travail*, Sainte-Foy, Les Presses de l'Université Laval, pp. 3–31.
Gauthier, Madeleine, (2000), "L'âge des jeunes: un fait social instable" in *Lien social et Politiques. Voir les jeunes autrement*, No. 43, pp. 23–32.

———, (2000), "L'insertion professionnelle des jeunes au cœur d'une nouvelle définition du centre et de la marge" in G. Fournier and B. Bourassa, Op. cit., pp. 59–82.

———, Marc Molgat and Louise Saint-Laurent, (1999), *Lien social et pauvreté: repérage et profil des jeunes précaires qui vivent seuls en milieu urbain*, Sainte-Foy, INRS-Culture et Société (research report).

———, dir., (1997), *Pourquoi partir? La migration des jeunes d'hier et d'aujourd'hui*, Sainte-Foy, Pul-IQRC.

Goblot, Edmond, *La barrière et le niveau*, (1925), Paris, Presses Universitaires de France.

Langlois, Simon et al., (1990), *La société québécoise en tendances 1960–1970*, Québec, Institut québécois de recherche sur la culture.

Lemieux, Nicole and Pierre Lanctôt, (1995), *Commencer sa vie à l'aide sociale*, Government of Quebec, Ministère de la sécurité du revenu, Direction de la recherche, de l'évaluation et de la statistique, 1995 (mise à jour en août 2001).

Ministère de l'éducation de Québec, (2001), *Indicateurs de l'éducation. Édition 2001*, Government of Quebec.

Pageau, Danielle, (2000), "Les étudiants changent mais les facteurs de réussite demeurent" in M. Gauthier et al., *Être jeune en l'an 2000*, Sainte-Foy, Les Éditions de l'IQRC, pp. 40–44.

Pageau, Danielle and Johanne Bujold, (2000), *Dis-moi ce que tu veux et je te dirai jusqu'où tu iras. Les caractéristiques des étudiantes et des étudiants à la rescousse de la compréhension de la persévérance aux études*, Québec, Université du Québec (research report).

Pageau, Danielle and Pierre Chenard, (1991), "De l'université au marché du travail: état de la situation des diplomées et diplomés québécois de premier cycle" in M. Diambomba, M. Perron and C. Trottier, dir., *Les cheminements scolaires et l'insertion professionnelle des étudiantes et étudiants de l'université. Éléments d'un bilan d'études au Québec*, Sainte-Foy, Université Laval, Les cahiers du Labraps, Vol. 10, pp. 133–250.

Rose, José, (2000), "Les jeunes et l'emploi. Questions conceptuelles et méthodologiques" in G. Fournier and B. Bourassa, Op. cit., pp. 83–116.

Roulleau-Berger, Laurence, (1999), *Le travail en friche. Les mondes de la petite production urbaine*, La Tour d'Aigues, Éditions de l'aube, 246 p.

Roy, Jacques, (1992), L'exode des jeunes du milieu rural: en quête d'un emploi ou d'un genre de vie," *Recherches sociographiques*, Vol. XXXIII, No. 3: 429–444.

Statistique Canada, (1971–2001), *Recensements du Canada*.

Tanguy, Lucie, dir., (1986), *L'Introuvable relation formation/emploi: un état des recherches en France*, Paris, Documentation française.

Trottier, Claude, (2000), "Le rapport au travail et l'accès à un emploi stable, à temps plein, lié à la formation" in G. Fournier and B. Bourassa, Op. cit., pp. 35–57.

———, (2000), "Questionnement sur l'insertion professionnelle des jeunes" in *Lien social et Politiques. Voir les jeunes autrement*, No. 43, pp. 93–101.

Veillette, Suzanne, Michel Perron and Gilbert Hebert, (1993), *Les disparités géographiques et sociales de l'accessibilité au collégial. Étude longitudinale au Saguenay–Lac-Saint-Jean*, Jonquière, Cégep de Jonquière, Groupe Écobes (research report).

Vincens, Jean, (1997), "L'insertion professionnelle des jeunes. À la recherche d'une définition conventionnelle," *Formation Emploi*, No. 60, October–December 1997, pp. 21–36.

PART TWO

INCERTITUDES AND REVERSIBILITIES IN BIOGRAPHIES

BABY BOOMERS IN TRANSITION:
LIFE-COURSE EXPERIENCES OF THE 'CLASS OF '73'*

Paul Anisef and Paul Axelrod[1]

This chapter is based on a panel study that closely charts the life-course pathways of an Ontario cohort of Grade 12 students in 1973 ('the Class of '73') to the leading edge of middle age in 1995. It employs a life-course theoretical perspective to assess the relative importance of structure and agency in the multiple school-to-work and life transitions made by one baby-boom cohort. Like other life-course researchers represented in this volume, we note that there have been tremendous social and economic changes over the past several generations (Heinz, 1999; Chisholm and Du Bois-Raymond, 1993; Evans and Heinz, 1994; Krüger, 1998). These changes—as we found in the case of the Class of '73—affected the values and directions taken by young people as they moved along uncharted pathways, constructing life scripts that were influenced by social-structural factors and individual circumstances. We anticipate that our findings will provide benchmarks for comparison with younger generations.

Our research is driven by two basic questions:

1. To what degree do social structural forces beyond the individual's control determine pathways to adulthood?
2. In what ways do agency and personal choices affect such outcomes?

In addressing these themes, this chapter draws on longitudinal survey data and personal interviews and focuses on the themes of social mobility, occupation, gender, and family life.[2]

---

* This research was made possible by the Social Sciences and Humanities Research Council of Canada under the Strategic Grants Program, Education and Work in a Changing Society. We would also like to acknowledge the contributions of other members of the Ontario Life Course Project Team to the development of ideas expressed in this paper.

[1] This paper was yet edited in V. W. Marshall, W. Heinz, Helga Krüger, A. Verma (eds), *Restructuring work and the life course*, Toronto, University of Toronto Press, 2001.

[2] Those surveyed and interviewed graduated from Grade 12 in Ontario high schools in 1973. They were surveyed six times. The last survey occurred in 1994–5 and included 788 of the original sample of 2,555. In 1995, they were in their early forties with some twenty years of labour-market experience. They were able to

Structure, agency, and the life course

Theorists and researchers who address the human agency-social structure debate vary in their approaches to the subject (Wyn and Dwyer, 1999). Some, like Lyotard and Baudrillard, contend that structural analysis has lost its validity and that the world has now entered a new postmodern epoch where patterns of behaviour and individual life chances have become less predictable than formerly (Furlong and Cartmel, 1997, p. 1; Chisholm, 1999). Beck argues that the influence of class, family, and gender on individual experience has diminished in modern industrial societies. Traditional social bonds and barriers, including social stratification, are weakened in a social and economic environment that is less enduring and less certain than in the past. 'The tendency is towards the emergence of individualized forms and conditions of existence, which compel people—for the sake of their own material survival—to make themselves the centre of their own planning and conduct of life.' (Beck, 1992, p. 88.) Others, such as Jones and Wallace (1992), are more cautious in interpreting social change. While they acknowledge a greater degree of uncertainty and a weakening of traditional ties in Western societies, they contend that life chances and experiences can still be predicted by knowing a person's location within social structures. Thus, while class effects may not be as strong in Britain today as they were in the past, 'pathways out of school are still structured by factors such as social class, family background, academic achievement . . . and opportunities in the local labour market' (1992, p. 45).

Roberts and colleagues (1994) compare youth transitions in Germany and England and conclude that a pattern of 'structured individualization' reflects the situation in both countries, whereby the movement to goals, the aims themselves, and the individuals' ability to realize them were products of their structural location (p. 51). Though agreeing that young people do face new risks and opportunities in the modern world, Furlong and Cartmel (1997) assert that the 'risk society is not a classless society, but a society in which the old social cleavages associated with class and gender remain intact; on an objective level, changes in the distribution of risk have been minimal' (p. 7).

---

review their school-to-employment and adolescent-to-adulthood transitions, and to reflect on their current family circumstances. This chapter reports selectively on the survey data and personal interviews.

Our study finds evidence of the *combined* influence of structural forces and individualized decision making. We maintain that personal agency is present in the transition from youth through to adulthood. Young people do make distinctive choices about their education and career pathways. These decisions are influenced by such individualized traits as interests, ability, personality, and ambition. But such decisions are not made in a vacuum. Structural factors—social class, gender, ethnicity, and location—play an important role in shaping the context in which personal choices are made. For example, our data demonstrate that youth from higher socio-economic strata are more likely than the less advantaged to pursue postsecondary education, and our interviews explore how young people—both those who pursue postsecondary education and those who do not—explain and understand their decisions.

Though the social structures within which young persons grow and mature operate 'above their heads,' they should not be thought of as necessarily constraining. In fact, social structures are simultaneously constraining and enabling. Though they may preclude the possibility of making certain choices, they also offer the very possibility of human choice (Hays, 1994, p. 65). For members of the Class of '73, social life was fundamentally structured as they made school-to-work transitions, and the choices they made usually tended to reproduce these structures. As Hays (1994) observes, 'That reproduction process, however, is never fully stable or absolute and, under particular circumstances, the structured choices that agents make can have a more or less transformative impact on the nature of structures themselves. Human agency and social structure, then, have a simultaneously antagonistic and dependent relationship' (p. 65).

As one ages, structure and agency continue to affect the life course, though not always evenly. Our data indicate that the importance of class and residence diminish once students enter higher education; their occupational pathways are affected more by the amount and type of education they obtain. At the same time, it is important to explore how individuals come to understand and then negotiate their location and social-class position as they pursue their educational and occupational aspirations. This effort itself is strongly influenced by individual traits, including clarity of choices, strength of commitment to life goals, and personal priorities and values (Anisef et al., 2000).

With regard to gender, occupational segregation continued from the 1970s through to the 1990s (Phillips and Phillips, 1993). Notwithstanding the growing participation of women in higher education, there were clear distinctions between the subsequent occupational profiles of men and women, and, individually, women made different decisions about the ways they would manage work and family life. As a number of researchers have noted, domestic responsibilities, orientations to marriage and family, and personal experiences can affect educational attainment, employment, and career opportunities, normally influencing the lives of women more than they do the lives of men (Wotherspoon, 1998, p. 168). We found that personality, interests, family matters, even health concerns influenced the varied decisions of members of the Class of '73. Structure and agency worked reflexively in their transition to adulthood, and personal choices were continuously being made and remade in the context of changing structural conditions (Anisef et al., 2000, especially chapter 7).

With Heinz (1995), we believe that it is important to interpret the meaning attached by individuals to conventional social forces (such as class) and their actual use. For this reason we conducted a micro life-course analysis for a selected number of respondents in the Class of '73 that charts separate trajectories and then links them with transitions and turning-points in the lives of individuals (Anisef et al., 2000, chapter 8). Furthermore, although the Class of '73 grew up in a society where status passages were governed by clear and explicit expectations, as they moved into their twenties and thirties they encountered instances of greater risk and uncertainty. We contend that there is no standard biography and that each person plays a critical role in writing her or his own life script. We therefore examine the type of individual decisions that were formulated in the various transitions between schooling, work, marriage, and parenting.

Our earlier work, which employed human-capital and status-attainment theories, has thus been enriched, we hope, by our use of life-course theory (Anisef et al., 1980; Anisef et al., 2000). Human-capital theory posits that through individual effort and investment in education, skills acquisition and credentials are normally converted into employment and career prospects (Livingstone, 1999, p. 162). The status-attainment model, though incorporating social-structural factors and individual traits, de-emphasizes social, economic, and historical contexts in analysing school-to-employment transitions (Boyd et al., 1985; Wotherspoon, 1998, p. 21). Useful as they are, these theories fail to capture the complexity of the transition process, the uncertainty flowing from a period of turbulent economic change, and the means by which individuals seek to assert control over their environment. For this reason we have turned to life-course theory.

Life-course theory, which attempts to explain the dynamic relationship between the individual and social order, allows researchers to examine a cohort's collective experience without reifying it and to remain attuned to individual differences without ignoring social context (Buchmann, 1989). More specifically, as Elder has noted, 'the life course refers to the pathways through the age-differentiated life span, to social patterns in the timing, duration, spacing, and order of events; the timing of an event may be as consequential for life experiences as whether the event occurs and the degree and type of change' (Elder, 1978, p. 21). Within this framework, school-to-work transitions are seen as constructed and negotiated by individuals within the context of social forces, educational selection, work experiences, and employment options. Decisions made by people are seen as both time dependent and more complex than is suggested by either the human-capital or the status-attainment model (Heinz, 1996, p. 7).

In our view, the concept of 'structured individualization' (Rudd and Evans, 1998, p. 61) best captures the theoretical model we have employed. The model indicates how structure and agency both shape the life course, intersecting continuously, as individuals construct their life 'scripts' in the context of conditions that are beyond their control (the state of the economy), and those which depend upon personal choices (marriage, having children, and seeking further education). The individual does her or his utmost, while at the same time recognizing that there is a kind of 'system' that might affect the available options and outcomes (Rudd and Evans, 1998, p. 61).

Class, education, and occupation

The analysis of findings in all phases of the study make it clear that structural factors, including class and region, have played a most significant role in shaping educational choices developed during the high school years. Our data show that those of high socio-economic origins were virtually four times as likely to obtain university degrees by 1979 as respondents with low socio-economic origins. Though the majority of respondents entered first jobs that were either skilled or unskilled, those who obtained postsecondary educational qualifications were more likely to begin their careers as professionals, semi-professionals, or mid-level/high-level managers.

For those lower-class youth who obtained higher education, the importance of class and region diminished with time. They achieved considerable success in the labour market as professionals, semi-professionals and managers, entering careers that were indistinguishable from those achieved by upper-class youth who had also pursued post-secondary education. Class mattered, but its impact on occupational attainment was tempered by the amount and level of education, clearly reflecting the underlying influence of agency.

While young people with high and low socio-economic origins started out with roughly similar occupational distributions with respect to first-entry jobs, they ended up with significantly different occupational distributions in 1995, differences that favour individuals from the high socio-economic group in terms of occupations concentrated in managerial and professional categories. While this shows that the impact of socio-economic origins was substantial, so too were the effects of educational attainment over the long term. By 1995, almost half of the university graduates were in high-level management and professional positions. Middle-management, semi-professional, and technical occupations drew heavily from all backgrounds including Class of '73 members with only high school education. Very few university graduates were found in either skilled or unskilled employment, whereas these sorts of occupations drew heavily from among those with community college or no more than high school education.

We also sorted 1973 high school region of origin into urban and rural and found that region of origin had a modest effect on first jobs, with the urban location favouring entry jobs in the two higher-status occupational categories. Having rural origins was strongly linked to the number of respondents starting out as farmers. By 1995, the occupational distributions of participants from cities and rural areas differed substantially, with even higher percentages of those with city origins ending up with occupations in the two higher-status occupational categories. We found that by 1995, for youth who started out with unskilled first jobs (white-collar and blue-collar), those with city backgrounds had been upwardly mobile into the managerial and professional ranks, while those with rural backgrounds had either been upwardly mobile into skilled occupations (white-collar and blue-collar) or remained in the unskilled occupational category.

Notwithstanding the impact of region on occupational destinations, the degree of occupational mobility for the Class of '73 was high.

In all likelihood, this was the combined result of stability and growth in particular occupation sectors between the mid-1970s and the early 1990s and the personal attributes and circumstances of individuals. After beginning their careers in low-level jobs, large numbers of employees were evidently still able to 'work their way up' the company or organizational ladder. The pathways forged by individuals varied significantly, however, as the following case studies indicate.

Navigating the life course

Neither of Jennifer's parents went to university or college, but they encouraged her to pursue higher education. 'I guess they wanted us to do better than what they had done themselves,' she said. Her mother was a secretary and her father a district fire chief. After finishing high school, Jennifer took a university degree in administrative studies. She then worked in secretarial jobs for which she was overqualified. But set as she was on paid employment, she 'took the first thing [she] could get.' After a year she was hired by a bank in a position where she was able to apply her university training. She eventually moved into a managerial position, where she remained in the early 1990s. The combination of parental encouragement and personal persistence (agency) and expanding opportunities in the service sector (structure of the economy) influenced Jennifer's life course.

By contrast, Frank, the youngest of five children of an Italian-immigrant working-class family, dropped out of Grade 13, worked as a surveying assistant, a job he disliked, and left. He then completed a Manpower retraining program in painting and decorating and worked briefly as a painting contractor, but quit following a dispute with his employer. For several years, he drifted, occasionally working with his mother at a laundromat, at times collecting unemployment insurance. He moved out of the family house at age 27 to marry, and has since worked as a maintenance man for a utility company. There have been many layoffs in the organization, and his job in 1994 was neither well paying nor assured, though he was hopeful that his seniority would secure his position. In Frank's case, the lack of postsecondary education limited his occupational options, though he was able to obtain some skilled training and employment. His commitment to assisting his mother and his difficulty in finding work that could sustain his interest contributed to the largely unrewarding vocational state. The recession of the early 1990s lurked in the background as an added source of pressure.

Frank's experience was quite different from Sam's, whose parents were also working-class Italian immigrants in a small Ontario town. His father worked as a garbage collector and his mother as a cook. Sam was a successful high school athlete and won a sports scholarship to an American university. Because he missed his family, he returned home, and then transferred to another American university. He played hockey while at college but did not pursue it professionally. Clearly, his interest in sports stimulated his pursuit of higher education, and he eventually received a bachelor's degree in business. He worked in hotels during the summer, where he met his then-future (now current) wife. Her father owned a restaurant/hotel in which Sam began to work. He 'moved up the ladder' and now manages the hotel. In the mid-1990s, he hoped one day to be the proprietor of his own hotel.

In Sam's case, the support he received from his parents to pursue his schooling, his special aptitude for sports, and his selection of a marriage partner all affected his career progress, facilitating to some degree his ability to surmount social-structural barriers. Elsewhere in our study, we document the particular determination of immigrant families to help improve the social status of their children (Anisef et al., 2000, chapter 6). This factor, too, affected Sam's outlook.

Consider also the case of Kelly, who grew up in a central-Ontario farm close to a small town. One of ten children, in a family that struggled financially, she finished high school and then a nursing program at a community college in another Ontario city. She did this despite the fact that her father did not value education highly. She was determined not to be a 'farmer's wife because farm women work too hard and they get no credit for it.' Still, she cherished country living, and resolved both to avoid the 'big city' and to live near her family. She moved back to the outskirts of her home town and has since worked part time in the local hospital, where secure full-time employment has been difficult to obtain. She married a builder/carpenter, who works irregularly; they have two children. Their very modest family income situates them at the low end of the socio-economic scale, though the mortgage on their house (which Kelly's husband built) is almost paid off. In 1995, Kelly remained very satisfied with rural life, which she considered superior to the frenetic pace of urban living. However, she was concerned about the future for her children, given the high level of youth unemployment, especially in economically deprived areas. She wanted them to continue living close by; however, with the gradual erosion of rural life in Ontario and the uncertain economy, she wondered how they would eventually support themselves.

In Kelly's situation, one can clearly see the combined impact of structure and agency. Like many other rural Ontarians, she did not attend university. In addition, she chose a traditionally gender-specific field of employment. But by undertaking college education away from home, she asserted her independence and increased her self-confidence. Employment conditions then limited her ability to work full time, but this was offset to a significant degree by the priority she placed on lifestyle and family concerns. The family lived modestly, but managed financially and revered its quality of life.

These examples illustrate the varied experiences of those from modest backgrounds. Status-attainment literature correctly notes that those who are born into more privileged families have a 'head start,' and generally maintain or improve their social status. Our study certainly supports this theory, but we explore as well individuals' particular experiences and perceptions, which are diverse, distinctive, and largely unpredictable.

Walter, for example, whose father was a professional and who grew up in a middle-class neighbourhood, recalled that 'there was never any decision to be made as to whether you would go to post-secondary education. It was more a function of when you would go ... [University was] a natural progression of events.' Still, his educational and occupational pathway was not entirely linear. He enrolled in science but performed rather poorly and did not complete his degree. He began to work part time for a large company as a computer operator, a skill he mostly learned on the job. He then took an auditing position with a bank. The job proved to be less interesting than advertised, and he was dissatisfied with his promotion prospects. He returned to university to complete a degree in economics and computer science. A subsequent job as an information-centre consultant for an insurance company lasted for a decade. But the 'shakeup of the industry,' which involved the 'elimination of huge layers of middle management,' led him to consider other possibilities. He left his job voluntarily and now works with a small reinsurance-facilitation company. He valued the autonomy he had gained in his work and the time it allowed for an active family life.

Coming from a middle-class background, Walter thus had the 'cultural capital' that enhanced his prospects for higher education. Although he did not initially complete his degree, he was interested in and able to find work in two areas of employment in which opportunities were expanding: computers and financial services. He eventually obtained his degree, inspired more by personal than by economic factors. He felt it important to finish a task that he had begun. The financial-services industry in which he worked has been subjected to major structural changes, though his experience and particular skills enabled him to work continuously and happily.

Gender, family, and the challenges of working life

Throughout the 1980s and early 1990s, members of the Class of '73 traversed their ways through the world of employment—a world in which opportunity and uncertainty coexisted. Without question, economic policies beyond the control of individuals affected their working lives (Krahn, 1996). Inflation, recession, free trade, the growth of the service sector, corporate downsizing, and public-sector deficit cutting all affected the availability and conditions of employment throughout the period. So, too, did the individual's social background, educational attainments, and gender. By 1995, the participation of women in the labour force had grown significantly—dual-income families were now the norm in Canada—but males and females still constructed their lives in distinctive, gender-specific ways.

However daunting the social and economic challenges, the men and women of the Class of '73 sought to ensure their personal autonomy and assert control over their working lives. Family life was a particularly important priority, and they were determined—women especially—to reconcile the demands of work with those of home and children.

As they looked back over the period from the perspective of our 1995 survey, the majority of respondents—66 per cent—declared themselves to be satisfied or very satisfied with 'the way things have turned out' with respect to *work or career*. Some 22 per cent were neither satisfied nor dissatisfied, and almost 12 per cent were dissatisfied or very dissatisfied. By contrast, more than 85 per cent were very satisfied or satisfied with their *family life*, and 5.7 per cent were dissatisfied or very dissatisfied. Some 83 per cent were similarly content with their *personal life* and slightly less than 5 per cent expressed dissatisfaction. Thus, in 1995, most respondents were positive about, or at least reconciled to, the reality of their working lives. But family life was a far greater source of fulfilment. Given the economic vagaries of the previous two decades, this attitude was understandable.

Overall, the respondents appeared to enjoy their work, with women experiencing a slight edge in job satisfaction. By 1995, job satisfaction bore no clear relationship to educational attainment, but those re- spondents who held high-level management/professional positions and middle-management/semi-professional jobs were more likely to express strong satisfaction than respondents who held skilled or unskilled jobs. (Anisef et al., 2000, chapter 4.)

Interviewees described, often in considerable detail, the conditions that both enriched and diminished the quality of their working experiences. The virtues of autonomy, diversity, flexibility, and creativity were highlighted by numerous people working in a variety of occupations. Where one or more of these conditions was absent, respondents might well have made changes, including voluntarily leaving their positions, in order to improve the quality of their work and their lives.

Ray, a chartered accountant, gave up a well-paying but 'boring' job with a large firm to start his own company. This was a 'risky' venture in the mid-1980s, given the fluctuations in the economy, but with the assistance of his wife, who helped with the books, he succeeded. He came to realize that accountants are employable in both good and bad economic times and that, to some degree, the profession is 'recession proof.' As a self-employed person, he came to cherish the control he gained over his hours and conditions of work.

Some, like Aaron, found it possible to fulfil their aspirations within a large organization. He dropped out of high school but later enrolled in university part time where he studied economics. Employed for several years by a major gas company, he had done economic forecasting and worked in both 'regulatory' affairs and policy development in the area of 'rate design.' He anticipated that he would refuse any promotions which reduced his independence and creative opportunities on the job.

While working as an occupational therapist, Jessica ran a small catering service at the hospital where she was employed. Entrepreneurial ambitions led her and her husband into the real-estate field where they worked successfully during the housing boom of the mid-1980s.

In one three-week period, they sold eleven houses. Her husband did the marketing and she worked closely with clients, a facet of her job with close parallels to her work in occupational therapy. In both fields she was required to 'hold [the client's] hand' and provide emotional support under stressful circumstances. She left the job to raise her children. Her husband continued in the real-estate business full time, while she worked with him 'in the background.'

Many women, as our survey shows, left paid employment, either temporarily or permanently, to bear and raise children. Some 81.5 per cent of women not employed in 1994–5 identified family responsibilities, including pregnancy and problems arranging child care, as reasons for being out of the labour force in 1994–5. Employed women frequently described the challenges of reconciling family and occupational demands, and those who successfully managed this were the most fulfilled. Others wrestled with the problem on a daily basis.

Stephanie, for example, enjoyed her current employment as a music teacher, which took her many years to obtain. But in 1995 she was experiencing stress. The mother of three children, her teaching job required her to offer programs in two schools, and she was feeling 'burned out' by the competing demands on her time. Having regularly banked a portion of her salary, she was preparing to take a year off from her job, though she 'remain[ed] passionate' about her career.

Our quantitative and qualitative data revealed that, within the household, married and cohabiting women still shouldered a greater burden of family responsibilities, including looking after children, cooking meals, cleaning the house, and shopping for groceries. Men and women shared responsibility for household finances and for disciplining children.

To realize their occupational aspirations and cope with labour-market pressures and family demands, women chose a variety of strategies. Laura, the mother of three sons, was married and living in suburban Toronto in 1995. She had switched to occasional relief work from the full-time secretarial position she had held at a utility company. But when her employer laid off its part-time staff, Laura was forced to register with a temporary-employment agency. She found travelling to downtown Toronto and looking after three children very stressful, and she decided to stay home full time. She was very involved in her children's school and sports teams, and although she found having primary responsibility for child rearing difficult at times, she derived considerable satisfaction from it. She described herself as 'Ms Chauffeur,' claiming to be much busier than when she was working now that her sons had so many activities. 'But I enjoy it,' she added.

Judy, whose job in the food industry required her to be at work very early in the morning, relied on her husband to feed and dress their two children, aged 7 and 3, and drive them to school. As her job ended at 1:30 p.m., she was able to take over child-care responsibilities for the afternoon. This reorganization was possible because her husband was unemployed for six months. During that time, as her workload increased, he took on more of the domestic duties. Although he eventually obtained full-time work, he continued to share many of the household tasks.

The concept of sharing such duties reflects the high proportion of respondents in dual-income families. However, female respondents were more likely than males to adapt their occupations to family needs by entering occupations long associated with the traditional female sphere—such as nursing and teaching—as well as various support services—such as clerical and secretarial work. Women in the Class of '73 were more likely to have married in their early twenties than men. However, it also true that many did not marry until their late twenties, and most waited to have children until they had been in the labour force for a number of years. Finally, unlike their parents, very few had more than three children, and most had two.

It is interesting to speculate on the extent to which these women's responses reflected their commitment to work and career rather than merely their need to adjust to the realities of their situations. Typically, with the birth of their second child, women made compromises with respect to the work setting and their place within it, even when they continued to work full time. This, of course, must be taken in the larger context of women's situation in the labour market, particularly with respect to their (lower) earning capacity. Given these practical but important matters, family decision making which accommodated the work and careers of men over those of women could be seen as rational and of general economic benefit to the family household. Extending this argument even further, not having children, or having only one child, would have paid greater dividends to women from a career standpoint. To fully understand the commitment of Class of '73 women to have and raise children, one must consider the combined influence of personal priorities, the intrinsic satisfaction attached to family formation, and the continuing impact of cultural pressures in reinforcing women's traditional domestic roles.

Conclusion

Both this chapter and the larger study from which it is drawn have sought to demonstrate the interactive role of structure and agency in shaping the life course. Employing the concept of 'structured individualization,' we argue for the importance of agency and, more specifically, individual traits, for understanding the choices and experiences of young people as they move from adolescence to adulthood. A close examination of personal biographies among members of the Class of '73 revealed important personal differences. Some articulated a clear vision of the future in their adolescent years, while others drifted through adolescence and early adulthood, giving little thought to the conscious pursuit of life goals. Those who drifted were more likely to succumb to the constraining aspects of social structures which operated around them, while those who articulated a clear vision and sought to enact their dreams were able to take creative advantage of the enabling aspects of these same social structures.

An examination of individual lives accentuated the unique ways in which people construct and negotiate their way within the context of existing social structures and the social and economic realities of the historical period within which they grew up. We have traced the ways in which the vagaries of the economy, socially constructed gender roles, and the importance of individual personality affected pathways from schooling to employment and to family life. Individuals found themselves in historical moments that shaped the context of their lives. Yet many were determined, through the choices they made, to determine the texture and substance of their daily experiences. For the most part, they believed they had succeeded. This final quotation reflects typical attitudes expressed in a distinctive voice.

> Despite what you may gather from this survey, I'm very happy with the outcome of my life: marriage, children and work. At some time, many of us wish for a better life! But I'm not complaining, considering the economy as such. Remember, to be fairly successful in life, no matter how much education or how many diplomas you acquire, you have to chase the dream whether it be happiness or wealth or both. Mind you, a great education helps immensely, and a good attitude toward life doesn't hurt either.

References

Anisef, P., Paasche, G., & Turrittin, A. H. (1980), *Is the die cast?: Educational achievements and work destinations of Ontario youth: A six-year follow-up of the critical juncture high school students*. Toronto: Minister of Colleges and Universities.

Anisef, P., Axelrod, P., Baichman, E., James, C., & Turrittin, A. (2000), *Opportunity and uncertainty: Life course experiences of the class of '73*. Toronto: University of Toronto Press.

Beck, U. (1992), *The risk society: Towards a new modernity*. London: Sage.

Boyd, M., Goyder, J., Jones, F. E., McRoberts, H. A., Pineo, P. C., & Porter, J. (1985), *Ascription and achievement: Studies in mobility and status attainment in Canada*. Ottawa: Carleton University Press.

Buchmann, M. (1989), *The script of life in modern society: Entry into adulthood in a changing world*. Chicago: University of Chicago Press.

Chisholm, L. (1999), From systems to networks: The reconstruction of youth transitions in Europe. In W. R. Heinz (Ed.), *From education to work: Cross national perspectives* (pp. 298–318). Cambridge: Cambridge University Press.

Chisholm, L., & Du Bois-Raymond, M. (1993), Youth transitions, gender and social change. *Sociology*, 27(2), 259–79.

Elder, G.H., Jr. (1978), Family history and the life course. In T. K. Haraven (Ed.), *Transitions: The family and the life course in historical perspective* (pp. 17–64). New York: Academic Press.

Evans, K., & Heinz, W. R. (1994), Transitions in progress. In K. Evans & W. R. Heinz (Eds), *Becoming adults in England and Germany* (pp. 1–16). London: Anglo-German Foundation.

Furlong, A., & Cartmel, F. (1997), *Young people and social change: Individualization and risk in late modernity*. Buckingham: Open University Press.

Hays, S. (1994), Structure and agency and the sticky problem of culture. *Sociological Theory*, 12 (1), 57–72.

Heinz, W. R. (1995), *Status passages as micro-macro linkages in life course*. Bremen: University of Bremen, Special Research Centre 186.

—— (1996), *The transition from education to employment in a comparative perspective*. Toronto: University of Toronto, Centre for International Studies.

—— (Ed.). (1999), *From education to work: Cross-national perspectives*. New York: Cambridge University Press.

Jones, G., & Wallace, C. (1992), *Youth, family, and citizenship*. Buckingham, U.K.: Open University Press.

Krahn, H. (1996), *School-work transition: Changing patterns and research needs*. Ottawa: Human Resources Development Canada, Applied Research Branch.

Krüger, H. (1998, May), *Social change in two generations: Employment patterns and their costs for family life*. Paper presented at the International Symposium on Restructuring Work and the Life Course, Toronto.

Livingstone, D. W. (1999), *The education-jobs gap: Underemployment or economic democracy*. Toronto: Garamond Press.

Phillips, P., & Phillips, E. (1993), *Women and work: Inequality in the Canadian labour market*. Toronto: James Lorimer.

Roberts, K., Clark, S. C., & Wallace, C. (1994), Flexibility and individualization: A comparison of transitions into unemployment in England and Germany. *Sociology*, 28 (1), 31–54.

Rudd, P., & Evans, K. (1998), Structure and agency in youth transitions: Student experiences of vocational further education. *Journal of Youth Studies*, 1 (1), 39–62.

Wotherspoon, T. (1998), *The sociology of education in Canada: Critical perspectives*. Toronto: Oxford University Press.

Wyn, J., & Dwyer, P. (1999), New directions in research on youth in transition, *Journal of Youth Studies*, 2 (1), 5–21.

VOCATIONAL INTEGRATION AND RELATIONSHIP TO WORK AMONG QUEBEC YOUTHS WITHOUT HIGH-SCHOOL DIPLOMAS

Claude Trottier, Mircea Vultur, and Madeleine Gauthier

Introduction

Within the current context, young people without a high-school diploma are confronted by a major challenge when it comes time to integrate within the workplace. These youths are faced with the possibility of being confined to the secondary labour market, with unstable employment situations, low-pay positions, mediocre working conditions and poor chances to be promoted. Furthermore, youths without a degree often have to suffer the competition of other more educated youths accepting jobs for which they are overqualified.

How do young people who have left high-school[1] with no diploma integrate into the workplace, compared with those who have completed their high-school studies? Is entry into the labour market easier for those who have matriculated? In what ways does the relationship to work differ between high-school graduates and non-graduates? This article aims at examining, within a comparative perspective, this article aims at examining the classic indicators of vocational integration, or simply put, integration into the work force. It also looks at other aspects concerned with the integration and relationship to work of young people with or without a secondary education diploma in Quebec. In order to mark the breadth of the phenomenon and to ascertain the position of youths between 15 and 24 in the population and on the job market, we thought pertinent to first examine the rates of youths exiting the education system without a high-school diploma.[2]

---

[1] In Canada, education falls under Provincial authority. In Quebec, the general secondary program comprises five years of studies after the six years in primary school and one year in nursery school. Usually, students enter secondary school at twelve and complete their studies at 17, although schooling is only mandatory up to sixteen years of age.

[2] This article was written within a larger study on vocational integration and the relationship to work of the young without a diploma. It will be published in an

1. *Rate for exiting without a diploma and rate for dropping out from high-school*

In the period 1999–2000, 28.7% of students did not get a diploma *within the youth sector or before the age of 20 within the adult sector* (MEQ, 2001a, chart 2.6). This rate of exiting without a diploma considerably diminished between 1975–76 and 1985–86, and then rose till the end of the decade, mainly because: a) the pass mark was raised from 50% to 60%, increasing the difficulty of getting the diploma, and b) the addition of one year of general education as a prerequisite to register with professional education courses. The rate decreased again from 1990 to 1995, to rise again slightly in 1997–1999. The rate of exiting without a diploma varied considerably between regions (from 21.2% for the Quebec City region to 36% in the Outaouais region, MEQ, 2001a, table 5.3). Furthermore, it is higher among men than among women and the gap between genders has tended to widen since 1975 (MEQ, 2001a, table 2.6).

It is important to underline the fact that the rate of exiting without a high-school diploma (the proportion of students from the youth sector or before the age of twenty in the adult sector who have not got a diploma) does not equal the dropout rate, which corresponds to the proportion of the population that does not go to school and has not received a high-school diploma at a given age. In 1999–2000, this rate was of 10.4%, 16.5% and 19.8% for the age groups of 17, 18 and 19 year old, respectively (MEQ, 2001a, chart 2.7). It was much higher among boys than among girls (24.6% versus 14.7% for 19 year old age group), and has diminished by half between 1980 and 2000 (40.5% versus 19.8%, still within the 19 year old age group).

Though it has diminished, the dropout rate among 19 year olds (19.8%) remains high in regard to the objectives established in the Action Plan for the Reform in Education (Department of Education, 2001) according to which 85% among the students of a generation should obtain a high-school diploma in 2010. On the other hand, if we compare the situation in Quebec with that of many countries of the OECD (MÉQ, 2001b), the rate of obtaining a secondary school diploma in Quebec (80%) ranks 15th among those countries,

---

enlarged version within the Colloquium proceedings: "Fragmenting, ruptures and segmenting the work force. The challenges of integration into the work force", presented in Montreal in October 2001. Many thanks to Diane-Gabrielle Tremblay for allowing us to publish the present version.

but is only slightly above their total average (79%).[3] This indicator should be interpreted with reserve and caution, however, given the difficulties inherent in the International Type-Classification of education, and the fluctuating quality of information systems and of the data communicated to OECD by the various countries.

Concerning the variables associated with the rate of exiting without a diploma or to the dropout rate, the *Youth in Transition Survey*–YITS (Bowlby and McMullen, 2002), focused upon a segment of young Canadians aged 18–20, allows us to compare youths with diplomas to high-school dropouts from the point of view of their family background, school performance, participation in school activities, working while studying, peer influence, and academic aspirations. According to this study, dropouts are more likely than others to a) have grown in a single-parent family, b) have parents who have not completed their secondary studies, and c) belong to a family whose parents have a rather low socio-economic status and work in the areas of sales, services, tradesperson, transportation, equipment operators, as well as the sectors of primary processing, manufacturing and utilities occupations. On average, they had obtained lower marks than the ones with a diploma and were more likely to repeat the year. Furthermore, compared to the students with a diploma, they showed a weaker commitment to school on the academic level (presenting homework on time, absences, relationship to teachers) as well as on the social level (participating in out-of-school activities), which shows that academic difficulties are not the sole reason for dropping out. As well, fewer of their friends had continued their studies beyond high-school, and they were also more likely to have consumed alcohol or drugs. Their main reason for dropping out was a failure of the school to keep them interested. But young men also mentioned their desire to work, and young women, pregnancy and child rearing. Contrary to what some might think, dropouts used to work less hours during their studies than the ones with a diploma, but when they did have a paid job, the dropout rate was lower when they were working a moderate number of hours per week, and higher when they were working full time. Finally, three-quarters of dropouts regretted their decision to quit school, and a wide majority indicated that they would like to complete secondary or university studies, eventually.

---

[3] This rate was obtained by dividing the number of "initial diplomas" granted in 1998 by the number of people aged 17, the age at which they are theoretically able to receive a high-school diploma.

2. Youths within the mainstream population and in the Quebec work force

Before comparing vocational integration between youths with or without a high-school diploma on the basis of the usual indicators (labour force participation, employment rate, part-time work rate, unemployment rate), we decided to first determine the proportion of youths aged 15–24 (with or without a diploma) in the population and in the work force.

The study of demographic tendencies shows that the population aged between 15 and 24 in Quebec has diminished since the beginning of the 80's, after having increased massively in the 60's and the 70's. In 1976, the proportion of youths aged 15–24 within the global population aged over 15 was 27.3%. In 1990, this proportion was of only 17.2% and in 2000, 16.2% (Statistics Canada, E-STAT).

As to youths within the work force, those aged 15–24 are less a part of it than before (see Table 1). Their *rate of participation in the labour force* decreased from 65.3% to 61.1% between 1990 and 2000. According to Human Resources Development Canada, (E-STAT, 2000), this decrease is mainly due to the fact that young people decide to delay their entry into the work force, stay at school longer, or go back to school to get a better preparation for the work force. From that perspective, it may be seen as an improvement. According to Lavoie and Béjaouie (1999), young people have sensed the new requirements in the work force generated by the globalization of the economy and technological changes, all of which demand new capabilities and privilege more qualified workers to an increasing extent. This structural factor could explain the decrease in the *rate of participation in the labour force*, much more than the contextual factor of the early 90's economic recession: this seems to have only had a minimal impact on the decrease in activity by young people who were working while doing their studies part-time (HRDC, 2000). Their *employment rate* has also diminished for the same reasons during the same period (from 55.6% to 52.6%). Concerning the *part-time employment rate* in that age group, it has raised considerably, from 34.2% to 44.5%, reflecting the changes in work organization and recruiting modes in companies. This tendency shows a deterioration of the youth situation within the work force, because "part-time jobs generally provide a lower pay and less benefits, as well as poorer chances of improving one's capabilities than full-time jobs" (HRDC, 2000: 6). As for the *unemployment rate*, it has decreased from 15.0% to 13.9%. On the other hand, it is important to underline that it has decreased only in the case of the 20–24 age group (14.1% versus 11.6%), and that in the case of the 15–19 age group, it has increased over 2% (from 16.4% to 18.5%). Such an increase during a period of strong economic resumption shows to what degree the work force requirements have risen in the last 10 years.

Table 1. Indicators of the integration into the work force, youths aged 15–24: 1999 and 2000

Age group	15–24 years	
Years	1990	2000
Participation rate in the labour force	65.3%	61.1%
Employment rate	55.6%	52.6%
Part-time employment rate	34.2%	44.5%
Unemployment rate	15%	13.9%
15 to 19 years	16.4%	18.5%
20 to 24 years	14.1%	11.6%

Source: Statistics Canada (2000) and E-STAT. Calculations by ISQ and the authors.

If we now examine the share of the Quebec work force held by the categories of persons (with or without a high-school diploma) which comprise the youths focused upon in the present article, we notice (Table 2) that close to one position in five (18.6%) was held by persons who did not complete their secondary studies, and one quarter of the positions by persons having successfully completed them (17.6%) or who have started part-time post-secondary studies (8.2%).[4] This data contradicts the common image of a work force dominated by the most educated, and it stresses the pertinence of research on high-schol graduates and non-graduates. However, one has to admit that between 1990 and 2000, the proportion of people in the work force without a high-school diploma has decreased by over 10% (from 29.5% to 18.6%), the percentage of people who have completed post-secondary studies has increased by 7.4% during the same period (from 29.0% to 36.4%), and the proportion of positions held

---

[4] According to Statistics Canada terminology, the post-secondary studies sector regroups a broad spectrum of pupils and students. This terminology concerns a) all school programs leading to vocational diplomas or certificates, including high-school diplomas in vocational studies, b) pre-university and technical college diplomas and certificates and c) university certificates and studies that do not lead to a degree such as a bachelor's, masters or doctorate.

Table 2. Employment according to highest level of education in Quebec (in %)

	1990	2000
Without high-school diploma	29.5	18.6
High-school studies completed	20.1	17.6
Post-secondary studies partially complete	8.2	8.2
Post-secondary studies completed	29.0	36.4
University studies successfully completed	13.2	19.2
Bachelor's degree	9.1	13.2
Degree superior to a bachelor's degree	4.1	6.0
Total	100.0	100.0

Source: Quebec Department of Education, 2001a.

by persons with a university degree has increased by 6% (from 13.2% to 19.2%).

3. *Indicators of youth vocational integration in accordance with having or not having a diploma*

In this section, we will attempt to examine various indicators of vocational integration by young people aged 15–24, specifically whether they have obtained a high-school diploma or not at the end of their schooling. What are the differences between people with or without a high-school diploma? Has their situation changed in the course of the last ten years?

In 2000, youths graduating from high-school show a much greater *labour force participation* than those without one (71.8% versus 45.4%). This data shows the importance of matriculating in both the decision of entering the work force or in accessing it, as well as the fact that young people without a diploma go back to school later. Ten years earlier, in 1999, *labour force participation* was also higher than in 2000, because the youths of that age were less inclined to continue their studies or go back to them after having left school.

The *employment rate* is also higher among youths with a diploma than among those without one in 2000, as in 1990; it is observed, however, that between those two dates, the differences, between youths with diplomas and those without, have become greater.

Data analysis of the *part-time employment rate* for 2000 reveal tendencies that are different from those observed in the case of the actual *employment rate*. The *part-time employment rate* is lower among

Table 3. Indicators of vocational integration for high-school matriculation: 1990 and 2000[5]

Indicators	With a diploma	Without a diploma
Labour force participation		
1990	76.6	54.7
2000	71.8	45.4
Employment rate		
1990	66.5	40.8
2000	61.5	35.4
Part-time employment rate		
1990	24.5	46.7
2000	35.6	45.9
Unemployment rate		
1990	16.4	21.6
2000	14.3	21.9

Source: *Quebec Statistics Institute*. Data compiled by the authors.

youths with a diploma than among those without one. As to the *unemployment rate*, in 2000, it is markedly lower among graduates than non-graduates. The same tendency is to be observed in 1990. Furthermore, the *unemployment rate* among non-graduates has not diminished since 1990 (21.6% versus 21.9%) despite a favourable economic context, which brings forth the idea that the standard relative to the necessity of a diploma as a condition to access employment has been reinforced.

Beyond those differences that concur with the usual indicators of integration into the workforce, other studies have highlighted differences between high-school graduates and non-graduates. Firstly, a national survey on Canadian graduates and non-graduates aged between 18 and 20 (Gilbert et al., 1993) has, among other matters, looked at various aspects of their entry into the work force. According to the survey, the non-matriculated are less likely to go back to their studies and retrain after leaving school than those with high-school diplomas. Once in the work force, the non-matriculated also have fewer opportunities to receive training from their employer. They are also more uncertain and indecisive about their career, and their vision of a long-term professional orientation tends to be less specific. Such

---

[5] Pupils of the first and second grades of high-school, as well as those registered in vocational training are not included in these figures.

orientation problems may prevent them from structuring their academic path and affect their motivation. Furthermore, the non-matriculated have a greater tendency to think that they have not received the kind of training they desire. On the level of employment seeking, regarding the type of actions undertaken, there are few differences between both groups. Nonetheless, the non-matriculated have a lesser knowledge of the various resources (federal and provincial programs) available and of the job-searching methods, and are less likely to turn to them. They rely on parents and friends rather than on job ads or the services of a career counsellor. The non-matriculated meet more difficulties when filling-out an employment application and, according to them, their shortcomings in reading, writing, and mathematics curtail their employment possibilities. More non-matriculated than those with diplomas receive welfare or unemployment subsidies.

Another comparative study (Charest, 1997) highlighted differences between matriculated and non-matriculated in general high-school education, and among these, students with adapting and learning disabilities (SALD) compared with those not suffering this disability. Indeed, half the matriculated in general high-school education have been active in the sense that since their exiting high-school, they have been working or studying without going through a transition of unemployment, whereas only one-third of non-matriculated are in that situation. Among those, youths with adapting disabilities were more subject to unemployment and inactivity than those who had learning disabilities. It is important to underline, though, that a return to education for adults is a common characteristic on the path of many non-graduating youths, particularly those who were not classified SALD or if they were, who had only met slight learning difficulties. Regarding the type of position held, graduates of general education are found in a much higher proportion in the trades and restaurant sector than non-graduates who are more present in the category of workers. Among that group, students who were SALD are present in a much greater proportion in the category of workers rather than the category of trade employees. Working conditions vary to a higher degree based upon gender rather than according to having or not having a diploma, as young women work fewer hours per week and are paid lower hourly and weekly wages. This difference can be explained by the fact that young women work at different types of jobs than young men. Salaries are lower in the areas of services and for shop assistants, where more young women are found, than in the industrial sector where the percentage of young men is higher.

4. *Interpreting the differences between graduates and non-graduates, in vocational integration*

How can one explain the fact that high-school graduates succeed better at integrating within the work force than non-graduates? Put simply: how does the diploma make the difference? Lacking the space to present an account of all studies on the matter, we will limit ourselves here to the two most classical explanations. According to the first, the diploma comes to mark the end of an educational course and attests to objective knowledge and capacities that can potentially be used at work and make the person with a high-school diploma more productive. The diploma also demonstrates cognitive capacities that give its holder a good predisposition to apprenticeship. For these reasons, holders of a diploma are traditionally given hiring preference and better work conditions. According to the second explanation, the diploma appears more as a signal, not of directly measurable capacities and capabilities, but a signal that allows the employer to distinguish among individuals according to their potential aptitudes. These non-observable aptitudes are not necessarily derived from the education received. The diploma then appears as an imperfect measure of productive capacities rather than a proof of capabilities. Employers in a hiring situation are not perfectly informed on the real aptitudes of employment seekers, but wish nonetheless to hire the most productive or those more likely to become productive; they therefore use the diploma as a filter to palliate the difficulties in directly collecting information on their future employee's aptitudes. This process confers an apparent legitimacy and may reduce the costs of recruitment.

Both theories are used not only to explain the differences in vocational integration not only between graduates and non-graduates, but also between young people exiting the education system at various levels, with or without a diploma.

Whatever the approach favoured, one must not overestimate the importance of the diploma as a factor explaining integration. Indeed, there is a relation between the fact of having a diploma or not, or between the level of education achieved, on the one hand, and indicators of vocational integration, on the other. But it is important to keep in mind that the diploma obtained or the level of education achieved at the time of the initial education are only part of the factors influencing access to employment. Several other factors need to be taken into consideration: the professional experience and the capabilities acquired outside of the education and production systems (self-training, volunteer or community activities), the availability of a network of relationships providing support, the area of the workforce (primary or secondary) into which youths are trying to enter, the types of jobs available to them, discrimination factors, latent or systemic, competition between youths—matriculated or not—after initial education and experienced workers or unemployed persons, working regulations that may privilege workers already in the work force, and the politics regarding employment and assistance to integration.

5. *Youth's relationship to work*

Relationship to work is a concept characterized by the wide variety of its uses. According to the most common one, this concept comprises the values and beliefs concerning the role of work within an individual's life, which serve as guidelines and shape attitudes. But it is also defined in terms of satisfaction derived from work.

Beathge (1994) adheres to the first conception of relationship to work, and identifies four ways in which youths define themselves in relation to work. Some base their main life orientations on work, and professional activity ranks first in their present and future projects. Others desire to build equilibrium between professional life and private life, aspiring to self-achievement wherein one does not supersede the other. The third type is the one that considers couple and family life as the structuring element of their life project. To them, work remains secondary. Finally, a fourth type of youth focuses on leisure for their life project. Some go as far as refusing to work, while others maintain a distance and don't invest much into work. In the present study, the two first types have appeared to be clearly predominant: work equals or surpasses couple and family life in importance.

Paugam (2000) defines relationship to work in terms of satisfaction and identifies three dimensions: a) the intrinsic qualities of work and the fulfillment it brings according to the individual's perception, b) the salary and material advantages provided by work and c) the quality of human relations initiated within the workspace and the working atmosphere. Regarding the first dimension, Paugam notes that satisfaction at work will vary mainly according to the socio-professional category. Non-qualified workers are less satisfied with the intrinsic qualities they find in work than managers are. Regarding salary, "youths under 25 say they are satisfied with their salaries more often than their elders, even though they receive a much lower salary on average" (Paugam, 2000: 51). This situation is caused by the fact that "youths have lower expectations, for what they essentially want is to prove themselves and to get recognition from the employer in order to keep their work position". The satisfaction degree in the area of human relations also varies according to the socio-professional category, non-qualified workers being the "most dissatisfied regarding their relationships to colleagues" (Paugam, 2000: 54). According to the author, age has a superior impact on salary than on the one related to the intrinsic qualities of work and the qualities of human work relations.

Nicole-Drancourt and Roulleau-Berger (Nicole-Drancourt and Roulleau-Berger, 2001) also wrote about the relationship to work of youth in a recent publication. The authors analyzed this relation's evolution under the angle of its instrumental, social and symbolic aspects, and found the emergence, since 1970, of the "precarious" youth type, for whom there is no balance between the three dimensions of the relationship to work. This category of youth "develops a relationship to work which is based on a principle of hesitation, ambivalence and reversibility" (Nicole-Drancourt and Roulleau-Berger, 2001: 156).

What of the relationship to work of young Quebecers or Canadians? Though the data currently available is fragmental and doesn't allow one to systematically compare high-school graduates and non-graduates, one can consider certain aspects on the basis of the work already completed.

Using the first conception of the relationship to work, Fournier and Croteau (1998), through a study on young Quebecers with a diploma in vocational training, technical studies, or an undergraduate university degree, reach the following conclusion: on a sample of young people, 50% consider work as more important than the other areas of activity; 20% place work at the second or third rank among their preoccupations, but work remains important in their view nonetheless; 10% consider work to be particularly important because they are at a stage in their professional lives when it has to be so for them to start their career, but they hope this is only a transition; 20% see work as of little importance and work only to earn a living, out of necessity. As for the significance of work for all-level graduates, a vast majority of them have an *expressive* conception of work, and expect it to be a source of self-fulfillment and personal development. A minority has an *instrumental* conception of work, perceiving it only as a source of income and a social obligation, a necessary ill.

In a study previously quoted from and, unlike the above, not dealing exclusively with graduates, but also with youths experiencing difficulties in learning or adapting, matriculated and non-matriculated youths in secondary education in Quebec, Charest (1997) found that two-thirds of all of these categories of youths give a particular importance to work as a means of personal development. The more practical aspects of work (salary and working conditions) come second. Nonetheless, non-graduates in general secondary education tend to adhere in a smaller proportion to this *expressive* conception of work. Among the non-matriculated, the ones who have met difficulties in learning and adapting are more prone to adhere to this conception. It seems they wish to receive more self-fulfillment at work than they were able to have at school. Furthermore, non-graduates in general education are less demanding than graduates regarding working conditions, though they share the same expectations salary wise.

As to the second satisfaction-oriented conception of relationship to work, a study by Gilbert et al. (1993) showed that high-school graduates and non-graduates were experiencing a very high degree of satisfaction concerning their jobs, but were dissatisfied with their financial situation—non-graduates even more so than graduates. Basing himself on the study following up young people going through their school/workforce transition between 1991 and 1995, Marquardt (1998) showed that young people who are working experience a high degree of satisfaction regarding their jobs, and that there was no difference between high-school graduates and non-graduates, nor between the latter and those who had undertaken postsecondary studies but had not completed them—university graduates showing nonetheless higher satisfaction. Marquardt also emphasized the fact that for all those groups, the most satisfying elements were intrinsic aspects of work (type of work, requirements relative to the job) rather than extrinsic ones (salary and other aspects). Finally, he showed that the higher dissatisfaction expressed by young people concerns intrinsic characteristics of work more than salary or working time issues. Within the perspective of their relationship to work, there is no notable difference between high-school graduates and non-graduates and those who have partly completed post-secondary studies.

In brief, having obtained a degree or not does not seem to affect young people's relationship to work. Graduates and non-graduates find work very important, have an *expressive* rather than *instrumental* conception of work, and a majority are satisfied with their work. There is no apparent split between the instrumental, social and symbolic dimensions of work as defined by Nicole-Drancourt and Roulleau-Berger. Studies on Quebec youths in a precarious situation (Gauthier, Molgat, Saint-Laurent, 1999) show that work remains a structuring value within their social world. It is nonetheless important to underline that data on Quebec and Canadian youths is fragmented, and, with regard to our initial objectives, does not allow for a systematic comparison between high-school graduates and non-graduates. Furthermore, one may wonder whether the relationship to work is not influenced more by the job's specifics (type of job, modes of work supervision, socio-economic status of the job) than by the fact of having or not having a diploma. On the other hand, the education level and the fact of having a diploma might impact on work indirectly by conditioning young people into types of jobs whose characteristics might influence the way young people define themselves in relationship to work.

Conclusion

We first attempted to take measure of the phenomenon of young Quebecers without a high-school diploma. We have determined young people's place within Quebec's society and highlighted their presence within the work force. Secondly, we analyzed the impact of having the high-school diploma on their vocational integration, basing ourselves on certain indicators. This analysis showed that: a) in general, the situation of high-school graduates is better than that of non-graduates; b) the impact of the diploma varies according to the integration indicators examined; c) there are wide variations among graduates and among non-graduates, and therefore, the relationship between these variables is not as simple and clear-cut as one might think; and d) it is worthwhile to examine the relationship between these variables, at the time taking into account various other explanatory factors of integration. In addition, we came to the conclusion that the way young people define themselves in relation to work does not vary much according to having or nor obtained a high-school diploma, and that this aspect also requires other explanatory variables to be explored.

We stress the fact that the influence of the level of education becomes more obvious if we compare young people having exited schooling at all levels, including university level. We have not systematically compared—and this is one limitation of our article—graduates and non-graduates at all levels of schooling.[6] But, in this conclusion, we would like to remind the reader that the assumption according to which the training/job adequacy would match "each type of job with a single training pattern" recognized by a diploma has been questioned for several years. Indeed, it is possible to reach a position through various training paths, with the exception of very specialized professions. From that perspective, having a diploma does not always seem to be a *sine qua non* condition to get a position, particularly in the case of non-specialized jobs. Furthermore, the basic education conferred by a diploma does not appear as the only means to acquire or develop the capabilities needed to reach a position. In that case, shouldn't we stop overstating the importance of the lack of diploma? One should also take into consideration that the relationship training/job is one to build upon and not one that is permanently established when one obtains the diploma, but "wrought", not just throughout the course of training, but also upon the professional trajectory, by all "actors" in the education and production systems on the societal level, and by the youths themselves in the work force. In short, many factors other than the diploma may contribute to facilitating the integration or, in the case of the relation to work, to shaping it.

Our analysis is an invitation to appreciate the whole significance of questioning the training/job postulate, and to come to realize that there is place within the work force for the less qualified, even if the working conditions are not ideal. Beyond that, one needs to take into consideration the whole of the variables related to the individual, to schooling and to the dynamics within the work force that impact on integration. With a plan of action in mind, while asserting that the diploma is important as a resource to "negotiate" entry or maintain oneself within the work force and encourage as many youths as possible to complete schooling in order to get the diploma, one has yet to admit that some among them have been marginalized

---

[6] On this topic, see the article by Gauthier in this same publication, wherein this comparison is mentioned.

through the school selection process and barred from the diploma, if not excluded from school; this group has developed an aversion for everything related to school. Beyond reinforcing programs for dropouts or for those who refuse to participate in such programs, we should be facilitating recognition for the capabilities and know-how they have acquired while working, and encouraging continuing education in companies, adapted to their particular situation, rather than relying only upon programs aiming at bringing them back to school.

Bibliography

Beathge, M., (1994), «Le rapport au travail des jeunes» dans G. Mauger, R. Bandit, C. Von Wolffersdorff (éd.), *Jeunesses et sociétés. Perspectives de la recherche en France et en Allemagne*, Paris, Armand Colin.

Bowlby, J. W. and K. Mc Mullen, (2002), *À la croisée des chemins. Premiers résultats pour la cohorte des 18 à 20 ans de l'Enquête auprès des jeunes en transition*. Ottawa: Développement des ressources humaines Canada et Statistique Canada.

Charest, D., (1997), *La situation des jeunes non diplômés de l'école secondaire. Sondage sur l'insertion sociale et l'intégration professionnelle des jeunes en difficulté d'adaptation et d'apprentissage et des autres jeunes non diplômés de l'école secondaire*. Québec: Ministère de l'éducation, Direction de la recherché.

Conseilsupérieur de l'éducation, (1996), *Contre l'abandon au secondaire: rétablir l'appartenance scolaire. Avis à la ministre de l'éducation*. Sainte-Foy, Québec.

Développement des ressources humaines du Canada et statisque Canada, (1993), *Après l'école- Résultats d'une enquête nationale comparant les sortants de l'école aux diplômés d'études secondaires âgés de 18 ans*. Ottawa.

Développement des ressources humaines du Canada. (1998 (1995)), *Le secondaire, est-ce suffisant?, Une analyse des résultats de l'Enquête de suivi auprès des sortants*. Ministère des travaux publics et des services gouvernementaux, Ottawa.

Développement des ressources humaines du Canada, (2000), *Profil des jeunes canadiens sur le marché du travail*. Ottawa, 2000.

E-STAT: http://estat.statcan.ca/

Fournier, G. and L. Croteau, (1998), «Attitudes des jeunes à l'égard du travail au cours des années 1980». *Psychologie du travail et des organisations* 3, no. 3–4: 89–108.

Gauthier, M., M. Molgat and L. Saint Laurent, (1999), *Lien social et pauvreté: repérage et profil des jeunes précaires qui vivent seuls en milieu urbain*, Québec, INRS-Culture et Société.

Gilbert, S., L. Barr, W. Clark, M. Blue and D. Sunter, (1993), *Après l'école, résultats d'une enquête nationale comparant les sortants de l'école aux diplômés d'études secondaires âgés de 18 à 20 ans*. Ottawa: Ressources humaines et travail Canada.

Giret, J.-F., (2000), «Le rôle du diplôme dans les premières années de la vie active». *L'orientation scolaire et professionnelle* 29 No. 2: 243–260.

Lavoie, C. and A. Béjaoui, (1998), *La situation de l'emploi des jeunes au Canada: Quelques explications et perspectives d'avenir*. Ottawa: Développement des ressources humaines Canada.

Marquardt, R., (1998), «Qualité d'emploi pour les jeunes», dans Développement des ressources humaines Canada (éd.), *Le secondaire, est-ce suffisant? Une analyse des résultats de l'Enquête de suivi des sortants, 1995*. Ottawa, pp. 49–56.

Ministère de l'éducation du quebec, (2001), *Indicateurs de l'Éducation*. Québec.

Ministère de l'éducation du quebec, (2000), *Le décrochage scolaire*. Bulletin statistique de l'éducation no. 14, Québec: Direction des statistiques et des études quantitatives.

Ministère de l'éducation du quebec, (2001), *La diplomation au Québec et dans les pays de l'OCDE*. Bulletin de l'éducation no. 21-janvier. Québec.

Ministère de l'éducation du quebec. (2001), *Plan d'action ministériel pour la réforme de l'éducation*. Québec.

Nicole-Drancourt, C., and L. Roulleau-Berger, (2001), *Les jeunes et le travail*, 1950–2000, Paris, Presses Universitaires de France.

Paugam, S. (2000), *Le salarié de la précarité*, Paris, Presses Universitaires de France, 2000.

Statisque Canada (2000), *Enquête sur la population active*. Ottawa.

'LONG TERM YOUTH': DISCONTINUITY IN LABOR PROFILES OF YOUNG SPANISH PEOPLE IN THE AGE OF INFORMATIONAL FLEXIBILITY

Juan Antonio Santos Ortega

In a recent publication, Loïc Wacquant (2000) analyses the living conditions of young people who reside in in the area of a black ghetto in Chicago. He centers his process of investigation in a boxing Gym where young people of the neighbourhood prepare themselves to fight and learn to confront danger and everyday street pressures. Initially, Wacquant's intention was to utilise the Boxing Gym as a 'window' from where he could observe the ghetto. During the course of his ethnographical study and of his being a participant observer—or rather that of a 'participating observer' as he himself refers to the intense immersion that brought him to live the life of boxing for three years—he became aware that the Gym and the Ring both were 'strategic places for research'—in the Mertonian sense—from where, in a privileged manner, the social atmosphere of the ghetto could be observed.

Taking advantage of Wacquant's metaphor of the Boxing Club being like a "window" from which one could observe a wider social reality, one could think of the youth question which concerns us here, as a window from which we can contemplate some of the most recent developments in the social structure of our fast paced, vertiginous and undetermined informational capitalism which is molding our societies. This heuristic potential of the youth question, and particularly in its labor aspects, has not escaped the attention of some of the principal European specialists on the sociology of Youth, who combined, since the eighties, the binomial of Youth and Work.[1]

Precariousness, labor instability and in the lives of the youth, the segmentation of employment, their attitudes concerning flexible work, all these aspects resound also in the works of the most important

---

[1] I point out only some of the more recent summaries that permit the updating of information on the question of juvenile employment: Roulleau-Berger and Gauthier (2001); Gauthier and Guillaume (1999) and Cachón (1999).

contemporary sociologists, an unmistakable sign of the relevance of this subject to endeavour to decipher the emerging labor tendencies of 'new capitalism'. A good example of this is the recent and attractive essay of Richard Sennett (1998) on the repercussions of the new flexible capitalism on employment. *The Corrosion of Character* is full of references regarding generational relationships, the roles of young people in the labor world and their changes in work profiles. The central thesis is that the new economy and the ideology of flexibility are dissolving the concept of a 'lineal career', typical of the old economy, and imposing a social and labor world ruled by incertitude in the work market. The relationships between the generations are marked by the "value of experience crisis": parental trajectories are failing to be a guide for the the present labor situation of their children. Sennett makes a diagnosis in which the work ethic is suffering the shake-up of an economic model where "it's absurd to work long hours and hard for a company that only thinks of liquidating the business and then leaving."

The consequences of these processes of change are yet to be seen; nevertheless, one of the preoccupations that Sennett allows to come through in his book, seems to consolidate itself in the present context of new capitalism. It deals with an extension of the state of insecurity that transfers itself from the work sphere to all aspects of social life. This criterion of instability spreads with greater intensity among the young and puts into action multiple defense mechanisims. Among those which stand out in the first place is the exaltation of their present situation and the fading away of any other lines of temporary action on their part: for the youth from the large cities—trapped by short term possibilities—consumerism and unbridled, nocturnal, free time leisure. Are they choices, or is it a manic defense that reveals a flight from the reality of the work crisis? In the second place, extreme and diverse individualism could be underlined, that although it is not exclusive to young people, reaches a special intensity with them. In this case, the most serious preocupation is the deep desocialisation that installs itself as the consequence of the processes of instability. Young people unsure of their future adopt the mentality of a besieged fortress and the popular fraternal saying "do unto others as you would have them do unto you" is transformed into a worrying "Do unto others before they do it to you". We will explore in this article how this process of desocialisation in the labor experiences of young Spaniards is expressed.

Sennett's analysis refers to American Society but to a greater or lesser degree, it could be extended to all countries whose central nucleus is capitalism. Although Spain is situated on the semi-periphery of this group it presents clearly the profiles that today identify the dark social side of flexibility in the new informational economy: impermanence and instability in employment; intensification and toughening of working conditions; growing inequality in salaries, with an increase in lower wages and *working poor*; chronic presence of persistent pools of unemployment.[2] The past twenty years of profound reorganisation of world capitalism is felt in Spain in an unquestionable way. The technological transformation, both productive and at work, guided by the slogan of flexibility, have produced a radiance of economic rationality and growth and, at the same time, a degradation of social rationality, that is manifesting itself in the extension of the vulnerablity of the most disfavoured sectors.

The expressive concept of *flexploitation* that Pierre Bourdieu is helping to extend in Europe and that we could translate into *flexible exploitation*, is a real terminological invention that permits the inscription of precariousness "into a new mode of domination founded on the institution of a generalised and permanent state of insecurity directed towards maintaining the workers in a state of submission and in the acceptation of exploitation" (Bourdieu, 1998).

To illustrate a panorama of the protagonism of young Spanish people in the dynamics of the *flexploitation*, I shall begin by presenting data on the trends of family and employment emancipation. Later, I shall choose two of the dimensions that now concern experts most about youth problems in Spain: on the one hand, the accumulation of low class professions on the most unqualified juvenile fringes and the profound transformation of the labor socialisation among them. On the other the strong indefinition, or vagueness, in the consolidation of of the professional careers of University students and the problem of over-education. We shall consider these questions by contributing data from recent investigations on these subjects and discussing their incidences on the changes in work profiles of young people in the age of informational flexibility.

---

[2] A panoramic view of these tendencies in the job market in Spain can be obtained in Alonso (2000).

The perennial young: delayed emancipation and employment break-down

The young people from the countries of Southern Europe present a model wherein the extended stay in the home of origin is one of the most outstanding characteristics. In the case of young Spaniards, this indicator reaches record levels. The previews of the latest reports of *Youth in Spain 2000* testify that the age limit where young people consider that they leave their youth behind is rising and reaches 34 years old. This subjective perception of the duration of the juvenile period is complemented by the objective situation of the stagnation in the process of emancipation. In the group aged between 25–29 years old, 50% of the young people still remain in the family home and the average age of obtaining domestic autonomy is about 27 years of age. The prolongation of juvenile permanence in the family residence is accompanied by a high degree of financial dependence: at 29 years of age, the statistical limit of juvenile age, one third of young people continue to have no type of self supporting income of their own.

Semi-autonomous situations, where young people can count on some type of income which, however, is not sufficient to establish projects for their independence have increased over the past years. This is a symptom that the youth are the principal providers of man-power for a flourishing market of low standard employment with poor salaries and temporary contracts. In the year 2000, 65 out of every 100 working young people were under temporary contract. The brevity of these jobs provokes a more and more intense turn-over which accentuates the idea of instability. The report cited shows how 30% of young working people have had more than four job experiences practically at the beginning of their working life, this already resembles more a list of discontinuous and erratic activities than a coherent and continuous curriculum.

The multiplying of work experiences among young people is showing that their temporary jobs are not a suitable means for establishing themselves in the work market. Unstable, short term, unqualified jobs which have no promotional possibilities do not really provide young workers with the experience they envisage to enable them to have access to a good job. Flexibility is a necessary, Spanish, economic, structural system and it exacts a very high price from young workers. At present, already normalised, it displays its disciplinary effects and control of man-power. Exploitation levels and labor irregularity grow due to this paradoxical situation of provisional permanency where the only promise for many young workers seems to be merely another short term job.

This period of assimilation is characterised, in general, by incertitude, the arbitrated salary and the comings and goings of work and unemployment. However, if we consider the social origins of the young workers, the situations are very diverse: from those who are socially and education-wise better placed and who can afford the strategic wait for quality employment, to those of the popular classes who with lower educational levels sub-employment is a frequent destiny. Very probably, our present class structures would need a less polarised analysis and with more nuances than this one. However, examining diverse Spanish studies which analyse the itineraries and strategies of youth (Martin Criado, 1998; Casal, 1997) one frequently observes how the prominent trajectories or trends are structured with this marked differentiation in class, where one can appreciate the effects of the social polarisation that has been accentuated in Spain over the past fifteen years. The widening of the distances between wages and salaries, the growth of the extremes of professional structures and the development of the dynamics of the service sectors in the framework of globalisation are gaining ground and settling among the groups of younger ages. The demands of business on young workers are reinforcing an intensive model in knowledge on one part and, on the other, intensive unqualified manual labor. The assessment of academic degrees in the competitive professional market shows similar symptoms: Qualifications for the new competition of the future global players, opposed to professional training 'without attributes' for the most 'proletariatised' services.

Evidence of the importance of the extremes in the occupational structures of young Spaniards is compiled in the study *Módulo de transición de la educación al mercado laboral* (INE, 2001). The employment obtained by young people who have finished their studies over the past ten years is analysed in this study. The resulting professional structure in this period is composed of 26% of scientific, intellectual, and technical support occupations and 32% of unqualified or semi-qualified positions in the service sector. These two polarised blocks accumulate a greater quantity of created job positions which manifest the presence of a highlighted polarization.

Taking into consideration all the reservations that the analysis of social classes impose at an incipient moment of informational capitalism, the two stronger and representative juvenile trajectories do not have to be understood as closed and homogeneous social groups, but they do seem to function as the most obvious poles of social attraction which mark the profiles of Spanish society. We shall analyse in the first place the itineraries of the juvenile social groups worse placed in the educative and professional structure: 'the children of de-regulation' and following this we shall focus on the segments that aspire to a social promotion which is not free of fears and risks: the youth of 'anxiety studies'.

'Children of de-regulation':
the undervaluation of the young in the working classes

The Spanish productive system generates an abundant quantity of non-qualified jobs in the service sector which are covered very frequently by young people coming from low-middle class social strata—with restricted educative trajectories or with little exchange value in the market and with tight economic family situations which force them into looking for early employment. These jobs which hardly require any qualifications have very low wages, added to the scarcity of opportunities for promotion, but they are accepted by young people as a source of provisional income to cover their most immediate living expenses. The low wage is not an impediment because they are still living in the family home. A kind of structural linking ties sub-standard jobs to the life conditions of the young people: It is not necessary to provide qualifications, nor experience; nor do they require great responsability; they allow a wide compatibility with studies and provide personal money, sometimes outside the obligations of a more stable contract.

The variety of cases is wide in the universe of juvenile substandard employment and also the expectations with which the young people face them: Few consider them as anything permanent or stable—above all those who reach higher levels of study—but the present growth portrays the consolidation of a fringe of non-qualified manpower destined to last over the coming years and in which many young people will be ensnared for more time that they would desire. In spite of the variety of cases these labor profiles configure a very frequent shared identity among the 'children of de-regulation'. Fernando Conde (1999) makes reference to this title when referring to the juvenile segments of low to low-middle-class origins that forge attitudes towards work marked by: nostalgia for work stability; accepted resignation towards the precariousness of employment, that is demonstrated in the often repeated saying "This is what there is"; the positive valoration of the work experience and the money that this early access to work provides; a decidedly submissive attitude to authority with bosses and heads of the business which make them feel the abuse that they frequently endure is 'normal', in avoiding confrontation with the boss, above all when his/her hierarchic arbitrariness does not make itself very explicit; finally, the relations with work companions presents a marked fragility at the base of solidarity, a functional situation is lived with the group but there is no identifying with the group itself.

These observations extracted from group dynamics carried out by Conde in his investigations show the negative tone and the claustrophobic nuances in the working lives of these young people. Their identity is related not to the the work itself but to the early availability of money in contrast to those other young people from the more accommodating classes, who continue to study and who do not work; opposed to those "parasites" who have it all made, are those who have to earn a living. Besides, this money allows them to spend and enjoy themselves. Whatever job they have it is all the same, the important thing is to live in the present, the idea of saving hardly enters into this discussion and what is first priority, is immediate spending: a type of economy based on barter between money coming from work proceeds and highly perishable consumer items.

These labor dynamics unchain a vicious cycle which commences with sub-standard jobs occupied by young people, followed by an accelerating spiral of juvenile spending on new consumer products and concludes with the acceptation and perpetuation of these sub-standard jobs that reproduce a cheap model of manual labor very present in the first stages of professional initiation. The aspirations of juvenile consuming contributes to a hive of cheap manpower for businesses and companies, which is nurtured on the progressive necessity of money on the part of the youth to continue the consumer spiral, and the impossibility to deprive themselves of this status of consumer once it has been reached. As they themselves declare: "Once you get your hands on money...".

This labor panorama has repercussions on the framework of studies and interferes in juvenile educational trajectories. On the one hand the number of young people who simultaneously work and study has increased over the past decade. This double role of student and worker exacts a high price in terms of utilizable time and bears negatively on academic performance. In the binomial of employment/school the latter is jeopardised and early withdrawals from the educational system are slowly making themselves seen. On the other hand, the glut of poor quality work and the difficulty in finding a job which coincides with the level of studies attained provoke attitudes of disappointment and undervaluation towards the education system: the promise of social promotion that this transmits decreases the desire towards the prolongation of studies among the less prosperous youth.

The progressing conflict among intermediate-high school students is a good indicator of educational undervaluation. The extension of compulsory school from 14 to 16 has served as an indicator of juvenile discontent and has revealed the wide spreading of situations of 'prolongation without accumulation' (Martin Criado, 1998), in which young people remain in the classrooms with very little hope of it producing any positive results for their future work cycle. The glut of sub-standard jobs confirm these negative expectations and youth is divided between those who withdraw from school in a depressed state and those who continue their studies 'lifelessly' dedicating themselves with a minimum of effort and not relinquishing pleasant free time and entertainment; the work future is, therefore, an uncertain territory over which they have no control, where luck and "good connections" will determine the outcome.

The meritorious discourse has not lost strength as a determining factor in the social place among all these young people, but it does not function for themselves and is applied only to those who obtain benefits and greater educational successes. Self-blame is a common reason among those who abandon their studies and do not obtain the results desired and they put into function a whole range of defense mechanisms, which go from the self-justifying stages to the type: "those who keep on studying are just lazy and will go onto unemployment without any experience" and go on to manic manifestations of flight through frentic entertainment and consumer pleasures based on the income, which this market of sub-standard juvenile employment provides.

Although it is too early to draw solid conclusions from the results of these dynamics, it could be argued that the young people involved in these juvenile trajectories, marked by the short term in their studies, temporary jobs and by the binomial of income-consumerism they could see one of their greatest nightmares converted into reality: the threat of permanent instability and being unable to obtain a secure 'real job' with guarantees and benefits. The flexibility in the informational economies seems to be imposing a circuit characterised by a cycle that maintains an important number of manual laborers captive in precarious situations. Some studious investigators have advanced data that strengthens the necessity to consider profoundly this hypothesis of the cyclical nature in the 'proletariatized services' (Esping-Anderson, 1999; Sassen, 1991). In Spain there is a great shortage of a system of stastical indicators which permits the analysis of the flexibile work market sufficiently and the trajectories of temporary work patterns so common today. Nevertheless, the data which we have to hand permits us to be assured that the prolonged stage of incorporation of these young people into the work market is marked by the proliferation of employment experience of little value that will not have a positive repercussion on their future labor position.

'Anxiety studies': the incertitude of professional promotion for young people

Contrasting with the trajectories that we have outlined of the 'children of de-regulation' we find those that appear mainly to be young people from middle and upper class social origins. In this case, the access to University studies and good academic results are converted into the threshold of key differences with respect to the previously discussed young people. In the year 2001, approximately 20% of young Spaniards were studying for a University Degree. The past fifteen years of massive access to Universities has continued to consolidate a segment of young people with extensive educational itineraries, and with high levels of studies. Social and statistical relevance has gained the strategy of educative valuation, consistent in prolonging studies and living in the family home until the arrival of the promised land of a good computer job where a University degree can be capitalised. Although the internal differences of this group are very significant, the greater part of these young people respond to a model that contrasts with that of the 'children of de-regulation'. The preference is, in this case, due to long term education and work, freedom from worry with respect to immediate cash, the lack of pressure for finding employment and family support up to very late ages. All these characteristics are shared by the majority of young University students, although among these there are very different attitudes: for some the University is a mere refuge against unemployment, for others it occupies a more creative role like the stage on which they will forge their professional future.

Professionally better placed than the 'children of de-regulation' the careers of these young people are not devoid of incertitude and 'anxiety'. The flexibility work syndrome also taints their first work experiences. Their work socialisation is governed by a new cognitive frame determined by flexibility, whose code the young people interiorise as "what the market demands and what the companies ask for". Marked by the new precepts on the management of Human Resources, the young people of 'anxiety studies' face new professional competition that the new companies demand: complete availability, maximum adaptability and a limitless involvement on their part. Never has so much been asked for and so little given in return. The semantics of informational flexibility offers a seductive image of the professional in the world business class or the champion in scientific and intellectual work. But behind this screen, the young people find too often, only a varied range of informational employment low qualified on the cutting edge of the *net economy*: Overworked supervisors in theme parks, stressed out operators on the switchboard of telephone companies, underpaid traders of new technological products. The new flexibility acts like a kind of intellectual 'speculative bubble' provoking an inflation of promising successful images behind which junk bonds of the precarious informational work are hidden.

A new career idea is opened with the rise of flexibility. Its principal consequence is the glorification of mobility, incertitude and change opposed to the, until very recently, stable, traditional organisation of the life course. Two examples serve to illustrate the more than justified preoccupations of young people of the 'anxiety terms'. The first is that of University students' scholarships: About 30,000 young people about the age of 22 finish their studies and enter this varied condition. Their situation could be considered privileged and adequate for the initiation of a career if it were not for the frequent precarious ups and downs that they have to suffer. Often the grants are like motorways through the dessert, they keep going and do not arrive anywhere in a professional sense. Economically, income is scarce and does not allow confrontation with a vital project, instability prevents for example, the accumulation of confidence to obtain a bank loan. Judicially, legal irregularity is very symptomatic; the people with grants are not included in the Spanish NHS and they cannot benefit from other employment rights like seniority, unemployment subsidies or maternity leave. Among the beneficiaries of grants/scholarships of the more advanced age groups, cases are increasing where those concerned do research in the mornings and work as waiters in the evening. This figure seems to represent well the general tendencies of the labor de-regulation that we are living, and the discontentment towards this type of informational precariousness manifests itself in some associations like the Federation of Young and Precarious Investigators.

The second example is that of the increasing over-qualification ticket that the working youth have to tolerate. While the level of studies of these subjects has continued to increase, an imbalance has been observed between the requirements of the employment and the training received. This phenomenon is so extended in Spain it would require a monograph study, but I shall only provide one piece of data: the synthetic index of over-qualification elaborated in a recent report on the juvenile work market, demonstrates that about 45% of young working people present situations of considerable over-qualification or very 'over-qualified' (Garcia and Peiro, 1999): the Spanish productive system does not create a sufficient number of positions to satisfy the needs of the capacities of these young people. Besides the economic waste which presupposes useless spending on an education which will not be utilised, over-qualification generates frustration and disappointment insofar as professional expectations are concerned on the part of graduates and puts into evidence the paradoxical situation of the training in our informational societies. By means of marketing, education has been overestimated insofar as virtual significance is concerned, obliging young people to consume obsessively and anxiously training which appears to be absolutely necessary—but later on it demonstrates itself to be for many, wasted and depreciated in its real significance and in its concrete usefulness on the part of the productive system.

Conclusion: recent processes in the generational changes of young Spaniards

Over the course of the past two decades labor instability has gone on configuring these *fin de siècle* juvenile trajectories that we have mentioned above. Among the interrogants which we could raise at these initial moments of the 21st century, although it may be in a tentative and provisional manner, we find that of knowing up to what point the defined labor dynamics of youth are changing the age barriers that define youth and their general models of access to adult life.

It seems more and more undeniable that the expectations of emancipation, according to the traditional model of transition to maturity, have become weakened among the young. The outline based on the sequence of study-work-a family of their own, that is chained to the youthful period and projects itself into the future, demonstrates evident imbalances today. Perhaps the inferior and superior extremes of the social scale follow processes of labor socialisation more in accord with this model, but the major groups of young people from the middle classes find themselves with the imbalance of being tied to this, with hypertrophies and dilatations constantly more obvious in the phases which lead them into adult life. In this sense, the transition from a model of youth to adult life from that of stationary youth is slowly accepted: a time in parentheses, hardly moving, without prospects for the future. Time of activities without projects, of action without strategies, except that of immediate pleasure in the space of consumerism and that of an undetermined waiting period. The words of young people leave an acute sensation of the disappearance of the future: "Here you've got no project, here you simply kill time". These experiences betray a present without apparent links with the future, one lives in the immediate present, the future does not appear, not even to complain about it.

In the extensive model of 'allongement de la jeunesse' (Galland, 1991), the middle class young people of the 80's seemed to protect themselves from the negative labor situation by prolonging their youth and confiding in a more benevolent future. It seems as if the future that today has arrived continues to produce an intense anxiety and these young people, who sought refuge in their training to provide content for their period of moratorium, are now beaten into retreat on the byways of consumerism and juvenile leisure time. Something seems to be changing in the model of 'successive approximation' to adulthood.

This turn-about from work to consumerism as the central code of juvenile language has been analysed in Spain by Fernando Conde (1999). His hypothesis is that what is actually taking shape among the young middle class, is a new condition which he denominates as 'adoyouth' and which alters even the traditional stastical frontiers of these ages. The fusion of the terms adolescent and youth indicates, therefore, the sense of change: first the juvenile age is anticipated and now has to be situated before fifteen years old; secondly consumerism is pointed out as a central variable of youth identity: thirdly the period "adoyouth" ends at about 23 years old, the moment in which a second juvenile stage opens which brings back to the center the traditional pattern of transition to adult life based on the preoccupation about work status and greater responsibility.

For Conde the principle indicator of entering into the 'adoyouth' stage is the access to the sphere of juvenile consumerism, where uninterrupted diversion and entertainment and access to group life are decisive. The precociousness of consumerism among young people today is evident even when they have no personal income. The 'adoyoung' synchronise their rhythm of consuming with their first part-time job experiences, destined to cover pocket money expenses. These experiences take place mainly when the family is unable to maintain the economic rhythm of their children. Therefore, work here is merely a source of income and does not demand a labor identity: work to satisfy pocket money necessities. Although this is a period when little sleep is had—above all during the week ends—the 'adoyoung' describe the moment as a kind of dream in which they cannot continue indefinitely and with the awakening they discover the future, which, until then, had been half asleep. The same young people de-limit the new age frontiers: "when you are 15 you can't see that within ten years you will be 25 but when you are 25 you do see that in 5 years you will be thirty".

Between 23–25 years of age a second phase begins during which the young start to get their "feet on the ground" insofar as the preocupations for work-stability and economic autonomy are concerned and become real. Nevertheless, the incertitude does not suddenly disappear and the period, up till the age of thirty, is characterised by a slow stabilisation that depends on the type of studies which have been completed. Even so, at this age, reports reveal how a quarter of less advanced young people have not attained full autonomy, and how a new pact has taken shape over the past two decades, displacing the future horizon of stable work towards the enjoyment of the present in consumerism contributed to by the cash proceeding from flexible youth employment.

Although it is too early to evaluate the effects of these dynamics on the social structure and on the lives of the young people themselves, their employment situations have been in the turmoil of a profound labor transition over the past two decades. The changeover from Fordism to risk, like that which Ulrich Beck (2000), characterised recently, carries with it an intense individualisation, de-traditionalisation, and fragmentation in the working world, and at the same time, an increase in consumerism as a generator of identity. In this sense, risk is a suggestive word to interpret the state of an important number of young Spaniards—work-wise adrift—and an exemplary representative of the new risks of informational societies.

Bibliography

Alonso, L. E. (2000), *Trabajo y postmodernidad: el empleo débil*, Fundamentos, Madrid.
Beck, U. (2000), *Un nuevo mundo feliz*, Paidós, Barcelona.
Bourdieu, P. (1998), *Contre-feux*, Liber, Paris.
Cachón, L. (ed.), *Juventudes, mercados de trabajo y políticas de empleo*, 7 i mig, Valencia.
Casal, J. (1997), 'Modalidades de transición profesional, mercado de trabajo y condiciones de empleo', *Cuadernos de Relaciones Laborales*, n° 11.
Conde, F. (1999), *Los hijos de la des-regulación. Jóvenes, usos y abusos en los consumos de drogas*, Fundación CREFAT, Madrid.
Esping-Andersen, G. (1999), *Social Foundations of Postindustrial Economies*, Oxford University Press.
Gauthier, M. and Guillaume, J. F. (1999), *Definir la jeunesse?*, L'Harmattan-PUL, Québec.
Galland, O. (1991), *Sociologie de la jeunesse*, Armand Colin, Paris.
García, J. and Peiró, J. (1999), *El mercado laboral de los jóvenes: formación, transición y empleo*, Bancaja-IVIE, Valencia.
Ine (2001), *Módulo de transición de la educación al mercado laboral*, Instituto Nacional de Estadística, Madrid.
Martín Criado, E. (1998), *Producir la juventud*, Istmo, Madrid.
Roulleau-Berger, L. and Gauthier, M. (2001), *Les jeunes et l'emploi dans les villes d'Europe et d'Amerique du Nord*, Editions de l'Aube, La Tour d'Aigues.
Sassen, S. (1991), *The Global City: New York, London, Tokyo*, Princeton University.
Sennett, R. (1998), *The Corrosion of Character: The personal consequences of work in the new capitalism*, W. W. Norton & Company, N.Y.
Wacquant, L. (2000), *Corps et âme. Carnets ethnographiques d'un apprenti boxeur*, Agone, Marseille.

EXPLAINING TRANSITIONS THROUGH INDIVIDUALISED RATIONALITY

Andy Furlong and Fred Cartmel

Introduction

The purpose of this paper is to outline a new theoretical perspective on youth transitions which avoids the dualistic approaches that have characterised previous theoretical paradigms. Recent changes in youth transitions have led to attempts to account for individual reflexivity and have been marked by a shift away from structuralist approaches. We accept the need to provide an adequate account of agency but argue that it is important to recognise the continued salience of social structures. Indeed, in previous work (Furlong and Cartmel, 1997) an attempt was made to use individualisation theory as a basis for understanding complex transitions in which young people's attempts to manage their lives and negotiate hurdles are often frustrated by the persistence of powerful structural barriers.

After reviewing changing perspectives on modern transitions we outline a theoretical model which explains the ways in which outcomes are achieved through the mobilisation of capacities within a market driven arena. The model utilises a variant of rational action theory that we refer to as rationalised individualisation. Finally, we use the model to explore the relationship between resources, agency and risk and illustrate the discussion through qualitative data from an ongoing Scottish study.

Perspectives on modern transitions

Youth research offers rich opportunities to study the impact of social change, analyse processes of social reproduction and develop new theoretical perspectives that an be applied across a broad spectrum of social life. However, with a few notable exceptions, relatively few researchers have fully exploited the opportunities to advance theoretical debate.[1] The more frequent occurrence is for youth researchers

---

[1] While the list is not exhaustive, as examples of researchers who have made

to apply and test theoretical perspectives developed elsewhere in order to explain trends within their own national, and occasionally cross-national, contexts. In this chapter we briefly examine modern theoretical perspectives on youth transitions before outlining a new model, rooted in rational action theory, which we suggest can be applied to all forms of social action.

In an earlier paper (Evans and Furlong, 2000), some of the main theoretical perspectives on youth were described and it was argued that the trends reflected the dominant theoretical paradigms. Beginning in the 1960s, we argued that with a buoyant labour market and the dominance of functionalist and developmental models, transitions from school to work were portrayed as being relatively straightforward and linear. With a rise in youth unemployment in the 1970s, researchers attempted to account for the increased complexity of transitions largely through an extension of functionalist perspectives. During the 1980s, structuralist perspectives were increasingly adopted to account for young people's labour market trajectories as transitional outcomes came to be regarded as being largely outside the control of individual actors. By the 1990s, reflexive and post-structural perspectives were increasingly adopted and attention turned to the navigational and negotiating skills of young people as factors that determined transitional processes and outcomes.

The position adopted in our book, *Young People and Social Change* (Furlong and Cartmel, 1997)[2] was that while it had become increasingly necessary to account for processes of reflexivity, it was important not to lose sight of the centrality of social structures. The position which we advanced involved the idea that Beck's (1992) individualisation thesis provided a useful starting point for an understanding of youth transitions and processes of social reproduction in late modernity. While it was argued that an increased complexity of experiences had resulted in youth transitions becoming more difficult to accomplish on a subjective level, an acceptance of the individualisation thesis was qualified by the view that underlying patterns of social reproduction had largely been preserved. It was argued that while collective identities may have weakened as a result of a greater

---

significant theoretical advances through the study of youth we would we cite the work of Robert Castel, James Coleman and Paul Willis.

[2] A summary of the position in French can be found in 'Penser autrement l'access a l'emploi des jeunes Britanniques', in Roulleau-Berger, L., et Gauthier, M. (2001) Les Jeunes et L'Emploi, L'aube editions, La Tour d'Aigues.

diversity of experiences in education and the labour market, young people's experiences were heavily conditioned by ascribed characteristics such as social class, gender and 'race'. In describing this mismatch between subjective and objective dimensions of transitions as the 'epistemological fallacy of late modernity', we recognised a tendency for the structural bases of action to become obscured as a result of the growing need for reflexive negotiation of lives in a world in which fixed points of reference were apparently lacking.

This argument, which was presented as a critique of the individualisation thesis, has occasionally been interpreted as a reassertion of structural interpretations of social reproduction and as a denial of the significance of agency. Our intention, however, was to move beyond dualistic approaches as reflected in our use of the term structured individualisation (Roberts, 1995). In this chapter we intend to correct some misinterpretations of this position and to present a theoretical perspective on youth transitions in more detail than was possible in the previous text.

In part, the need to refine theoretical perspectives on transitions emerged as a result of a growing consensus that youth transitions had become increasing protracted and complex. Among modern youth researchers there is no vocal dissent from the view that complex modern transitions have resulted in a situation where few individuals will follow identical sets of transitional routes and in which they are faced with the need for reflexive interpretation and constant negotiation in an increasingly unpredictable social world. While we accept that proposition, two qualifications must be made. First, new evidence (Goodwin and O'Connor, 2001) has led to an acceptance of the view that earlier British research on transitions (Ashton and Field, 1976; Carter, 1962) had tended to understate the level of complexity which characterised youth transitions in the 1960s and 1970s. Researchers tended to concentrate on macro-level analysis, highlighting class (and occasionally gender) specific patterns of reproduction while neglecting individual-level complexities and processes of negotiation. The notable exception to this being Willis (1977) who managed to illuminate some of the ways in which the everyday lives of working class boys involved forms of action, negotiation, penetration and resistance which were central to processes of social reproduction.

Our second qualification relates to the levels of complexity characteristic of modern transitions. Here we suggest that the case for the de-linearisation of transitions has been over-stated. Indeed, evidence from a study of 16 to 23 year-olds in the west of Scotland (Furlong et al., 2001) suggests that about half of the age cohort made transitions defined as linear. Whereas members of the earlier generation of youth researchers may have focused on structure at the expense of agency, in the rush to embrace late modern or post-modern perspectives, many contemporary researchers have over-stated the significance of processes of reflexivity and life management. In this context we agree with Roberts' (1997) argument that theory has started to run ahead of empirical evidence.

Mobilising capacities

To develop a theory of social reproduction which avoids dualistic explanations, our starting point is the recognition that any transitional outcome (in education, the labour market or households, for example) requires a (conscious or unconscious) mobilisation of capacities within a market driven arena. What we refer to as the mobilisation of capacities incorporates structural resources (such as economic, social and cultural capital) as well as capacities that tend to be regarded as signifying agency (such as motivation, drive and determination). Both dimensions are inter-linked and essentially involve an ability to draw on scarce resources (consciously or unconsciously) in order to attain a specific outcome.

With the mobilisation of capacities occurring in a local and global market, we need to recognise that effective mobilisation is spatially and temporally constrained. In other words, demands vary according to the conditions existing at a specific time in a particular market place. The types of resources that would have facilitated a particular outcome at one point in time may be less effective in a different spatial or temporal environment even when other factors (such as social and economic capital and levels of motivation) remain constant.

In addition to these factors, it needs to be recognised that both markets and individual capacities can be affected by critical incidents. Constraints and opportunities can arise through chance events that touch the lives of individuals, groups or markets. Individual careers, for example, can be affected by the ill health of themselves or those close to them while an event occurring in a far corner of the globe (such as a plan worked out in a cave in Afghanistan) can affect stock prices that in turn lead to job losses in the local community.

The mobilisation of capacities can be either conscious or unconscious although no individual is ever fully aware of the conditions under which they act, the resources they are utilising and the constraints on their actions. We also suggest that individuals usually have at least a partial awareness of the resources available to them and of obstacles that they may encounter. What Willis (2000) refers to as 'partial penetrations' or what we have referred to as an 'epistemological fallacy' incorporates this recognition that individuals are neither fully aware of, nor fully blind to, the conditions of life in late modernity.

Rational action

Any adequate theoretical model of transitions has to recognise that any mobilisation of capacities is preceded by rational (or rationalised) action. In speaking of rational action, we must be clear about the definition adopted and of how it fits into the overall model being proposed. As Goldthorpe notes, there are a 'whole family' of rational action theories as well as 'family resemblances' (2000: 115). Although there are weak and strong versions, Goldthorpe (2000) suggests that what they have in common is an attempt to show how 'regularities are created and sustained or, perhaps, modified or disrupted, through the action and interaction of individuals' (2000: 116). Under the 'weak' version of rational action theory proposed here, action can be construed as rational if it is appropriate given the situation faced by an actor and the beliefs that they hold. Thus if a young person living in a depressed labour market resists attempts to make them join a training scheme or activation measure in the belief that participation is unlikely to lead to employment, these actions could be construed as rational. Here we agree with Elster's view that 'people are rational in the normatively appropriate sense' (1989: 3).

Like Goldthorpe, we are not suggesting that recourse to rationality can avoid distortion or that 'all actors at all times act in an entirely rational way' (2000: 116). However, while Goldthorpe argues that such distortion can only be overcome through 'the law of large numbers' (2000: 116), we suggest that the identification of the 'normatively appropriate' requires recourse to qualitative approaches. Goldthorpe may view 'with a radical scepticism' 'the capacity of social scientists to gain access to actors' values, beliefs, attitudes, goals or preferences' (2000: 89), but recourse to central tendencies and 'large numbers' leads to the risk of making inferences which are far removed from the normative rationalities of groups of individual actors and can leave the social sciences divorced from lived realities.

We are not suggesting here that cause can necessarily be derived from close observation of individuals. Rather that the logic of rational action suggests that some credence be given to the rationalisations put forward by actors. However, given that social scientists are rarely able to observe rationality in real time, it is important to be aware that individual accounts will involve some post-hoc rationalisation. Obviously rationalisation will involve some distortion as individuals seek to reconstruct events and biographies in ways which give their lives an overall meaning and consistency (Heinz, 1991). Rationalisation may to lead to an exaggeration of agency over structures given that actors may not be as fully aware of the existence of constraints as they are of personal actions. It could also be argued that the relative weight placed on structure or agency in explaining outcomes will vary according to the perceived desirability of that outcome. For example, individuals may be more likely to blame negative outcomes on external forces or conditions while giving themselves credit for achieving more favourable outcomes.

Rationalised individualisation

In the model developed here, the relationship between rational action, the mobilisation of capacities and the emergence of outcomes is portrayed as dynamic. In a capitalist society, rationality is developed and transformed in the context of attempts to mobilise capacities within markets and shaped by past experience of secured or frustrated outcomes. Thus the rationalisation of a secured or frustrated outcome feeds back into the ongoing process of rational action as new goals are framed or aspirations modified.

The 'weak' and 'situated' variant (Goldthorpe, 2000) of rational action theory we apply here is referred to as rationalised individualisation. We use the term 'rationalised' rather than 'rational' in recognition of the dynamic and reflexive nature of the process. With action being framed by past experience, an element of rationalisation is always present. The term 'individualisation' is used to draw attention to the fact that the permutations of structural and situational capacities are virtually infinite. The process may act in such a way as to lead to social class-based formations, but the differences between the formations are almost as varied within them as between them. As a result, class structures are inevitably obscure.

The new model, outlined in Figure 1 (below), describes the process in some detail. The first recognition is that quantitative perspectives on transitions (or on any social processes) are only able to focus on the extent to which quantifiable capacities impact on outcomes and account for various external effects such as labour market and opportunity structures. They carry the assumption that such external contexts can lead directly to an outcome (line marked B in Figure 1) whereas in reality such a link is always indirect. Young people entering a buoyant labour market, for example, do not automatically secure jobs: a process of mediation is necessary in which various capacities are mobilised and rationalised. In a quantitative model, any rationality can only be inferred, perhaps using knowledge derived from other sources on norms and priorities of specific social groups. Analysis of this type is powerful and capable of showing, for example, the extent to which economic resources or opportunity structures are associated with a variety of outcomes (such as getting a job or becoming unemployed). Analyses of this type are used extensively in the social sciences and the intention is not to detract from their usefulness.

Examples of the use made of quantitative analysis in our current study include claims that for those who make direct entry to employment at age 16, it is not uncommon to encounter a protracted period of unemployment after a relatively long spell in employment. This analysis can be extended and it can be argued that long-term unemployment is strongly associated with poor school leaving qualifications (Furlong et al., 2001). Thus it can be argued that a resource (qualification) is associated with an outcome (unemployment). It can then be inferred that employers place a premium on educational qualifications (as a signal of ability, competence or motivation). The limitation inherent in such models is that while they can show sequences of events which are linked to successful job entry (such as participation on training schemes, the acquisition of further qualifications etc.), they cannot tell us very much about the ways in which individuals re-frame priorities or embark on courses of action which bring about certain results. No 'law of large numbers' or 'central tendencies' can answer such questions.

Figure 1

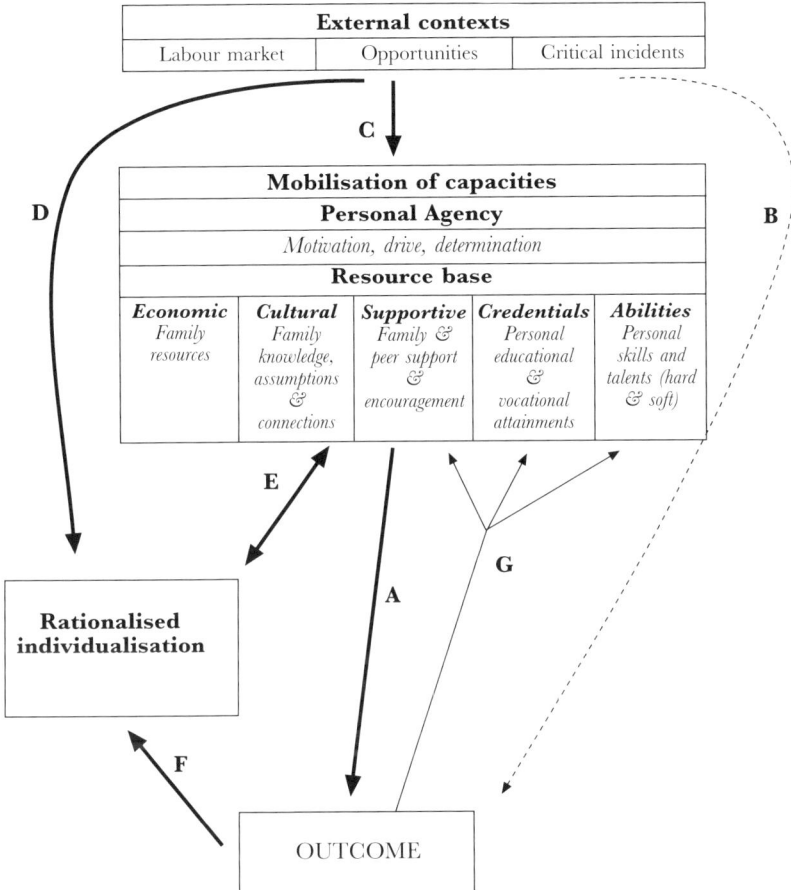

It is not being suggested here that individual subjectivity in the form of rationality is a sufficient force to secure goals. The view is that outcomes are largely determined (and therefore can be predicted) by a set of resources and contexts which are largely structural, but which also involve personal agency. However, in our view, rationality is an essential link in the chain. Outcomes are never secured without some rational intervention by actors and are always subject to post hoc rationalisation in which individuals seek to explain an outcome by reference to some combination of personal action, constraint and/or opportunity.

The model begins with the recognition that capacities must be mobilised in order to secure an outcome (A). The core capacities involved in young people's labour market transitions include various components of the resource base to which they have access such as the economic and cultural resources of the family (social class) as well as personal resources such as academic attainments, skills and talents. Personal agency is also central to the mobilisation of capacities and includes factors such as motivation, drive and determination. External factors, such as the structure of labour markets, opportunities and critical incidents can be seen as both constraining and facilitating the ways in which capacities are mobilised (C). These external factors also shape assumptions, are rationalised (D) and in turn feed back in ways which also affect the mobilisation of capacities (E). Lastly, few outcomes can be seen as final resting places. Young people may mobilise capacities to secure forms of education or training or may secure a job that represents a step in a broader process of career progression. As such, outcomes (positive or negative) are rationalised (F) and can affect the resource base leading to an increase in motivation (G). In a positive situation, for example, we may find that a job may result in the attainment of additional qualifications or skills and may lead to the upward revision of goals. In a negative sense, for example, a period of unemployment may directly lead to a reduction in levels of motivation.

Resources, agency and risk

With both resources and personal agency being central to the mobilisation of capacities, it is important to reflect further on the ways in which these factors interact. This relationship is illustrated in Figure 2 (below) and elaborated through preliminary analysis of qualitative interviews conducted as part of our current study of youth transitions. Sixty qualitative interviews were conducted in 2001 among 28/29 year-olds living in the West of Scotland. The individuals selected had been long-term participants in a longitudinal study of young people who were surveyed regularly between the ages of 15 and 28/29 (the West of Scotland Twenty-07 study). Each young adult talked at length about their experiences in education and the labour market and of key events which may have had an impact on their lives.

The first point is that few young people who had access to a rich resource base (either in terms of personal attainments or family resources) *and* displayed evidence of strong personal agency (motivation and determination) (A) had failed to secure outcomes at age 28/29 which they themselves (and most outside observers) would define as desirable.

Typical of this dually advantaged group is Tony. Tony's parents owned a shop and his first job was obtained via family contacts in a firm with which his father did business. His brother helped him obtain his second job making pizzas. Subsequently he and his brother set up their own café in premises owned by their father. Despite these advantages, Tony was determined to see his business thrive, took risks and made sacrifices. 'We put in a lot of hours, you know, with more or less no return, but we stuck at it'. While Tony's business is now very successful, he still works fourteen hours a day, seven days a week.

David is another example of someone who was able to draw on a strong resource base, but was also highly motivated. However, David's prime resources were a personal academic ability and a supportive family rather than an economically advantaged class position. Having completed his Highers[3] and intending to go to university, he attended a Careers presentation by Scottish Power.[4] Impressed

Figure 2

	Personal Agency	
	+	−
Resources +	A Very Low risk	B Some risk
Resources −	C Some risk	D High risk

---

[3] Highers are a Scottish examination in which the appropriate level of attainment can secure university entry.
[4] The central corporation responsible for the generation and supply of electricity in Scotland.

with the training and career opportunities, he successfully applied for a traineeship. His parents, however, were unwilling to let him leave education without seeing a written contract detailing the training which was to be provided. While working for Scottish Power, David completed a Scottish National Certificate in business administration through day-release. However, he went on to sit an HNC and various professional diplomas in his own time in order to develop his career prospects.[5] He currently holds a managerial post at Scottish Power.

At the other extreme, those who had few resources and weak personal agency (D) tended to have had extremely problematic transitions. Martin, for example, has had over 15 jobs (mainly short-term), numerous periods of unemployment and has been on a range of training programmes (usually at the insistence of employment office staff). At age 29 he was unemployed and living with his parents. He has few qualifications and admits that he played truant from school frequently from the third year of secondary school (age 14) onwards. The training programmes he has attended, including the New Deal, were regarded as a 'waste of time', together with other trainees he 'clocked on' and then spent most of the day 'sitting in the pub across the road' or 'on a good day.... went out and played football' as 'even the tutors didn't turn up'. Martin has some artistic abilities and makes small amounts of money from selling paintings or playing in a band, however, while he would like to make a career in art or music, he says that his problem is 'getting up tomorrow and actually doing something'.

Jimmy is also an example of someone with few resources and a lack of drive and motivation. He grew up on a deprived estate in Glasgow and left school at 16 with no qualifications although he had rarely attended since the age of 13 having had to care for an alcoholic mother. He has had a number of short-term jobs, often undertaken whilst in receipt of unemployment benefit, been on training schemes and had several long periods of unemployment. Many of his jobs have been casual and he has had his benefits suspended on more than one occasion for not declaring such work. He has not completed his training courses and has a negative attitude towards them—'but it was a fruitless thing an all. I ended up finished it before its term. I just thought it was pointless because after the two

---

[5] These are advanced vocational qualifications at the sub-degree level.

years or whatever, you were back on the dole again'. Jimmy's aspirations are limited 'just to have maybe a full-time job, a full-time steady job' and job applications have been completed without much thought as part of a signing-on process. 'It was like standard practice with the careers office and jobcentre and what not, you had to fill in certain application forms anyway'. However, despite his apparent lack of success, he is not totally disappointed with the way his life has turned out. 'I could have been a lot worse, you know. I could be an alcoholic, a junkie, you know what I mean'.

In both of these cases, a poor resource base combined with weak personal agency has resulted in a set of post-school experiences which neither Martin, Jimmy, or outside observers would describe as completely satisfactory. However, relatively few of those interviewed occupied this position of dual negativity and among the cohort both of these examples represent extremes.

In a less predictable position are those who have motivation and drive but lack resources (C) and those who have access to resources but lack motivation (B). The majority of our sample can be seen as occupying one of these two positions. Both of these groups tend to encounter difficulties and frequently made adjustments: few, however, encountered long periods of unemployment or faced social or economic exclusion. From the analysis we would suggest that those who have access to resources but lack developed agency are more likely to secure the outcomes they desire and tend to have a 'smoother ride'.

Lisa is an example of someone who has access to a weak resource base but who exhibits signs of highly developed personal agency. She left school with few qualifications after having decided that further study was futile. Since then she has moved jobs several times in order to secure advancement, moving when 'I couldn't have gone up any further'. This has sometimes meant travelling fairly long distances to work. Although she has had little in the way of training from any of her employers, she has taken it upon herself to learn all aspects of the job. Whilst working in an engineering firm, for example, she felt that she needed a better grounding in the machine parts she was dealing with in a sales capacity. To develop this knowledge she said that

> when the factory works late on a Tuesday and Thursday I would put my overalls on and would go out on the factory floor and build the tools with the boys. Because I was serving spare parts and giving advice, I had to be able to picture the tools stripped down in sections.

Lisa's career was largely shaped by her own drive and determination although in the process her resource capacity was enhanced as she developed skills which eased the process of transition to subsequent jobs. It is also clear that her motivation could be translated into positive outcomes as a result of the availability of opportunities in the local labour market and it could be argued that she had the 'soft skills' necessary to make an initial entry into the labour market.

In contrast to Lisa, Mike displayed virtually no personal agency during his early labour market career. In terms of resources, while he left school after having failed all of his O grades,[6] he was able to rely on a highly supportive (even directive) family. Although lacking in economic resources, his family used knowledge and social capital to control virtually every aspect of Mike's access to jobs and training. Mike's key interest was in golf and prior to leaving school he spent virtually all of his spare time in pursuit of his hobby. On leaving school he decided that he should accept a job as a greenkeeper as if he was working there 'I can play more and get more practice'. His Dad, however, had other ideas and 'pushed' him into a youth training programme in a local sports centre.

> The decision was made for me ... (my Dad) ... contacted the training officer and said "have you got anything there" and they got me a place. So it was really down to my father what I did. I mean, I didn't have any objections, I couldn't have cared less as long as I was out of school.

Mike was eventually offered a permanent position and his father persuaded him to take an opportunity to study for an HNC in Leisure Management on a day-release basis. 'Not that I particularly wanted to do it, I just wanted to earn more money and have, you know, a peaceful life. But he kind of pushed me to sort of further my education'. As a result of these early experiences, Mike eventually built up a resource base that included personal skills and credentials and which enabled him to develop a career in leisure management.

Examples of young people who have a strong resource base and weak personal agency cross the full spectrum of socio-economic classes and personal attainments. Helen attended an expensive private school in Glasgow and went on to be a doctor. 'It was kind of expected that ... you would either go and be a doctor, accountant or lawyer'.

---

[6] Examinations taken by all young people at age 16.

She never considered anything other than medicine. 'Quite a few of my friends went into medicine as well. They all went to university, nobody went and got jobs'. Here we suggest that Helen's 'drift' into medicine despite the absence of strong personal agency was only possible due to her having access to an extremely rich resource base.

Many of the examples provided here are extremes which have been used to illustrate the variety of ways in which individuals utilise a range of different resources and display varying levels of drive and motivation. Among the sample, there were very few who were totally lacking in resources of any kind and few who showed a total absence of personal agency. Many, however, had to cope with some resource or agency deficit that had an impact on labour market outcomes. Some of the resources described here can remain latent and are mobilised when other resources prove insufficient to secure a desired outcome. A young person, for example, may have strong personal skills and academic credentials and might not need to operationalise other aspects of their resource base (such as family connections). The point, however, is that each facet of the resource base provides a potential safety net: deficits in one quarter can be counter-balanced by surpluses in another. Of course, the actual currency of each of these resources is wholly dependent on external contexts (such as labour markets, opportunities and critical incidents) which have the potential to deflate the value of the resource currency.

Conclusion

In this chapter we have tried to illustrate the multi-faceted ways in which individuals secure outcomes in modern labour markets. In other papers derived from this study, we have attempted to quantify the strength of some of the aspects of the resource bases described here and have illustrated some of the processes involved through qualitative analysis. While the purpose of this chapter is to develop a theoretical model through which transitional outcomes can be explained, several important conclusions can be drawn from the discussion.

The first point is that the effective mobilisation of capacities (which is central to smooth transitions) operates within a set of external constraints and tends to involve both resources and personal agency. A deficit in either of these two dimensions increases the risk of 'negative' outcomes. It is important therefore that any policies which aim to smooth transitions address aspects of agency, such as motivation, as well as the different aspects of the resource base (education, training, knowledge, support etc.). If a set of policies fail to treat the mobilisation of capacities in a holistic manner, then their overall effectiveness will be weakened.

Second, interventions are unlikely to be effective unless they address the rationalising processes through which individual transitions are driven. Here it is necessary to develop partnerships between external agencies and individuals, to act with them rather than attempt to impose outcomes on them. There are plenty of examples provided by the qualitative interviews of individuals who had been allocated to jobs or training programmes without much regard for their own perspectives: our study suggests that such interventions are rarely effective in the long-term.

Third, while recent British policies, such as the New Deal, have given a central role to personal advisors, they can only act as a poor substitute for the supportive and cultural resources of families. Where we have examples of strong families which have helped individuals to secure desired outcomes, our respondents suggest that these interventions work as family members know what they are like, what they want and what they are capable of and work with the individual to develop an effective plan of action. In contrast, contact with officials tend to be more fleeting and the relationship is underpinned by the knowledge that sanctions can be applied.

Fourth, the model described can be equated to a complex engine that occasionally requires a 'kick start' but which from there on tends to develop a momentum of its own. Here we have plenty of examples of individuals who incrementally develop their resource base in a work context as they develop both hard and soft skills. This resource capacity loop ensures that, given the opportunity for skill development, future transitions and processes of career development entail lower levels of risk.

Finally, we suggest that those researchers who are beginning to conclude that the impact of social class on young people's transitional outcomes have become weaker, or even lost its significance, are basing their conclusions on an inadequate conceptualisation of social class as a central dimension of the resource base. Our analysis suggests that further research is necessary in order to test our model and determine the strength of the various components of the resource base and its interaction with personal agency and processes of rationality.

Acknowledgements

We would like to acknowledge the financial support provided by the Scottish Executive and Scottish Enterprise for the project 'Reconceptualising Youth Transitions: Patterns of Vulnerability and Processes of Social Inclusion' under which this analysis was undertaken. We would like to thank our co-workers on the project, Andy Biggart, Helen Sweeting and Patrick West, with whom some of the ideas have been discussed. The paper was also strengthened as a result of comments by David Raffe and Gerda Reith.

REFERENCES

Ashton, D. N. and Field, D. (1976), *Young Workers*, Hutchinson, London.
Beck, U. (1992), *Risk Society*, Sage, London.
Carter, M. P. (1962), *Home, School and Work*, Pergammon, London.
Elster (1989), *Solomonic Judgements: Studies in the Limitations of Rationality*, Cambridge University Press, Cambridge.
Evans, K. and Furlong, A. (2000), 'Niches, transitions, trajectories: De quelques theories et representations des passages de la jeunesse' *Lien Social et Politiques*, Vol. 43.
Furlong, A. and Cartmel, F. (1997), *Young People and Social Change: Individualisation and Risk in Late Modernity*, Open University Press, Buckingham.
Furlong, A., Cartmel, F., Biggart, A., Sweeting, H. and West, P. (2001)
Goldthorpe, J. H. (2000), *On Sociology: Numbers, narratives and the Integration of Research and Theory*, Oxford University Press, Oxford.
Goodwin, J. and O'Connor, H. (2001), working paper
Heinz, W. (1991), *Theoretical Advances in Life Course Research*, Deutscher Studien Verlag, Weinheim.
Roberts, K. (1995), *Youth and Employment in Modern Britain*, Oxford University Press, Oxford.
——— (1997), 'Structure and Agency: The New Youth Research Agenda', in Bynner, J., Chisholm, L. and Furlong, A. (eds.) *Youth, Citizenship and Social Change in a European Context*, Ashgate, Aldershot.
Willis, P. (1977), *Learning to Labour*, Saxon House, Farnborough.
——— (2000), *The Ethnographic Imagination*, Polity, Oxford.

PART THREE

YOUTH, EMPLOYMENT POLICIES AND
SOCIAL PRACTICES

THE NEGOTIATION OF VOCATIONAL EDUCATION QUALIFICATIONS: AN EFFICIENT ALTERNATIVE TO THE DEREGULATION OF THE YOUTH LABOUR MARKET?

Eric Verdier

1. *Introduction—The viability of vocational training for young people called into question*

The construction of qualifications is a major coordinating mechanism linking social and economic actors. In a period of persistent employment crisis, and of rapid and chaotic changes in productive systems, the question facing this form of public action can be expressed as follows: is the certification of vocational training still able to provide effective reference points for the protagonists in the training-employment relationship, whether at the inter-industrial, industrial or micro-economic (firms and individuals) levels? The debate is a topical one, since it puts the spotlight on the effectiveness of institutional modes of regulation compared with that of the predominantly market mode of regulation that prevails in the process of globalisation.

Several types of reasons and arguments are commonly adduced in order to cast doubt on the relevance of youth training systems based on preparation for trades and professions.

- Initial vocational training is frequently stigmatising, since it is generally held to reflect prior failure in the general education system. From this perspective, any attempt to democratise access to education should focus principally on extending general education.
- The new productive paradigms give priority to general competences, which are often described as behavioural (ability to take initiatives and to work independently, aptitude for teamwork etc.). The acquisition of such competences is said to depend more on the quality of basic education; consequently, the aim should be to encourage individuals to go on to higher levels of general education. In this way, they would be better able to deal with the growing complexity of technologies and products.

- Vocational training is based to a greater or lesser extent on a set of more or less compartmentalised occupations and/or areas of economic activity which, in the light of the increasing instability of unemployment and the consequent uncertainty as to the nature of the activities individual workers will be called upon to undertake, have proved to be too narrowly defined.
- There appears to be very little space between the development of general education, for which the State must take responsibility because of the positive externalities it generates, and the skills market, in which firms are the prime movers for reasons of efficiency and effectiveness, for the regulation of vocational training which, in those countries that still have a developed training system, generally requires a tripartite mode of regulation involving employers, trade unions and the public authorities that is a constituent part of the exercising of an individual and collective right to vocational training.

The advent of the "learning society", to quote the title of a White Paper published by the European Commission (1995), is said to justify efforts to dismantle costly and inflexible institutional apparatuses that are incapable of producing productivity symbols that can be readily interpreted by employers in business and industry.

The analytical framework
Drawing on comparative analyses of national education and training systems (Buechtemann, Verdier 1998), three ideal types are advanced as means of analysing the interrelationships between vocational training programmes and configurations of actors: an "occupational" convention, a "meritocratic" convention and a "market" convention. This societal approach (Maurice, Sellier, Silvestre 1982) also draws on the institutional approach of convention theory, which emphasises the plurality of modes of coordination (cf. Eymard-Duvernay 1989 on the problems of product quality). Since the issues around the construction of training systems are primarily macro-social in nature, we will begin by adopting a "conventionalist approach" that can be used to examine modes of coordination from a macroeconomic perspective. Although the conventionalist approach is far from being settled at this level, an approach based on "public reference points" can be adopted subsequently in order to take into account national specificities in the modes of coordination.

Each underlying convention serves as a springboard for constructing a specific definition of the overall objective of the training process, the instruments and rules on which each convention is based, the configurations of actors that each convention mobilises, the modes of coordination it brings into play, the place of vocational training in the organisation of the various educational pathways and, finally, the various "recognition spaces" it opens up as "portals" into the labour market.

Each of the societal constructions (Germany, France, the United Kingdom) is based primarily on one of the three conventions (occupational, meritocratic and market) that structure the linkage between the particular societal concept of vocational training and the actions of the actors involved. In reality, however, the various modes of regulation draw on a mix of these three conventions.

The main characteristics of the three conventions as regards youth training

Convention	Occupational	Meritocratic	Market
Certification	Recognised qualification	State-validated diploma	Ratified competence
Nature of the programme	Negotiated regulations	Academic norms	N/A
Objective of the training	Occupational rules	Aptitude signals	Human capital
Privileged recognition space	Occupational market	Internal market	External ("spot") market
Key actor in the training process	Firm	Vocational lycée	Service provider
Key actor in institutional regulation	Social partners at industry level	State	Employers

2. *Is the development of individual competition and the meritocratic principle irresistible?*

At the European level, the changes that have taken place in several countries in which vocational training has traditionally made a significant contribution to skill formation and, more broadly, to labour market regulation would, at first sight, seem to provide evidence in support of the argument that youth training systems, and hence the bargaining rights and/or spaces associated with them, are irredeemably obsolete.

2.1 *The United Kingdom, France and Germany: an upsurge in the competition principle*

In Great Britain, the apprenticeship system that provided training for skilled manual workers collapsed in the mid-1980s. It is true that this structural adjustment was the result of decisions taken by the Conservative government, which saw the apprenticeship system as both a symbol of and resource for the trade unions, whose power the government was seeking to reduce. At a more fundamental level, however, the apprenticeship system was at the mercy of forces pushing it into irresistible decline unless it underwent considerable structural modification. The system was helping to keep in place a rigid system of occupational demarcation that was increasingly out of step with changes in work organisation that required greater functional flexibility and initiative. It was also proving to be too costly because of the considerable increase in apprentices' wages relative to those of manual workers (for more details, see Ryan 1995).

In France, considerable efforts had been made since the mid-1980s to enhance the economic and social value of vocational and technological education and training. The introduction of the vocational *baccalauréats* symbolised the whole undertaking, but within higher education, the considerable expansion of the *brevets de techniciens supérieurs* (BTS—a post-18 vocational training certificate) and of the *diplômes universitaires de technologie* (DUT—a 2-year diploma in a technical subject) also played its part. Mention should also be made of other innovations, such as the establishment of university institutes of vocational studies (IUP), which award degrees requiring four years' post-*baccalauréat* study, and the introduction of masters' degrees in science and technology and of the *diplômes d'études supérieures spécialisés* (DESS—one-year postgraduate diplomas in an applied subject awarded after five years' higher education). Furthermore, unlike the British government, the French public authorities at both central and regional level made efforts to promote apprenticeships at the various levels of the education system. Nevertheless, despite some encouraging results, it has to be said that the dominant characteristic of these past 15 years has been an unprecedented expansion of general education. The number of university students doubled in 13 years, as did the proportion of young people attaining the *baccalauréat*, which now stands at two thirds of each age cohort. What is more, the percentage of young people gaining a DUT and then continuing their studies exceeded the 60% mark before the mid-1990s. Thus level of educational attainment has continued to be the main principle driving the changes in the education and training system, at the expense of vocational specialisation (for a more detailed study, see Verdier 1996).

In Germany, the celebrated dual system, which is based on an apprenticeship scheme providing training for approximately two thirds of each age cohort and is regarded as essential to the maintenance of German product quality, has come under pressure from various directions. Since the beginning of the 1970s, under the aegis of the federal State, it has operated in accordance with a mode of regulation based on the "private governments" (Hilbert, Streeck 1997) formed by employers, trade unions and the chambers of commerce. These "governments" lay down the practical rules governing youth training. Since the end of the 1980s, the dual system has been riven by tensions, caused, among other things, by young people's growing preference for general education, due largely to the decline in job opportunities for those completing an apprenticeship, the difficulty in finding places within the training system for young people with a poor educational record, particularly those from immigrant families, and the relative withdrawal from the system of manufacturing firms, particularly the larger ones. This manifested itself during the recession of the mid-1980s in a more rapid decline in the number of training places than in jobs, a marked departure from the counter-cyclical role traditionally played by the apprenticeship system. The disengagement of larger firms was further compounded by the shortage of training places in the new *Länder* of Eastern Germany. Thus the system's social and economic legitimacy, based on the mutual commitments given by the social actors, has been quite seriously undermined by these developments (see Buechtemann and Verdier 1998).

These national trajectories have given rise to a certain degree of convergence towards a mode of regulation governing young people's entry into the labour market based on individual competition. This competition unfolds in two stages.

– The first stage takes place within the education system, where the fairness of the competition must be guaranteed by the State. Academic performance is the standard used to establish the merits of each individual pupil. Its use as a criterion seems all the more justified since its supposed neutrality forms part of the quest to accumulate the knowledge required to establish a society that is both fairer and more efficient. Thus it was that "an approach to education that relied on the scientific detection of each individual's aptitudes developed in France at the beginning of the (20th) century" (Duru-Bellat 1992). One of the results of this approach is to create a "civic" justification for the formal separation of the education system from the economy. These general characteristics confer on the education system a considerable responsibility, since it is charged not only with the task of educating young people but also with establishing a ranking of individuals, which consequently takes on a very particular social importance. As a result, the school becomes the locus for differentiated family strategies which, de facto, reintroduce an important social dimension into the results of competition. These strategies revolve around the need for young people to distinguish themselves from others as much as to learn, with judgments being made on the basis of the "noble" criterion par excellence, namely the individual accumulation of general knowledge. In consequence, any other form of knowledge or modes of training will necessarily be a degraded, "impure" form of general education. For some authors (d'Iribarne and d'Iribarne 1993), the power of this meritocratic notion of society is such that they speak of the "academic nobility" (see Bourdieu 1989) which, in their view, has replaced the hereditary nobility of the Ancien Régime). It represents, as it were, a synthesis between hierarchical social structure and the Republican ideal of an elite legitimated by its knowledge. Clearly, France epitomises this type of societal construction, although these characteristics tend to be shared with other countries. Was not Lutz (1992) drawing attention to the risks of a drift towards meritocracy in Germany when he alluded to the "French mode" of labour market entry!

– The second takes place in the labour market, where there is increased competition for jobs among individuals intent on signalling their suitability for the stable jobs offered by companies' internal labour markets. To do this, they rely on the acquisition of qualifications within the education system in order to jockey for position in the "queue" for access to these stable jobs. In this "job competition" (Thurow 1975), the relative level of educational attainment plays a more important part than the absolute level in determining the chances of being selected. This filtering system based on educational qualifications has the effect of increasing young people's eagerness to pursue their studies within the general education system as jobs become more severely rationed. In the youth labour market, this competition is coupled with a "selective exclusion" mechanism (Garonna and Ryan 1989) which, in a very different way depending on the level of educational attainment, controls access to internal labour markets after the acquisition of initial work experience, which is often gained in lower status jobs. Clearly, in macroeconomic circumstances unfavourable to employment, these modes of regulation governing young people's entry into the labour market are reinforced, thereby intensifying the competition both within the training system and in the labour market.

2.2 *The deregulatory effects and the induced costs of the competition principle*

The effects have been described at length elsewhere (cf., for example, Lefresne 1999), and some of them have already been alluded to above.

– The education system and individuals seem to increase their investment in the production of signals that enable employers to select the most "capable" of those waiting in the jobs queue on the basis of vaguely defined criteria of "professionality", with level of educational attainment being used as an incomplete and unsatisfactory indicator. The production of real "human capital" may be called into question, at least partially; this tendency is all the more pronounced the higher youth unemployment becomes and the less constraining the modes of access to higher education are, whether in terms of cost (low enrolment fees) or selection for entry.
– Uncertainty as to the real productive capabilities of young people serves to reinforce the downgrading processes (relative to level of educational attainment) that come into play on recruitment and which are already sustained by general job rationing (Forgeot, Gautié 1997); similarly, such uncertainty stimulates the creation of precarious jobs in which young people's productive competences can be tested.
– Recruiting young graduates to do low-skilled jobs very considerably increases the risks of long-term unemployment, if not social exclusion, for the less well-educated or trained.
– Even though its quality is recognised, vocational and technological training suffers from an endemic trend among young people and their families, who continue to privilege general education to

the detriment of the status accorded to vocational or technological qualifications in the labour market.
- Failure rates in the general education system can be very high, which causes much painful disillusion. For example, more than 100,000 young people in France, out of an annual cohort of some 700,000 individuals, enter the labour market with just the *baccalauréat* after failing to gain a qualification after one or two years' higher education.
- The severity of this twofold competition within the education system and then in the labour market for new entrants has made the integration of young people into the job market "a matter for the State". In order to try to offset the effects of selective exclusion, the State is forced to put in place a series of measures intended to help young people entering the labour market. The objectives can be summarised as follows: to make good the failures in basic education and training, to encourage a better match between individual skills and employers' expectations, in particular by opening up access to initial work experience, and to lower the (relative) wage costs of young people. In countries in which "selective exclusion" predominates, public intervention of this kind has become structural, to the point of institutionalising those precarious jobs which, in the high-growth era, marked out the route to the more secure jobs offered by internal labour markets for those least well endowed with educational capital. Thus subsidised jobs have replaced those jobs in the private sector which used to give young people their first work experience (Germe 1986). Despite its massive scale (800,000 young people under the age of 25 are involved in France, more than an annual cohort), such public intervention is subject to the filtering and competition principle already identified in the case of primary jobs: those young people least at risk from exclusion are generally the ones most likely to take part in the programmes offering the highest levels of training and qualifications (Aucouturier, Gélot 1994).

Faced with such difficulties and risks, the individual and collective returns to education and training, and particularly to vocational training, may decline to such an extent that it may be justified, in certain cases, to speak of "overeducation" (Sicherman 1992): the recruitment of university graduates into junior posts in the public service is an example that typifies the French situation.

Ultimately, the disparities between insiders and outsiders tend to increase, to the particular detriment of those young people least well endowed with educational capital.

It is clear that combating these selective tendencies in the labour market and the education system is a particularly tricky task.

- Over and above the competitive mechanisms underpinning its development against a background of job rationing (a temporary difficulty, let us hope), the general education system is responding to individual aspirations by extending the range of possible choices; early vocational specialisation, on the other hand, brings with it the risk of excessively restricting future prospects.
- Firms' pursuit of organisational flexibility militates in favour of qualificational reference systems that are sufficiently broadly defined to encourage convergence between the expectations of individuals and those of employers.
- The rationing of jobs for young people and the ensuing competition for jobs have proved to be more socially acceptable and the legitimate than explicit restrictions on access to general education, particularly higher education, even if this means defending the value of formal qualifications, whether gained in the university system or through vocational and technological training.

3. What are the alternatives to the mix of meritocratic principle and competitive regulatory?

Clearly, simply calling for the establishment and/or defence of (neo)-corporatist modes of regulation (Streeck 1996) based on cooperative mechanisms, such as those that prevail in German-speaking countries, is inadequate, for two main reasons.

- As we have seen, considerable uncertainty hangs over the future of this type of societal arrangement even though, in general terms, it is holding out against increasing short-termism in business and industry, a trend that is at odds with investment in vocational training for young people.
- The specificity of this societal construction means that it is not readily transferable, particularly because it is based on a configuration of actors whose complexity and characteristics, which have developed gradually over a long period of time, scarcely facilitate its "export".

So what alternatives are there to the mix of meritocratic principle and competitive regulatory, whose harshness can otherwise be attenuated countercyclically only through a vigorous programme of job creation?

3.1 *The dead ends of the market mode of regulation*

One initial, market-oriented approach would be to develop a highly operational concept of the certified competences, focusing mainly on an individual's immediate performance. Such an approach involves breaking down an individual qualification into a multitude of basic competences or "building blocks" (modular concept). For the advocates of such an approach, its advantage is that it makes human capital more liquid, so much so, indeed, that it becomes identifiable and manageable just like any asset in any portfolio.

As d'Iribarne (1986) stresses, the underlying aim of this concept, which informs the European Commission's White Paper, is to effect the transition from a paradigm based on flexibility to one based on the liquidity and fluidity of the human factor, with a view to making it as mobile and malleable as the assets and capital that are being expected to increase in value within ever shorter periods of time. This approach logically demands investment in the processes of certification and the norms that underpin it, rather than in the training programmes themselves. Furthermore, training organisations, whether public or private, would be free to choose their methods and programmes within the framework of the competitive principle.

Consequently, efforts have to be made to eliminate the "rent" automatically derived from credentials or formal qualifications by objectifying capabilities and, preferably, bringing them into line with the particular requirements of individual jobs, as in earlier skill and work organisation systems. The influence of the credential principle, which is considered excessive in French society, for example, is said to give rise to socially unjustified rents and to rigidities in the social sphere and in occupational status that conflict with the need for more adaptable skills and competences. The situation is said to encourage the acquisition of credentials rather than skills or competences.

This approach developed by the European Commission was very closely modelled on the British system of National Vocational Qualifications, which was originally driven by this quest for fluidity, although attempts were also made to reconstruct the requirements of individual jobs as identified on an industry-by-industry basis (the building trades, for example).

It is certainly beyond the scope of the present paper to embark on an overall assessment of the British system (see Ryan 1995, Bertrand 1997, Lefresne 1999). Nevertheless, bearing in mind the observations made above, mention should be made of certain factors that reveal the limits of an approach in which competences are managed as if they were mere products that acquire their value in the marketplace.

- The breaking-down of competences is not necessarily consistent with the ability to cope with a workplace situation acquiring responsibility and initiative. The construction of skills centred around the immediate requirements of individual jobs brings with it the risk that individuals will be less able to adapt to changing circumstances in the world of work.
- The importance of knowledge and know-how in understanding work situations has probably been underestimated, and the overall mode of regulation governing the system leads to a downplaying of the role of basic knowledge in preparing for certification. Recent evaluations and developments seem to acknowledge the limitations of this short-term approach, which encourages training organisations to concentrate on less expensive competences and skills (on these points, see Steedman et al. 1994).
- For these reasons in particular, it has been difficult to establish the intrinsic credibility of the system, both among employers, who make little reference to it in their recruitment process, and among individuals, who prefer to undertake courses of study that place greater emphasis on the acquisition of knowledge.

In sum, the doubts expressed by many social and economic actors about the quality of the competences produced by the NVQ system have reintroduced a considerable degree of uncertainty about the transferability of the skills thus acquired, which flies in the face of the aim of creating greater transparency.

3.2 *The principles governing the negotiated construction of vocational training for young people, or the creation of an individual and collective right*

If young people were to acquire a right to vocational training that counteracts the fluidity of the market with a collective solidarity based on common, shared and negotiated referents, while at the same time avoiding the meritocratic principle driving the acquisition of academic qualifications and competition within the education system, of what might that right consist and on what might it be based?

An attempted definition
Let us offer the following general definition: the aim is to provide access to a recognised vocational training covering a sphere of activity sufficiently broadly defined to avoid confinement within a narrow speciality, which vouches for an indisputable level of education, which is the product of a mix of school-based and workplace-based training combining general and specific competences and which, over the course of the working life, leads to recognised qualifications. Is there not a connection here with Weber's notion of "Beruf" (trade or occupation) which, as Lefresne (1999) reminds us, is itself connected with the ways in which German-style on-the-job/off-the-job training has been implemented? Indeed, "there are three aspects to this notion: the tasks a person's job involves, his level of education and training and his opportunities for acquiring income and security from the societal point of view".

Through the exercising of this right, it should be possible to lay the foundations for the establishment of "occupational autonomy", which would protect individuals from both the precariousness associated with inadequate skills and the dependency resulting from the possession of competences wholly specific to an internal market. While the first risk is a fairly obvious one, it should be stressed that the second one has weighed particularly heavily on the regulation of internal labour markets which, like those in France, were based on seniority, which led to the acquisition of skills specific to the firms that were ensuring stability of employment. The possibility of external mobility would have exposed individuals to the risk of downgrading and/or long-term unemployment because of the non-transferability of the skills they had acquired. Consequently, insiders were given greater protection, often to the detriment of the recruitment of young people.

3.3 *The conditions for the effective implementation of young people's right to vocational training*

The first thing that must be stressed is that it would be futile, in a society in which social individuality tends to outstrip the narrow confines of occupational or professional solidarities, to develop an approach based on a one-to-one correspondence between training and employment, in which individuals who had trained in a particular speciality would necessarily and "rationally" be destined for the corresponding type of job. Ultimately, the "building blocks" approach adopted in the European Commission's White Paper systematises this one-to-one approach, in a way that is reminiscent of the attempts made in France in the late 1960s and early 1970s, in a completely different political and institutional context, to put in place a school-based system of vocational training. Clearly, such an approach is incompatible with the exercising of a legitimate right to mobility.

Secondly, this right to vocational training, which would be likely to facilitate integration into the labour market, should apply not only to pupils in secondary education but also to all young people leaving the education system. For example, it has already been noted that dropout rates from first-stage university courses in France are particularly high; furthermore, even when they have obtained a general qualification, many of these young graduates find that their vocational skills are inadequate and that, more generally, they lack the training required to work in organisations subject to flexibility demands. What is more, the act of conferring *an automatic right to "training for work" as an indispensable corollary to all general education*, would undoubtedly be one way, albeit inadequate on its own, of giving vocational training a greater degree of social legitimacy. This might reduce the incentive to pursue courses of general education with virtually no tangible prospects and, conversely, increase the incentive to opt for vocational training at an earlier age. This type of trade-off will play a part more frequently since vocational training will be less subject to the principle of maximising the level of educational attainment, which still predominates in France.

That said, this type of arrangement, and the incentives it creates, have no chance of gaining credibility unless there are opportunities within the continuing training system to build on initial vocational training. The meritocratic principle that is so dominant in France derives its strength from the fact that continuing education has remained in an embryonic state; consequently, each individual can rationally take the view that "everything is settled before the age of 25". Against this background, therefore, "lifelong learning" is at best merely an uplifting slogan. If the German dual system has long enjoyed widespread legitimacy and, until the recent past at least, fulfilled the expectations of individual workers and employers, it is primarily because it has been able, through the development of continuing training programmes certified and recognised at federal level, to provide access to supervisory jobs in both manufacturing and services, as well as to technicians' jobs.

A recent French ministerial report (Office of the Junior Minister of State for Women's Rights and the Right to Vocational Training 1999) advocates a widening of access to *the certification of vocational skills*. Several routes can be envisaged. Firstly, recognised processes of certification for vocational skills could be established at industry level. Secondly, occupational experience could be validated, conceivably in such a way as to provide access to initial training qualifications, particularly in those countries in which such qualifications enjoy a particularly high level of legitimacy. Moreover, these two arrangements could complement each other, with the first, for example, leading onto the second.

A combination of school-based and workplace training is an essential element in the construction of a vocational training system, "since there are things that cannot be acquired in school without help from the workplace, whatever the quality of the practical training provided there, and, conversely, there are things that cannot be learnt in the workplace without getting help at school . . ." (Lichtenberger 1995). In this way, the vocational training system could respond dynamically to the challenge of the competences principle that is being advocated by employers, and more particularly in France by the MEDEF (ex-CNPF).

Any attempt to assess the issues at stake in developing such a combination of school-based and workplace training, particularly with a view to supporting occupational autonomy, must take account of *certain lessons to be learnt from the German case* that have a general applicability beyond the societal specificity of the German system.

– The first of these issues relates to the fact that the quality of youth training is maintained by a network of actors operating at different levels in the regulatory system: the national level, where the overall rules of the game are laid down (the need to define a minimal reference system for any firm providing training, even for just one apprentice, in a specified occupational area and in accordance with relatively highly formalised procedural rules), the industry level, which is the privileged space for the implementation of joint

regulation, the local level, where there are opportunities for adapting general legislation to the particular characteristics of firms in the region and, finally, the firm, where the delicate task of striking a balance between the transferability stipulated in the legislation and the acquisition of firm-specific knowledge and know-how will have to be performed.
– This complex configuration underlies the entangled relationship between the construction of specific skills (firm level) and that of skills that are, if not general (national level), then at least transferable from one firm to another (industry level): the quality of one set of skills determines that of the others, and vice versa (Franz, Soskice 1994). The objective here is to prepare workers for a career in an internal labour market while at the same time developing a potential for external mobility that may help to safeguard each (young) worker's future and occupational autonomy.
– The provision of school-based and workplace training for workers under contract raises the delicate question of the funding of vocational training. Since such training has a high level of specificity, i.e. its effects can be appropriated privately, it is on the face of it logical that firms employing apprentices should contribute towards the cost (Becker 1964). However, individuals benefit from transferable training, and this very transferability is a disincentive for firms since they may well be unable to get any return on their investment if the recipients of training then leave. Any contribution they make may well be reflected, for example, in low rates of pay for apprentices (which may be lower than their productive contribution to the firm). Ultimately, in view of the positive economic externalities associated with it, the establishment of a basic training system requires public funds. The funding issue reveals the extent to which the establishment and viability of a high-quality vocational training system depends on an intricate and delicate balancing of interests (particularly since it is perfectly possible to demonstrate theoretically that firms can justifiably be called on to fund part of general training [cf. Franz and Soskice 1994]).
– From this point of view, the question of the recognition of vocational training in wages and agreements ensues from what has gone before, which is essential to the stability and realisation of the right in question. Once again, the Franco-German comparison is instructive. In France, where vocational training is largely school-based, the tripartite agreement on the content of qualificational

reference systems is separate from any recognition of qualifications in collective agreements. As a result, the implications of any mutual commitments are subject to considerable uncertainty, which hardly helps to increase the social legitimacy, and therefore the attractiveness, of vocational training. In Germany, the dual system of school-based and workplace training is jointly regulated, and this is reflected in the recognition of vocational qualifications in collective agreements, provided that the job held equates to the occupation for which training has been received. The lesson that should be learnt from this is that the right will be all the more effectively implemented if the vocational training system is constructed cooperatively and sustained by mutual commitments.

Even then, the joint resource thus constituted must have sufficient credibility. That credibility is indissociable from confidence in the reliability of the capabilities and competences thus constructed. True, the combination of school-based and workplace training is itself a favourable factor but this characteristic is not sufficient in itself. There are two other essential aspects. Firstly, the quality of the basic knowledge imparted must be guaranteed by regular evaluation of the capabilities of those undergoing training. Secondly, the reference systems must be revised periodically by establishing a somewhat awkward compromise between two requirements, namely incorporating into the reference systems major changes in work organisation and technologies[1] while at the same time ensuring that the qualifications remain sufficiently stable to make them credible signals or, even better, rules for the protagonists in the training process and the wage relationship.

The manner in which the reference systems of qualifications are constructed has a crucial role to play in the quest for this compromise, a role that has two major aspects.

– Firstly, the various social interests have to engage in constructive dialogue in order to reach a compromise that will make vocational qualifications one of the rules governing the organisation of the labour market, and not simply a signal that acquires its value in a market, with all the attendant uncertainties. In Germany, for example, employers traditionally argue in favour of narrowing the scope of qualifications in order to make trainees operational imme-

---

[1] This technological aspect is all more important since expertise in the technologies reinforces the general nature of the qualifications.

diately, while the trade unions have always been in favour of extending the scope of the reference systems in order to give future employees as much autonomy as possible vis-à-vis their first employer. The result is a lasting compromise as to the mode of skill formation (cf. Möbus and Verdier 1997).
– Secondly, each reference system must offer young people a global approach to the activity in question in order to set it apart from "the repeated performance of discrete tasks that characterises on-the-job learning" (Kuda 1997).

Conclusion

This paper has sought to pursue two types of arguments relating to the vocational training on young people and the associated rights.

– In the first type, we have attempted to show that a system of vocational training whose mode of institutional regulation brings into play social and economic actors has retained its relevance despite two pronounced trends, namely the emphasis on general competences, associated a priori with the general education system, and the destabilisation of the institutional constructions in which the training of young people for particular trades or occupations had an important place. In particular, maintaining a system of vocational education that is regulated in the public space may serve as a defensive measure against the development of the meritocratic principle based on twofold competition—within the education system and in the labour market for access to jobs—that is reflected in the excessive capital derived from the most prestigious courses of general study and the recurrent devaluing of vocational and technological training. Denunciation of the capital automatically derived from credentials or qualifications, and of the inequalities associated with it, have led to calls in certain quarters for the establishment of a "free market in competences" that will make it possible to combine efficiency and fairness. The risks of subordination for wage-earners arising out of a human capital that has been made as "liquid" as possible require, by way of counterpoint, the establishment of collective reference points, in which a recognised system of vocational training could be an essential fermenting agent.
– In the second, we sought to identify some of the conditions likely

to make the negotiation of vocational training viable and credible. It emerges from this that vocational training can provide the basis for a "virtuous" social and economic compromise if it encourages the construction of occupational autonomy among trainees/wage-earners. The following characteristics of a negotiated system of vocational training can contribute to the production of such a compromise.

1. The generalisation of access to vocational training at the end of the various degree courses will help to entrench the social legitimacy of vocational training.
2. The linkage between initial vocational training and continuing training leading to further qualifications will encourage occupational trajectories that are not limited to careers in corporate internal markets.
3. The generalisation of on-the-job/off-the-job training is crucial, since it underpins several essential aspects of the system: the linkage between theoretical (general) and vocational knowledge, between transferable and specific knowledge; the balancing of funding sources and of the forms of social and occupational recognition for the training; the establishment of social compromises at central, industry and local level.
4. The quality and credibility of the training provided can be guaranteed by an ex ante evaluation that finds material form in sufficiently broadly defined qualificational reference systems and an ex post evaluation that guards against the risks of obsolescence.

Thus the effective implementation of a right to vocational training for young people would result in a very complex social construct based on a multiplicity of compromises at national and local level and on an acute sense of negotiation and compromise on the part of the numerous actors involved. Consequently, it has neither the simplicity nor the clarity of increasingly compelling solutions derived from the meritocratic and market conventions and sustained by increasing short-termism. It might reasonably be feared, therefore, that its prospects are slight. That said, the worst does not always come to pass! Let us reiterate that an effective right to vocational training would benefit individuals (occupational autonomy and opportunities for retraining), firms (better management of the consequences of economic instability and ability to deal with technical-economic change), the various trades and occupations (better flow of competences than when specific skills predominate) and society as a whole (better return on investment in training and reduction in the risks of exclusion). This co-operative approach is dependent on the outcome of (unlikely) negotiations, which are likely to be particularly difficult in the new and rapidly developing sectors such as services, particularly personal services, where the capacities for collective organisation are usually limited, not to say nonexistent.

Bibliography

Aucouturier A.-L., Gelot D. (1994), "Les dispositifs pour l'emploi et les jeunes sortant de scolarité", *Economie et Statistique* n° 277-278. INSEE, 75-93.
Becker Gary (1964), *"Human Capital"*, Columbia University Press.
Bertrand Olivier (1997), « *Certification et Validation des compétences, une approche internationale* », UNESCO.
Bourdieu Pierre (1989), « *La noblesse d'Etat: grandes écoles et esprit de corps* », Ed. de Minuit, Paris.
Buechtemann Christoph, Verdier Eric (1998), "Education and Training Regimes: Macro-Institutional Evidence", *Revue d'économie politique*, vol. 108 (3) mai-juin, 292-319.
Cahuc Pierre (1998), *La nouvelle micro-économie*, collection Repères, La Découverte, Paris.
Commission Europeenne (1995), "*Enseigner et apprendre. Vers la société cognitive*", Livre Blanc, Office des publications officielles des Communautés européennes, Luxembourg.
Duru-Bellat M. (1992), "Evaluer les trajectoires sociales a l'aune de la 'méritocratie'", *Savoir* n° 3, 24-42, Paris.
Forgeot G., Gautie J. (1996), "Insertion professionnelle des jeunes et processus de déclassement", *Economie et Statistique*, n° 304-305, pp. 53-75.
Franz W., Soskice David (1995), « The German Apprenticeship System » in Butler F., Franz W. Schettkat R., Soskice D. (eds.) « *Institutional Frameworks and Labor Market Performance* », Routlege, London and New York.
Garonna Paolo, Ryan Paul (1989), "Le travail des jeunes, les relations professionnelles et les politiques sociales", *Formation Emploi* n° 25. La Documentation Française, 78-90.
Germe Jean-François (1986), "Employment policies and the entry of young people into the labor market in France". *British Journal of Industrials Relations*, vol. 24 n° 1. London.
Gospel Howard (1998), Le renouveau de l'apprentissage en Grande-Bretagne, Examen de trois secteurs, *Formation Emploi* n° 64, 25-42.
Hilbert Joseph et Weber Hajo La régulation de la formation professionnelle en Allemagne: une relation tripartite, les corps intermédiaires in Möbus Martine et Verdier Eric (eds.) *Les diplômes professionnels en Allemagne et en France, conceptions et jeux d'acteurs*, Paris, L'Harmattan, 1997, 93-103.
d'Iiribarne Alain (1996), "Une lecture des paradigmes du Livre blanc sur l'éducation et la formation: éléments pour un débat", *Revue européenne de formation professionnelle* n° 8-9, CEDEFOP, 23-32.
d'Iribarne Alain, d'Iriabarne Philippe (1999), "Le système d'éducation comme expression d'une culture politique", *Revue europeenne de formation professionnelle* n° 17, mai-août, Cedefop, Thessanoliki, 27-39.

Koch Richard (1997), *La rénovation des formations professionnelles réglementées: instrument majeur de moderni-sation du système dual depuis les années 1970* in Möbus Martine et Verdier Eric (eds.) "Les diplômes professionnels en Allemagne et en France, conceptions et jeux d'acteurs", L'Harmattan. Paris.

Kuda Eva (1997), *Le renouvellement des formations industrielles de la métallurgie* in Möbus Martine et Verdier Eric (eds.) "Les diplômes professionnels en Allemagne et en France, conceptions et jeux d'acteurs", L'Harmattan. Paris.

Lefresne Florence (1997), "Renouveau de l'apprentissage et débat sur la formation professionnelle au Royaume-Uni", *Chronique Internationale de l'IRES*, n° 51, mars, pp. 17–22.

——— (1999), "*Systèmes nationaux d'insertion professionnelle et politiques publiques de l'emploi en direction des jeunes: une comparaison européenne*", Thèse pour le doctorat de sciences économiques, Université de Paris I.

Lichtenberger Yves (1995), "Alternance en France et qualification professionnelle" in Lichtenberger Y., Luttringer J.-M. et Poupard R. "*Alternance et formation professionnelle, les enjeux*". Ed. d'Organisation.

Lutz Burkart (1992), "Le système allemand de formation professionnelle: principes de fonctionnement, structure et évolution" in Möbus M. et Verdier E. *Le système de formation professionnelle en République Fédérale d'Allemagne, résultats de recherches françaises et allemandes*. Collection des études, n° 61. Cereq. Marseille.

Marsden David (1998), Apprentissage, le Phénix renaît-il de ses cendres? La formation professionnelle en Grande-Bretagne, *Formation Emploi*, n° 61 pp. 35–57.

Möbus Martine, Verdier Eric, eds. (1997), *Les diplômes professionnels en Allemagne et en France, conception et jeux d'acteurs*, L'Harmattan, Paris.

Ryan Paul (1995), "Education et formation professionnelle au Royaume-Uni: changements institutionnels", *Formation Emploi* n° 50, La Documentation Française, 41–62.

Sicherman N. (1991), "Over education in the Labor Market", *Journal of Labour Economics*, vol. 9, n° 2, 101–122.

Secrétariat d'Etat aux Droits des Femmes et à la Formation Professionnelle (1999) "La formation professionnelle: Diagnostics, défis et enjeux", mimeo. Paris.

Streeck Wolfgang (1996), "Le Capitalisme d'Etat: existe-t-il? A-t-il des chances de survivre?" in Crouch Colin et Streeck Wolfgang "*Les Capitalismes en Europe*", coll. Recherches, La Découverte, Paris, 47–76.

Throw Lester (1975), "*Generating inequality: Mechanics of Distribution in the US Economy*". Basic Books. New York.

Verdier Eric (1996), *L'insertion professionnelle des jeunes 'à la française': vers un ajustement structurel?*, Travail et Emploi n° 4, La Documentation Française, 37–54.

JUGGLING YOUTH UNEMPLOYMENT AND EMPLOYMENT PRECARIOUSNESS IN CANADA AND QUEBEC: FROM A SOCIAL TO A MORE LIBERAL APPROACH TO EMPLOYMENT POLICIES?

Diane-Gabrielle Tremblay

In recent years, many have questioned the employment policies developed in North America, comparing them in particular with the policies developed in Europe. While European policies are often considered to be of a more "social" nature and North American policies more liberal, we would like to show in this article that the situation is somewhat more complex in Quebec and Canada and that Europe does not necessarily have a monopoly over the more social approach (see Le Queux, Biddle, and Tremblay, 2002). Although recent policy developments in Canada are moving towards a more liberal approach, they are still very different from those observed in the United States. Moreover, historically, Canadian policies have differed radically from their American counterparts.[1]

It should also be noted that the specific contours of unemployment differ widely in Europe, for youth as well as other groups, and that the policies developed to deal with unemployment trends also differ from one country to another. There may be a dominant model of more social intervention, particularly in the Nordic countries, but there is also a diversity of policies, many of which have evolved over recent years in the context of European integration. Although we will keep this comparative perspective in mind, we will focus on the Canadian case.

Youth employment policies of Canada and Quebec, in contrast with those of the U.S., are more in line with the Nordic countries and, to a certain extent, are characterized by a social or collectivist tradition. Many programs developed over the years, particularly in the 1970s, are influenced by this tradition. Social partnerships are highly developed in Quebec (Tremblay, 1995), where there were numerous concertation initiatives from the 1970s to the 1990s, although

---

[1] As was shown in Tremblay, Biddle, Burguess and Le Queux (2002).

their influence appear to have declined more recently. Also, Canadian unions are still quite strong, contrary to what is observed in the U.S., and many of these unions intervene in these matters, though often only through a consultative board.[2]

In the following pages, we will discuss employment policies in Quebec and Canada more fully and defend the thesis that in the 1970s and 1980s these policies, which have had positive results, tended to be relatively original and somewhat social in nature. However, we will also indicate that beyond the stabilization of youth unemployment and a high level of youth participation in the labour market, there is still a strong risk of exclusion of certain categories of youth, as well as a risk of dualization of the youth labour market. It should also be noted that the ideological context of recent years tends to be influenced by developments in the U.S. There is an observed tendency, particularly in English Canada, towards a more liberal vision which questions legal protections and the collective representation of workers by unions. Moreover, the unions have tended in many cases to exclude youth or at least not to defend their place in the labour market very strongly.

In Canada, but even more so in Quebec, the youth unemployment situation changed radically in the 1970s. Youth unemployment was not very high until the mid-1970s, when it suddenly jumped to high levels following a general increase in unemployment. However, the consequences were even greater for youth whose unemployment rates increased to more than twice those of adults, at times reaching over 20%. Of course, some regions and groups, such as less educated youth, were much more affected than others. Unemployment therefore increased significantly in the early 1980s, when yet another economic crisis struck the Canadian labour market, hitting youth hardest.

It is in this context that many programs were developed to try to integrate youth into the labour market. Youth initiatives and similar programs appeared to be the solution to the exclusion of young people from standard employment situations. This was the begin-

---

[2] The *Commission des partenaires du marché du travail* and the *Conseil consultatif du travail et de la main-d'œuvre* are both consultative bodies, where representatives of unions and employers sit and discuss various social and employment issues. Although their discussions often lead to general agreements and publications on various issues related to the workplace (training, the work-family balance, etc.), they do not have the authority to impose any decision on workplaces, which considerably limits their impact.

ning of a long series of programs that offered jobs related to community initiatives, or what is now called the "social economy."

In the 1990s, the reduction in the absolute numbers of youth contributed to a decline in their high unemployment rates. However, the policies developed over the years have to a certain extent contributed to a destandardization of youth employment, creating a certain distance from collective union representation and protection and the fringe benefits usually associated with traditional standard forms of employment. Indeed, the strong presence of youth in non-standard employment has largely contributed to their more marginalized position in the labour market and minimal fringe benefits (retirement plans, medical and dental plans, etc.), since the latter are usually not associated with forms of non-standard work. Before turning to youth employment policies, however, let us draw a portrait of the Canadian employment context.

1. *Youth employment in Canada*

In addition to the official numbers of unemployed, many social assistance recipients could be included in the numbers of unemployed, or totally excluded youth. However, because of risks of double counting, it is difficult to give a definite number or percentage. Of course, youth unemployment is always very sensitive to variations in economic activity and is usually 1.5 to 2 times greater than that of adults. In 2000, youth unemployment was 15% in Quebec, compared with 8.5% for adults, and in the first three quarters of 2001, it was 12% compared with 8% for adults. However, the last quarter, in the aftermath of September 11, saw increases in total unemployment, which reached 8.9% in Quebec and 7.5% in Canada as a whole. Youth, both male and female, are still very affected by precarious employment. Women tend to be affected later in life while older men (25-45 years) are gradually integrated into more regular forms of employment.

Exclusion from the labour market can take many forms. Although long-term unemployment is one of them, short employment spells interrupted by unemployment may constitute exclusion. It often translates into precarious employment, that is, a succession of short-term, contract or part-time jobs.

We do not have the space here to present all the data available on youth employment (Tremblay, 1997), so we will focus on a few key elements. It should first be noted that 43% of youth aged 15–24 worked on a part-time basis in 1999 (35% of men and 51% of women in this age group). These percentages are higher than those observed in the labour market in general, since 25.7% of all women aged 15 and over worked on a part-time basis, compared with 9.6% of men.

Table 1 below, which shows the distribution of employment for workers of various ages according to type of employment, reveals the more precarious situation of youth in Quebec. Indeed, it can be seen that only 41.9% of all youth aged 15–24 have a permanent salaried full-time job, or what can be considered a typical job.

A total of 58.1% of youth aged 15–24 are involved in atypical employment. Of this group, 23.2% work in a permanent salaried job, but only part time; 14.3% are full-time temporary workers, and 17.1% are part-time temporary workers. In addition, 1.7% are full-time self-employed workers and 1.8% are part-time self-employed workers. Although part-time work in Canada is defined as less than 30 hours per week, in many cases these jobs are limited to approx-

Table 1. Distribution of workers aged 15–64 according to the characteristics of their job (typical or atypical), gender and age, Quebec, 2000

Sex and age	All workers		Typical	Atypical					
			Salaried permanent full-time	Total	Salaried permanent part-time	Salaried temporary		Self-employed	
						Full-time	Part-time	Full-time	Part-time
	'000s	%			%				
Men	1,860.6	100.0	67.3	32.7	4.8	7.5	3.3	15.5	1.6
Women	1,540.8	100.0	59.6	40.4	16.0	7.5	6.1	7.9	2.9
15–24 years	**507.9**	**100.0**	**41.9**	**58.1**	**23.2**	**14.3**	**17.1**	**1.7**	**1.8**
25–54 years	2,592.9	100.0	69.0	31.0	7.2	6.4	2.3	13.1	2.0
55–64 years	300.4	100.0	55.5	44.5	10.7	5.1	3.1	20.8	4.9
15–64 years	3,401.2	100.0	63.8	36.2	9.9	7.5	4.6	12.1	2.2

imately 15 hours per week, especially in the service and trade sectors. It should also be noted that the characteristics of precarious employment tend to aggregate. For example, youth working in temporary jobs also often find themselves working part time, thus combining two dimensions of precarious employment.

As concerns the usual number of working hours, youth are concentrated in the short workweek (under 30 hours), 42.3% have what is considered a normal workweek (35 to 40 hours), and very few (6.7%) have a long workweek. Also, long workweeks are more often the lot of men (20.5%) than women (6.5%), of older workers (18%) than younger ones (15% for those aged 25–54) and of self-employed workers (44% of whom have long hours, that is, over 40 hours per week). Considering the fact that many youth now enter the labour market through self-employment, towards which many have a positive attitude, although often over 24 years of age, this may be a trend that will affect them more in the future. It is interesting to note that 58.9% of self-employed persons with employees work long hours, as compared with 34.2% of self-employed persons without employees.

Few data are available on the number of people holding two jobs simultaneously, but youth aged 15–24 years represent 20% of all people in this situation.

It is clear that non-standard employment situations are more and more common and it is thought that today's youth will be more concerned with this situation than the previous cohort, just as the latter were more concerned with this than their parents had been. Indeed, the service sector's growth in the economy translates into more and more evening and night jobs, as well as weekend work.

Employment policies should be aimed at getting youth into the most favourable situations but, as we shall see below, it is not clear that they can actually attain those objectives. It will be all the more difficult since it seems that in 20 years, the proportion of atypical employment will be greater than that of the typical employment of today. The stark reality of the labour market shows that there are many precarious, temporary, self-employment situations that do not necessarily give access to the best situations. To conclude this section, let us recall the major problems confronting youth and which policies should address:

1. The lack of standard, full-time, year-round jobs. Over the years, various changes in the Canadian economy have translated into a

strong incidence of part-time and contingent employment for Canadian youth. Clearly, full-time standard jobs are more difficult to come by, especially for those who are less qualified.

2. Youth jobs are often low skilled jobs, which do not lead to future training or real careers. This is clearly related to the first point, i.e. that youth are more represented in non-standard precarious jobs, including, as was seen above, part-time jobs.
3. The low earnings and low or non-existent fringe benefits of youth jobs. This makes it difficult to plan for the future, to build a family and so on. While many youth do not resent this situation while they are still studying and working part time, it becomes more constraining and difficult to accept as they move into their 30s and often still find themselves in non-standard precarious jobs.
4. In relation to the low wages, it should be pointed out that many unions have collective agreements which provide for lower wages for young people entering the same jobs, but more recently. In Quebec, these are called "orphan clauses," and many youth resent what they see as a refusal by unions to defend the rights of young people in favour of preserving the privileges enjoyed by older workers.
5. The low level of unionization and, related to this, low levels of employment protection for youth. Youth have tended to be in more non-standard and precarious jobs, as indicated previously, but these jobs have also tended to be in firms or sectors of the economy (trade, services) with low unionization rates. All these factors translate into a difficult situation for youth, even if the labour market of the 1990s has been better for most workers than it had been in previous decades.

2. *The Canadian-Quebec youth employment policies*

Canada has a federal government structure and therefore employment policies have been traditionally defined at the federal level, with possible variation in their implementation depending on each province's initiative and the existence of additional power (for example, Quebec has recently been given greater autonomy in the area of vocational education, including for youth). Overall, Canadian youth employment policies have shifted from active intervention in the 1970s to a more passive intervention, centred more on the labour supply (developing competencies and qualifications of youth). Over the years, attention has been paid to integration initiatives (Fontan and Rodriguez, 2000), as well as to the development of new attitudes and social competencies. The view that supports this vision is apparently that youth unemployment is largely due to individual characteristics that are considered inappropriate, rather than to lack of demand. Job creation or support is thus not favoured as much as it was previously (Tremblay, 1998). However, this is being reconsidered in the aftermath of September 11th. The Canadian federal budget at the end of 2001, for example, included supplementary spending in defence and related areas. With this overall picture in mind, special attention will be given to the case of the province of Quebec, more specifically, its unique approach through a so-called *économie solidaire* (social economy or solidarity economy).

It should first be noted that Quebec and Canada have a long tradition of intervention in the field of employment policy, particularly as regards youth. It was in Canada that some of the first youth employment programs were developed in the 1970s, most of them oriented towards job creation in the community or associative sector. Many projects favoured the development of community organizations that today are seen as part of the social economy.

The 1970s were thus marked by a strong focus on job creation or, in other words, intervention on the labour demand side. This type of intervention can be regarded as being similar to the social-democratic intervention of Nordic governments. The governments of the time adopted an employment strategy centred on the direct creation of jobs for what were then called "target groups." The goals of the job creation programs were threefold: to reduce or counter the discriminating effects to which youth may be subject because they are young; to adopt job creation measures; and lastly, to avoid long-term youth unemployment since it was feared that this could have a negative impact on the work ethic of young people.

These programs appeared in the form of financial support for start-up activities in the fields of social services (day care, for example) and services to individuals (information on eligibility for unemployment insurance, social assistance and other similar programs). The grants resulted in a proliferation of community groups which saw this as an opportunity to obtain a funding base for youth services, services to women (abortion support centres, victims of violence, etc.), immigrants and others.

2.1. *From a demand-side to a supply-side policy*

The 1990s led to a policy shift to the supply side. Neo-liberal arguments increasingly predominated even though the employment situation seemed to have improved. Like the Canadian government, the Quebec government seemed to think that it was better to adopt American-style approaches since a liberal economy and market forces appeared to provide the solution to unemployment which, despite everything, still persisted, particularly in Quebec where unemployment was always higher. In the 1980s and early 1990s, the fight against inflation first became the priority, followed by efforts to reduce the deficit. Thus, although the Quebec state had generally engaged in quite a strong degree of interventionism in the field of employment, in the 1990s it evolved towards a degree of liberalism which, although certainly less striking than in the United States, was nevertheless more pronounced than it had been in the 1970s.

The state continued to support job creation in some well-targeted fields, in particular new technology and multimedia, which it wanted to attract to Montreal, specifically to the *Cité du Multimédia*. However, the employment policy was generally shifting towards the labour supply side. There was less effort to create jobs to compensate for a shortage of jobs offered. Rather it was thought that jobless young people were excluded because they did not possess sufficient skills or qualifications to compete in the labour market and that their attitudes were often poor. It was within this context that support for training and integration through training and employability programs aimed at improving the qualifications, attitudes and skills of individuals came to predominate in the strategies intended for youth.

The Quebec government reformed social assistance and sought to integrate youth through training programs and employability improvement programs (Tremblay, 1997a). Academic upgrading, workplace training, and various job integration measures were offered to young people. Social assistance recipients were particularly urged to participate in these programs. However, participation remained voluntary since the federal public assistance plan forbids coercion.

In recent years, there has been considerable concern about "excluded" youth, that is, those who go on social assistance and stay there. In 1996, the government experimented with the OPTIONS program. Then, in September 1999, it implemented a pilot project called *Solidarité Jeunesse* (youth solidarity) which is currently being evaluated. The program, which is intended to prevent youth from coming to rely on income security, was extended for two years, from September 2000 to 2002. During a maximum period of three months, the youth participates 20 hours per week in counselling and services aimed at fostering motivation, self-knowledge, and the identification of his or her potential as well as difficulties or problems. The aim is to give the young person the incentive to actively search for employment or to go back to school. The second phase includes follow up and support activities for a maximum of one year after starting the program. The income support thus comes from either a job or employment assistance, to which is added an employment assistance allowance. Youth recipients are identified by the local job centres and the program is run by the youth employment organizations. The program seems to have positive results at a personal level but does not often lead to jobs. Moreover, there is some concern that the government may make the program mandatory in order for youth to obtain allowances. It nevertheless falls within the "social" or collectivist tradition of Quebec.

2.2. *Towards a more active involvement of firms*

The government has also attempted to encourage firms to play a greater role in vocational training by adopting a law designed to provide them with the incentive to carry out training. The government would also like to intervene less in job creation, instead giving firms primary responsibility in this area. Like the federal government, Quebec is trying to encourage employers and unions to consult each other in sectoral committees, which have been created to develop labour training in their sectors (Tremblay, Doray and Landry, 2000). Though this approach does not reflect a form of pure liberalism, firms are nevertheless playing an increasing role in the definition of programs and training, thus contributing to bringing the education sector and the business sector closer together so that, in principle, the demands and needs of firms will be better met (Tremblay, 1997a).

This growing emphasis on the needs of firms, which seems to form a central reality in Quebec, obviously has an influence on the situation of youth. Young people who have studied in the growth areas (ICT, biotechnology, multimedia and so on) are in a relatively good position, even though they often hold precarious jobs at the start of their career. However, those who are less qualified face great difficulties and are seen, in a way, to be the cause of their own problems because they have not chosen—or could not afford to choose—better training programs. At the same time, changes made to the unemployment insurance program have also affected youth, that is, people who quit their jobs voluntarily no longer receive benefits. As youth often experience periods of unstable employment or job entry and exit, this affects them greatly, especially those in precarious and low-paid jobs.

Thus, in the past decades one can see the transition from an approach in which state intervention played a determining role (the 1960s and 1970s) to one in which the onus has been put on individuals—in our particular case, youth—to integrate into the labour market. Their inability to integrate is attributed to their individual characteristics, such as their lack of qualification, technical skills, social skills, formal education, etc. However, it should be added that while the state seems to be evolving towards a more individualist vision of responsibilities for unemployment and its solutions (employability and integration programs), at the same time it is striving to delegate to the third sector—community or social economy organizations—a large part of its intervention in the field of employment as well as in the field of social services.

The picture is thus somewhat ambiguous. Certainly young people are expected to be more responsible and accountable with regard to unemployment and job insecurity, and employment policy interventions are mainly centred on employability and integration. However, job creation measures are being taken in two opposite economic "poles." In the new knowledge-based economy, support is being provided for job creation in the multimedia sector (jobs mostly held by young people). Job creation measures are also being implemented in the proximity service and social economy sector. The characteristics of the population holding jobs in the social economy sector are currently not known, apart from the fact that they are mostly women, especially in non-profit organizations and slightly less so in co-operatives. Young people are certainly not the only ones involved in the social economy jobs, but many of them do not have the qualifications required by the new economy, and thus it seems that the social economy is an important employment opportunity for them. The "social" tradition therefore continues to serve youth even though policies have been shifted towards the supply-side.

2.3. *Youth integration through the community and social economy sector?*

Given the difficult economic context of the last two decades and the persistent difficulties of "unqualified" or "problem" youth who have been, in many respects, abandoned by the state and especially by firms, other organizations have been set up to compensate for these shortcomings. Thus, over the years in Quebec, a great number of community organizations have become involved in this field and the community sector has become an important actor in the development of employability and training to improve the qualifications and attitudes of individuals. It is therefore relevant for us to examine community intervention *strategies* (Tremblay and Fontan, 1994).

The approach of community or social economy organizations in the field of employment and training is to deal with individual factors and those related to the social and economic context at the same time. This is what distinguishes these interventions from the traditional governmental programs that often tended to consider only individual factors which were viewed as personal problems or individual shortcomings in need of correction. However, as community and social economy interventions are subject to evaluation by the governments to have their funding renewed, they must in general move towards the indicators or measurements set up by the government.

This is a great challenge for these organizations. There are currently two types of intervention. The first type relates to interventions in the area of employability to develop the skills of individuals and groups; they are mainly associated with interventions in attitudes and training which are adapted to the needs of individuals and the environment. The aim of this *first strategy*, which focuses on youth as individuals, is to develop social or vocational skills. Numerous activities can be grouped under this category, which mainly relates to improving employability. These activities range from those encouraging individuals and groups of youth to take charge of themselves in order to improve their general living conditions to all forms of support for job integration: acquisition of a minimum educational level, training adapted to firms and community projects, vocational training, strategies to reduce school drop outs, retraining and upgrading of employed workers who are likely to be downgraded, counselling, support and follow up in job search, etc.

The aim of the *second strategy* is to provide more direct support for integration. This intervention strategy, which is more collective or community-based, favours economic activity as a means of integration. Workplace training, efforts to hire locally, and integration firms are part of the means developed at the micro-territory level. Integration firms are structures created to combine technical learning with social learning within a real workplace. They can thus be designed according to diverse needs and particular clients. These structures, which are increasingly found in Quebec and are nowadays recognized through a state policy of recognition of integration firms, can take the form of firm-schools, work co-operatives which include technical learning, or community or social economy businesses which offer services to residents.

Although it was more easy for some youth to enter the labour market in 2000, things are becoming more difficult for them again in 2002. In this context, many less skilled youth remain excluded. Thus, two aspects should be underlined: first, the importance of appropriate support for measures of integration into the labour market through, among other things, community initiatives aimed at integration; and second, the importance of collective measures which ensure that the greatest number of youth are integrated into the labour market on a more stable basis. In fact, although many patterns of integration can be deemed successful in terms of short-term integration into the labour market, it seems that long-term integration and mobility towards better quality jobs are still difficult to achieve. This implies that concrete measures of direct support for employment, mobility and employment stability might be necessary in order to ensure long-lasting labour market integration for youth and avoid social dualization.

3. Conclusion

From the 1970s to the 1990s, the trajectory of Canada's employment policies was linear, moving from state intervention related to national macro-economic policies and based on active programs of job creation or employment assistance to a more liberal approach that gave priority to regulation by the market and to micro-social or micro-economic solutions, such as those of the social economy in Quebec. This shift from the demand-side to the supply-side strategy, the transition from a public response to youth unemployment to the individual responsibility of the young unemployed, asserted itself in a more radical way in the United States than in Canada but the change was nevertheless visible.

Canada is experiencing a certain decline in the universalistic vision of many as the so-called state welfarism erodes, social benefits are reduced and more coercive measures sometimes resembling workfare are implemented. The recent changes to the Unemployment Insurance program have partly reduced the eligibility for benefits of precarious workers, many of whom are young people. In 1990, some three quarters of unemployed youth had access to unemployment benefits, and in 1997 this proportion had dropped to roughly 25% (CSN, 1999).

From a social to a more liberal view?

What can be concluded from all of this is that beyond a collectivist or social tradition of concertation (Tremblay, 1995), employment guarantees can sometimes be fragile. Moreover, although present developments cannot be considered as a definite change, changes in unemployment insurance benefits translate into social impacts and social realities that are presently more difficult for youth, particularly the most disadvantaged such as those who are less qualified.

Clearly, the changes observed show that the liberal solution of workfare, low wages and little training do not result in full employment, and even less so in employment stability for youth. On the other hand, Quebec's very strong development of the social or solidarity economy does not necessarily hold all the promises. It still integrates youth (and many women) under conditions of work that are way below those of the regular adult (male) labour market. It is clear that even if the discourse on the social economy jobs and the community service vision of these jobs are very positive, the stark reality is that most of these are still unskilled jobs with few possibilities of promotion or even of mobility towards better paying and better qualified jobs. To a certain extent, even after only a few years of development, it must be acknowledged that the social economy does not hold promise of a better world of work for the youth and women who form the majority of its workers (for example, in support for the elderly, disabled persons, social housing, etc.).

Other criticisms of these low-paid jobs underline the fact that previously, in the context of a Keynesian approach, the state would have been the one to provide these social support services. For some, it follows that the social economy jobs for youth represent a form of discrimination since the "good jobs" of the past, with good pay and fringe benefits as well as job security, have given way to low paid, insecure jobs in the social economy. This may be an overly critical view, but there is no doubt that many young people resent the present situation which offers them, at best, these types of social economy jobs, and at worst, more insecure and even more precarious jobs in the trade or proximity service sectors. Already in 1994, Statistics Canada reported that the revenue of young people aged 20 to 24 was 20% less than those in the same age group 20 years previously. More recent data have not been found, but it is highly improbable that things have changed considerably.

What does the future hold for youth?

Although deregulation and recourse to community work conceal obvious risks of exploitation and ghettoization, the emphasis placed on the employability of youth in "deficit" and their systematic marginalization on the labour market often translate into a feeling of guilt and alienation whose psychological and social effects can sometimes be devastating. This is undeniably cause for concern.

This dualization is becoming more pronounced among youth, between those who have been able to specialize in skills that are in demand—for example, in IT—and the growing cohorts of overqualified and debt-overloaded students without guarantee of a job, those who are in vocational training programs devoid of real qualifying content, the losers of the education system, most of whom are employed under minimal conditions, in particular in the retail and hospitality industries. Lastly, there are the excluded, whose numbers are always hard to estimate because they are "zero-status" youth who are left out of the statistics.

The market is producing many losers with few prospects, which points to the need to return to more mixed employment policies, including the re-implementation of a form of welfarism that is adapted to a more occasional participation in the labour market and that can respond to the vulnerability of youth in employment.

References

CSN (1999), *L'urgence d'une meilleure intégration des jeunes pour une société plus forte et solidaire—La situation des jeunes au Québec: portrait, analyse et enjeux*, Montréal: CSN.

De Terssac, G. and D.-G. Tremblay (eds.), (2000), *Où va le temps de travail?* Toulouse: Editions Octares, pp. 5–25.

Fontan, J.-M. and P. Rodriguez (2000), *Recension des entreprises d'insertion dans la région de Montréal*. Montréal: UQAM.

FTQ (2000), *Branchés sur une même solidarité*, Montréal, January, http://www.ftq.qc.ca/ftq.html.

Le Queux, S., Biddle, Burgess, and D.-G. Tremblay (2002), Does Europe have a monopoly of heart? Youth employment policies in Australia and Canada. In Serrano, Pascual, A. (ed.), *Youth Employment policies in Europe and abroad*. Brussels: ETUI.

Lipsett, Brenda, and Mark Reesor (1997), *Flexible Work Arrangements: Evidence From the 1991 and 1995 Survey of Work Arrangements*. Ottawa: Human Resources Development Canada.

Serrano, Pascual, A. (ed.) (2000), *Tackling youth unemployment in Europe*, Brussels: ETUI.

Tremblay, D.-G., P. Doray and C. Landry (2000), Les comités sectoriels du Québec: un signe de rapprochement économie-éducation en matière de formation professionnelle? In A. Alcouffe, et al. (2000), *Efficacité versus équité en économie sociale*. Volume 2, pp. 63–74.

Tremblay, D.-G. (ed.) (1998), *Objectif plein emploi: le marché, la social-démocratie ou l'économie sociale?*, Québec: Presses de l'Université du Québec.

——— (1997), *Economie du travail. Les réalités et les approches théoriques*, Montréal: Éditions Saint-Martin.

——— (ed.) (1997a), *Formation et compétivité économique; perspectives internationales*, Québec: Éditions St-Martin.

——— (ed.) (1995), *Concertation et performance économique*. Québec: Presses de l'université du Québec.

THE YOUNGER GENERATION OF SPANISH MOTHERS IN THE FAMILY AND IN THE WORKPLACE

Constanza Tobío

Introduction

For most of the 20th century up to the sixties—and even early seventies—there was a clear negative correlation between fertility patterns and female labour activity in Europe. The Northern European countries were characterized by both the lowest fertility rate and the highest proportion of women in the labour market. Conversely, fertility remained high in Southern Europe until the last quarter of a century whilst female activity was low. The interpretation of this North-South duality was generally based on the idea of a coherence between the traditional demographic and social patterns, where women exclusively dedicated to the home and children were the most fertile and female labour activity was associated with modernity, one characteristic of which was a lower fertility rate.

The situation was to change during the eighties, and now in the nineties we can say that the reverse is true: Southern European countries, especially Spain and Italy have the lowest level of labour activity (36.7% and 34.8%) (Eurostat, 1998) and the lowest fertility rate (1.15 and 1.22 respectively). On the other hand, in Northern Europe there is a higher proportion of women working (in Sweden 56.5%) and these have more children than the average European.

The paradoxical contrast between the hyperactivity of the women in the North, both in the productive and in the reproductive sphere, faced with the apparent inactivity of the women in the South can perhaps be more easily understood if we take into account the recent evolution regarding the participation of Spanish women in the labour market, as well as the attitudes of the women themselves, and those of society in general, to female employment. The global activity rates overshadow the remarkable increase in the number of women working among the younger generations, given the reduced activity among the older ones. There has been a generational breakdown between women over 40–50 years of age, the majority of whom are and have been housewives for most of their lives, and younger women who, in the main, have joined the labour market (Garrido 1993) and continue in it even when they become mothers, thus changing the old gendered family model that conceived motherhood and employment as incompatible.

Therefore, it can be said that we are living in a period of transition from the old model of woman and family, characterized by a marked division of gender roles, to a new model based on the incorporation of women into the labour market. Nonetheless, what has essentially become a reality—a new normality founded on the fact that the majority of women will work throughout their life—has not yet been recognized and assumed by Spanish society. It has failed to recognize that this, from a social point of view, is both a change and a problem that makes the redefinition of the forms of social organization from the smallest scale (family life) to the largest (social policies, work, time and space) imperative.

In the following pages, I will look at generation, rather than age. The younger generation of Spanish working mothers represents the first generation for which this double role is the norm. They are facing new problems that the previous generations of women did not have to face. They are giving solutions and finding answers, even if often these are not the best possible ones. They are beginning to demand that the social organisation as a whole adapt to the new reality of dual earner families as the new normality.

The first part of this chapter deals with the patterns of female labour activity as well as with the general reasons why the new generations of women have chosen to work. The second part presents the public policies that exist in Spain in an effort to make family life and work life more compatible and, lastly, it raises the question of how Spanish working mothers, who most intensely personify the contradiction between work and family life, carry out their double role in two worlds so far apart.

1. *New roles in the workplace. Why do women work?*

For a long time women's work outside of the home has had a cyclical nature, dependent on economic, military and even biological factors. For example, during the First and Second World Wars they occupied the positions, above all in factories, that the men had had to leave when sent to the front. However, during the post-war period, a redeployment of women back to the home could be observed as could a rise in the fertility rate. Female activity generally rose in moments of economic recovery and declined during recession, acting principally as a shock absorber during economic cycles. A similar occurrence can be noted with biological cycles as female labour activity reached a peak at around twenty five years of age and then waned during the years of highest fertility. In short, labour activity and fertility appeared to be conflicting activities, not easily combined.

Over the last twenty years Spain has witnessed an important increase in activity among the generations that are currently under forty years of age. Especially significant is the increase in activity between the ages of 30 and 40, an age at which the majority of women have young children. Whilst in 1981 less than a third of the women in this age group were active, the latest data from 1999 show that this figure has risen to over two thirds (Fernández Cordón, 1999).

If the working mother is the new social normality, the question that arises is why do women work? The investigation on which this work is grounded, the Family-Employment Compatibility Survey[1] (FECS), has come up with some answers to this question. All the people interviewed for this survey were working mothers with at least one dependent child. Their attitude towards their own work was very positive. Almost two out of every three women interviewed (62%) stated that "They liked their job and would not leave it willingly", as opposed to slightly more than one third (38%) who asserted that "If they could they would leave their job and dedicate themselves to their family". The most influential factor in the attitude towards work was the socio-economic level.[2] There were pronounced differences, with 78% of interviewees in the high socio-economic bracket affirming that they liked their job but only 44% of those in

---

[1] The data presented in this part of the paper are based on Tobío, Arteta and Fernández Cordón (1996) and on Tobío, Fernández Cordón and Agulló (1998). The first investigation was based on twenty five in-depth interviews and six discussion groups with working women between the ages of 20 and 49, with a partner and at least one child under 18. The field work was carried out from February to June 1995 in Madrid, Barcelona, Valencia and Bilbao. The second investigation was based on 1,200 representative interviews of Spanish working mothers who had at least one child under the age of eighteen still living in the family home. The field work was carried out from March to June 1998. Both research projects were financed by the Spanish Women's Institute of the Ministry of Social Affairs.

[2] This was determined based on the occupation of the interviewees.

the low socio-economic group stating the same. However, one interesting point was that even in the most unfavourable situations, almost half the mothers interviewed that occupied low-qualified positions and had at least one child under eighteen still residing in the family home asserted that they did not wish to give up work.

When asked about the reasons why they worked, the most common response given was family economic necessity with almost 55% stating this as the main reason. This declined to 26% when the three main reasons were accumulated. In earlier qualitative studies this had appeared repeatedly, as had the opinion among women from all social classes that today work was an obligation imposed by economic necessity, as only one income was no longer sufficient to support a family. What is more, on starting out younger families believe two jobs to be the norm. Notwithstanding, there were certain subtle variations among the social classes with respect to the content of this economic need. For women from the lower-classes it was a case of need in the strictest sense of the word, and yet middle and upper class women considered their work as necessary if family level of consumption that was characteristic of their environment was to be maintained.

The second reason given, although this was considerably less popular than the former (14% gave this as the main reason and it went up to 17% when the three main reasons were accumulated), was individual economic independence. This reason differs greatly in nature from the first, although it does also have an economic aspect. In this case work is an individual strategy of women, a basic support which provides security both for the future in case of separation and divorce and for the present by strengthening their position inside the family.

The third consideration given (9% chose this as the principal reason) in answer to the question of why women work was in order to practise their profession, directly related to the logical sequence of professional training-activity. Women who have studied for a degree believe that they should put the knowledge acquired to use, as otherwise it is seen to be a waste.

The fourth most popular reason stated as the main cause (by 8% of the interviewees) is the actual pleasure that is gained from working. In this case work is not a tool used to achieve other aims but by itself constitutes an objective or goal. From this point of view, work is seen to be a rewarding and welcome activity for those who carry it out, desirable and pleasurable in itself.

On asking the general opinion of the women themselves regarding the ideal employment situation for a woman with children, the majority, exactly half of those surveyed, stated that part-time work would be ideal as long as the children were small. The ideological spectrum and implicit demands are clearly defined by this question. Approximately one fifth of the working women in our country adopt the traditional posture that mothers should not work.

The option of "working when the children are older" appears to point to the sequential model of distribution between work and family life, which exists in other countries such as Germany and France. The demand implicit in this case is for parental leave which makes childcare possible during early childhood, thus later allowing or facilitating the return to work. Part-time work[3] is the situation preferred by the majority of working women while their children are still small, specially among the younger working mothers. This, nonetheless, is at odds with the narrow margin the majority of those interviewed claimed to have to relinquish a part of their salary, should they be offered this opportunity. Full-time work even when the children were small was considered desirable for a small number of the interviewees, and this represented the most progressive option: that both children and labour activities constitute two equally important and compatible aspects for a woman.

Nevertheless, the predominantly positive opinion regarding paid work expressed by working mothers when asked about the ideal situation for women dramatically declined when enquiring about what was best for the children. Almost half the women interviewed consider that it is in the best interests of the children for their mothers not to work, whereas only 9.5% believe that the ideal situation for children is for the mother to work full time. This means that more than a quarter of the total women interviewed (28.5%) show conflicting views regarding what is better for the mother (work) and what is in the best interests of the children (that the mother does not work). The reverse—those who believe that a full time working mother is in the best interests of the children but not of the mother herself—

---

[3] This is the model in Anglo-Saxon countries such as the United Kingdom, the United States and Australia and, to a great extent, the model in practise in Nordic countries where despite the importance of policies on equal opportunities, the promotion of female labour activity and the high level this has achieved, half of the women work on a part-time basis (Letablier, 1995).

is almost non-existent (less than 1%). 62% of the cases coincide on what is in the best interests of both the mother and the children. When these interests do not coincide it is largely due to those opinions that reflect the idea that it is better for the children if the mothers do not work at all or work less.

There exists, therefore, a contradiction between the plurality of individual and family, practical and personal identity reasons which induce women to carry out labour activity and the perception of what is better for the children. Female employment as a new social normality represents modernization; the preferred option of maternal childcare almost certainly represents the inertia of the traditional model and indicates that the assumption of new work roles by the mothers has not been accompanied by a new positive childcare model.

2. *Public policies for the reconciliation of work and family life*

In the latter part of 1999 a law known as the *Reconciliation of work and family life for working individuals* (Law 39/1999 dated November 5) that transposes the Spanish regulations to the European guideline 96/34/CE regarding parental leave was passed. The new law organized and brought together the many disperse regulations existing at that time regarding maternal leave, extended leaves of absence and reductions in working days for childcare reasons, as well as other specific leaves for family reasons (Villa Gil and López Cumbre, 1999). In addition, it increased the cases in which leave can be taken by either the father or the mother in an attempt to promote equality between the sexes. As far as parental leave is concerned, apart from the sixteen weeks of maternity leave—ten of which can be taken by the father—, this law established that an extended leave of absence of up to three years could be taken in order to take care of children under eight years of age. This can be taken by either the mother or the father, and this period of time is counted as time worked as far as length of service is concerned.

This law represents the first recognition of the problems created by the growing incorporation of women into the workplace, and in many aspects it is open and flexible. It does, however, have one important limitation in that the leaves of absence are unpaid, and for this reason, few fathers and mothers will be in a position to take advantage of them. According to data from Eurostat in 1995 only

2% of Spanish women with children under three years of age were on parental leave, compared to 10% in Germany and 9% in France (Deven et al., 1997: 55–56).

Crèches and schools should be one of the chief resources called upon to help combine the employment and childcare. From the quantitative point of view these are of critical importance. According to FECS data, 73% of working mothers who have at least one child under four years of age use the services provided by crèches and nursery schools. Despite the high proportion of working mothers making use of these centres for their small children, only 1.5% of those interviewed stated that these constituted a facilitating factor for reconciling labour activity and the family responsibilities. The majority of these centres, above all the public ones, have not yet recognized that the housewife who is available to take care of the home and the children at all times is no longer a social normality. Social organization has not kept up with this new reality of two working parents, which will soon be the case in the majority of households. This is apparent regarding three main problems: a lack of coordination between school and work timetables, school holidays, which are considerably longer than those enjoyed by workers, and lastly, children's illness.

The FECS provides information on the relationship between school and work timetables. Almost one third (29%) of children with working mothers start nursery school after their mother's working day begins. This lack of coordination becomes even more apparent when children finish nursery school as in 58% of the cases children leave school before their mothers have finished work. This situation does not improve, indeed it gets worse, when the children go to primary school. 33% of the women interviewed begin work before their children under the age of 12 years start school and 60% of them leave when their young children have already finished their day's schooling.

Another source of incompatibility between the educational and working world is the long school holidays. Half of the women interviewed stated that solving the problem of childcare during the holidays was difficult to a greater or lesser extent: 10% stated that this was very difficult, 15% said it was moderately difficult and 23% asserted that it posed some difficulty. The perception of difficulty was heightened among the interviewees with longer working days and among the younger ones because they have a higher proportion of small children.

The third problem to be taken into account regarding schools was how to deal with sick children. The surprise factor, an unexpected event which frequently appears out of the blue, makes this a source of worry and anxiety. For 60% of working mothers taking care of a sick child presented some type of problem: 18% considered it a big problem, another 18% asserted that it was relatively problematic whilst 24% stated that it supposed a problem to a certain extent. There is no general regulation that covers this type of situation. The new Reconciliation Law includes two days paid leave, which already existed, for a serious illness, accident or the hospitalisation of a child or other family member, but it fails to cover less tragic, everyday situations. Thus, there is a considerable gap regarding this issue in the current regulations governing leaves of absence to take care of children.

In Spain there is no form of childcare in the home of the carer as exists in France (assistantes maternelles) or in the United Kingdom (child minders). What is much more frequent is paid domestic help. Unlike in France, no specific aid programme for this form of childcare[4] exists (Fagnani and Rassat, 1997; Fagnani, 1998). Whilst there is no aid or tax exemptions for families with two working parents who hire somebody to care for their children, there is, however, a special Social Security regime which has made it possible to improve the working conditions of domestic workers and take the sector out of the underground economy to a large extent.

This is practically all that is available regarding public policies directed towards facilitating and favouring reconciliation between work and family life, although other types of policies—economic policies, urban growth among others—may also affect the relationship between these two worlds. The following paragraph deals with the practical and working strategies used today by working mothers in an effort to overcome the problems that arise from their two roles.

3. *The strategies employed by Spanish women to combine their work and family life: substitute mothers*

In a context where there are few public policies that favour the double working and family role, Spanish women have devised a variety of principally private and individual strategies in order to maintain

---

[4] Allocation de garde d'enfant à domicile (AGED).

their presence in both worlds. They do not wish to return to the old models of the past and their new role as a worker represents a path they wish to follow: real equality between men and women in all areas of life, but what is less clear is which positive family model corresponds to this new situation. There is a strong inertia left over from the traditional family in many respects, above all regarding everything connected to childcare or the quality of family life (home cooked food associated with health, family rituals, etc.). This probably explains the importance of the strategies based on the substitution of the mother by another women who takes on her role during her absence, this may be a relative, most frequently the maternal grandmother, or someone who receives payment in exchange for this service.

Today's working mothers represent the first generation of women in which the majority form part of the labour force, and their mothers represent the last generation of women who were, on the whole, housewives. Today's mothers are faced with new problems and they are finding the help they need from the earlier generation. Many of today's mothers would not be able to work if they could not count on their own mothers to help them with childcare. According to the Family-Employment Compatibility Survey of 1998 (Tobío, Fernández Cordón and Agulló, 1998) 77% of working mothers have a close relative living in the same area, and in 56% of the cases this is their own mother. The help provided by grandmothers is generally transmitted through the female side of the family: 54% of the women interviewed whose mothers live nearby receive the latter's help with the household chores on a daily basis. The help received from the family network, and above all from the grandmothers, takes on even more importance during unforeseen events (when a child gets ill, during school holidays, etc.): 65% of the women interviewed receive help from their mothers, 40% from their fathers, 36% from their mothers-in-law and 12% from their fathers-in-law.

Among working mothers from the lower classes the help provided by grandmothers and family network is the most important strategy for childcare as the margin of choice is extremely narrow. Middle class mothers more frequently choose family members to take care of their children, preferring this option to leaving them with "strangers" either at home or in a nursery school. The upper classes, on the other hand, generally use paid home help, but even in these cases grandmothers carry out an important role controlling the organization of their daughters' homes or helping out during unforeseen events.

Age also makes a difference in the perceived importance of kinship support. Among working mothers below thirty the help of the family network is considered in 37% of the cases to be a necessary condition for them to keep their jobs; for another third it is considered to be very important.

During the sixties and seventies domestic help was on the decline in Spain and the way it had been organized up to this time, as a form of unregulated, casual labour was substituted by a greater professionalization and delimitation of the working day. This came about within the context of the generalized modernization of both the economy and the society which, on the one hand, was due to the mechanization of many household chores through the increased use of electrical appliances and, on the other hand, was due to the lesser availability of female labour force in this sector. But the nineties saw a return of domestic help, mainly immigrants, brought about by the new demands associated with the strong rise in female labour activity, above all with regard to the care of children and the elderly.

6% of Spanish working mothers have full-time paid domestic help, which take on practically all the domestic chores. Another 19% of women have paid help for a certain number of hours every week, which deal with the more difficult chores or cover moments when schedules are incompatible (taking the children to school or nursery school when the parents go to work, spending some time with them in the evenings, etc.).

In short, help from the family network and paid domestic help are strategies based on the assumption by women that they are responsible for care. The mother is substituted by another woman who carries out her role in her absence, but basically the association between women and taking care of the home and the children has remained, as stated by Leira (1994) and Windebank (1996). Thus it would seem that the possibility of women joining the professional world depends greatly on the existence of other women available to take care of the home and the children. This may be interpreted as a contradiction, strongly associated with economic, social and professional position, between women who are freed from everyday work in the home and other women whose principal activity is taking care of the home and the children, be they theirs or other women's'.

4. Other strategies

According to data from the Family-Employment Compatibility Survey in Spain working mothers that live with their partner note a considerable inequality in the distribution of chores. Less than a third of the women interviewed (32%) believe that the domestic chores are shared equally, as opposed to two thirds who consider that they carry out the majority of the chores. A little more than half (53%) believe that men should participate to a greater extent with the household chores. The perception of equality clearly relates to age. Among the younger group of women those who think that domestic work is shared equally with their husbands or partners double those over forty who think so.

Out of the eighteen chores studied none were carried out chiefly by men and only three were dealt with by both parents the majority of the time: getting up at night to see to the children, helping the children with their homework and spending time with them after school, although it is worth pointing out that in a fourth of the homes nobody dealt with the last two tasks. The chores that are more frequently carried out by the interviewees alone are loading and putting on the washing machine (77.1%), ironing (76.4%), cleaning the bathrooms (69.9%), hanging out the clothes (68.4%), preparing the meals (66.5%) and cleaning the windows (65.0%). The chores least likely to be carried out by men alone are: cleaning the bathrooms (1.9%), ironing (2.0%), dusting (2.7%), loading and putting on the washing machine (3.0%), making the beds (4.3%) and taking the children to the doctor (4.7%).

The professional level of the women interviewed has an influence on the chores carried out by men as it introduces more equal patterns, as well as the occupational level of the man, although this affects the division in a very different way. As the professional level of their partners rose, the women interviewed carried out domestic chores less frequently, this, however, did not lead to an increase in chores carried out by the men. In these cases it is people other than the couple themselves who carried out the majority of work in the home. Another influential factor is age. Younger working mothers have more co-operative partners, specially in tasks related to the children.

There are complementary strategies related to distance (looking for work close to home, moving to live close to grandparents, etc.), to time (working part-time, using nights, early mornings or weekends to cook, clean, iron, etc.) or to simplifying domestic chores (applying Taylorist methods for food preparation, eating out, reducing the amount of clothes that have to be ironed, etc.). There are also extreme strategies, which are not wholly satisfactory in making labour activity and childcare compatible. These strategies mean the partial or incomplete sacrifice of a part of these two worlds; they are used when there is no other possible solution and are not the preferred option in any case. Extreme strategies are, for example, taking the children to work when there is nowhere else to leave them, missing work for reasons related to the children or leaving the children alone in the house.

Delaying motherhood or a reduction in the number of children is an indirect strategy. There is, on the whole, no direct relation between the number of children the interviewees had or expected to have and paid work, as this is associated to a greater extent with the economic situation. The number of children will thus depend on the economic capacity of the families. Nonetheless, there is an indirect link between the work of the mother and the number of children she has, however, this link does not function in a simple inverse fashion, i.e. the more the woman works the less children she has, it is in fact far more complicated. The desire to have more children exists, but this requires a level of dedication on the part of the woman which would make it impossible for her to continue working, yet if this were to happen the resulting economic situation would forestall the arrival of more children. Thus, work is not the reason why women have less children, on the contrary it actually makes it possible for them to have one or two at the most, more are rarely possible.

Conclusion

The incorporation of women into the labour force is now the norm and represents generalized behaviour in the generations under forty years of age, both because the family economy has made this necessary and because the women themselves wish this to be the case. Everything points towards their remaining in the job market for their whole life, and in this way their work patterns will become more and more similar to those of men, as has occurred in the majority of European countries. The old association between high levels of fertility and low levels of female labour activity belongs in the past; any scenario that envisages the recovery of fertility should start off from the premise that female activity is now a fact.

However, the ever-increasing and soon-to-be majority participation of women in employment points to a social change of enormous relevance, which will affect social organization as a whole. Spanish society appears unable, or perhaps even unwilling, to accept the fact that if women assume new roles as workers, others (men, the state, the market) will have to also accept that the old ways regarding housekeeping and care for those who need it will have to change. The effects of generalized female labour market participation affects social organization in its entirety, and consequently society must take on the new problems that today's women are forced to solve using informal and provisional methods as their own. Some of the strategies in use today in an attempt to combine work and family responsibilities do not constitute the future models, as is the case with help received from grandmothers. The increased availability that they enjoy today will be considerably reduced in the future when the current generations of working mothers reach this age and will most likely continue their professional activities until it is time for them to retire. On the other hand, it is also arguable whether a childcare model based on grandmothers/grandfathers is in fact desirable. Other strategies are only within the means of few women, such as is the case with paid domestic help. In other instances, the problems of compatibility between childcare and employment are being solved through a series of practices, negative for both the children and the mothers, such as leaving them alone at home when they are still young or taking them to the workplace. The organization of educational centres must adapt considerably to the new situation characterized by the fact that the majority of women now work. Aspects such as the coordination of school and work schedules, offering play activities or activities to supplement schooling during the holidays are of the utmost importance if the everyday life of women who are both mothers and workers is to be made easier. Care for sick and very young children requires both services and resources in order to avoid situations where the reconciliation of work and family life becomes impossible. Today we are living in a period of transition, led by the younger generations of women, between the old model, which belongs to the past, and a new one whose definition is a task to be assumed by all.

References

Deven, F., Inglis, S., Moss, P. and Petrie, P. (1997), "Revisión de las investigaciones realizadas en Europa sobre conciliación de la vida laboral y familiar para hombres y mujeres y calidad de los servicios de atención" Final report of the Equal Opportunities Unit of the European Commission. The Spanish versión is available at *Materiales de Trabajo*, 40, Ministerio de Asuntos Sociales, Madrid.

Eurostat (1998), *Labour Force Surveys* 1997, Luxemburg.

Fagnani, J. and Rassat, E. (1997), "Garde d'enfant et/ou femme à tout faire? Les employées des familles beneficiaires de l'AGED" in *Recherches et Prévisions*, 49, 51–58.

Fagnani, J. (1998), "Helping mothers to combine paid and unpaid work—or fighting unemployment? The ambiguities of French family policy" in *Community, Work and Family*, Vol. 1, 3, 297–312.

Fernández Cordón, J. A. (1999), "Mujer y protección social: la situación sociolaboral de las mujeres" Fundación Alternativas, Madrid.

Garrido, L. (1993), *Las dos biografías de la mujer en España*. Instituto de la Mujer, Ministerio de Asuntos Sociales, Madrid.

Leira, A. (1994), "Concepts of caring, loving, thinking and doing" in *Social Service Review*, June 85–201.

Letablier, M. T. "Emploi-Famille: des ajustements variables selon les pays" in *La Lettre*, Centre d'Etudes de l'Emploi, nº 37, París, 1995.

Tobío, C., Arteta, Q. and Fernández Cordón, J. A. (1996), "Estrategias de compatibilización familia-empleo. España años noventa" Departamento de Humanidades, Ciencia Política y Sociología, Universidad Carlos III de Madrid, (investigation report).

Tobío, C., Fernández Cordón, J. A. and Agulló, A. (1998), "Análisis cuantitativo de las estrategias de compatibilización familia-empleo", Departamento de Humanidades, Ciencia Política y Sociología, Universidad Carlos III de Madrid, (investigation report).

Villa Gil, L. E. and López Cumbre, L. (1999), "Adaptación de la legislación española a la Directiva 96/34/CE sobre permiso parental" en Revista del Ministerio de Asuntos Sociales, Número Extraordinario, 41–69.

Windebank, J. (1996), "To what extent can social policy challenge the dominant ideology of mothering? A cross-national comparison of Sweden, France and Britain" en *Journal of European Social Policy*, vol. 6, 2, 147–161.

LABOUR MARKET POLICIES AND YOUTH IN GERMANY FROM THE EARLY 50s UNTIL TODAY

Frank Braun

Since the mass unemployment of the 1920s *Jugendsozialarbeit* in Germany has been the central social agency for addressing unemployment and inadequate training facilities among young people. The German term *Jugendsozialarbeit* will be retained here because, translated literally as "youth social work", it fails to point to two aspects unique to such work in Germany: first, *Jugendsozialarbeit* aims to place young people, especially "disadvantaged" young people, in the job market; second, although usually financed by the state or by unemployment insurance, it is implemented on a semi-private basis, by the welfare organisations, associations and local initiatives that are subsumed in Europe under the term "third system" and by training schemes instituted by private-sector industry.

A recurrent lack of training opportunities and continued mass unemployment since the 1970s have repeatedly made *Jugendsozialarbeit*'s work in implementing employment policy the subject of specialist controversy. One extreme theory holds that *Jugendsozialarbeit* acts as a selective controlling agency by separating those who can be placed in the job market from those who cannot and by neutralising, even steering, the latter's potential for social conflict (Galuske, 1998). The present paper will analyse the functions and tasks that have been accorded or attributed to *Jugendsozialarbeit* by those responsible for regulating the job market, especially the Bundesanstalt für Arbeit (Federal Institute of Labour; BA) and its predecessors. This will involve outlining the history of employment policy in relation to young people in the Federal Republic of Germany, from the "jobless youth" years immediately after the Second World War, via the long period of full employment and labour shortages that ended in the first half of the 1970s, to present-day problems surrounding the placement of young people in the job market. The analysis addresses the relationship between *Jugendsozialarbeit* and employment policy at a federal level, as reflected in laws, guidelines and commentaries, and at a local level, where the increasingly regional orientation of employment policy has led to the formation of cooperative undertakings, to rivalries, to wider scope for action and to dependencies. The paper closes with a look at the current debate on the "future of labour" and the changes and the challenges it may entail for employment policy and *Jugendsozialarbeit*.

Employment policy and Jugendsozialarbeit *in the post-war years: compensating for lack of training opportunities and for regional and sectoral imbalances*

Employment policy in the late 1940s and early 1950s was dominated by measures designed to combat the effects of war. Cities, infrastructures and industrial plants had been subjected to widespread destruction, and economically backward areas such as Bavaria, Lower Saxony and Schleswig-Holstein had become the main place of refuge for the flood of refuges from the east. While jobs and training opportunities were in short supply almost everywhere, in certain industrial regions (the Ruhr District, for example) and in agriculture demands for workers and apprentices could not be met (Schelsky, 1952). Discussion among experts was dominated by fears that the hard conditions of life in the post-war years might make young people not only "rootless" but also "work-shy". It was felt that " 'flitting' from one job to another and 'making do' [might] appear to young people as a rather more effective way of coping with everyday life" (Münchmeier, 1989, n.p.).

An enquiry conducted among unemployed young men at the time resulted in a negative assessment of their willingness to work. Four per cent of the men were said to be wholly willing to work, fifty-one per cent less than wholly willing, thirty-three per cent fairly unwilling and twelve per cent extremely unwilling. The author of the study concluded that young people should be permitted to receive unemployment benefit only if they participated in training schemes or found employment of some kind. Accordingly, long-term maintenance was to be avoided (Wurzbacher, 1952, p. 314).

The measures introduced to combat what, in the language of the day, was the "danger" represented by "needy" young people who were "unemployed, untrained and uprooted" (Will, 1979, p. 133) still belong among the provisions of *Jugendsozialarbeit*. Those measures were:

- Hostels for young people. In regions offering adequate numbers of jobs or training opportunities the hostels served as accommodation, while in regions with high unemployment the hostels themselves provided training, apprenticeships and jobs (BAG JAW, 1952, pp. 120–21). By 1958 the number of hostel places had risen from 11,000 to 120,000 (Lenhartz, 1952, p. 7; Reschke, 1999, p. 11).
- Basic training courses. According to the guidelines issued in connection with the Bundesjugendplan (Federal Youth Plan; BJP) in 1951, these courses were to acquaint participants with the material normally learned during the first year of "proper training as apprentices in skilled manual, commercial, industrial and agricultural jobs" (BAG JAW, 1952, p. 126). For young women in particular, basic training courses often took place in the context of hostels or other institutions, offering the institutions an opportunity to acquire money by engaging participants in simple domestic, horticultural or agricultural chores. Courses for young men involved greater expense: it was thought necessary to equip them, unlike their female counterparts, with tools and machinery (ibid.).
- Jugendgemeinschaftswerke (Youth Community Works). These voluntary work camps were set up especially in the so-called refugee regions—Bavaria, Lower Saxony and Schleswig-Holstein—as a means of offering young people the opportunity of "extra work in non-profit-making organisations" (ibid.).

These measures were financed by the federal states, the labour administration and the BJP. A study carried out by the labour administration in northern Bavaria found that the provisions were "successful for girls", because housekeeping classes and sewing workrooms were inexpensive and easy to set up, but more problematic in the case of adolescent men, since "experience has shown that handicraft workshops... are of little value as preparation for entering the job market" (Schirmer, 1950, p. 17). Hence, 5,380 adolescent women made use of the 174 opportunities offered by the provisions, but only 302 adolescent men.

Until the mid-1950s youth employment policy was committed to the following:

- setting up hostels in an attempt to reduce the imbalance between regions with a surplus of jobs and training opportunities and structurally weak regions with high unemployment,

– offering basic training courses and other external means of acquiring qualifications as compensation for the lack of company-based training facilities,
– creating jobs in non-profit-making organisations or additional temporary employment as compensation for the lack of job opportunities.

These provisions were aimed at young people well-equipped for training and employment. Employment policy expressly denied responsibility for young people at a social or educational disadvantage (Busold, 1952, p. 245).

*Full employment and labour shortage:
mobilising labour reserves in a deserted job market*

Increased demands for labour in the mid-1950s brought about a change: "more support for young people unfit for work" was now the order of the day (Giggel, 1956, pp. 1–4). In order to meet the growing "requirements of the West Germany economy", from 1955–56 increasing numbers of special training courses were set up for "uncompetitive" young people who had previously been denied vocational support. "All mentally and physically fit young people [should be equipped for] training or for an active role in the national economy, so as to meet increased labour demands now and in the future" (ibid., p. 1).

This reorientation in employment policy was not given a fundamentally new basis in law until the passing of the Arbeitsförderungsgesetz (Promotion of Employment Act; AFG) in 1969. The responsibilities of the BA were expanded to include combating, reducing and compensating for unemployment and below-value employment resulting from economic, structural and technological developments or from physical disability on the part of employees (Kost, 1974, p. 282). People—including young people—wishing to engage for the first time in employment subject to compulsory insurance now had a legal right to assistance.

This employment policy, aimed at offering vocational support to the widest possible range of people, including the "disadvantaged", was pursued until the mid-1970s. In 1974, for instance, the expansion of the BA's measures to prepare people for entry into the job market—catering for 11,000 people in 1973–74 as opposed to 1,400 in 1968–69 (Kost, 1974, p. 288)—was explained with reference to "our constitutional law", which guaranteed everyone "the right to free development of their personality, to the cultivation of their talents and abilities, and to freedom in their choice of vocation and workplace" (ibid., p. 284). In other words, young people with physical, mental or social disabilities, young people suffering from bodily ailments, impaired performance ability and learning disorders, should "not be denied the right to appropriate personal development" (ibid.).

Lack of training opportunities and jobs for young people: compensating temporarily before establishing a system of temporary assistance

Between 1970 and 1975 the number of company-based training vacancies placed with the vocational counselling service shrank by fifty per cent. From September 1974 to January 1975 the number of unemployed under the age of twenty rocketed from approximately 70,000 to more than 123,000 (Meisel, 1976, p. 240). With these developments in mind, and in view of the fact that those born in years with high birth rates were approaching the end of their schooling, a team of researchers from the Institut für Arbeitsmarkt- und Berufsforschung (Institute for Job Market and Vocational Research) warned of a "crisis threatening training opportunities" that would lead to long-term "congestion in applications" and the "displacement of applicants by those with higher qualifications" (Kühlewind, Mertens and Tessaring, 1975, p. 10).

Expanded job preparation measures were the response to this problem, with a focus on basic training courses of the kind familiar from the immediate post-war period. Subsequently, the demands on those involved in *Jugendsozialarbeit*, who offered such courses and, increasingly, job creation schemes for young people, stayed relatively constant with regard to the content of their work and the numbers of its beneficiaries. Obligatory curricula were devised for the implementation of the measures, the ratio of training specialists to trainees was fixed and the scope for expanding or developing the provisions was circumscribed rather strictly. An element of uncertainty remained, however, because the BA, at a time of vast increases in expenditure, adjusted the number of its training opportunities in accordance with developments in the education system, rather as a tube expands or contracts depending on the amount of material passed to it from another tube to which it is connected. Job preparation and provision on the part of *Jugendsozialarbeit* acquired the character of a "permanent temporary measure". While the continuity of the tasks undertaken by *Jugendsozialarbeit* increased its professionalism, their provisional nature and the frequently uncertain funding of *Jugendsozialarbeit* and its workers adversely affected its efficiency.

The forecast made in 1975 that the lack of training opportunities would not disappear within a few years and would result in the long-term exclusion of young people with educational and social disadvantages remained without consequences until 1982. That year, the Bundesbildungsministerium (Federal Ministry of Education; MBW) instituted a programme of assistance for the disadvantaged. Young people who had attended pre-job training courses or suffered from "personal disadvantages" and were unable to find a place in a company-based training scheme were now given the opportunity of receiving full training at external institutions. This became an established field of activity for those involved in providing training and for those engaged in *Jugendsozialarbeit*. For years, implementation of the new programme lived with two lies intended to emphasis its complementary character vis-à-vis company-based training schemes but in fact revealing the inherently ambivalent nature of this type of centralised employment and qualifications policy. First, training for the disadvantaged was described not as "external" training (though that is exactly what it was), but as "industry-wide training"—a term that gives the deliberately false impression that the programme complemented, rather than replaced, company-organised training. Second, the general principle that training for the disadvantaged was to take place externally for one year and thereafter in a company context was—and is—observed only in exceptional cases.

Regionalisation of the job market:
using Jugendsozialarbeit *as a coordinator*

From 1974–75 onwards, a notable feature of political responses to unemployment among young people was the conception, funding and implementation of employment and qualification measures by a number of bodies in addition to the BA: at an international level, the EU, supplying money and devising programmes for reducing regional imbalances; at a federal level, the MBW and the Bundesarbeitsministerium (Federal Ministry of Employment); at a state level, the employment, education, arts and youth ministries, often operating in competition with one another; and at a local level, various economic organisations along with social security offices and youth services (Braun, 1996, pp. 11–12). In the training system, established coordinating processes and bodies ceded importance to new authorities, which, however, were not consulted about decisions taken within the system.

The result for some young people was a "programme career" (Kraheck, 2002; Lex, 1997; Raab, 1996). In no special order, these people participated in a number of programmes offered by various bodies, without coming any closer to their goal of finishing training for a job recognised as requiring such training.

Until the early 1980s expert opinion saw employment and qualification policy as the responsibility of central government and the individual state governments (Hegner, 1986, p. 121). Reactions to the subsequent tendency for employment policy to become the province of local government were ambivalent. On the one hand, this development was viewed as a typical instance of "passing the buck" of problems caused by central government or by society as a whole without providing the resources necessary to tackle them (Krüger, 1985, p. 28). On the other hand, the deficiencies noted above in connection with the system of temporary assistance could be eliminated only at a local level (Braun, 1996), the lack of financial means requiring a careful husbanding of resources that was easier to accomplish in a local context that at the level of central government (Krüger, 1985, p. 28).

The associations and expertss involved in *Jugendsozialarbeit* interpreted the perceived deficiencies in coordination at local levels as a challenge for them to adopt the function of coordinators (SEAJ, 1990). An experimental programme devised to test the viability of this strategy revealed its limitations. *Jugendsozialarbeit* was able to perform local tasks assigned to it only when job centres or local government took an active part in implementing employment policy. In places where employment policy had not become an established area of political activity *Jugendsozialarbeit* was unable to fulfil an effective coordinating function (Braun, 1992; Braun, 1996).

The regionalisation of employment policy was given fresh impetus by the replacement in 1998 of the AFG as the basis of job incentive schemes by the new legislation contained in the *Sozialgesetzbuch III* (Social Welfare Statute Book III; SGB III). The closer monitoring of success introduced in SGB III in effect made *Jugendsozialarbeit* and job centres competitors, entailing a danger that "promising cases" would receive greater attention and support (what Nicaise and Bollens, 1998, p. 128, call "creaming of the poor") while the genuinely disadvantaged—*Jugendsozialarbeit*'s "real" target group—would face increasing marginalisation.

Employment policy and Jugendsozialarbeit *in eastern Germany*

After the reunification of Germany young people in the area of the country formerly occupied by the German Democratic Republic were abruptly faced with unemployment and a lack of training opportunities. The state responded with a massive deployment of the policy resources at its disposal (Felber, 1997). State intervention in the form of additional training programmes and the subsidisation of company-based training schemes became the norm. Nevertheless, increasing numbers of young people had no chance of finding a job either because they had not been able to complete their vocational training or because the qualifications they had gained were not those required by employers.

The scope of employment policy resources deployed in the new, eastern states, and the speed with which they were implemented, was not without consequences for the way training was offered there and for the creation of an infrastructure for *Jugendsozialarbeit*. On the one hand, training institutions from western Germany established themselves quickly in many eastern parts of the country using the organisation and methods practised in western Germany (and often occupying all administrative posts with people from the west). On the other hand, local initiatives and projects, developed almost in slow motion, became an important means of pursuing the aims of *Jugendsozialarbeit* (DJI, 1998).

New working lives = new demands on employment policy and Jugendsozialarbeit?

The current debate on "the future of labour" has produced highly contradictory forecasts with regard to the amount of available paid labour, to quantitative and qualitative developments in various areas of qualification and to the extent to which various population and labour groups will be integrated in the job market or risk vocational and social marginalisation. On some issues, however, experts agree, especially with respect to the effects that changes in the job market will have on working lives. It is thought that:

- working lives will be marked by more frequent change, of employer, of vocation and of status;
- working lives will be interrupted more often, by unemployment and by periods of training and employment that turn out to be dead ends in terms of vocational advancement, setbacks on the path to integration in the job market and society;
- working lives will involve new patterns in the combination of different kinds of work, with men engaging not only in kinds of employment traditionally associated with them, but also in kinds that had previously featured strongly in women's biographies, such as domestic work and subsidised public service jobs.

Such changes have already begun to affect young people handicapped by a lack of training opportunities and jobs. Disadvantaged young people, in particular, frequently reach employment via paths other than the classic progression school—training—job. Not only has the number of stages on the road to employment increased; their sequence has also become less standardised, with the consequences of opting for a particular alternative often unforeseeable at the time the decision is taken. Although young people remain attached to the idea of a "normal" biography, emphasising that that they wish to earn their living by gainful employment (Bertram, 1997; Raab, 1996), they are forced to develop strategies for coping with discontinuity and uncertainty. They integrate periods without training or employment more or less easily into their working lives. Hence, work, unemployment and training are combined in new patterns (Kraheck, 2002).

One opinion repeatedly voiced in connection with the "future of labour" is that, with the job market dominated by uncertainty, support for disadvantaged young people should no longer focus on employment (Krafeld, 1998). Yet the proposed solution, "preparation for unemployment" rather than "preparation for employment", is not a viable alternative. Discontinuous employment and subsidised employment, too, require qualifications. Young people should be prepared for meeting the demands of employment and they should be prepared for not seeing themselves as "victims" when unemployed. They need to develop their employment potential. However much the requirements of skilled labour may change and new qualifications be demanded as a result, young people depend on qualifications for "biographies worth living". Subsidised and unpaid work, participation in qualification and employment schemes, demand proven skills if the activity is to be worthwhile in human terms.

Translated from the German by Michael Foster

BIBLIOGRAPHY

BA, Bundesanstalt für Arbeit (ed.), (1975), "Übersicht über die Lehrgänge der Bundesanstalt für Arbeit für Jugendliche", *Die Heimstatt* 23, 1975, pp. 197–202.
——, Bundesanstalt für Arbeit (ed.), (1976), "Berufsvorbereitende Massnahmen: Ergebnisse aus dem Berichtsjahr 1974/75", *Informationen für die Beratungs- und Vermittlungsdienste der Bundesanstalt für Arbeit*, Nuremberg, 1976, pp. 419–30.
BAG JAW, Bundesarbeitsgemeinschaft Jugendaufbauwerk, ed., (1952), "Ordnung der Begriffe", in *Fünfzig Jahre BAG JAW im Spiegel von Zeitzeugen und historischen Dokumenten*, Bonn, 1999, pp. 120–36.
Bertram, B. (1997), "Keine Wende zum Heimchen am Herd! Erfahrungen und Orientierungen von ostdeutschen Frauen in Beschäftigungs- und Qualifizierungsmassnahmen", Munich and Leipzig, March 1997, working paper written in connection with the pilot project 'Jugendsozialarbeit and the Job Market'.
Biermann, H. (1990), "Berufsausbildung in der Produktionsschule: Konkurrenz oder Kooperation im Ausbildungssystem?", in P. Collingro, ed., *Glücksfall Arbeit*, Wetzlar, 1990, pp. 47–55.
Braun, F. (1992), *Die Modellprojekte im Bundesjugendplan: Modellprogramm "Arbeitsweltbezogene Jugendsozialarbeit" als qualifizierungs- und arbeitsmarktpolitische Akteure*, Munich, 1992.
—— (1996), *Lokale Politik gegen Jugendarbeitslosigkeit*, Munich, 1996.
Brinkmann, C. (1999), *Zielkontrolling und Evaluation im Rahmen der Arbeitsförderung*, Institut für Arbeitsmarkt- und Berufsforschung: Werkstattbericht 2, 1999.
Busold, K. (1952), "Zum gegenwärtigen Stand der Berufsnot der Jugendlichen", *Das Arbeitsamt* 3, 1952, pp. 243–45.
DJI, Deutsches Jugendinstitut, (1998a), *Arbeitsweltbezogenen Jugendsozialarbeit: Modellversuche zur beruflichen und sozialen Integration von benachteiligten Jugendlichen*, Munich and Leipzig, 1998.
—— (1998b), *Vom Modell zur Alltagspraxis: Dokumentation zur Abschlusstagung des Modellprogramms "Arbeitsweltbezogenen Jugendsozialarbeit" 1994–1997*, Munich and Leipzig, 1998.
Felber, H. (1997), *Berufliche Chancen für benachteiligte Jugendliche? Orientierungen und Handlungsstrategien*, Munich, 1997.
Fülbier, P. (1989), Quo vadis, Benachteiligtenprogramm? Stand und Perspektiven der Berufsausbildung benachteiligter Jugendlicher", *Die Heimstatt* 37, 1989, pp. 67–74.
Galuske, M. (1998), "'Abkehr von der heiligen Kuh'! Jugendberufshilfe nach dem Ende der Vollbeschäftigungsillusion", *Jugend Beruf Gesellschaft* 49, 1998, pp. 6–14.
Giggel, E. (1956), "Verstärkte Betreuung auch nicht berufsfähiger Jugendlicher", *Das Arbeitsamt* 7, 1956, pp. 1–4.

Hegener, F. (1986), "Handlungsfelder und Instrumente kommunaler Beschäftigungs- und Arbeitsmarktpolitik", in B. Blancke, ed., *Die zweite Stadt*, Opladen, 1986, pp. 119–53.
Kost, W. (1974), "Berufsvorbereitende Massnahmen als Hilfen zur beruflichen Eingliederung noch nicht berufsreifer Jugendlicher", *Die Heimstatt* 22, 1974, pp. 282–90.
Krafeld, F. J. (1998), "Bewältigung von Zeiten der Arbeitslosigkeit als Sozialisa-tionsaufgabe?!", in P. Becker and J. Schirp, eds., *Jugendliche Arbeits- und Lebensverhältnisse in Zeiten der Deregulierung: Jahrbuch 1997/98*, Marburg, 1998, pp. 49–64.
Kraheck, N. (2002), *Karrieren jenseits normaler Erwerbsarbeit: Abschlussbericht*, Munich, 2002.
Krüger, J. (1985), "Kommunale Sozialpolitik in der Krise des Wohlfahrtsstaates: Zur Verortung der sozialpolitischen Dezentralisierungsdebatte", in J. Krüger and E. Pankoke, eds., *Kommunale Sozialpolitik*, Munich, 1985, pp. 11–45.
Kühlewind, G. Mertens and Tessaring, M. (1975), *Zur drohenden Ausbildungskrise im nächsten Jahrzehnt: Eine Modellrechnung zur Aufnahmefähigkeit des berufsbildenden Bildungssystems für Übergänger aus dem allgemeinbildenden Schulsystem bis 1990*, Nuremberg, 1975.
Lenhardt, G. (1979), *Der hilflose Sozialstaat: Jugendarbeitslosigkeit und Politik*, Frankfurt am Main, 1979.
Lenhartz, R. (1952), "Dreieinhalb Jahre Bundesarbeitsgemeinschaft Jugendauf-bauwerk", in *Informations-Rundbrief zur sozialen Lage der Jugend*, reprinted in BAG JAW, ed., *Fünfzig Jahre BAG JAW im Spiegel von Zeitzeugen und historischen Dokumenten*, Bonn, 1999, pp. 6–8.
Lex, T. (1997), *Berufswege Jugendlicher zwischen Integration und Ausgrenzung*, Munich, 1997.
Meisel, H. (1976), "Jugendarbeitslosigkeit—Ausbildungsstellenmangel: Lösungsmöglichkeiten aus der Sicht der Bundesanstalt für Arbeit", *Die Heimstatt* 24, pp. 238–55.
Münchmeier, R. (1989), "Vierzig Jahre Jugendhilfe", *DJI-Bulletin* 13, 1989.
Nicaise, I., and J. Bollens, (1998), "Training and Employment Opportunities for Disadvantaged Persons", in CEDEFOP, ed., *Vocational Education and Training: The European Research Field—Background report 1998*, vol. 2, Thessaloniki, 1998, pp. 121–53.
Raab, E. (1996), *Jugend sucht Arbeit*, Munich, 1996.
Reschke, W. (1999), "Fünfundzwanzig Jahre Jugendaufbauwerk: Ein Weg zur Chancengleichheit für junge Menschen in Beruf und Gesellschaft—Gekürzte Fassung der Festansprache aus dem Jahr 1974" in BAG JAW, ed., *Fünfzig Jahre BAG JAW im Spiegel von Zeitzeugen und historischen Dokumenten*, Bonn, 1999, pp. 9–14.
Schelsky, H., et al. (1952), *Arbeitslosigkeit und Berufsnot der Jugend*, 2 vols., Cologne, 1952.
Schirmer, A. (1950), "Erfahrungen in Nordbayern", *Das Arbeitsamt* 1, 1950, pp. 17–18.
Seaj, Sachverständigenkommission zur Erstellung des Achten Jugendberichts (1990), *Bericht über Bestrebungen und Leistungen der Jugendhilfe*, Bonn, 1990.
Will, H.-D. (1979), "Die verlorene Schlacht der Jugendhilfe: Die Stellung des Jugendamtes während der Jugendarbeitslosigkeit 1950–1955", in G. Lenhardt, ed., *Der hilflose Sozialstaat: Jugendarbeitslosigkeit und Politik*, Frankfurt am Main, 1979, pp. 130–73.
Wurzbacher, G. (1952), "Das Verhältnis der männlichen jugendlichen Arbeitslosen zu Arbeit und Beruf", in H. Schelsky et al., 1952, pp. 237–314.

PART FOUR

WORK, YOUTH AND IMMIGRATION

REGIONAL YOUTH OF IMMIGRANT ORIGIN IN QUÉBEC: INNOVATIVE RELATIONSHIP TO WORK*

Myriam Simard

Immigration to non-metropolitan regions[1] is a relatively recent phenomenon in Québec that has been subject to little analysis to date, given that a regionalization policy was only introduced in the 1990s. This policy is intended to ensure a more geographically balanced distribution of immigrants throughout Québec, and to encourage the sustainable settlement of immigrants outside the Montreal metropolitan area, where the majority of new arrivals tends to concentrate.[2]

Although over ten years have passed since this policy was adopted, few studies have examined, from an intergenerational perspective, the integration process of immigrants living in non-metropolitan regions. As I am particularly interested in the practices* of youth from immigrant families settled in non-metropolitan regions, in 1987 I undertook a study of these young people living in less urbanized regions. Do they stay in these regions or leave them for Montreal or other large cities? What sense of belonging do they have in terms of their region? By what process do they integrate socially, economically and culturally into these communities that are characterized by cultural and ethnic homogeneity?

Some of the results of this study have already been presented in other papers, particularly the findings concerning their migration patterns, identities and occupational integration trajectories (Simard et al., 2001; Mimeault et al., 2001). This purpose of this paper is to

---

* I wish to thank the Social Sciences and Humanities Research Council of Canada (SSRHC), Canada's Secretary of State and Emploi-Québec for their financial contribution to this research project on regional youth of immigrant origin in Québec. I would also like to thank my translator, Leslie Macdonald, for her diligent collaboration.

[1] The concept of *region* is a complex one and denotes a multiform reality. In Québec, it refers to the 17 administrative regions that are usually described as remote, intermediate (midway between urban and rural) or central in terms of their location relative to the Montreal metropolitan area. In the context of this paper, I concentrate on remote and intermediate regions; therefore, the term "regional youth" refers to youth originating from one of these two regions.

[2] I have already discussed the issues and paradoxes involved in this policy of immigration regionalization in another paper (Simard, 1996).

explore in greater detail the particular relationship these regional youth of immigrant origin have with respect to work. It examines the importance and meaning of work in the minds of youth that llive outside the major urban areas. In a regional context, do they attach particular significance to work? Attempting to answer this question necessitates going beyond the usual categories of analysis and broadening the issue.

1. *Brief overview of this study*

Conducting a study of young people of immigrant origin living in non-metropolitan regions requires considerable caution in terms of the concepts to be used (Aubert et al., 1997) and factors to be considered. In this regard, I have already criticized the "second generation" concept and proposed a multifactorial perspective in order to identify clearly the particular characteristics of integration in the non-metropolitan context, as well as the heterogeneity of youth (Simard, 1999). I will not reiterate these points here, as my interest lies more in exploring the original and dynamic relationship of youth to work.

It is, however, appropriate to review the main features of this study. It focused on young people of immigrant origin living (or having lived) in non-metropolitan regions of Québec, specifically, young people who either arrived in the country with their parents at school or pre-school age or who were born here. The main purpose is to shed light on the overall integration process—scholastic, occupational, social and cultural—of these regional youth, as well as on their migration patterns.[3] A total of 66 in-depth conversations lasting an average of two hours were held with young people between the ages of 18 and 29.

The regions retained included two intermediate regions (Mauricie–Bois-Francs and Estrie) and two remote regions (Bas-Saint-Laurent and Abitibi-Témiscamingue), as well as the two main cities in the

---

[3] This study of young people of immigrant origin is related to the work of a multi-disciplinary, interuniversity team concerning the internal migrations of young Quebecers, carried out under Madeleine Gauthier. For an overview of the problem as a whole, see Gauthier (1997). The word *migrations* refers to the independent movement—without their families—of youth from the age of 15 on, *outside* their region of origin. Intra-regional movements, which were minimal in the study conducted, were not considered to be migrations. A minimum duration of four months outside the region constituted the main inclusion criterion for a migration.

province of Québec that are migration destinations, i.e. Montreal and Québec City. The group studied was distributed more or less equally among these three types of regions; however, looking at the two urban migration destinations, the groups were underrepresented in Montreal compared with Québec City. A little over half of the young people interviewed were of European origin (55%), while the remainder came from a variety of other origins (45%)—African, Asian, Latin American and Haitian. Lastly, 80% stayed in their non-metropolitan region for more than ten years, such that their assessment of regional life is based on a sound knowledge of the community and sufficient objectivity.

A bias exists in the group studied inasmuch as all respondents were connected to families who stayed in the non-metropolitan regions, and whose integration was successful, from both the social and occupational standpoints.[4] The route taken by young people from immigrant families that stayed in non-metropolitan regions for a few months or years and later moved elsewhere in Québec, Canada, the United States, has not been investigated and therefore remains largely unknown. Moreover, the relatively high socio-economic status of the parents of the young respondents in this study cannot be overlooked.

2. *Precarious entry into the labour market*

The entry into the labour market of regional youth of immigrant origin is generally characterized by precariousness: alternating between employment/unemployment, intermittent work, irregular and unstable wages or salary, etc. The jobs held vary widely, and include social worker, chef, CEGEP teacher, waiter, farmer, factory worker, nurse, electromechanical technician, and chambermaid. Youth of non-European origin appear to be more affected by this precariousness, as it is sometimes coupled with certain forms of racial discrimination toward "visible" minorities. They usually describe this discrimination as "minor" (Mimeault et al., 2001). Rejection due to

---

[4] Professional immigrant parents were overrepresented in the non-metropolitan regions, primarily in the teaching and health fields, for the period concerned. These immigrants in fact came to the regions to fill positions created during the Quiet Revolution of the 1960s, mainly with the opening of the public colleges (CEGEPs) and the establishment of the Québec university network and the regional health and social service networks.

their accent or foreign name, verbal insults, harassment and exclusion were mentioned, a finding consistent with the national and international literature on this subject (Aubert et al., 1997). Only very few highly educated individuals with certain specialities, such as young doctors, seemed to benefit from more stable and remunerative working conditions, right from the start of their careers.[5] These results are not surprising as they concur with the many studies conducted on the difficulties youth face in integrating into the labour market of post-industrial society.

Moreover, these young people have to cope with the transformations taking place in the labour market and the crisis of work that has prevailed in North America and Europe since 1975 (Castel, 2001; Furlong and Cartmel, 1997). They have to be resourceful in order to find jobs with adequate salaries, particularly in the non-metropolitan regions, where jobs are even scarcer. Piecemeal employment in the form of temporary or casual jobs, self-employment, seasonal work, work on-call, part-time work, replacement work, commission-based work, night or split-shift, and short-term contracts in fact constitute the conditions under which the vast majority of the young people interviewed began their working life.

Paradoxically, most of the respondents reported their satisfaction with their work situation, even if, as they put it, "it's not always easy," and even though, for some, a number of objective criteria of precariousness persist in terms of duration of the work, hours worked, salary, and so forth. They envisage an improvement in their work situation and consider that their careers are moving in the right direction. Even those in the most precarious positions expressed satisfaction in terms of a number of subjective evaluation criteria, such as cordial work relations. They appear motivated to improve their occupational situation, primarily through plans to return to school when needed. A legacy of family values regarding education is noted here, as immigrant parents appear to be demanding in terms of their children's academic progress.

A key factor in the young respondents' positive assessment of their occupational integration is the importance of a work atmosphere that

---

[5] In this paper, the analysis of occupational integration is based mainly on the testimonials provided by the young workers (slightly over half of the group studied), although the occupational aspirations of those who were students were also taken into consideration. The analysis of relationships to space (urban, rural, regional), is based on the comments of all the young people interviewed, both students and workers.

is at least pleasant and warm, even if it is not stimulating. This is indicative of the importance of sociality at work, particularly in the absence of work that is even minimally interesting and in which young people might be able to express their creativity. This "good atmosphere," to use their term, makes it easier for them to accept the uncertain, often boring conditions. The importance they place on the social aspect of work concurs with Rainer Zoll's analysis of the communicational and playful attitude of young people toward work. According to this author, "the quest for fun"—in remunerated work and elsewhere—often replaces, at least to a certain degree, the quest for meaning (Zoll, 2001). This refers directly to the socio-cultural transformation in the meaning of life and work in which self-actualization becomes crucial in the post-modern context of heightened individualism (Zoll, 1992). Few regional youth of immigrant origin appear to be demanding working conditions that involve permanent status or fringe benefits. Do these conditions seem to them to pertain to more prosperous times from the past? In this regard, their critical remarks about unions suggest a discomfort with an institution that stands in defence of workers' rights, an institution which to them appears inadequate as we enter the 21st century. Clearly for them, salaried work is no longer the only preferred way of giving meaning to life. What emerges here is a transformation in the relationship between work and life outside work.

3. *Pluriactivity and overall quality of life*

Aware of the current restructuring of the labour market, combined with precariousness and the need for flexibility, young people are developing a pragmatic approach to work by not making it the sole value of their lives. They are thus seeking to take advantage of their greater leisure time to participate in other types of activities[6] pertaining to their desire for personal fulfilment and the concerns of their own age group. Friendships, entertainment, mutual assistance networks, family life, travel, these and other activities, over and above work, must also be taken into account in analyzing their relationship to work. This pluriactivity is witnessed mainly when the desired employment proves to be unavailable or uninteresting. It allows young

---

[6] For the distinction between work, employment and activities, see Annie Fouquet's article (1998).

people to fulfil themselves nevertheless, outside the context of remunerated work. Unlike preceding generations, their lives are not essentially focused on their professional careers, but rather on the acquisition of new social, cultural and occupational experiences that enable them to create an overall quality of life for themselves. Does this represent a way of protecting themselves against disappointments and disillusionment regarding occupational integration? The question remains open. The concept of *overall quality of life* is thus crucial. Yet this pluriactivity represents one of the innovative forms of self-expression in which young people have the opportunity to mobilize their resources and relational abilities.

In the regional (non-metropolitan) context, involvement in local and regional development associations is highly valued. However, an examination of the various activities of regional youth of immigrant origin reveals that they are not yet very involved at this level. Their immediate priorities and values drive them more to spend their energy in sociability relationships, personal self-fulfilment projects or activities closely related to the realities of their age group. Moreover, the time and energy required to look for work and involved in holding several small jobs must be taken into consideration. From this emerges the paradox of regional development and immigration regionalization policies, at least in the short term, for they focus on the initiatives of local social actors, both young and older, to revitalize the regions (Simard, 1996, 1997).

However, this does not mean that young people are completely disinterested inn regional community life, as they can in fact be creative actors regarding the issues that affect them most closely. It seems that it is only later, once they have had children of their own, that they begin participating actively in regional community life, initially, through school or leisure activities, as has been shown in another of my studies. In this respect, they will be following the model of their parents' overall participation in the local community (Simard, 1995). A future study of the various ways in which these young people participate in regional life at the economic, as well as social, political and cultural levels, will explore the extent to which their involvement may take other forms, through original, informal contributions likely to pave the way for local and regional revitalization.[7]

---

[7] An analysis of the participation of young people of immigrant origin in regional life is currently under way, and the definitive results are expected to be available in 2003.

A. *Quality of life crucial*

A key factor in this pluriactivity is the concept of overall quality of life.[8] Frequently cited by the majority of young people, this concept refers to a set of features—economic, social, cultural, and environmental—each with a different value placed upon it, depending on whether the young person has decided to settle and travel within the region, or in a highly urbanized centre such as Montreal. Significantly different relationships to space are observed, depending on the quality of life sought. However, all young people share an overriding concern with finding a quality of life that meets their values, aspirations and desire for self-fulfilment, regardless of the work they perform.

The comments made by the young people living in non-metropolitan regions are significant. They rarely criticize the fewer job opportunities, the remote location, the distances and the lack of variety in activities and services. Instead, what pervades their interviews are their positive comments about *nature*: the peace and quiet, vast spaces, ready accessibility to nature, fresh air, and so on. This reflects youth's current passion for environmental issues and a variety of outdoor sports.[9] They also speak about factors pertaining more to the modes of interaction that are present in the regional setting, including a more personalized knowledge of the community and its networks, warm contacts, and mutual assistance networks. Lastly, they refer to a number of other positive features of non-metropolitan regions, such as greater safety, the absence of traffic and criminality,

---

[8] This notion is different from that of "lifestyle." Several research centres around the world (notably, in the USA, Canada, Denmark, and Great Britain) are dedicated to studying the issue of quality of life. Quality of life is observed through a set of indicators, mainly mental and physical health, social/family/love relationships, leisure activities, participation in community life, self-esteem and well-being, autonomy, and relationship with the environment (c.f. see the multi-dimensional definition of quality of life given by the University of Toronto, at www.utoronto.ca/qol/concepts.htm). For an overview of studies on this subject, refer to the review of the literature in Frank A. Andrews (ed.), *Research on the Quality of Life*, Ann Arbor, Michigan: University of Michigan Press, 1986. Jean-Louis Paré, one of the professors on the interuniversity team researching the internal migrations of young Quebecers, is currently analyzing the quality of life of youth in relation to migration. See his article "L'intégration du migrant par les loisirs," in *Pourquoi partir? La migration des jeunes d'hier and d'aujourd'hui*, edited by M. Gauthier, 189–212, Québec City: PUL-IQRC, 1997.

[9] An examination of young people's expenditures on leisure activities indicates a significant increase in the portion of their income used to acquire sports equipment (canoes, kayaks, bicycles, dryland skis, rock-climbing equipment, sailboards, etc. (Bureau de la Statistique du Québec, *Habitudes de consommation, 1996*).

less stress, access to a variety of services, numerous outdoor activities, and proximity to grandparents. Evident here is their concern with maintaining a balance in their lives and not sacrificing family and social life for an all-consuming career.

All these factors create a "quality life" context, a vital prerequisite in the minds of these young people, in addition to that of interesting work that offers them a decent standard of living. In this regard, they are no different from regional youth of old stock, for whom this overall quality of regional life is the main criterion for settling in the region. To preserve this quality of life, they are prepared to accept a narrower range of services and fewer job opportunities. When they reach the stage of contemplating a family of their own, this quest for quality of life extends to the conditions conducive to raising children in a safe environment in close proximity to a solid intergenerational family network. A genuine attachment to the land of their childhood can be noted.

Regarding their relationship to the Montreal metropolitan area, it appears to be ambivalent, including both points of attraction and detractors in the minds of these young people who stay in non-metropolitan regions. On the one hand, they mention the greater availability of jobs and services, the wide variety of cultural activities, the diverse cultures and the considerable broadmindedness found in the big city. On the other hand, in their opinion, these advantages do not outweigh the negative impacts of a large city: crowding and lack of green spaces; stressful pace of life; high rate of criminality, pollution and traffic, and the high cost of goods and services. They also comment frequently on the poor quality of human relations, condemning the indifference and coldness of Montreal urbanites and the existence of immigrant ghettos.

These last two aspects concerning the impersonal nature of relationships, as well as the different types of status given to immigrants in Montreal and the means whereby they integrate, appear to be decisive factors in the choice these young people make—especially those of non-European origin—to return to live in non-metropolitan regions after completing their studies in urban centres.[10] The negative aspects

---

[10] Due to the nature of the Québec school system, young people who wish to pursue a specfic program of studies must to all intents and purposes leave the regions of their childhood to undertake, elsewhere—usually Montreal, Québec City or Sherbrooke—the CEGEP or university-level studies most relevant to their occupational goals.

of urban living seem to trigger an awareness of their attachment to their region of origin, where they feel not only well integrated, but also like full-fledged Quebecers. In contrast, they condemn the ghettoized ethnocultural groupings and Montrealers' stigmatizing attitude toward immigrants that they witnessed during their stay in the city. Paradoxically, it appears that these young people feel more visible and labelled in a cosmopolitan environment than they do in the more homogeneous region where they grew up. The long time they have spent in their regions, the relatively young age at which they arrived, the quality of their integration into the region, as well as the overall quality of regional life, would appear to explain, at least in part, their return to their region.[11] As the first place where they experienced personalized relationships with "old-stock" residents, the region of their childhood would seem to be a place that is conducive to putting down roots and developing a sense of belonging to Québec.

With regard to regional youth of immigrant origin who have settled in Montreal or Québec City, what emerges is a diametrically opposed position with respect to space. The characteristics that define overall quality of life will therefore be different for them. In their case, it is the urban and metropolitan setting that offers the greatest attraction, with its myriad of services and activities and its wide range of jobs, whereas the non-metropolitan regional space is more problematic, mainly owing to its demographic imbalance (the exodus of friends, etc.), and its poorer capacity to satisfy occupational aspirations and diversified tastes. While youth who settle in non-metropolitan regions regard the impersonal and individualistic nature of urban relationships as a disadvantage, young people in the group who have left the non-metropolitan regions value the anonymity afforded by big cities. A certain distancing from the region where they grew up, which is not offset by their attachment to family, is noted here. Montreal's ethnic diversity and the freedom to be a nonconformist and assert one's opinions are also factors that are appreciated. Might this in part be attributable to the fact that these young people of immigrant origin regard it as easier to blend in amidst such a cosmopolitan, impersonal crowd, much like the Haitian Montrealers who migrate to New York seeking to merge with the more numerous black Americans and thus become less visible? (Morin, 1993).

---

[11] The high percentage of "returning young people" (36%) was an unexpected finding of the study.

B. *Mobility, transnationalism and openness to the world*

Of the myriad of activities pursued by youth today, one particular type attracts greater attention. It has to do with experiences abroad: adventure travel, overseas study sessions, third-language learning (e.g. Spanish or English), and humanitarian aid trips, among others. Regional youth of immigrant origin are far from being isolated and shut off in a hermetic regional environment with no openness to the world beyond. In fact, the majority of them benefit from significant *mobility*[12] from early childhood on, as they usually spend their summer vacations in their parents' country of origin. In addition, some of them set off to explore the world on adventure trips ranging from six months to one year in length. Their desire for different experiences abroad leads them mainly to Europe, but also to Central or South America, and sometimes to the Middle East and India.[13] This mobility demonstrates to what extent immigrants are not confined to a single space, as shown by Alain Tarrius with his concept of *"territoires circulatoires"* [circulatory territories] (1992), and by other authors such as Kearney (1995), Glick Schiller et al. (1995) with the notion of transmigration, and Hannerz (1996), with the notion of transnational connections.

This contact with different countries, primarily the countries where their parents were born, constitutes a definite aspect of their family heritage. It helps these young people develop awareness of new horizons, broadens their skills and enriches their "social and cultural capital," in the sense given to this expression by Bourdieu (1979). It also constitutes an asset in the current context of globalization, for it opens the doorway to acquiring new knowledge and skills, such as resourcefulness and flexibility, which can be useful in their occupational integration. Through their transnational links with family in the country of origin or around the world, these young people benefit

---

[12] Maintaining the distinction made by Madeleine Gauthier's team between *internal migration patterns* and *mobility* in reference to young Quebecers, the word *mobility* is understood here to mean a temporary, usually short-term trip lasting a few months at most, primarily for the purpose of discovering the world or having an adventure.

[13] The adventure-travel destinations of these regional youth of immigrant origin differ from those of the regional youth of old stock who were investigated in the study conducted by Ms. Gauthier's team. The latter in fact travel more to western Canada (mainly Vancouver and Banff in British Columbia), or to the United States. A number of factors come into play here, including proximity, the absence of international family migration, the non-existence of extended family networks abroad, and differences in social class.

from a "window to the world," as do the Montreal youth of immigrant origin studied by Meintel (1993). This extended family network appears to serve not only as a destination, but also as a reassuring transition point or stopover haven during their journeys. It constitutes a social space replete with numerous resources that help them in their travels. In fact, these young people seem more interested in having new experiences and discovering the world than they do in pursuing a nostalgic search for roots as part of a quest for identity. As Meintel has bserved, this transationality is far from being counterproductive in terms of successful integration into the host society.

To what extent is this experience of travelling abroad common to all young people in Québec? Is it a feature of social class, given that these young people of immigrant origin generally speaking come from families with a high socio-economic standing and who are usually well educated? A few authors have shown that the children of international elites adopt certain values and practices resembling those described here. Thus, Wagner analyzes the "international culture" of foreign executives living in France, and observes that the latter do not want to "relinquish the benefits of having accumulated numerous cultural references" (1998: 216). The children of these executives praise diversity and the opportunity to learn several languages, value their family heritage, and seek global horizons and openness. This same phenomenon can be observed in regional youth of immigrant origin in Québec. Notably absent, however, is the severance and enclave effect observed in youth with elite immigration status in France who attend exclusive schools. Yet few authors have undertaken a comparison for the purpose of identifying the similarities and differences between the practices of youth of immigrant origin and youth of so-called "old stock" (descendants of the first colonists, in this case, mainly French and British) in this regard. This question has yet to be investigated, particularly in relation to the globalization context that fosters these international connections.

What conclusion can be drawn from this pluriactivity? In my view, one of the challenges presented by the contemporary problems young people face in their social and occupational integration is that of ensuring that the free time now available for new activities does not turn into "empty time," to use the expression coined by Jean-Louis Laville (1996: 67), either out of desperation or for want of doing something, with the concomitant risks of isolation and relative "desocialization" noted by Galland in unemployed youth (1991: 218).

Another challenge is to ensure that this individualization of occupational life-courses does not lead to profound disparities between youth who have the required skills and resources and others who, owing to a lack of "capital" as used by Bourdieu, are unable to cope with increasingly competitive and uncertain situations (Castel, 2001; Furlong and Cartmel, 1997). The data collected in this study do not allow for a more refined analysis of attitudes toward work in relation to the diverse social categories of youth. The weight of social determinants in this regard warrants further investigation.

4. *Innovative relationship to work*

The practices of youth in terms of work and their pluriactivity indicate the need to go beyond the traditional, restrictive concept of regular salaried work to encompass a multitude of other activities that bring a sense of meaning and personal fulfilment. Apart from formal work, it is therefore important to take into account their various other activities—volunteering, leisure, community, activitist, humanitarian, etc.—in order not to underestimate young people's relationship to work, nor to sideline activities that may have decisive importance in terms of meeting their needs for emancipation and fulfilment. A close interdependence exists between these varied modes of work, mainly through innovative links between the economic, social and cultural, as well as public and private, spheres in post-modern society.

Sociocultural transformations are unquestionably taking place in terms of the meaning of work, changes that are related to young people's desire for personal fulfilment and self-esteem (Cannon, 1994; Furlong and Cartmel, 1997; Kergoat et al., 1998; Roulleau-Berger, 1999; Zoll, 1992), as well as the search for new "identity spaces." Their search for a meaning to life goes beyond work, even if the latter remains an important referent in the construction of their social identities and their overall integration into society. New values underlie their relationship to work, among them, freedom, autonomy, creativity, self-fulfilment, social usefulness, intercommunication, and openness. These ultimately culminate in a "quality of life" which young people wish to be "overall," i.e. present in all aspects of their daily lives. This distance taken by youth toward salaried, formal work is noted in several countries, as evidenced in the comparative analysis carried out by Laurence Roulleau-Berger on youth and employment in Europe and North America (2001). The distancing process is fostered by the emergence of new values over and above the market and money. This disenchantment with salaried work is accompanied by a *"désengagement subjectif"* [subjective disengagement], to use Gorz's expression, marked by "the desire to balance work-employment by self-determined activities, the desire to be in charge of one's time, life, and choices and the achievement of one's goals" [translation] (Gorz, 1998: 37).

The search for a balance between two spheres (personal life/work), which was marked by a split in the preceding generation, the importance of informal activities and of personal fulfilment, control over one's time, the quest for quality of life, these are the key ideas needed to grasp this sociocultural transformation. The relationship to work is increasingly defined in terms of quality and freedom, even if young people are having to assume greater risk and uncertainty, as shown by Roulleau-Berger mainly through her concept of *"cultures de l'aléatoire"* [cultures of uncertainty] in a disintegrating wage-based society (1999), and by Furlong and Cartmel in their analysis of the "risk society" (1999). This relationship to work implies a new assumption of control by youth over their lives, as well as societal redefinition, a new choice of society which recognizes both the value of pluriactivity and the differentiated significance of metropolitan or regional (non-metropolitan) spaces in terms of quality of life, or the vital importance of control over one's time. Days and weeks are no longer structured in terms of salaried work alone, but also in terms of a host of other activities which offer greater freedom. This is particularly applicable in post-industrial societies, where increasing free time and time for oneself is becoming a growing priority for individuals (Zoll, 1992).

In a context of uncertainty where salaried work "ceases to be the pedestal on which each person can construct his life's project" [translation] (Gorz, 1998: 33) and find recognition for his varied skills and his dignity, young people are trying, in their own innovative ways, to invent and reconstruct the foundations for their societal recognition. And in a regional (non-metropolitan) space, this recognition will mainly be rooted in so-called "proximity" activities, as has already been observed by Castel (1996: 682), since young people will be able to fulfil themselves as social actors in terms of both their personal destiny and the future of their region (Simard, 1996, 1997). The original nature of this relationship to work thus becomes even more evident in the case of youth of immigrant origin who are living in non-metropolitan regions, since it overlaps with, for the most part, little analyzed aspects, such as the relationship to minimally urbanized spaces, nature, and the environment. An analysis of the relationship to work in non-metropolitan regions thus reveals a complex, rich and dynamic reality by bringing to light other facets than those usually examined in the metropolitan context. It adds nuances, primarily underscoring the different significance attached to "quality of life," depending on whether the young person lives in Montreal or a non-metropolitan region.

Bibliography

Aubert, France, Maryse Tripier and François Vourc'h (eds.). *Jeunes issus de l'immigration. De l'école à l'emploi*. Paris: CIEMI and L'Harmattan, 1997.

Bourdieu, Pierre. *La distinction. Critique sociale du jugement*. Paris: Les éditions de minuit, 1979.

Cannon, D. *Generation X and the New Work Ethic*. London: Demos, 1994.

Castel, Robert. "Les jeunes ont-ils un rapport spécifique au travail en France?" In *Les jeunes et l'emploi dans les villes d'Europe et d'Amérique du Nord*, edited by L. Roulleau-Berger and M. Gauthier, 287–298. France: Éditions de l'aube, 2001.

———. "Travail et utilité au monde." *Revue internationale du travail* 135, no. 6 (1996): 675–682.

Fouquet, Annie. "Travail, emploi, ou activité?" In *Le monde du travail*, edited by J. Ketgoat, J. Boutet, H. Jacot and D. Linhart, 228–238. Paris: Éditions La Découverte, 1998.

Furlong, Andy and F. Cartmel. *Young People and Social Change: Individualization and Risk in Late Modernity*. Buckingham: Open University Press, 1997.

Galland, Olivier. *Sociologie de la jeunesse: l'entrée dans la vie*. Coll. U. Série Sociologie. Paris: Armand Colin, 1991.

Gauthier, Madeleine (ed.). *Pourquoi partir? La migration des jeunes d'hier et d'aujourd'hui*. Québec City: Institut québécois de la recherche sur la culture, 1997.

Glick Schiller, Nina, Linda Basch and Cristina Szanton Blanc. "From Immigrant to Transmigrant: Theorizing Transnational Migration." *Anthropological Quarterly* 68, no. 1 (1995): 48–63.

Gorz, André. "Le travail fantôme." In *Le monde du travail*, edited by J. Kergoat, J. Boutet, H. Jacot and D. Linhart, 30–39. Paris: Éditions La Découverte, 1998.

Hannerz, Ulf. *Transnational Connections. Culture, People, Places*. London and New York: Routledge, 1996.

Kearney, M. "The Local and the Global: The Anthropology of Globalization and Transnationalism." *Annual Review of Anthropology*, no. 24 (1995): 547–565.

Kergoat, Jacques, Josianne Boutet, Henri Jacot and Daniele Linhart (eds.). *Le monde du travail*, 40–49. Paris: Éditions La Découverte, 1998.

Laville Jean-Louis. "Jeunesse, travail et identité sociale." *Sociologie et Sociétés* XXVIII, no. 1 (Spring 1996): 63–71. Special issue on youth, edited by Jacques Hamel.

Meintel, Deirdre. "Transnationalité et transethnicité chez des jeunes issus de milieux immigrés à Montréal." *Revue européenne des migrations internationales* 9, no. 3 (1993): 63–79.

Mimeault, Isabelle, Josianne LeGall and Myriam Simard. "Identités des jeunes régionaux de parents immigrés au Québec: métissage et ouverture sur le monde." In *Cahiers de recherche sociologique*, no. 36. Montreal: Université de Québec à Montréal, 2001.

Morin, Françoise. "Entre visibilité et invisibilité: les aléas identitaires des Haïtiens de New York et Montréal." Edited by M. Elbaz and F. Morin. *Revue européenne des migrations internationales* 9, no. 3 (1993): 147–176.

Roulleau-Berger, Laurence. *Le travail en friche. Les mondes de la petite production urbaine.* France: Éditions de l'Aube, 1999.

———. "Les jeunes et l'emploi dans les villes d'Europe et d'Amérique du Nord: entre affiliations, désaffiliations et résistances." In *Les jeunes et l'emploi dans les villes d'Europe et d'Amérique du Nord*, edited by L. Roulleau-Berger and M. Gauthier, 5–23. France: Éditions de l'Aube, 2001.

Simard, Myriam. "La régionalisation de l'immigration: les entrepreneurs agricoles immigrants dans la société rurale québécoise." *Recherches sociographiques* (Université Laval) XXXVI, no. 2 (May–August 1995): 215–242.

———. "La politique québécoise de régionalisation de l'immigration: enjeux et paradoxes." *Recherches sociographiques* XXXVII, no. 3, (1996): 439–469.

———. "Le discours entrepreneurial de l'État québécois et la rétention des jeunes en région." Chap. 7 in *Pourquoi partir? La migration des jeunes d'hier et d'aujourd'hui*, edited by M. Gauthier, 163–188. Sainte-Foy, Que.: PUL-IQRC, 1997.

———. "Définir la jeunesse d'origine immigrée: réflexions critiques à propos du concept de deuxième génération." Chap. 7 in *Définir la jeunesse? D'un bout à l'autre du monde*, edited by M. Gauthier and J.-F. Guillaume, 121–143. Sainte-Foy, Que.: PUL-IQRC, 1999.

Simard, Myriam, Isabelle Mimeault and Maryse Lévesque. "Insertion en emploi et pratiques migratoires des jeunes d'origine immigrée en région au Québec." In *Les jeunes et l'emploi dans les villes d'Europe et d'Amérique du Nord*, edited by L. Roulleau-Berger and M. Gauthier, 229–242. France: Éditions de l'Aube, 2001.

Tarrius, Alain. *Les fourmis d'Europe. Migrants riches, migrants pauvres et nouvelles villes internationales.* Paris: L'Harmattan, 1992.

Wagner, Anne-Catherine. *Les nouvelles élites de la mondialisation. Une immigration dorée en France.* Paris: PUF, 1998.

Zoll, Rainer. "Jeunes, sens du travail et nouvel individualisme en Allemagne." In *Les jeunes et l'emploi dans les villes d'Europe et d'Amérique du Nord*, edited by L. Roulleau-Berger and M. Gauthier, 261–271. France: Éditions de l'aube, 2001.

———. *Nouvel individualisme et solidarité quotidienne. Essai sur les mutations socio-culturelles.* Paris: Éditions Kimé, 1992.

WORK, YOUTH AND IMMIGRATION IN FRANCE

Claire Schiff[1]

France, like the Unites States, can be regarded as a Nation of immigrants, despite notable differences in these countries' historical narratives and national identities. The overall ratio of foreign born and citizens of immigrant descent as percentages of the total population is indeed quite similar on either side of the Atlantic ocean.[2] So too is the trend towards increasing numbers of arrivals from non-European countries.[3] Consequently, it appears that differences in ideological and political representations serve to explain the major contrasts between the two countries modes of inclusion and exclusion of immigrants and minorities more so than do factual and statistical considerations.[4]

In the American context, notions such as race and ethnicity are widely used when analyzing the situation of immigrants and minorities and when distinguishing various groups from one another. In France however such concepts are only just beginning to emerge in academic discussions and in the public sphere. Indeed, the dominant discourse still focuses mainly on the necessary 'assimilation'[5] of those who are still regarded first and foremost as foreigners. The idea that ethnic and racial minorities might exist as an integral but distinct part of French society is still perceived as a threat to the Republican ideal of a universal undifferentiated citizen, defined first and foremost by his or her legal status, and devoid of any particular cultural or ethnic allegiance.

Yet at the same time as this ideal of colorblindness and universal equality among citizens remains very much a part of French national identity, underlying and deep-seated cultural images of a

---

[1] Member of the Center for Sociological Analysis and Intervention (CADIS), teaches sociology at the University Victor Segalen in Bordeaux.
[2] Noiriel, G., *Le creuset français*, Le Seuil, Paris, 1988.
[3] Lebon, A., *Rapport annuel sur l'mmigration et la présence étrangère en France*, La Documentation Française, Paris, 1998.
[4] Horowitz, D. L., and Noiriel, G., (eds.) *Immigrants in Two Democracies: French and American Experience*, New York University Press, New York, 1992.
[5] Although the term 'integration' is more widely used nowadays.

racialized uncivilized Other, stemming from France's colonial past, are constantly being revived through stereotypes relating especially to second and third generation youth of African descent (from North and West Africa and the French West Indies). This tension or paradox between the generous undiscriminating, albeit somewhat ethnocentric, aspect of the French model of 'integration' and expressions of fear and rejection, often directed at the most culturally assimilated segments of the population of foreign descent, lies at the root of France's 'immigrant problem'. This contradiction reminds us of the 'American Dilemma' unveiled by Gunnar Myrdal's analysis of the treatment of blacks in the United States.[6] Although it is less pronounced in France, because not embodied in actual legal and political discrimination against a racially defined group.

In this paper we therefore propose to examine a few of the forms and consequences of the particular French 'dilemma' regarding the treatment of immigrant and minority youth as far as their modes of identification and their experiences of schooling and employment are concerned.

Old minorities and new immigrants: an uneasy cohabitation

Perhaps one of the more characteristic aspects of the particular French bind regarding its most visible ethnic minorities is the way in which the terminology used to designate racially stigmatized groups still largely reflects assimilationist categories. This is particularly true of those individuals originating from former French colonies. Although most young people of Arab origin living in France are not immigrants per say but native born minorities, they are still regarded as new arrivals. Consequently, the terms 'immigrant' or 'foreigner' have become euphemisms for those minorities whose membership in mainstream French society is often suspected of being partial because of their color, their historical link to former colonized people and their concentration in disadvantaged urban areas. Problems such as juvenile delinquency and school failure, which are more frequent in neighborhoods where one finds a high concentration of immigrant families, are spontaneously interpreted as signs of cultural incom-

---

[6] Lapeyronnie, D., 'Assimilation, mobilisation et action collective chez les jeunes de la seconde génération de l'immigration maghrébine', *Revue française de sociologie*, vol. 18, 1987.

patibility between the youth's family or community of origin and the values of the French middle-class, and rarely as a consequence of discrimination or as a side-effect of rapid acculturation.[7] The term 'jeunes de banlieue',[8] which is a common way of designating lower-class, mostly non-white youth, without overtly referring to any particular ethnic identity, reveals the extent to which issues of race, class, generation and urban segregation are intertwined in the French debate over questions that are nonetheless still largely subsumed under the label of 'le problème de l'intégration des immigrés'.

As for the young people themselves, it is interesting to observe the manner in which they deal with this tension between, on the one hand, their adherence to the national emphasis on assimilation and their departure from traditional immigrant culture and values, and, on the other hand, their experience of segregation and their feeling that they will never be considered fully French. The most salient aspect of these second and third generation youth's mode of identification is its ambivalence. It is at one and the same time open to racial, ethnic and cultural diversity and confined to rigid and entrenched oppositions between their own very localized community and those of wealthier neighborhoods as well as between their immediate peer group and the overall adult population (teachers, employers and parents).[9] Be they of Arab, African, West Indian or even French descent, when one asks these urban youth what is at the root of their sense of group membership they tend to downplay racial oppositions while emphasizing territorial and generational ones.

> Fabrice: Things work by neighborhood. What they call 'tough neighborhoods'. Each neighborhood is really stereotyped. It doesn't matter what you are, white or whatever... as a matter of fact there's less racism in those neighborhoods because the kids are often together. It makes no difference if the guy is white or arab, as long as he belongs to the neighborhood. If he's got a problem with someone in another neighborhood, his neighborhood will stand behind him. It's not a question of race, it's a question of clans, of neighborhoods, of gangs...

---

[7] Thomas, W. I. and Znanieki, F., *The Polish Peasant in Europe and America 1918–1920*. Ed. E. Zarensky. Chicago, University of Illinois Press, 1984.

[8] The American equivalent would be 'inner-city youth'. In France the term 'banlieue' (suburb) has somewhat the same connotation as the term 'ghetto'.

[9] Schiff, C., *Situation migratoire et condition minoritaire. Une comparaison entre les adolescents primo-arrivants et les jeunes de la deuxième génération vivant en milieu urbain défavorisé*, Thèse de Doctorat de sociologie, sous la direction de Michel Wieviorka, EHESS, 27 janvier, 2000.

Jean-Luc: For example, you have French guys in a project (cité) who grew up with blacks (les blacks). Well you wouldn't think they were really French. I know some guys, white guys, when we talk to them we call them "negro", because they're just like us. I mean they're white, but the way they dress, with the pants down to their knees, all that, you'd think they were black. There are those who've been hanging out with Arabs ever since they were born: it's like they're more Arab...

Tidiane: It's the same thing everywhere. It's not because I have a French friend that I won't help him if he's in trouble with guys from Ivry. It's not because we're always together, blacks and Arabs, that we don't like other races. We all grew up together. It's like they took the blacks and the Arabs and put them aside and all the kids grew up together. So it's normal that they're always together... Even when you go to Paris and you get in trouble with some other guys: you just have to tell them that you come from the 'banlieue', and if they're also from the 'banlieue', they understand and they leave you alone. It's a way of being, of dressing, of talking, of walking too. We recognize each other.

While in middle-class French society, overt references to racial, ethnic or religious traits are still somewhat taboo, these young urban minorities speak very freely about issues such as color, precisely because such characteristics are considered to be less significant than membership in the local urban community of multi-ethnic youth. Their modes of participation and identification both reflect and subvert the Republican ideal of 'integration'. In these neighborhoods the 'right of birthplace' (droit du sol) prevails over the 'right of parentage' (droit du sang) in the same way that the Republican model of citizenship emphasizes political participation over kinship ties. Yet one also observes a reversal of roles between the majority French (white) population and those minority groups generally considered to be the least likely to fully assimilate. Within the framework of popular culture, 'arabness' and 'blackness' become acquired traits, almost questions of taste and style characterising the majority of urban youth, and thus potentially shared by all those who are considered by society at large to be on the wrong side of the social and urban divide.

Because public attention is so exclusively focused on the 'problems' posed by these minority youth of African descent, little is known or written about the newest waves of immigrants, arriving mainly from third world countries such as Turkey, China, or the Indian continent, and who, in contrast to their predecessors, share no common history with the French. Initially these groups often settle in the same disadvantaged neighborhoods still inhabited by the previous generations of post-colonial immigrants, who are the parents and grandparents of todays minority youth. The contrast between the two populations is striking. These new immigrants have much stronger links to countries other than France. Because they often belong to international diasporas, they rarely identify with their local neighborhood community. Moreover, they often have no previous knowledge of the French language. They are often part of strong ethnic networks which provide them with jobs in specific sectors (garment trade, construction, restaurants).

As in the United States, changes in the composition of the immigrant population, increasing economic polarization, and worsening urban segregation all heighten the risk of downward assimilation for the children of immigrants.[10] For the most recent arrivals, the alternative is often between remaining in the safe haven of their relatively closed immigrant community and family network, or integrating within the juvenile community of their disadvantaged neighborhood. Moreover, lack of facility with the French language, as well as the absence of a colonial complex re French society, distinguish the newest arrivals from earlier non-European immigrants. For all the above reasons acculturation is both more difficult and less desirable for the most recent groups who are generally less sensitive to the opinions and assimilationist incentives of the majority population than are older minorities.

The second and third generation minority urban youth, previously cited, regard these new arrivals with a mixture of condescension and envy. While the dominant French discourse on immigrants still assumes that cultural assimilation is the prerequisite for economic success and upward mobility, these youths see for themselves that their new neighbors, while remaining culturally distinct, often suffer less from unemployment than they themselves do. They consider themselves to be culturally superior to groups such as the Turks or the Asians, because of their fluency in the French language and moores and their multi-racial social relations. Yet these second and third generation blacks

---

[10] Portes, A., and Zhou, M., 'The New Second Generation: Segmented Assimilation and its Variants', *Annals of the American Academy of Political and Social Science*, vol. 530, nov. 1993.

and North Africans also feel somewhat resentful of the fact that, having played according to the rules of the assimilationist Republican model, they do not reap the economic benefits which they and their parents were led to expect.

> Yasmina: The Hindus[11] have done better than we have. They know how to fend for themselves . . . They came just like the Arabs and the blacks. They had nothing, and now look at them: they're the ones who have more.

> Sandrine: You see them with Mercedes and everything. They stick together. I went to ask some Hindus for a job. They said: "No, we take only Hindus". They always work together, usually in the same family. They're not liked. Maybe it's jealousy because they've made out better than the others. The blacks, the Arabs, the Africans or whatever, who arrived before the Hindus, didn't make it like them. They don't help each other. There's no solidarity. A black guy thinks first about himself; not about helping someone else. If he has a job he's not going to say "I've got some work" or "There's a company that's hiring over there". He's more likely to give the job to a French person than to a black one.

The co-existence of these two different groups in disadvantaged and stigmatized neighborhoods occasionally leads to inter-ethnic conflicts or rather to scape-goating on the part of local youth who express their frustration through more or less organized forms of bullying and racketeering of recent immigrants and refugees.[12] Such violence has never however reached the same proportions as for instance the black-Korean conflict in American cities such as Los Angeles. Despite similarities in immigration trends and in the general transformation of the national economies, living conditions and the extent of racial segregation in the most disadvantaged urban areas of France are still much less severe than those encountered in inner-city ghettos in the United States.[13]

---

[11] This term is used by the urban youth to designate anyone from the Indian continent, regardless of nationality or religion.

[12] Schiff, C., 'Nouvelles jeunesses immigrées en France et aux Etats-Unis', *Agora-débats/jeunesses*, n° 22, 2000.

[13] Wacquant, L., 'Pour en finir avec le myte des 'cités-ghettos'. Les différences entre la France et les Etats-Unis'. *Les Annales de la Recherche Urbaine*, n° 54, 1992.

Trends in the schooling and employment of immigrant and minority youth

Having presented a few of the ways in which the French immigrant and minority experience, particularly that of urban youth, compares to the American one, let us now examine some current trends of inclusion and exclusion as they appear through data on schooling and employment.

First of all it is important to stress how much the accumulation of reliable data has been hindered by the traditional resistance to even considering the existence of minority groups, or the possible influence of ethnic factors on the academic and economic progress of immigrants and their children in French society. Until very recently, large scale surveys accounted mainly for differences between French nationals and foreigners (i.e. legal status) and between the various social classes as measured by occupation. The result is that, within the framework of academic research, immigrants and minorities, and especially young people, are defined essentially by their legal or social status.[14] Rarely are the effects of ethnicity or of factors such as age on arrival seriously analyzed as possible causes of mobility or lack thereof. Moreover, comparative analyses tend to stress differences between the main stream French population and the immigrant population taken as a whole in an attempt to 'measure' the latter's distance from the norm and its progress along an evolutionary path towards complete assimilation. Research systematically comparing different immigrant or minority groups amongst themselves is virtually nonexistent.

A few recent quantitative studies do, however, offer some information regarding differences between the academic and professional achievements of first and second generation youth belonging to the various immigrant minorities. One such study carried out by the demographer Michèle Tribalat raised a very heated debate because it proposed to distinguish between French youth born of immigrant parents and immigrant youth and between a few of the main ethnic groups present within certain nationalities (such as the Arabs vs. the Berbers, the Kurds vs. the Turks, etc.).[15] Much of the criticism

---

[14] Silberman, R., 'French Immigration Statistics' in: Horowitz and Noiriel (eds.), op. cit.

[15] Tribalat, M., *Faire France. Une enquête sur les immigrés et leurs enfants*. Paris, La Découverte, 1995.

directed at this study was based not so much on scientific evaluation of its methodology and representativity, but rather on political and ideological concerns. Many critics denounced the risk of a 'balkanisation' of French society, considered to be an inevitable consequence of demographic categorizations which take immigrant descent and ethnic factors into account.[16] Another large-scale study on the educational achievement of first and second generation immigrant pupils examines the effect of previously ignored factors on progress in school, such as the number of years spent in the country of origin prior to emigration.[17]

In addition to these statistical surveys which make it easier to distinguish between the social trajectories of the different ethnic groups and between the various generations of young people born of immigrant parents, an increasing number of qualitative ethnographic studies analyze the effect of the local environment in disadvantaged neighborhoods on schooling and economic opportunities available to immigrant and minority youth and the particular forms of discrimination from which they suffer.[18] These works offer a much more complex picture of the situation of young people born of immigrant parents than the traditional image of a homogeneously 'disadvantaged' group.

All other things being equal, when one observes academic progress over the long term, second generation status constitutes a slight academic advantage for the major ethnic groups (North African, African, Asian, Southern European).[19] The most discriminating factor is age on arrival, especially among such non-French speaking groups as the Turks, the Southeast Asians, and the Portuguese. Those arriving after the age of twelve are more likely to leave school without having obtained a high-school level diploma.[20] Moreover, recent arrivals

---

[16] Le bras, H., *Le démon des origines. Démographie et extreme droite*. Paris, L'Aube, 1998.

[17] Vallet, L.-A. et Caille, J.-P., *Les élèves étrangers ou issus de l'immigration dans l'école et le collège français*. Les dossiers d'éducation et formation du Ministère de l'Education Nationale, n° 67, Avril 1996.

[18] Payet, J.-P., *Collèges de banlieue. Ethnographie d'un monde scolaire*. Méridiens-Klincksiek, 1995.

Roulleau-Berger, L., *Le travail en friches. Les mondes de la petite production urbaine*, Editions de l'Aube, 1999.

Tarrius, A., *Arabes de France dans l'économie mondiale souterraine*, Editions de l'Aube, 1995.

[19] Vallet et Caille, op. cit., p. 112.

[20] Brinbaum, Y., *Age d'entrée en France et situation professionnelle des immigrés*. Mémoire de DEA de sciences sociales, Université de Paris V et Lasmas, septembre 1994.

have a much higher chance than other pupils of being tracked into special education classes which are not adapted to their particular situation since they are meant for children with intellectual deficiencies or rather severe psychological problems.[21] Academic achievement as measured by the length of study and the proportion of young people who go into the non-professional high-schools, leading to the more prestigious general baccalaureate, as opposed to the professional ones, leading to vocational or blue-collar training programs, is highest among pupils of African, especially Algerian, descent. This latter group appears to be the only group in which arrival during childhood actually constitutes an additional advantage in terms of social mobility, since foreign born Algerians are more likely than their French born counter-parts to obtain a university diploma and to reach white collar status, even though they overwhelmingly come from working class households.[22] Clearly, higher achievement motivation among first generation children and adolescents, as compared to second generation pupils, account for this difference. To the extent that Algerians are at least partially francophone upon arrival, the language barrier does not impede the positive attitudes towards schooling associated with the experience of emigration the way it does for recent arrivals from the Asian continent for example, who despite equally high achievement motivation, suffer from their lack of familiarity with the French language.

These observations lead us to conclude that in its overall treatment of first and second generation immigrant youth, the French school system does not so much discriminate according to racial or ethnic membership as it does according to immigrant status or language fluency in French. Compared to the American school system, French methods for teaching to language minorities and procedures for progressive integration of immigrant pupils in mainstream classes are indeed very inadequate. In most schools little is done to evaluate the students' level in their own language upon arrival and most teachers unconsciously regard poor mastery of French as a sign of low academic potential, often even as a sign of intellectual deficiency.[23] This is a result of the strong assimilationist ideology entrenched in

---

[21] Vallet et Caille, p. 152.
[22] Tribalat, op. cit., pp. 143–147.
[23] Schiff, C., 'Les adolescents primo-arrivants au collège. Les contradictions de l'intégration dans un univers en tension', *VEI enjeux/migrants-formation*, n° 125, juin 2001.

the French public school system, and of the belief that differential treatment of pupils, especially regarding factors linked to foreign status, inevitably lays the ground for inequality and discrimination. In such a rigidly 'egalitarian' system, which leaves little time and space for the necessary adaptation of late arrivals, immigrant pupils must either sink or swim. Indeed, the schooling patterns of recent immigrants youth indicate two major alternatives: early dropout and rapid entry into the lower echelons of the job market for the majority or marked success and over achievement within the academic institution for a minority of recent arrivals.[24]

Compared to first generation immigrants, second and third generation youth, particularly those belonging to the most visible minorities, tend to remain in school even when they are experiencing difficulties. Indeed, they hope to eventually gain access to intermediate or higher level diplomas which they consider necessary for their successful entry into the job market, especially given their lack of social networks and the absence of economic niches among immigrants of African descent. Until fairly recently, the fact that Arab youth tended to persevere in their studies despite their working class origins was considered to be a premonitory sign of assimilation to the French middle class. However, recent studies which analyze the link between schooling and employment indicate that young people of Algerian and to a lesser extent of Moroccan descent suffer from a notable discrepancy between educational achievement and economic integration.[25] While those who do find work often enter white collar or professional occupations, the rates of unemployment are particularly high, reaching 40% among those aged twenty to twenty-nine born of Algerian and Moroccan parents.[26] Unemployment rates are even higher among black African youth, especially among foreign born young women (47%) who suffer from obstacles linked to their sex (female unemployment is generally 10% higher than male), their color and their lack of efficient economic networks. This situation seems particularly worrysome when compared to that of Portuguese youth, who, regardless of whether they are born in France or abroad, experience particularly low rates of unemployment (5%

---

[24] Vallet et Caille, op. cit.
[25] Silberman, R. 'Formation scolaire et insertion professionnelle des enfants d'immigrés', *Formation Emploi*, n° 65, 1999.
[26] Tribalat, op. cit., p. 175.

less than youth born of French parents), even though their educational achievements are lower than their North African counterparts. Similarly to the Portuguese, young Turks, who are mostly foreign born and who usually enter vocational training, have relatively low rates of unemployment since they easily find jobs in the garment industry and in construction, where their networks lie.

Many young people, especially those who have not obtained a high-school or university degree, spend several years in various vocational training institutions, government assisted programs and apprenticeship jobs before their professional situation becomes stable. The French system offers a wide variety of intermediary measures meant to ease the transition between school and work, some of which have relatively weak links with the actual job market. A detailed analysis of the distribution of the various immigrant groups across these different training programs reveals two different patterns of introduction into the job market.[27] Young people of Algerian and West African descent are over represented in government sponsored placement programs mostly connected to the public sector, while the Portuguese, and to a lesser extent the Turks, the Asians and the Moroccans more often have access to apprenticeship jobs that require the young person to find an employer by his or her own means in small and medium sized businesses, often owned by compatriots. It is therefore possible to distinguish between those who depend upon public assistance programs for their initial introduction into the job market and those who depend upon their community's informal ethnic networks. The first group is made up essentially of the children of post-colonial immigrants whose parents were employed mainly in large industry before the massive downsizing which took place during the seventies and eighties. The second group is made up of more recent immigrant youth whose parents are more likely to be ethnic entrepreneurs, or to be employed in the growing informal or service sectors.

It appears thus that the link between educational achievement and entry into the job market is not necessarily a linear one for immigrant and minority youth, as it is for youth born of French parents for whom higher academic acheivement is almost always correlated with lower rates of unemployment. Contrary to popular belief, culturally assimilated minority youth of African descent are not particularly disadvantaged in schooling, certainly no more so than other

---

[27] Lebon, 1995/96, op. cit., p. 51.

pupils of working class origin. However, they do suffer from disproportionately high rates of unemployment. Inversely, recent arrivals, particularly from non-French speaking countries are clearly handicapped within the school system, yet their access to jobs (albeit precarious and unqualified ones) often seems better assured than second and third generation youth. This paradox in and of itself undermines the Republican model of integration which stresses equal opportunity based solely on individual merit regardless of creed or color, and which most second generation youth have come to believe in quite strongly as a result of their socialization within the French school system. Indeed, research increasingly shows that ethnic and racial factors do influence mobility, especially within the job market.[28] This threat to the French model of integration may be stronger than that posed by scientific attempts at counting or categorizing according to race or ethnicity.

The case of minority youth in apprenticeship programs

The contradiction between a school system which refuses to openly acknowledge differences linked to ethnicity or immigrant status and a job market, which increasingly exploits and reinforces racial differences as determining factors in the distribution of economic roles and function, creates a particular dilemma for minority youth. This is most apparent in instances when the two systems must interact such as is the case with apprenticeship training programs requiring young people to alternate between work and school. Our study of two such institutions offering training in various service trades to approximately 1500 young people aged 16 to 25 living in a disadvantaged urban district of the Parisian periphery, revealed systematic forms of racial discrimination and profiling in several types of occupation.[29]

The director of one of these trade schools explained how difficult it was to find internship positions for her non-white apprentices (approximately 50% of the student population).

> It's obvious, in hairdressing, the employers (maîtres d'apprentissage) prefer white youngsters. They explain this by saying that it's because of the clientele, given the nature of black women's hair, they're likely

---

[28] Bataille, P. *Le racisme au travail*. Paris, La Découverte, 1995.
[29] Schiff, 2000, op. cit., pp. 287–318.

not to know how to deal with people who don't have kinky hair. There are, however, a lot of North African girls in hairdressing. It's just that the bosses ask them to change their first name at work, which they accept fairly easily. (...) Some of the black girls find internships in Afro-Caribbean salons. That works out really well. The problem is that what they learn here in our training program doesn't prepare them for doing that sort of hair styling. When the girls get into afro salons they're delighted, because after that they have an easier time finding employment. If we had more of them it would be much easier for us to place our apprentices. (...) In beauty salons there is a distinct preference for whites. Employers never say that they themselves don't like them (non-whites), but always that it's because of the clientele. In sales, there's a clear rejection of the entire black and North African population. If they're accepted, they don't come in contact with the clients. Except for sportswear stores, where we succeed pretty well in placing the black boys. They are well aware of what their 'market' is. Not when they leave school, but after the training program. Sometimes in sales employers say: "I'll take one (non-european apprentice) if its not too obvious". In the bakery trade it's impossible to place blacks and Arabs in sales positions (where they take only girls), but sometimes we do in production jobs.

The director of the other trade school was much more reserved about the issue of racial discrimination, considering this problem to be beyond the scope of her function as an academic administrator. While she acknowledged the existence of widespread discriminatory practices among potential employers, she rejected the idea that the school's training and placement program should take such a reality into account. For example, regarding the placement of black girls in hairdressing salons, she emphasized the fact that the requirements for obtaining the diploma after a two year training period did not include Afro-Caribbean styling techniques. She concluded from this that it would be undesirable to increase the number of such salons in their partnership program.

In effect, since these girls have very few chances of finding apprenticeship positions outside of ethnic salons, what they learn in school is of limited use in their job search and what they learn during their internship is not acknowledged by the examination program's requirements. Such a double-bind illustrates the paradox created by the passage from a school system whose credo is identical treatment of pupils regardless of actual differences, into a job market that gives more credence to ethnic and racial profiles than it does to acquired knowledge and experience.

Conclusion

As in the United States, the contradiction between the aspirations born of cultural assimilation and the economic reality of a relatively segregated job market creates a context in which strategies of selective assimilation become increasingly attractive for recent arrivals as a way of avoiding unemployment and integration into the local urban communities of frustrated minority youths.[30] While initially, most recent immigrant teenagers express a strong desire to find work outside of their community, when the time comes for them to enter the job market, and given the obstacles (particularly the language barrier) to their educational pursuit, they have little choice but to depend upon the economic niches created by the previous generation, and often find themselves in a better situation than native born non-european youth.

One of the major differences between the French and American situation regarding the comparative academic and professional prospect of immigrant and minority youth, lies in the fact that in France there does not yet exist a social and racially defined group such as inner city blacks, disadvantaged both in schooling and employment. In this sense French born youth of North African descent do not clearly constitute an 'involuntary' or 'caste' minority as defined by John Ogbu,[31] since many continue to display specifically immigrant characteristics, such as high achievement motivation in school, and characteristics which are typical of discriminated minorities, such as heightened sensitivity to racial and ethnic stereotyping and occasional participation in collective forms of political mobilization against various forms of discrimination.[32] The main problem for these young adults is the discrepancy between the experiences and expectations developed in school and the reality they face upon entering the job market. It is quite possible however, that for those presently still of secondary school age, increasing awareness of the existence of a job

---

[30] Gans, H. J., 'Second-generation decline: scenarios for the economic and ethnic future of the post-1965 American immigrants', *Ethnic and Racial Studies*, vol. 15, n° 2, april 1992.
Fernandez-Kelly, P., 'Divided Fates: Immigrant Children in A Restructured US Economy', *International Migration Review*, vol. 28, n° 4, 1994.
[31] Ogbu, J., *Minority Education and Caste: The American System in Cross-Cultural Perspective*, Academic Press, 1978.
[32] Lapeyronnie, op. cit.

ceiling will become an incentive for them to develop anti-school sentiments and more entrenched forms of oppositional ethnic identities than one finds among their elders. Indeed those who have recently come of age often experience a form of blocked mobility which prolongs their adolescent status making it difficult for them to leave the parental household. For instance, young women of Algerian descent experience particularly high rates of celibacy,[33] since they tend to reject the traditional immigrant practice of arranged marriages with men living in their country of origin, yet find few economically independent partners among their male peers.

A significant proportion of post-colonial second and third generation youth are thus trapped in an ambiguous position between on the one hand assimilation to the French norms of consumption and values of individualism and on the other their identification as 'outsiders' by the majority population. Such a mismatch between aspirations and imposed roles, between identity and identification are particularly apparent among those living in disadvantaged urban settings.[34]

Today French society is only just waking up to the fact that the national consensus concerning the necessary 'integration' of its non-European minorities, besides being a rallying call for French Republicanism, might also be a very contradictory injection and an often painful process for those most directly involved. One might hope that increasing awareness of the discrepancies between social reality and national ideology might encourage the French, not so much to revise their universalist ideals, as to pay closer attention to those daily injustices which undermine the foundation of their democracy.

---

[33] 38% of young women of Algerian descent aged 25 to 29 are married, against a national norm of 48%, Tribalat, p. 181.

[34] Roulleau-Berger, op. cit., pp. 118–126.

CHANNELING LATINO YOUTH INTO THE LOW-WAGE TRAP: RACE AND CLASS POLARIZATION IN CALIFORNIA

Julio Juan Cammarota

In the United States, the rise of service industries and global economic restructuring has polarized the general occupational structure as well as social relations. This new economy produces jobs that fall primarily into diametrical—high and low skill—categories. I argue that 'job market polarization' along with low levels of educational attainment may contribute to channeling young Latinos into low skill jobs. Because entrance into high skill employment requires a college degree, low educational attainment among Latinos could explain their tendency to fill low-wage positions. In addition, I discuss how California restructured its economy, integrated into global markets, and expanded the service sector with a general reduction in wages and immigrant labor from Latin America. With the general depression of wages and the employers' desire for cheap immigrant labor, Latinos in California encounter the bulk of their employment opportunities in low-skill job markets. Severe racial inequalities in the California education system prevent Latino youth from attaining the credentials that would help them move up the occupational structure. Because job options for Latinos remain limited to low-wage services and whites continue to receive better educational and occupational opportunities, race and class polarization has emerged as a distinctive feature of California's social composition.

A report on youth in California indicates that Latinos will make up 42% of all adolescents in the state by 2005, thus becoming the largest racial group of young people in California (Fernandez 2000). With new immigrants and children of immigrants adding to this rapid population growth, young Latinos undoubtedly will become a significant portion of the workforce and play a major role in the state's future.[1] However, with the restructuring of the economy from

---

[1] The 2000 Census shows that Latinos contributed to three-fourths of California's 4.1 million population growth over the past decade, from 1990–2000 (Ness 2001). Half of the new Latinos (2 million) added to the state population within this period

manufacturing to service industries, they will enter a challenging world of work that bears the distinct structural feature of employment 'polarization' (Sassen 1998). In the service economy, job growth occurs either within low-skill/low-wage employment, including food preparation, cleaning, or domestic services, or high-skill/high-wage employment in finance, technology, or communication. Because schools often fail Latino students and high-skill employment requires a minimum of a college degree, they will most likely end up in jobs on the low-skill side of the occupational structure.

As young Latinos continue to encounter limited employment and educational opportunities, low-skill service jobs might become somewhat exclusive destinations for them. A high concentration of Latino youth at the bottom of the occupational structure may signify the emergence of an 'apartheid-like' political economic system. Although racial and ethnic diversity abounds in California, Latinos and whites are the two largest population segments yet maintaining the most extreme differences with regards to wealth and income status. One of the fastest growing segments of the population (i.e. young Latinos between the ages of sixteen and twenty-four) tends to fill the jobs with the worst pay and conditions while the diminishing white population retains access to better and higher paying positions.

This article describes how the 'polarized' organization of labor in conjunction with low levels of educational attainment may limit young Latinos' choices when negotiating their future in the world of work. I discuss, specifically, the way in which the global political economy tends to lower Latinos to the bottom of the workforce by relying on Latino (immigrant and non-immigrant) labor to expand low-wage job markets in the United States. California is a prime example of an economic region within the Unites States that expands low-wage job markets by using Latino workers. The discussion also examines the education system's role in engendering racial polarization between whites and Latinos by perpetuating the academic success of the former and failure of the latter. Schools continue to confer to white students the credentials they need to secure high-paying employment

---

were new births. A study by David Hayes Bautista, director of the Center for the Study of Latino Health and Culture at UCLA, discovered that 64% of Latino mothers were first generation immigrants (John 2001). In California, 43% of all children younger than 18 are Latino (Ness 2001). Latinos now comprise one-third of the entire California population; immigrants and children of immigrants greatly contribute to this rapid population growth among Latinos in the state.

yet fail to promote the educational attainment of Latino students, which relegates them to the low-wage trap. The challenges Latinos face as they enter the workforce include significant economic and educational barriers that can prevent them from moving up the occupational structure.

Polarization and the channeling of Latinos into the service economy

Following the 1940s in the postwar era, young workers frequently secured high-paying and skilled employment with no more, or sometimes less, than a high school education. Good paying jobs requiring minimal education often helped many poor or working class individuals achieve middle class dreams. However, today it is somewhat rare to attain social and economic mobility without a college degree or though work experience alone. In the contemporary service-based economy, job growth moves in two diametrical directions, what sociologist Saskia Sassen describes as 'polarization' in the organization of labor (Sassen 1991; Sassen 1994; Sassen 1998). This polarization generates only two job markets: a primary market with high skill/wage jobs in financial, business, communication, and technological services, and a secondary market with extremely low skill/wage jobs in food services and preparation, house and child care, retail, etc. Most jobs in the primary market require a college education while a formal education is often unnecessary for employment in the secondary market. An intermediary market with positions for skilled workers without a college education is almost non-existent in contemporary service industries. Furthermore, most new jobs added to the US service-based economy appear in the low-skill secondary market. Sassen reviews projections from the US Bureau of Labor Statistics that indicate that service industries "will account for about half of total US employment growth between 1992 and 2005" (1998, 143). The job category that will see the greatest expansion is low-wage services, with almost half of these jobs being positions in food-related work (Sassen 1998, 143 footnote 6).[2] Entering the service workforce without a college degree leaves young workers few, if any, options for obtaining work with descent wages.

---

[2] One estimate has fast food jobs rising to an amazing total of 250,000 by 2006 (Mead 1998). Employment projections produced by the Bureau of Labor Statistics

Moreover, the US workforce is not only polarized by job markets but also by race. People of color, particularly Latinos, tend to be over-represented in low paying service jobs in the United States.[3] In food preparation and service occupations alone, Latinos (sixteen years old and over) represent almost 17% of the workforce; their share dramatically increased from 7% to 17% between 1983 and 2000 (Statistical Abstract of the United States 2001). On the other pole of the labor force, things look somewhat different. For example, while the share of Latino fast food servers witnessed an intense seventeen-year period of growth, the share of Latino systems analysts rose only from 2.7% to 3.6%, less than one percentage in seventeen years.[4] Statistics from 1997 show that this job category was still over-represented by white males, whereas Latinos were failing to head in that direction in the new, bifurcated service economy. The contemporary opportunity structure is significantly marked by a polarization between races, necessitating specific attention for understanding why Latinos tend to fill low-wage service jobs.

Before delineating the economic circumstances pushing young Latinos into the service workforce, it is important to discuss the dramatic shifts in the US economy over the last two decades that led to the financial pressures facing immigrant families. As a result of the crisis of postwar capitalism and rise of foreign competitors, the US economy integrated into multiple global markets (production, consumer, and labor). The globalization of the economy as well as the rise of service industries imposed a downward push on wages and an increase in demand for immigrant labor. The following section discusses how these economic processes developed in California and affected the Latinos living there.

---

indicate that food preparation and service occupations will provide more new jobs than any other service occupation, almost 5 million new openings between 1996 and 2006. See table 2, Employment by Occupation, 1996 and Projected 2006 (US Bureau of Labor Statistics 1997).

[3] According to economist Charles Lieberman, nearly 40% of those filling new jobs in 1996 were Latino, yet they comprise only 10% of the US population (1997).

[4] Systems analyst is the 'work' that economist Robert Reich referred to in *The Work of Nations* when he argued that the strength of the US economy depended not on the wealth of America's corporations but on the type of work its citizens contributed to the global economy (Reich 1991). While he was right about the economic importance of data manipulation in the new millennium, he also predicted that the Latino percentage of system analysts would increase (1991, 179).

Transforming the economy and establishing flexibility in labor

In the postwar period, the Fordist model of mass production and consumption shaped the US economy, with economic prosperity hinging on a steady growth of domestic markets, high levels of employment, and decent wages. During the 1970s, Fordist production, however, encountered a profound crisis that unleashed a series of problems requiring economic restructuring. The US domestic market reached a point in which effective demand for consumer-durable goods began to tail-off because more products existed than people capable of consuming them. This 'saturation' of consumer and production markets led to disastrous consequences, including over-production, unused productive capacity, surplus of goods and money, and high unemployment rates (Davis 1986). By 1973, these conditions had fully emerged and the steady, unmitigated growth that rendered the US economy number one in the world ran into the constraints.

External pressure of foreign competition compounded the effects from these constraints. Western Europe and Japan were also experiencing saturation and began to look for overseas markets for their excess production. The destination for much of this surplus was the United States, location of largest consumer market in the world. The sluggishness of the US economy, the availability of cheaper foreign goods and, as Robert Reich asserts, "sometimes at higher levels of quality" meant the arrival of full fledged competition (1991, 70).

The response to save high profits from the competition and saturation was limited by what geographer David Harvey calls 'rigidity' within Fordist production (Harvey 1990, 142). The increased competitive environment forced US firms to adopt an approach to production organized around the notion of flexibility, which meant firms had to become 'lean,' reduce costs for high profits, and set pricing to contend with global competitors (Piore and Sabel 1984). The primary means for achieving low costs was the reduction of wages at all levels of production. Therefore, leanness and cost reduction were accomplished at the expense of gains achieved by labor during the postwar era. Standing in the way of cost reduction were collective bargaining, long-term labor contracts, high wages, benefits, and large payrolls. The strategy to reduce costs turned into "a matter of flexibility in who is hired, for how long, for how much, and for which tasks" (Bernhardt and Bailey 1998, 19). However, 'working class power' precluded any major adjustments for lowering wages and limiting most labor contracts to temporary or part-time arrangements (David 1986; Harvey 1990; Lash and Urry 1987). Therefore, the political economic project for firms interested in retaining high profits despite global competition necessitated the busting of unions and the weakening of labor power.

US industries accomplished this project through three cost reduction and labor weakening strategies: expanding into third world labor markets; relocating production from the Northeastern manufacturing centers to the Southwest region (most notably California); and allocating new domestic jobs to immigrants (primarily from Latin America). These strategies rolled back the gains in worker rights and wages attained though unionization during the post-war period.[5] In the post-Fordist age of flexibility, wages dramatically fell in all sectors as a consequence of the weakening of labor.

While the Great Lakes region served as a center for postwar manufacturing, California undoubtedly became the center for Sunbelt development, with its wide variety of industries and economic potential (manufacturing, high tech, aerospace, computers, agriculture, tourism, finance, service, etc.). By 1990, the California economy was larger than the economies of most countries in the world, as gross domestic product reached almost 800 billion dollars (California Statistical Abstract 1997). Between 1979 and 1988, a critical moment of Sunbelt development, California added 2.6 million jobs, 1/6 of all new jobs in the US (Walker 1995, 44). Most of these new jobs were added to retail and service industries, which contributed to over half of California's 12 million jobs. Between 1991–95 a recession hit California and poverty rates soared to 17%, unemployment reached 10%, and job loss figures climbed to 400,000. Despite the recession's severity, California quickly returned to preeminence, maintaining one of the strongest economies in the world. Gross state product declined by an average of 1% (in constant dollars, 1992) yearly throughout the recessionary period, but by 1994 the recession was

---

[5] The representation of unions throughout America's workplace declined rapidly; from the late 70's to the early 90's, union membership fell from 24% to 16% of the workforce (Topolnicki, 1993). In that same period, the average wage for a production worker dropped 9% (Ibid.). Therefore, an attendant drop in overall wages appeared with the decline in union membership rolls. At the height of postwar prosperity (1955–1970) real wages, adjusted for inflation, grew on the average of 2.5% annually (Kacapyr, Francese et al. 1996). A different story emerged between the years of 1971 and 1994: average wage growth barely reached 0.3% a year (Ibid.).

waning as growth jumped back up to 2% annually (California Statistical Abstract 1997). Between 1997 and 1998, the state added 375, 000 new jobs while unemployment reached its lowest point in eight years (California Budget Project 1998). In that same period, personal income rose by 7.3 percent (Ibid.). The recession was clearly in decline after 1995 and growth had again returned to the California economy.

A price reducing, flexible allocation of labor has been critical for economic growth in California's multiple economic sectors. Many California employers kept labor costs down and prices competitive by avoiding long term contracts of unionized labor and acquiring temporary and part-time workers, sub-contractors, women, and most importantly, "less expensive and more malleable" immigrant labor (Rouse 1995, 365). The close proximity of Mexico and "almost half of its workforce unemployed or underemployed and real wages plummeting under the current IMF austerity" positioned the country as a primary source for California's thirst for cheap labor, giving the low wage workforce its Latino character (Davis 1986, 221).

Not much can disguise the fact that the employers' demand for Latinos is predicated on labor exploitation and the elevation of profits. From 1980 to 1990 profits from hiring Latino workers rose from 25 billion to 85 billion (Walker 1995, 64). The California Department of Employment Development reports that Latinos (sixteen years old and over) in California comprise a significant percentage of workers in several occupational categories: 60% of private household services (i.e. domestic workers, gardeners, etc.); 48% of cleaning and building services (i.e. janitors); and 36% in food preparation and services (i.e. cooks, dishwashers, etc.).[6] The rise of immigrant labor in California was accompanied by a decline in union representation. According to the state's Division of Labor Statistics, 40.8% of Californian workers in 1954 were in unions. By 1989, the number was halved to 19.1%. The decline of unions and rise of immigrant labor depressed wages while the economic growth and profits resulting from wage depression benefited only the wealthiest segment of the state's population.

By repressing worker power and avoiding unionization, the employers' use of immigrant workers became the third cost reduction

---

[6] I would suspect that these percentages are low, since undocumented labor is quite common within these occupations. Undocumented workers are not usually reported to the state, so their numbers would not be included in official occupation totals.

strategy that achieved lower labor costs. A 1997 study by Karen Hossfeld revealed that high tech companies in San Jose's Silicon Valley hired immigrant women for low-paid work simply "because they complain less" and "don't organize unions."[7] By hiring non-union immigrant workers, employers have greater flexibility over various aspects of the labor process, including wages, length and kind of contract, work hours, application and skill requirements. An employer in Silicon Valley admitted that he prefers migrants because "people don't get as upset as if you were laying off regular workers."[8] Racism against immigrant groups encourages society in general to be indifferent toward the plight and workplace conditions for immigrant workers, thus colluding with their exploitation.[9] The passage of state propositions 187 (denying undocumented immigrants public resources) and 227 (removing bi-lingual education from public schools) are clear examples of political forces within California attempting to deny Latino immigrant groups entrance into the American citizenry and render them nothing more than cheap laborers. The tenuous social position of immigrants makes it difficult for them to take action against employers.

Class, race, and Latino families in California

Although California's economy is among the world's best, the absence of a defined middle income strata imposes the graphic image of an hourglass onto wage distribution patterns. Since the 1980s, the state has experienced a continuous widening of the income chasm.[10] Almost twenty years after the opening of this chasm, the other end of the income distribution remains a dismal reality. After an adjustment for inflation, wages in California have been in steady decline since 1989

---

[7] Karen Hossfeld's study of immigrant women workers in Silicon Valley is reported in Manned by Women *San Francisco Examiner*. July 14 1997: C-1.

[8] Ibid.

[9] Kevin R. Johnson provides a useful and general discussion of racism against Latinos and Latino immigrants in the United States (1998).

[10] Richard Walker states, "the yawning chasm between the classes that opened in the United States in the 1980's left it with the most unequal income distribution of all the wealthy countries, and California led the pack along with the rest of the Sunbelt states. Those who owned capital did spectacularly well. California's jetstream of fast track entrepreneurs and rentier families more than doubled to over 340,000 millionaires" (1995, 48).

(California Budget Project 1998).[11] The decline in wages and disparity of earnings between the top and bottom has maintained California's hourglass income distribution. This wage gap occurs from the rising income of the state's wealthy and from a steady decline among workers in the middle to lower income brackets (Reed 1999).

Income disparity and wage depression have placed many Californian households in financial trouble. The poverty rate in California, increasing 63% since 1980, climbed above the national rate to 18% of the population in 1993, placing California in the top seven states in poverty rates. Although the 2000 Census reports that the California poverty rate has declined to 16%, the rate of poverty in California is still higher than the national average of 13.3%. Unsurprisingly, because of wage depression, most poor families in 1996 had at least one or more adults employed at some point during the year (California Budget Project 1996). Within California's low wage environment, even a full-time worker in a poor household cannot provide enough income to change substantially the family's economic situation. Some 63% of the adults in working-poor families were employed full-time during the previous year (Ibid.). Contrary to popular belief, poor families in California receive most their income from wages and not government assistance. For those poor families with at least one employed individual, 88% of their income derives from wages; government assistance provides only 5% of the income for working families living in poverty (Ibid.).

Since immigrants significantly fill California's low-wage markets and at least 20% of the state's population are foreign born from Latin America, it is hardly surprising that Latinos represent a substantial portion of the working poor (Reed 1999). Fifty-three per cent of California's working poor families are of Latin American origin (California Budget Project 1996). The portion of working poor Latinos rises to 66% among working families with children (Ibid.). The economic situation for many Latino families living in California is somewhat distressing, because Latino workers often hold jobs with wages that confine them to poverty. Therefore, the income hourglass is

---

[11] From 1979 to 1997, wages have dropped for the bottom 80% of California's income earners, while the top 10% escaped the wage depression syndrome (California Budget Project 1998). Male workers in the bottom 25% saw wages drop by 40% in the last two decades (Reed 1999).

polarized racially in California, with darker shades primarily filling the bottom half.[12]

Tomas Almaguer claims that historically, beginning in the nineteenth century, race relations in California exhibited a complicated, hierarchical pattern with numerous "racial fault lines" (1994). In the 21st century, however, the stark division between the income of the two largest social groups (whites and Latinos), along with the coalescence of race and class, renders racial 'polarization' a more apt description of the social organization of Californian society. 'Stratification' or 'hierarchy' evoke a sense of multi-layered inequality, but social and economic relations in California appear more two dimensional and polarized. Latinos represent one-third of the state population yet more than half of the state's poor families. Whites, on the other hand, are decreasing in population size, barely holding on to a slim majority, but still overwhelmingly outnumber other racial groups in the state's wealthiest segment. The drastic rift between these racial groups is none the more apparent than when entering any of California's fine dining establishments. With some degree of consistency, one will see whites sitting at the dining tables while Latinos are cooking and cleaning for them in the kitchen. The clear separation of socio-spatial locations between white and Latinos within the restaurant context is indicative of the wider social reality of polarization. The frequent repetition of this type of race/class division, not only in fine restaurants but numerous other businesses, establishments, and workplaces, gives the impression that California is rapidly adopting a social composition similar to many third world countries.

Working youth in Latino immigrant families

The service-based economy and global economic restructuring have encouraged employers to push wages down and pull immigrants from Latin America into the low-skill job sector to minimize labor costs. Consequently, the general depression of wages has negatively affected

---

[12] Robert G. Mogull reviews census data and provides smooth estimates and projections of poverty rates for various racial groups in California. Although African Americans are still among the poorest in the state, their poverty rates have been in decline since 1959. The poverty rates for white have been relatively low—one of the lowest in the state. However, "the overall poverty within state borders is expected to increase markedly into the next century. The projected increase is due primarily to the dramatically rising incidents of poverty among the state's Hispanic population and its offspring (Mogull 1998, 634).

Latino immigrant families by requiring not only two but sometimes multiple earners, including children, for survival. If a parent or both parents hold low-wage jobs chances are their earnings would barely support themselves, let alone a family of four or more. Many Latino youth, therefore, feel the economic pressure to take jobs in low-wage services and contribute to their families' survival. My research in Oakland, California reveals that young people in Latino immigrant families often become the second, third, or fourth option in most of the multiple earner arrangements.[13] In most cases, young Latinos receive information about employment through kin-based social networks. In the service-based economy, particularly within secondary markets, firms hire through social networks instead of internally or through an open labor market (Sassen 1995). This hiring practice increasingly places the household or community at the center of local labor market formation (Ibid.). Given the class specific dimension and locational characteristics of networks and their importance in hiring, poorer Latinos often are embedded into social networks with information leading primarily to low wage jobs. If by chance the social network accesses only information about jobs in the secondary market, then job opportunities become limited to this option.

Thus, financial need and easy access to low wage jobs guide Latino youth into dead end service occupations. The US Census Bureau reports that 75% of all employed Latino youth between the ages of sixteen and nineteen work in the wholesale, retail, or service industries; many of these jobs are in eating and drinking establishments. In my study, Latino youth who worked in fast food restaurants frequently felt that their jobs would not lead to advancements or better opportunities. Twenty-year-old Fast food worker Fernando Alvarez describes the limitations of his job:

> Some jobs help you with the future because you are learning something that can help you earn more money. But only flipping burgers, all your life you're going to stay right there. Doing the same thing and sweating, like $5 all your life.

Many fast food workers quickly realize that their job is no more than a dead-end. According to nineteen-year-old Nestor Cruz, fast food work is not much of a "real" opportunity:

---

[13] My dissertation research was based on an ethnography of Latino youth from Oakland, California, focusing on their perceptions and experiences of work. See "First Jobs: the perceptions and experiences of work among Latino youth" dissertation: UC Berkeley, 2001.

> If you stay there forever, that's not a good thing. You get hassled too much, and they still ask for more work from you and you get paid less. It is hard to get good pay. You have to ask them every six months. If the manager sees that you're doing your job, they might give you a little raise, 10 cents if you're lucky. That's not a lot for six months.

Nestor's words caution that a long tenure in fast food could lead to the possibility of being caught in a process that sustains low-wage existence. The testimonies and experiences of other fast food employees support Nestor's perspective. Many in the study feel that fast food work fails to meet the expectation of an opportunity that would lead to a better future. On the contrary, workers frequently describe their work experiences in terms analogous to a dead-end course, with no way out from the low-wage trap.

Educational attainment and labor market status

The correlation between educational attainment and labor-market status may shed light on why young Latinos might remain in the low end of the bifurcated job market. Most indicators for labor outcomes suggest that labor market position improves with higher levels of educational attainment.[14] Indeed, education levels influence participation rates and labor force status, but the critical economic indicator of income correlates with years of schooling. For the general US population, a high school graduate earned only 57 cents for every dollar a college graduate made in 1990, a decline from 64 cents in 1972 (Topolnicki 1993, 10). Earnings for Latinos rise with level of education as well. For example, the Latino income for those above 25 years-of-age and without a high school diploma averaged about $15,832 a year in 1999 (Statistical Abstract of the US 2000). With a diploma, income jumps to $20,978 a year. The greatest disparity is between high school and college graduates: Latinos with a bachelor's degree earned 15,000 dollars more per year (average of $35,014) than Latinos who had only a high school degree.

---

[14] US Bureau of Labor Statistics revealed that unemployment rates for Latinos in 2000 decreased incrementally according to level of education: 8.3% for those with less than high school diploma; 4.6% for high school graduates; and 3.2% for college graduates (Statistical Abstract of US 2001). In that same year, labor force participation rates for Latinos increased with education: less than high school is 69.9%; high school graduate at 78.5%; college graduate at 87%.

The wage disparity between those with college degrees and those with only a high school diploma is attributed to better paying, high-skill jobs requiring a college education. Employment projections to 2006, estimated by the Bureau of Labor Statistics, show that high-skill occupations in computer and technological related fields will witness growth rates above 100%, but these new jobs will require a minimum of a bachelor's degree. Educational attainment may reliably indicate which side of the bi-polar job market a worker will end-up on.

The generally poor educational picture for Latinos suggests that they would most likely attain jobs in the low skill employment sector. Among all racial groups in the United States, Latinos have the lowest educational attainment rates, implying that they would fail to meet the basic credential requirements for entrance into the high skill/paying job markets. High school graduation rates for the US population show that Latinos lag behind other racial groups in the United States.[15] Latino figures for college achievement are equally discouraging.[16] Because college facilitates access to the high paying side of the polarized job market, many Latinos must contend with poor labor market status resulting from low achievement levels in higher education. Without a college degree in the new service economy, job opportunities for young Latinos become limited to a single alternative: the expanding low wage service sector.[17]

---

[15] In 1994, only 57% of Latinos between the ages of 18–24 graduated from high school, compared to 77% of African Americans (Bruno and Curry 1996). The dropout rate for the same age group among Latinos was 35%, whereas the white dropout rate reached 13%. While the high school graduation rate improved for African Americans in the last twenty years, graduations for Latinos have actually gone down. In 1975, 60% of African Americans between the ages of 18 and 21 graduated from high school; Latinos were not that far behind with a 57% graduation rate (Statistical Abstract of the US 2001). But in 1999, Latinos not only failed to catch up but moved farther behind African Americans by dropping to a 56% graduation rate while African Americans improved to 70%.

[16] In 2000, 11% of Latinos 25 years and older had completed at least 4 years of college, whereas whites were 26% and the Asian completion percentage was an astounding 44% (Statistical Abstract of the US 2001). Among the non-Latino population within the same age group, 18% had a bachelor's degree compared to 7% of the Latino population (Ibid.). In the last twenty years college enrollment has gone up for African Americans while enrollment for Latinos has declined. In 1975, 25% of African Americans between 18 to 21 years of age were enrolled in college. In that same year, Latino enrollment was 24%, somewhat equal to African Americans. However, college enrollment numbers have changed for both groups since then. According to 1999 figures, African American percentage rates rose to 36% while Latinos dropped to 23% (Statistical Abstract of the US 2001).

[17] A recent Education Testing Service study indicates that, "Millions of young

Racial inequality in California schools

California schools unfortunately do not offer a way out of the low-wage trap for Latino youth. In some ways, the Californian education system contributes to channeling them into low-wage services because it fails to lead them to a college education. Although Latinos represent the majority in California's K-12 public schools, they are some of the least likely to attend college.[18] A Latino child enters an education system with profound racial inequalities, a system that is more effective at ensuring his or her failure than success. However, the system is extremely adept at meeting the needs and interests of white students and preparing them for college.[19] With the polarization of the service workforce and college requirement for entrance into high paying jobs, schools in California, by default, help to perpetuate racial inequalities by continuously failing Latino students while promoting the academic success of white students.

Harvard education scholar Gary Orfield contends that the main educational barrier for Latino students in California is that they are more likely to attend segregated schools than any other racial group (Orfield and Eaton 1996). Segregated schools often exhibit many negative characteristics (i.e. tracking, unqualified teachers, lack of resource, culturally irrelevant curriculum, etc.) that education researchers have identified as the reasons for low achievement among Latino students (Olsen 1997; Orfield and Eaton 1996; Perez and Salazar 1993; Trueba 1999; Valencia 1991). Perez and Salazar state that segregated schools for Latinos

> tend to lack resources to provide students with a competitive education; that the curriculum in predominantly minority schools move away

---

Latinos who are qualified for college never attend, often becoming stuck in dead-end, low paying jobs" (College Education Gap Hurts Latinos, Study Finds. *San Francisco Chronicle* September 30, 1999: A13).

[18] The Department of Education, Educational Demographics Unit reports that in the 1998–99 school year (the last year reported) Latinos were the largest racial group in the public school system, representing 41.3% of the students enrolled in K-12 public schools (2000). Whites are the next largest group at 37.8%. However, in that same year, only 22.1% of Latino high school graduates were eligible to apply for college in the California public university system, whereas 40.6% of white graduates were eligible.

[19] In 1997, state enrollment figures for California colleges and universities show that whites represent almost half of all college students in the state while Latinos barely reach 21% of the California college student population (Statistical Abstract of the US 2001).

from advance-level work and toward low-level work; and that teachers in such schools have less education and experience than their colleagues in predominately white schools (1993, 220).

A highly segregated school system in California suggests that Latino and white students move through divergent and unequal academic trajectories. The Academic Performance Index (API), which the California Department of Education produces to measure the performance of schools and students within the state, verifies the divergence and inequality between Latino and white students. Presenting an almost inverse relationship, Latinos represent 75% of the students enrolled in the lowest performing schools in the state, whereas white students make up 74% of the students enrolled in the highest performing schools (California Budget Project 2001). The key significance of this performance differential is that white students are far more likely to receive a better education than Latino students.[20]

Severe inequalities in the educational system cut against the grain of the standard belief in the possibilities and expectations of schooling. Many Americans wholeheartedly accept the modern discourse of how academic achievement theoretically can overcome barriers imposed by social inequality. Out of necessity immigrant families often accept the key premise within this discourse, using it to rationalize immigration to the United States. Parents expect education to result in better opportunities for their children and serve as a way to avoid their path, thus breaking from a life of toil and paltry earnings. America would mean providing their children with a good education and better opportunities. Unfortunately, the school system, if anything, is less about making Latino youth college bound and more about placing them in lower tracks, including those that eventually lead to low-wage services. Without a college degree, a young Latino in California will experience far greater challenges to earning high wages than anywhere else in the nation.[21]

---

[20] A report by the Public Policy Institute of California indicates that on the average Latino students are enrolled in schools with almost 12% of the teachers not fully certified, whereas white students attend schools with less than 4% of teachers not fully certified. The report states that "whites are being taught by teachers who are more experienced, better educated, and more likely to be fully credentialed, relative to the teachers who teach black and Latinos" (Betts, Rueben et al. 2000, 88).

[21] Julian R. Betts reports that a worker receives a higher return to education in California than any other state. He points out "[t]he wage gap between those with a bachelor's degree and those with only a high school diploma... widened more in California than elsewhere" (2000, 61).

Conclusion

This paper raises some important concerns about recent economic developments and the future of Latino youth in California. For many young Latinos, coming-of-age in California during the 1990s included the unfortunate experience of social marginalization through processes of globalization. Throughout the decade, racial politics reared its ugly head in the form of anti-immigrant (Proposition 187), anti-affirmative action (Proposition 209), and anti-bilingual education (Proposition 227) state ballot initiatives. These propositions targeted the state's Latino population as a way to reinforce a subordinate relationship to the dominant economic interests. The 90s' political onslaught to contain the 'brown tide' suggested to many Latinos that dominant forces would attempt to control their future by ensuring that the growing size of the Latino population within the state would not translate into increased social and economic power. Therefore, the impending future is clear: young Latinos would have to suffer the eventual fate of living under an 'apartheid-like' political economy. This political economic system intends to segregate and cordon them off as a subservient class denied access to the better resources and opportunities and relegated to the status of cheap labor to satisfy the economic interests of those in power. Stephen Steinberg, author of *The Ethnic Myth: Race, Ethnicity, and Class in America* states that "policies of apartheid" appeared more than fifty years ago in housing and economic development policies implemented throughout US cities (Steinberg 1991, 744). Now apartheid moves directly and pervasively within the political economy through the "missed opportunity to upgrade the skills of marginal workers and lower racist barriers throughout the workplace" (Ibid.). With apartheid looming on the horizon, many Latinos, young and old, must find the political resources and strategies to push past the occupational and educational impediments and challenge their subordination within the new millennium.

REFERENCES

Almaguer, Tomas (1994). *Racial Fault Lines: the origins of White Supremacy in California*. Berkeley, University of California Press.

Bernhardt, Annette, and Thomas Bailey (1998). Improving worker welfare in the age of flexibility. *Challenge*. 41: 16.

Betts, Julian. R. (2000) The Changing Role of Education in the California Labor Market. San Francisco, Public Policy Institute of California: 145.

Betts, Julian R., and Kim S. Rueben, et al. (2000). Equal Resources, Equal Outcomes? The Distribution of School Resources and Student Achievement in California. San Francisco, Public Policy Institute of California: 347.

Bruno, Rosalind R., and Andrea Curry (1996). School Enrollment-Social and Economic Characteristics of Students: October 1994. Washington, D.C., US Bureau of the Census, Current Population Reports, pp. 20–487.

California Budget Project (1996). Working, But Poor, In California. Sacramento: 49.

California Budget Project (1998). Unequal Gains: The State of Working California. Sacramento: 13.

California Budget Project (2001). What Do The 2000 API Results Tell Us About California Schools? Sacramento: 8.

California Department of Education (2000). CBEDS, California Statewide Profile. Educational Demographics Unit.

California Department of Employment Development (1994). Race/Ethnicity Within Occupational Group. Labor Market Information Division.

California Department of Finance (1997). California Statistical Abstract. Financial and Economic Research Unit.

Castells, Manuel, and Jeffrey Henderson (1987). *Global Restructuring and Territorial Development*. Newbury Park, Sage.

Davis, Michael (1986). *Prisoner of the American Dream: politics and economy in the history of the US working class*. London, Verso.

Fernandez, Geovanny (2000). California: State of Our Children. Oakland, Children Now: 62.

Harvey, David (1990). *The Condition of Postmodernity: an enquiry into the origins of cultural change*. Oxford, Blackwell.

John, Kelly St. (2001). Latino Births Signal Future for California: babies born in state increasingly Hispanic. *San Francisco Chronicle*. December 19: A-21.

Johnson, Kevin R. (1998). "Race, the immigration laws, and domestic race relations: A 'Magic mirror' into the heart of darkness." *Indiana Law Journal* 73(4): 1111–1159.

Kacapyr, Elia, and Peter Francese, et al. (1996). "Are You Middle Class? (definitions and trends of US middle-class households)." *American Demographics* 18(10): 30–6.

Lash, Scott, and J. Urry (1987). *The End of Organized Capitalism*. Cambridge, Polity Press.

Lieberman, Charles (1997). Immigrant Assistance (Chase Securities economist Charles Lieberman's report on the positive economic impact of Latino immigration to the US). *Economist*. 342: 28.

Mead, Walter R. (1998). At Your Service: the new global economy takes your order. *Mother Jones*. 22: 32–41.

Mogull, Robert G. (1998). "The Incidence of California Poverty by Population Segment (Special Issue: Focus on Governance)." *Social Science Journal* 35(4): 627–35.

Ness, Carol (2001). Hispanics Now Make Up Third of Californians. *San Francisco Chronicle*. March 30: A-1.

Olsen, Laurie (1997). *Made in America: immigrant students in our public schools*. New York: New Press.

Orfield, Gary, and Susan E. Eaton, et al. (1996). *Dismantling Desegregation: the quiet reversal of Brown v. Board of Education.* New York: New Press.
Perez, Sonia M., and Denise De La Rosa Salazar (1993). "Economic, Labor Force, and Social Implications of Latino Educational and Population Trends." *Hispanic Journal of Behavioral Sciences* 15(2): 188–229.
Piore, Michael J., and Charles F. Sabel (1984). *The Second Industrial Divide: possibilities for prosperity.* New York, Basic Books.
Reed, Deborah (1999). California's Rising Income Inequality: Causes and Concerns. San Francisco, Public Policy Institute of California: 101.
Reich, Robert B. (1991). *The Work of Nations.* New York, Vintage.
Rouse, Roger (1995). "Thinking Through Transnationalism—Notes On the Cultural Politics of Class Relations in the Contemporary United States." *Public Culture* 7(2): 353–402.
Sassen, Saskia (1991). *The Global City: New York, London, Tokyo.* Princeton, NJ, Princeton University Press.
——— (1994). *Cities in a World Economy.* Thousand Oaks, Calif., Pine Forge Press.
——— (1995) "Immigration and Local Labor Markets" in *Economic Sociology of Immigration: essays on networks, ethnicity, and entrpreneurship.* New York, Russell Sage Foundation: 87–128.
——— (1998). *Globalization and Its Discontents.* New York, The New Press.
Steinberg, Stephen (1991). Occupational Apartheid. *Nation.* 253: 744–47.
——— (2001). *The Ethnic Myth: race, ethnicity, and class in America.* Boston, Beacon Press 3rd Edition.
Storper, Michael, and Richard Walker (1989). *The Capitalist Imperative: Territory, Technology, and Industrial Growth.* New York, Basil Blackwell.
Topolnicki, Denise M. (1993). The American Dream: economic myths and realities. *Current*: 4–10.
Trueba, Enrique T. (1999). *Latinos Unidos: from cultural diversity to the politics of solidarity.* Lanham, Md., Rowman & Littlefield.
US Bureau of the Census. (1990). 1990 Census of Population and Housing. Washington, D.C.
——— (1998). Statistical Abstract of the United States. Washington, D.C.
——— (2000) a. 2000 Census of Population and Housing. Washington, D.C.
——— (2000) b. Statistical Abstract of the United States. Washington, D.C.
——— (2001). Statistical Abstract of the United States. Washington, D.C.
US Bureau of Labor Statistics (1997). Occupational Projections to 2006. *Monthly Labor Review* (November).
Valencia, Richard R. (1991). *Chicago School Failure and Success: research and policy agendas for the 1990s.* London; New York, Falmer Press.
Walker, Richard (1995). "California Rages against the Dying of the Light." *New Left Review*: 42.

MAKING IT IN URBAN AMERICA: CHALLENGES AND PROSPECTS FOR THE CHILDREN OF CONTEMPORARY IMMIGRANTS[1]

Min Zhou

Contemporary immigration to the United States has had a lasting effect on the growth and composition of the general U.S. population. The 2000 Census records 281.4 million people residing in the United States. Even though America's population has grown 13% over the past decade, such an increase is uneven among its racial minority sub-populations. Overall, the country has witnessed stagnant growth of non-Hispanic white population (3%), moderate growth of non-Hispanic black population (21%), and rapid growth of Hispanic and Asian-origin populations (61% and 76%, respectively) due in large part to international migration that has accelerated since the 1970s.

Varied rates of population growth and international migration have significantly altered the racial composition of the U.S. population, making it racially more diverse than in the past. As of 2000, non-Hispanic whites share 69% of the total U.S. population as of 2000, down from 76% in 1990, while non-Hispanic blacks, 12.6%, at the same level as that in 1990. In contrast, Hispanics have drawn virtually even with non-Hispanic blacks as the nation's largest minority group. The Hispanic population now comprises 12.5% of the total U.S. population, up from less than 9% in 1990. The Asian-origin population has remained relatively small but its share of the total population jumps from 2.8% in 1990 to the current level of 4.4%.

Because of the recentness of contemporary immigration, a new generation of immigrant children and children of immigrant parentage is coming of age. The Current Population Survey (CPS) for the period 1994–1998 shows that almost 40% of the second generation is under 18 years of age, in contrast to 28% of the general U.S. population. This new second generation is not only disproportionately young, but also ethnically diverse. In the second generation,

---

[1] This chapter draws heavily on my previously published work in Zhou 1997, 2001a, 2001b; Zhou and Logan 2002; and Zhou et al. 2000.

more than a third are Hispanic and 7% Asian. If it were distributed randomly across America's urban landscape, the new second generation would not be of great interest since it is relatively small in absolute numbers. However, historical and contemporary patterns of immigrant settlement suggest that immigrants and their children are highly concentrated in just a handful of metropolitan regions. How immigrant children are making it in urban America has become a central issue of concern. This chapter uses the U.S. census data (CPS in particular) and some qualitative observations to examine generational and ethnic differences in educational attainment and labor market incorporation of the children of new immigrants in five largest immigrant-receiving centers, New York, Chicago, Los Angeles, San Francisco, and Miami. It begins with a discussion of the challenges confronted by the new second generation in their quest for entry into mainstream American society. It then provides a demographic profile of the new second generation, followed by a series of comparative analyses that address: a) toward which direction—upward or downward—the new second generation is likely to move, and b) to what extent the children of immigrants from different national origins achieves parity with non-Hispanic whites. It finally discusses the implications of these patterns on the assimilation of the new second generation.

The challenges confronted by the new second generation

Classical sociological theories about immigrant adaptation predicts a linear trajectory, in which the children and grandchildren of immigrants eventually move beyond the first generation's socioeconomic status and become indistinguishable Americans. The assumptions that underlies this assimilationist paradigm are: that there is a natural process by which diverse and initially disadvantaged ethnic groups come to share a common culture and to gradually gain equal access to the opportunity structure of the host society; that this process consists of gradually deserting old cultural and behavioral patterns in favor of new ones; and that, once set in motion, this process moves inevitably and irreversibly toward assimilation (Warner and Srole 1945). National origin groups remain ethnically distinguishable from one another depending largely on the lengthy of time since arrival and the degree to which ethnic groups gain inroads into the host society and become merged into native-born population. Nevertheless, distinctive ethnic characteristics will eventually fade, or become merely symbolic, with each of the succeeding generations (Gans 1979; Gordon 1964).

As in the past, the journey to America and their adjustment to the new land have always been extremely hard for the children of immigrants. The parents' low socioeconomic status makes it difficult for the children to succeed, even though both parents and children desperately want to get ahead. The environment in which the children find themselves further limits the chances: too many live in inner-city neighborhoods that are poor and socially isolated. For example, a typical immigrant neighborhood in Los Angeles is characteristic of overconcentration of racial/ethnic minorities, the foreign born, and the poor (Zhou et al. 2000). The proportion of racial/ethnic minorities residing in Los Angeles' Chinatown, Koreatown, and Pico Union (a Mexican/Central American neighborhood) is more than 90%, while the proportion of the foreign born is over 70%. Also, median family incomes in these neighborhoods are less than two-thirds those of the city as a whole and most adults lack education, job skills, and social capital that facilitate access to resources and opportunities in mainstream American society. The situation in Los Angeles immigrant neighborhood mirrors that in other larger immigrant-receiving metropolises, with the exception of some newly emerged middle-class immigrant communities in suburban areas (Fong 1994; Zhou and Kim 2002).

Living in poor immigrant neighborhoods in the inner city pose some serious risks for families and children. The most obvious risks are associated with the socially disruptive environment beset by poverty, substandard living conditions, unsafe streets, and economic distress, and inadequate or even turbulent schools. These contextual risks are further exacerbated by other risk factors associated with immigrant disadvantages. On such risk factor is family disruption through migration, which undermines the customary measure of social control. Migration disrupts normal patterns of social relations, making it difficult to reinforce the family's values, norms, and behavioral expectations, especially when these values, norms, and behavioral standards are at odds with those of American society.

Another risk factor is the lack of adult supervision at home. The majority of immigrant children live in families with both parents working full time. In many cases, those parents are working several jobs and on different shifts, and many enduring long hours of commuting to and from work. Therefore, parents do not have enough time to be with their children in their waking hours, much less to supervise them.

A third, and perhaps most devastating, risk factor is the erosion of parental authority. Often parents worry that their children have too much free time, too little adult supervision, and too many risks on the streets, but they do not have the authority to exercise parental power. Parents' lack of English ability pushes children into parental roles. Children read the report card for parents or tell the parents what goes on in school the way they want to present it, and interpret for their parents at teacher-student conferences. In one often-cited case, a teacher was puzzled at the smiling face of a parent when she told him that his son was suspended from school. What the teacher did not know was that her student interpreted her words to his father as meaning that he was doing so well in school that the teacher decided to give him a vacation. When the parents use their own way of disciplining their children (often corporal punishment), they are threatened by their children's power of calling 911. They are then at risk of being jailed for child abuse.

A fourth factor is the language problem among the children themselves. Many children have difficulty in understanding teachers or expressing themselves in the classroom—thus making the education of immigrant children a very challenging task. Some of the children, especially those who arrive as teenagers, had already dropped out of school, or had completed their minimum schooling, in their homelands upon arrival. They are thus likely to be considered high school dropouts even if they have never even dropped in (Venez and Abrhamse 1996). Some have simply enrolled in school behind their grade levels and then drop out because they cannot keep up with the work.

To all these difficulties are added the generic problems of second generation acculturation, aggravated by the troubles associated with coming of age in an era far more materialistic and individualistic than encountered by immigrant children in years gone by. Today's second generation often finds itself straddling different worlds and receiving conflicting signals. At home, they hear that they must work hard and do well in school in order to move up; on the street they learn a different lesson, that of rebellion against authority and rejection of the goals of achievement. Today's popular culture, brought to the immigrants through the television screen, exposes children to the lifestyles and consumption standards of American society, raising their expectations well beyond those entertained by their parents. As a result, the children are not as "willing" as their parents to work at low-paying, low-status jobs; but at the same, many may not have the education, skills, or opportunities to do better. This mismatch between rising aspirations and shrinking opportunities can either lead to "second-generation decline" (Gans 1992) or provoke "second-generation revolt" (Perlmann and Waldinger 1997).

So do immigrant children manage to traverse the difficult social terrain they encounter? Or do they fall into one of the many traps that afflict young people—especially those of socioeconomically disadvantaged or minority background—in contemporary America? Next, I explore these questions through a series of analyses of the 1994–98 CPS data, focusing on the school and labor market experiences of the second generation.

School and labor market incorporation

One way of examining how well immigrant children fare in the U.S. Society is by looking at how well members of the second generation appear to be adapting to the American educational system and the labor market in comparison to their first generation counterparts and third-plus-generation counterparts, focusing specifically on the effect of generation. Another way is by examining whether or not the children and grandchildren of different national origin groups have achieved parity with the native-born population. In the following analysis of the CPS data, I focus on addressing these two interrelated issues—whether the second generation advances or declines and to what extent the second generation achieves parity with the native-born population.

A demographic profile of the new second generation

What does the new second generation look like relative to first and third-plus generation and to the old second generation? Corresponding to the immigration surge in the past three decades, a new generation of immigrant children and children of immigrant parentage has become the fastest growing and the most ethnically diverse segment of America's child population. The timing and composition of contemporary immigration suggests that today's second generation is spatially concentrated in just a few metropolitan regions, following the settlement patterns of the first generation. Figure 1 illustrates the relative size and distribution of three immigrant generations in five metropolitan regions—New York, Chicago, Los Angeles, San Francisco, and Miami—as well as the rest of the United States.[2] Historically, New York and Chicago have been the most popular destinations of new arrivals. In the past 30 years, Los Angeles, Miami, and San Francisco have emerged as the most immigrant important receiving centers. These five metropolitan regions comprise one fifth of the total U.S. population but share over half (55%) of the total foreign born population.

As the top panel of figure 1 shows, within each region, the size of the first-generation (foreign-born) and second-generation cohorts are at least twice at large as those residing elsewhere in the country, which is not surprising given the prominence of these metropolitan areas as preferred destinations of contemporary immigrants. The difference between old and new immigrant-receiving centers is remarkable. New York used to be the number one immigrant city, but has lost its dominant position to Los Angeles in terms of the absolute as well as the relative size of the first-generation cohort and to Miami in terms of the relative size. Chicago, once second to New York in receiving immigrants, has significantly reduced its share of the foreign born population. Nonetheless, its foreign stock in absolute numbers is still quite large given the size of the metropolitan population. By contrast, the first-generation cohort makes up nearly a third of Los Angeles' population and more than a third (37%) of Miami's population. San Francisco lies somewhere between the old and new centers. Like Los Angeles and Miami, San Francisco was never a major immigrant center until the 1960s, but historically, it was a major entry port for immigrants from Asia, who made up only a tiny fraction of the total arrivals at the turn of the century.

The distribution of the second generation within each region corresponds to that of the first generation. Generally, the size of the second generation in all urban centers, except for Chicago, is more than twice that elsewhere in the country, accounting for about one-fifth of the total population. Correspondingly, the third-plus generation is relatively smaller in immigrant receiving centers than that elsewhere, except for Chicago.

---

[2] These are Consolidate Metropolitan Statistical Areas (CMSA) designated by the U.S. Census Bureau.

Figure 1. Distribution of immigrant generations in major immigrant receiving centers

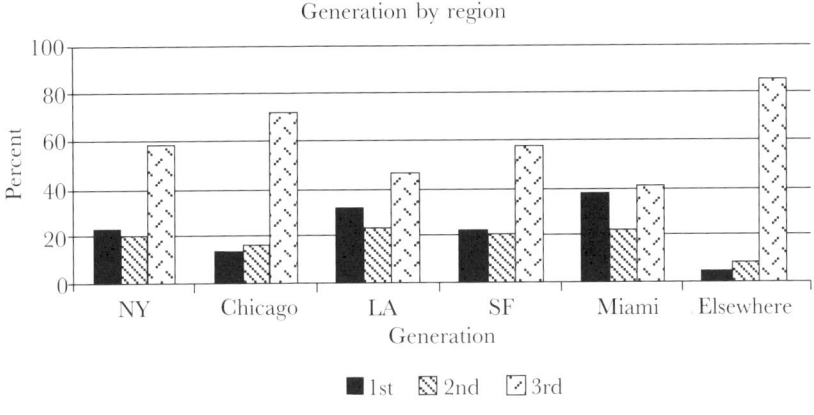

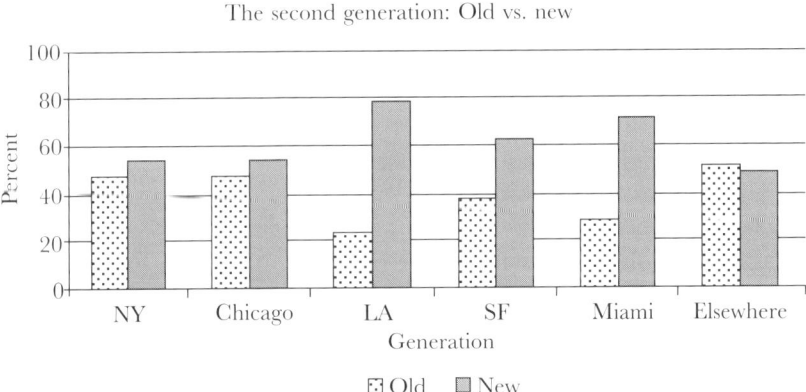

Source: Current Population Survey: 1994–97.

The bottom panel of figure 1 shows the contrast between the old and new second generation. In the this chapter, I roughly define the younger cohorts of the children of immigrant parentage, under 35 of age and born in after 1960 when contemporary immigration began to pick up momentum, as the *new* second generation, and the older cohorts, aged 35 and over, as the *old* second generation. Reflecting the nature of contemporary immigration, the new second generation is disproportionately large in new immigrant receiving centers. In Los Angeles, in particular, the new second generation is more than three times as large as the old second generation.

Contemporary immigration has also altered the racial and ethnic composition of metropolitan populations. In the mid-1990s, the U.S. population is about 70% non-Hispanic white, 10% non-Hispanic black, 9% Mexican, 6% other Hispanic, 3% Asian, and 2% other races. However, immigrants of different national origins are not randomly distributed across urban America. Historically, immigrants have concentrated in just a few metropolitan regions, and within each region in just a few local communities. Earlier European immigrant groups most settled in big cities in the Northeast and the mid-West. Today's linguistically and ethnically diverse immigrant populations are just as geographically concentrated, but in different urban centers. For example, Dominican, Haitian, Jamaican immigrants tend to concentrate in New York, while Mexican immigrants tend to concentrate in Los Angeles and big cities in the Southwest, Guatemalans and Salvadorans in Los Angeles, Cubans in Miami, and Asians in San Francisco. The settlement patterns of new immigrants have given today's new urban centers ethnic mosaics different from those in old centers.

Figure 2 illustrates the distribution of major racial or ethnic groups by generational status. As shown in the top panel, the first generation is less "white" and more "colored" with Mexican-, other Hispanic and Asian-origin groups making up the majority (about three quarters). The ethnic composition of the second generation mirrors the diversity characteristic of the first generation, but with a much higher proportion of non-Hispanic whites, that belongs to the older European stock. In contrast, non-Hispanic whites dominate the third-plus generation. Grandchildren of Hispanic and Asian immigrants were almost invisible. These patterns suggest that most of the young people of Hispanic and Asian origins are either immigrants or children of immigrants.

The bottom panel of figure 2 zooms in on difference in the racial and ethnic distributions between the old and new second generation.[3] In general, second-generation non-Hispanic whites are mostly children of immigrants from the earlier waves of European immigration and thus tend to be older. As shown, the old second generation is primarily made up of the children of earlier European immigrants. The children of non-European origins are almost invisible. The new second generation—the children of immigrants under

---

[3] The old second generation refers to the children of immigrants who are 35 years or older and the new second generation under 35 years of age.

Figure 2. Distribution of major racial/ethnic groups by generation

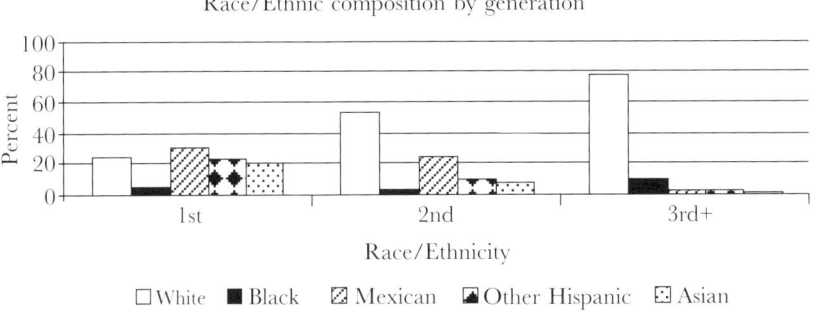

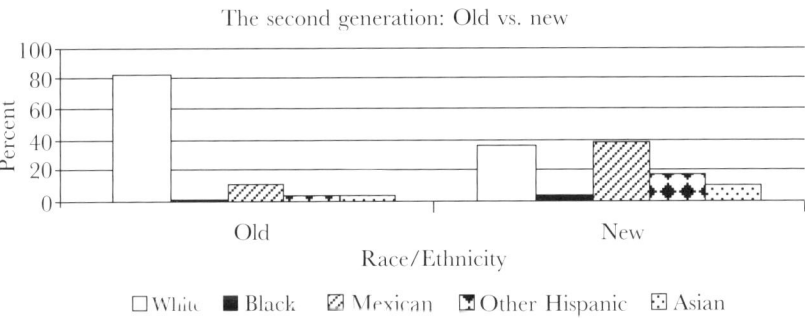

Source: Current Population Survey: 1994–98.

35 years of age, in contrast, is strikingly different in its racial and ethnic makeup. What is remarkable about the new second generation is its high level of diversity, which fundamentally alters the white-black dichotomy. For example, 37% of the new second generation is Mexican, 16% other Hispanic, and 11% Asian, compared to only 31% white and 5% black.

The demographic patterns discussed above suggest that the new second generation is still in the making, but is expected to come of age rapidly in the next decade or so, and that this new second generation is not only highly concentrated in regions of first-generation settlement but also extraordinarily diverse in national origin. Since race or ethnicity is strongly associated with class status, the spatial patterns of different immigrant groups may have significant bearing on the mobility prospects of the new second generation.

Educational attainment of the new second generation

For the children of immigrants, acquiring skills and credentials is a crucial step toward upward mobility in American society. Thus, failure to complete high school is generally considered a risk factor adversely impacting a person's future life chances. Beyond high school, college attendance is considered an important measure for adaptation, as it enhances a person's competitiveness in meeting the skill demand for higher ranking jobs in the labor market. I classify all of those youths aged 16 to 19 (within school age but old enough to legally quit school), who are neither currently enrolled in school nor high school graduates, as "dropouts," and all those youths aged 18 to 24 (not counting high school students), who are currently enrolled in college, as "college attendees."

Figure 3 illustrates the percentage distribution of high school dropout among youth aged 16 to 19 and college attendance among young adults aged 18 to 24 by generational status, region, and race. First-generation youth are in big trouble on this count, as can be seen from the top left panel in figure 3. I note that "dropout" may not be the most appropriate label for foreign-born children, as many of them may never have "dropped into" high school to begin with, heading straight to the labor market as soon as they set foot on U.S. soil. This minor qualification apart, failure to attend or complete high school among foreign-born youth clearly looms large. But that generalization does vary somewhat depending on how one cuts it. Relative to their second or third generation counterparts, immigrant youth are a good deal more likely to be "dropouts" in every region save Miami, which also happens to be a southern metropolis that also boasts the relatively largest black third-generation—in other words, a place where black youth are particularly likely to be confronting school difficulties. On the other hand, there are some clear regional disparities, with Chicago, and most disturbingly, the two largest immigrant regions of Los Angeles and New York, places where high school attendance and/or completion is all too uncommon among foreign-born children.

Taking a somewhat different view, the foreign-born disadvantage, though still perceptible, looks very different as one compares with the major ethnic categories (top right panel). The gap between first and later generations is greatest among Mexicans, mainly because the first generation "dropout" rate is so high. These high first gen-

MAKING IT IN URBAN AMERICA 275

Figure 3. Educational outcomes by generational status: inter-regional and inter-group comparison

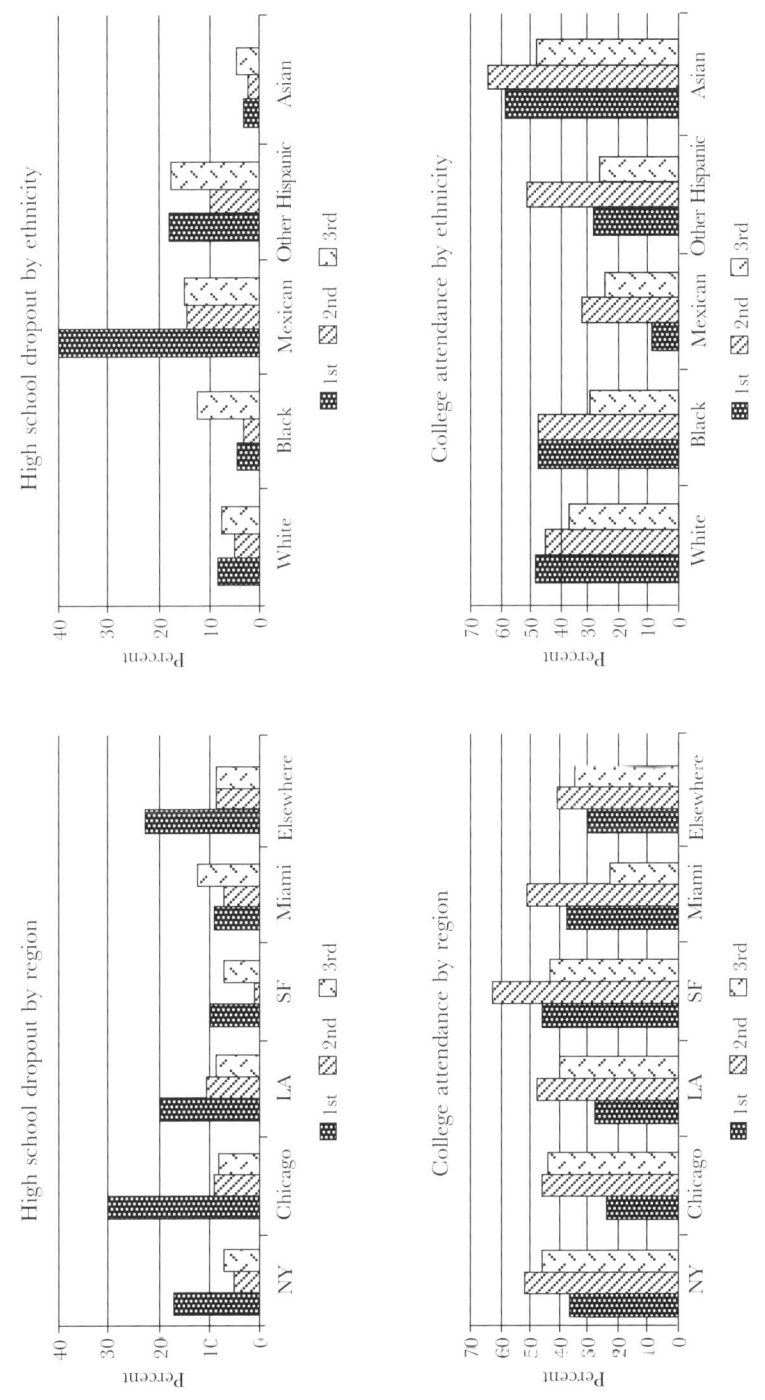

Source: Current Population Survey: 1994–98.

eration dropout rates imply that this indicator will not provide evidence of second generation "decline," pointing, rather, in the opposite direction. Not surprisingly, Mexicans show the greatest improvement, though this change qualifies as "improvement" only in relation to the depressing first generation pattern: second generation Mexicans attend and/or complete high school at rates that compare unfavorably with third generation blacks; third generation Mexicans do still slightly worse. In contrast to the first generation, second generation outcomes more clearly vary across the regions, with second generation youth less likely to dropout than their third generation counterparts in San Francisco, New York, and Miami, and more likely to do so in Los Angeles or Chicago. Part of the regional variation is undoubtedly related to each region's distinctive ethnic mix, the impact of which is most visible in San Francisco, the only region with a sizeable Asian second-generation group, and thus, the beneficiary of the extraordinary low dropout rates among second-generation Asian youth.

Ideally, high school graduates will go on to college, for which the relevant population consists of those aged 18–24. This indicator again highlights the foreign-born disadvantage, as the bottom panel of figure 3 shows; however, one would be hesitant to qualify the gap as inherently disastrous. If immigrant youth never drop in to high school, all the more so for their slightly older counterparts, many of whom are drawn to the U.S. by the opportunity to get right down to work. In some regions, with San Francisco again leading the pack, the foreign-born are attending college at remarkably high rates; even at the lowest level, recorded in Chicago, foreign-born college attendance rates are not much worse than the pattern for native-born blacks—which puts the matter in some perspective. Ethnic differences are again more dramatic, with more than 60 percent of all Asian-born youth attending college, as opposed to less than 10 percent of their Mexican-born counterparts.

But college attendance rates for second-generation young people do strike a stronger blow against the hypothesis of "second generation decline": not only does the second generation attend college at considerably higher rates than the first; it does better than the third generation as well. Clearly, the regional patterns are deeply confounded with a compositional bias: the very high college attendance rate for San Francisco is almost certainly related to the high college attendance rates among Asians, whereas the stark fall-off in second to third generation rates in Miami is likely a reflection of the problems encountered by blacks in this relatively poor southern metropolis. Nonetheless, the regional patterns are roughly consistent with the intergenerational differences *within* ethnic categories: only one category shows decline from first to second generations, but this happens to be whites; and though college attendance rates appear the same among first and second generation blacks, stability cannot count as evidence of "decline."

Labor market incorporation among young adults aged 16 to 34

Schooling is strongly associated with socio-economic attainment, and more so today than ever before, since the steady educational upgrading of the economy puts at risk all those who fail to attain the societal norm. To examine generational patterns of labor market incorporation, I focus on three measures among young adults aged 25 to 34: labor force marginalization, employment status, and occupational achievement. Labor force marginalization refers to being idle in society and is interpreted as a temporal outcome of maladjustment. I classify all working-age adults who are neither enrolled in school nor participate in the labor force as social "idlers," marginal both to their peers who are attending school and those who are working. Among those who are in the labor force, I examine their employment status and occupational achievement. I classify all those who are sufficiently employed as having adequate employment, as opposed to those who are underemployed with insufficient hours of work or minimum wages, and those who are unemployed. Occupational achievement is a dummy variable, coded 1 for those who have achieved executive and professional occupations as opposed to all other occupations.

In a sense, the discussion over immigrant incorporation takes place in the shadow of the "underclass" debate, with much of the immigration anxiety linked to the possibility that the newcomers and their descendants may fall to the bottom of the society and stay there. Though the "underclass" has always been a nebulous formulation as a concept, it clearly implies a thoroughly marginalized population, neither involved in schooling nor in gainful employment. As the top panel of figure f shows, marginalization is most common among the first generation. As one might expect, marginalization appears most common among first-generation Mexicans, though the ethnic differentials on this count are much smaller than the gaps we observed when examining the educational indicators above. By contrast, the second generation is more clearly integrated into the labor market, with the distinctive patterns associated with San Francisco and with Asians, noted earlier, showing up again.

Once in the labor force, the disadvantage associated with foreign birth persists to negatively impact employment positions and occupational achievement. Among those participating in the labor force, the first generation experience considerably lower rate of adequate employment than the second or third generation across regions (center-left panel of figure 4). Though regional variations are minimum, Los Angeles seems to be especially unfavorable for first-generation workers. Among ethnic groups (center-right panel), blacks and Mexicans trail behind their white or Asian counterparts regardless of generational status, despite improvement from the first generation. This indicator highlights the persistent foreign-born disadvantage, with the immigrants the least likely to have jobs of adequate quality in every place, and in every region and every racial or ethnic category. Likewise, it points up the progress that immigrant offspring are making relative to those of foreign birth. While second-generation Mexicans do a good deal better than the foreign born, they are doing about as well as third-generation blacks—which is less than satisfactory from the view of structural assimilation.

Finally, I examine a more selective indicator of labor market success, namely levels of professional and managerial employment (see bottom panel of figure 4). The now-familiar pattern—of first generation disadvantage, second generation improvement, and mild third generation decline—reappears, though with some variations among regions and among groups. San Francisco leads in the rate of second-generation upper-white-collar employment, followed by New York and Miami. Even though the situation in Chicago and Los Angeles is not nearly as impressive, the overall level is not unimpressive. Clearly, a substantial portion of the second generation, as well as the third generation, is moving well beyond bottom-most rungs. Of course, access to these higher-level jobs varies greatly by group. Mexican second-generation workers are doing much better than the foreign-born; nonetheless they appear at a greater relative disadvantage on this count than on any of the employment indicators examined so far; and there is a very great gap separating U.S.-born Mexicans from their white or Asian counterparts. The extremely low occupational status of first generation Mexicans corresponds to the nature of unskilled Mexican labor migration. Although second-generation Mexican Americans manage to uplift themselves more

Figure 4. Labor market incorporation by generational status: inter-regional and inter-group comparison

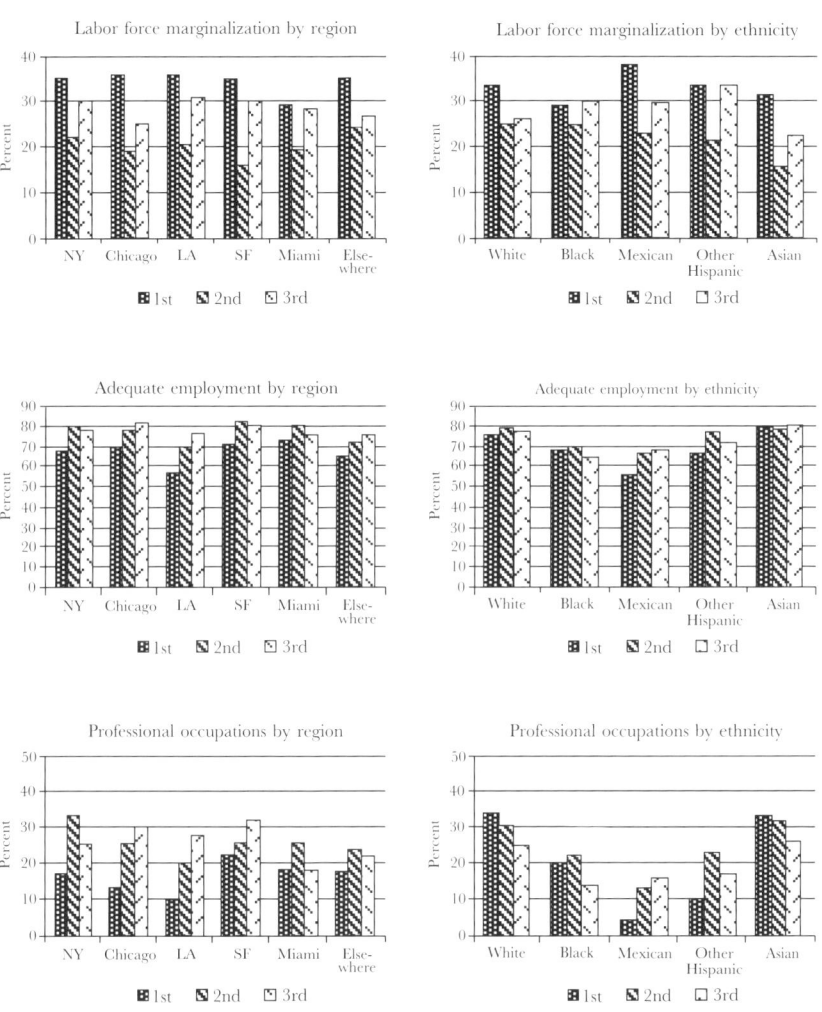

Source: Current Population Survey: 1994–98.

than twice from the first generation status and at a rate far greater rate than other ethnic groups, they still trail behind other group by a significant margin. By the third generation, Mexican and other Hispanic Americans achieve parity with blacks, and Asian Americans with whites. Moreover, the trend of third-generation within each ethnic group decline is striking.

The above descriptive analyses have suggested that the second generation is moving upward, doing far better than the first generation and, in many cases, than the third-plus generation across regions and across major ethnic groups. The effect of time is dramatic between the first and second generation, but matters less between the second and third-plus generation. These intergenerational patterns all point to an optimistic trend of second-generation progress and a somewhat troubling trend of third-generation decline. Nevertheless, there are certain persistent inter-group differences at both intra-regional and inter-regional levels. Overall, Mexicans faring the worst of all ethnic minority groups and Asians the best in all the measures discussed. Findings about blacks and other Hispanics are quite mixed depending on the region. These results imply that space is interacting with both generational status and ethnicity. In particular, the higher rate of second-generation dropout in Chicago and Los Angeles, and the lower rate of third-generation college attendance in Miami blur the prospects of intergenerational mobility. But it remains unclear whether these generational or ethnic differences are a function of demographic characteristics and socioeconomic backgrounds of the individual or of time, ethnicity, and space.

Conclusion

As I have shown in this chapter, the leading cadre of the "new second generation" is now entering the labor market, its presence particularly noticeable in the major immigrant centers of the United States. Several important findings about the new second generation in major immigrant receiving centers emerge from the analyses. First, foreign birth does exert a severe penalty for upward social mobility of young people, even after controlling for measurable demographic and socioeconomic factors. Second, there is a consistent trend of drastic second-generation progress beyond the status of the first generation across regions and ethnic groups. And members of the new second generation generally fare as well as, and in many cases better than, their third-plus-generation counterparts. Moreover, in the third-plus generation, there is a clear convergence of Asian Americans toward the socioeconomic status of non-Hispanic whites and a persistent gap between Mexican or other Hispanic groups and non-Hispanic whites, which resembles the black-white gap. Furthermore, immigrant centers distinguishes themselves from elsewhere and are themselves distinct from one another. These urban centers offer opportunities as well as impose disadvantages on immigrants and their offspring of different racial and ethnic group memberships.

Although my analyses do not directly test the hypothesis of second-generation decline, the findings clearly show that the second generation is advancing in big strides. More troubling is the trend of decline of the third-plus generation, even among Asian Americans whose progress is believed to approach parity with the dominant social group in society. This trend reflects the enduring influence of ethnicity and structural impact of the ethnic stratification system, which implies a high probability of segmented assimilation (Portes and Zhou 1993). Some portion of the ethnic and ethnic-regional disparities that I have detected is probably related to class differentials that I have not been able to adequately assess with the data at hand. I suspect how the third-plus generation of ethnic minorities respond to the structural disadvantages varies by ethnicity. Some may respond to structural disadvantages in an active and empowering way as to reject the dominant groups standards. Others may rely on the ethnic community or ethnic networks of social relations to overcome structural disadvantages and achieve structural parity with the dominant group. Ultimately, however, the value of using ethnicity as an important determinant of intergenerational mobility depends on the extent to which those born or reared in the United States continue to hold a distinctive cultural identity, the extent to which this distinctive identity provides an advantage, rather than a disadvantage, in meeting the challenges of American life and promotes integration (Zhou and Bankston 1998).

In any case, the ethnic effects are sufficiently large and consistent to persist, which lead to a central question for today's research: how to account for ethnic differences. Though accounting for ethnic differences connects the scholarship on today's immigrants to the still-changing literature on their predecessors, it is also a subject with which many contemporary researchers evince more than a little discomfort. As I have argued in the past, groups that both maintain a distinctive identity as well as social structures that promote continued cohesion, have a leg up in the race to succeed. I see nothing in the evidence presented in this essay to suggest a different point of view. Grappling with this claim, and the competing contentions about ethnic differences and their import, remains at the top of the agenda for today's research on tomorrow's second generation.

References

Fong, Timothy P. 1994. *The First Suburban Chinatown*. Philadelphia: Temple University Press.
Gans, Herbert J. 1992. "Second-Generation Decline: Scenarios for the Economic and Ethnic Futures of the Post-1965 American Immigrants." *Ethnic and Racial Studies* 15 (2): 173–192.
Gordon, Milton M. 1964. *Assimilation in American Life: The Role of Race, Religion, and National Origins*. New York: Oxford University Press.
Perlmann, Joel and Roger Waldinger. 1997. "Second Generation Decline? Immigrant Children Past and Present—A Reconsideration." *International Migration Review* 31 (4): 893–922.
Portes, Alejandro and Min Zhou. 1993. "The New Second Generation: Segmented Assimilation and Its Variants." *The Annals of the American Academy of Political and Social Science* 530 (November): 74–96.
Vernez, Georges and Allan Abrhamse. 1996. *How Immigrants Fare in U.S. Education*. RAND: Institute for Education and Training, Center for Research on Immigrant Policy.
Warner, W. Lloyd and Leo Srole. 1945. *The Social Systems of American Ethnic Groups*. New Haven: Yale University Press.
Zhou, Min. 1997. "Growing Up American: The Challenge Confronting Immigrant Children and Children of Immigrants." *Annual Review of Sociology* 23: 63–95.
———. 2001a. "Second-Generation Fate: Progress, Decline, Stagnation?" Pp. 272–307 in Roger Waldinger (ed.), *Strangers at the Gate: New Immigrants in Urban America*. Berkeley: University of California Press.
———. 2001b. "La 'Nouvelle Second Generation' aux Etats-Unis: Reussite Scolaire, Acces au Marche du Travail et Assimilation Segmentee." Pp. 243–258 in Laurence Roulleau-Berger and Madeleine Gauthier (eds.), *Youth and Employment in North American and European Cities*. Editions de l'Aube.
Zhou, Min with Jo-Ann Adefuin, Angie Chung, and Elizabeth Roach. 2000. "How Community Matters for Immigrant Children: Structural Constraints and Resources in Chinatown, Koreatown, and Pico-Union, Los Angeles." Project final report submitted to the California Policy Research Center.
Zhou, Min and Carl L. Bankston, III. 1998. *Growing Up American: How Vietnamese Children Adapt to Life in the United States*. New York: Russell Sage Foundation.
Zhou, Min and Rebecca Kim. 2002. "A Tale of Two Metropolises: Immigrant Chinese Communities in New York and Los Angeles." In David Halle, ed., *Los Angeles and New York in the New Millennium*. Chicago: University of Chicago Press.
Zhou and Logan. 2002. "School Segregation and Its Implications for the Education of the New Second Generation." Unpublished manuscript. Department of Sociology, UCLA.

PART FIVE

YOUTH AS SECOND-CLASS WORKPLACE CITIZENS

WHY DO WORKING YOUTH WORK WHERE THEY DO?[1]

Stuart Tannock

Introduction

Youth in the United States work predominantly in low-end jobs in the service sector—often in "dead end jobs" or "McJobs" located in restaurants, malls, retail outlets, warehouses, offices, movie theaters, theme parks and so on. Working minors are especially concentrated in low-end service work, with over a third finding employment in restaurants and grocery stores alone (National Research Council 1998). Many youth in their late teens and twenties likewise find themselves continuing in jobs much the same as those they had while in high school. Indeed, low-end service work has become naturalized as an extended rite of passage for American youth. Whole segments of service sector employment are widely stereotyped and easily identifiable as being appropriately "youth" forms of work.

Why do working youth work where they do? How did youth employment in America come to look the way it does today? In this article, I point to four key factors. Contemporary youth work in low-end service jobs because: (1) this is where youth have always worked; (2) there has been a broad shift in our society from an industrial to a post-industrial economy; (3) structural transformations within the low-end service sector have favored the employment of youth; and (4) the rise of consumerism and commodification of youth via mass advertising have increased both the supply of and demand for young service sector workers. Consideration of all four of these factors is critical for those who would wish to transform and improve what are all too often marginalized and exploitative youth working conditions.

---

[1] This paper is supported with a report from the Young Worker Project. The Young Worker Project is an effort to bring together academic researchers, labor and community organizers, students, youth and educators who are concerned with improving youth work conditions in the San Francisco Bay Area. The Project is housed at the Center for Labor Research and Education at the University of California, Berkeley, and is coordinated by Sara Flocks, Nato Green, Warren Mar and Stuart Tannock. Sara Flocks, Warren Mar, Nato Green and Robin Gryczman all provided invaluable assistance on the writing of this paper.

A long history of youth in service

One simple answer to the question of why youth today work in low-end service jobs is that young people have always performed such work. Standard histories of children, youth and work typically construct narratives of radical transformations over the past two centuries. An initially agrarian society—in which children and youth worked within household-based production and farming, and young men took on apprenticeships to learn skilled trades—was fundamentally reshaped by the ravages of the industrial revolution in the nineteenth century. Youth were pulled into waged employment; craft-based apprenticeships gave way to the mass and brutal reality of unskilled child factory labor. Subsequent technological, economic, social and political shifts gradually led to the end of the era of children working in factories. Over the course of the first half of the twentieth century, the spread of child labor laws and compulsory education removed more and more youth from the full-time wage labor market altogether. During the second half of the twentieth century, youth increasingly returned to the wage labor market, only now as part-time student workers, who combined formal studies with temporary and seasonal stints in low-end service work.

Such stories of sweeping change belie an enduring continuity. For even at the height of concern with child factory labor at the end of the nineteenth century, only a minority of working children were ever employed in manufacturing and mining (Nardinelli 1990). The large majority of working children worked, as they long had, in agriculture and in the service and distributive industries (Kett 1977). Nineteenth and early twentieth-century cities, according to historian David Nasaw (1985, 48), provided an over-abundance of low-end service jobs for child workers:

> [Children] provided city workers and residents with their afternoon and Sunday papers, their gum, candy, pencils, and shiny shoes. They helped out at home with the cooking, cleaning and laundry. They ran errands and made deliveries for neighborhood tradesmen, carried messages for downtown businessmen who could not yet rely on on their customers to have telephones, and did odd jobs for shopkeepers and local manufacturers.

In the grand department stores that were born in this era—such as Macy's and Marshall Fields—fully "one-third of the labor force was composed of cash girls and cash boys, young children busily involved in transporting money and goods between sales clerks, the wrapping desk, and the cashier" (Zelizer 1985, 63). Moreover, many of the children who worked in manufacturing and mining were in actuality employed there in order to perform service tasks in support of adult production workers. For example, in one typical glass factory at the end of the nineteenth century, over 40% of the workforce were boys. The tasks for which these boys were reponsible, however, consisted of much the same sort of delivery work such as was performed by their peers working as messenger boys and newsies in the city streets, or as cash boys and girls in city department stores: "'Take-out boys' and 'snapper-ups' carried the blown glass in tongs from the blowers to the finishers; the 'carry-in boys' picked it up from the finishers and placed it in the cooling ovens to harden" (Nasaw 1985, 44).

In pre-industrial times, young children from poor families were frequently "placed out" in wealthier families to serve as maids, servants and helpers—indeed, domestic service remained the largest employer of young women throughout the nineteenth century (Ben-Amos 1995; Kett 1977; Nasaw 1985). As was the case in manufacturing settings, children and youth who worked in household-based production and agriculture typically found themselves performing service and support tasks (cleaning, carrying, fetching, etc.) for adult kin. While apprentices of this period were in theory placed under the control of master craftsmen in order to learn a skilled trade, an all too common complaint from young apprentices was that they were taught no skilled trade at all, but were instead expected to perform rote, mundane, unskilled and dead-end service and support work (Hine 1999). (This, of course, is a complaint one hears to this very day from youth who take on low-paid or unpaid "internships" in the often frustrated hope of learning about and gaining entry to prestigious and high paid occupations in media, law, finance, and so forth.)

In the early twentieth century, child labor laws focused on removing children from industrial employment, while more enduring and traditional forms of youth service and delivery work (exemplified in the era by messenger boys and newspaper carriers) continued to be considered widely acceptable (Zelizer 1985). The spread of compulsory schooling undeniably had an enormous impact on removing children from the full-time waged workforce. Yet child and youth part-time and seasonal service work continued to be an integral part of American society and economy. Thus A. B. Hollingshead (1949, 267), in *Elmtown's Youth*, his classic study of the lives of American adolescents in the 1940s in the mid-western U.S., could write that:

> The Elmtown economy has relied upon the labor of boys and girls since frontier days. The language is sprinkled with descriptive terms indicative of the roles boys have played in the mines, mills, stores, and offices: grocery boys, butcher boys, mine boys, water boys, engine boys, barge boys, stable boys, donkey boys, printer's devils, office boys, dray boys, ash boys.... The working girls' roles have been limited traditionally to housemaid, nursemaid, ribbon clerk, office girl, waitress, seamstress, and barmaid.

Hollingshead noted that "Elmtown's economy [had] changed radically in the last two generations" (p. 267); and that "unions no longer allow thirteen- and fourteen-year-old boys in the coal mines, the Mill, or the Foundry" (p. 268). However, Hollingshead also pointed out that "there are no union pressures to keep [boys] out of any small business,... nor has the union closed the door to girls who wish to work in restaurants, stores, and homes" (p. 268). "Today," wrote Hollingshead in 1949, "the distributive and service aspects of the economy have as much need for adolescent employees as in an earlier era, perhaps more" (p. 268).

Why have working youth and children been consistently concentrated in low-end service work? The answer has less to do with any innate capacities (or lack thereof) or affinities that young people have for performing service work, and more with what Phil Cohen (1999) talks of as a labor market system of "patriarchy," and what Diane Elson (1982) describes as a labor market system of "seniority." Focusing on the issue of child labor, Elson (1982, 479) argues that occupational hierarchies in society are constructed not just along lines of race, gender and class, but also of age:

> Children's labour power is systematically differentiated from the labour power of adults working for capitalist enterprises. The most obvious and universal differentiation is that children's labour is remunerated at a lower rate than that of adults. There is also differentiation within the labor process, where children generally have a different status from adults—they are 'trainees', 'apprentices', 'casual' or 'temporary' labourers, helpers or 'mates' of adult workers, subject to the authority of adult workers, as well as to the owners or managers of the enterprise.

Age hierarchies structure remuneration and status within occupations, as well as age-based stratification across occupations. The kinds of tasks that comprise low-end service work have long been seen as low in status, value and skill—and, in fact, unlike even the most menial forms of agricultural and industrial labor, as hardly even constituting "real" work. Such tasks, consequently, have historically been consigned to those groups who are most disempowered and marginalized: women, minorities, immigrants, as well as children and youth (Glenn 1992; Macdonald and Sirianni 1996).

Working youth have been confined to low-end service work in large part through their being explicitly excluded, both institutionally and ideologically, from higher wage and higher status occupations. Seniority rules, limited openings in apprenticeships and professional schools, minimum age limitations, and compulsory schooling (that restricts school age youth to part-time employment) have all been used by adults (especially white males) as ways to protect their own interests in the labor market and exclude youth from good and stable forms of employment (Osterman 1980). Prejudicial stereotypes of youth as being immature, ignorant, incapable, unstable and unreliable have long been invoked to argue that youth are fit for little more than the most mundane, unskilled forms of entry-level service work (Tannock 2001). Condemning youth to tedious and routine service sector jobs has further been justified by popular beliefs in the "school of hard knocks" and the value and necessity of "paying one's dues." Even the most unpleasant and intolerable forms of child and youth work have been constructed as being "character-building" and valuable for the socialization and education of younger generations (Greenberger and Steinberg 1986; Nieuwenhuys 1986). The long history of youth in service has produced—and itself been reproduced by—a constellation of beliefs and practices that today lead many adults and youth alike to see the contemporary concentration of working youth in low-end service work as being natural, inevitable and altogether unremarkable: for this, after all, is what young people do and have always done.

Post-Industrialism, educational expansion and the rise of the student worker

To say that there have been continuities in the lives of working youth through history is not to deny that there have simultaneously been radical changes. One of the most significant has been caused by the broad shift in the United States, over the last several decades, from an industrial, manufacturing-based economy to a post-industrial, service and information economy. While employment numbers and conditions in America's manufacturing sector have been eroded through a combination of technological change, managerial restructuring, deunionization, global competition and capital flight, low-end service jobs have proliferated almost endlessly. Job categories such as cashiers, drivers, security guards and sales clerks continue to be predicted by the U.S. Bureau of Labor Statistics to be among the largest growing for the foreseeable future. Already, over three quarters of Americans of all ages are employed in the service sector, a good many of them in low-end, low-wage jobs (Herzenberg, Alic and Wial 1998). In a telling sign of the times, Wal-Mart, which has been for several years the largest private employer in the United States, passed Exxon Mobil in January 2002 to become the nation's largest company in terms of revenue.

The shift from an industrial to a post-industrial economy has had its primary impact on the lives of working-class and minority youth, and on youth over the age of seventeen (working minors, after all, have rarely been employed in manufacturing, since the passage of child labor laws and spread of compulsory secondary education in the early twentieth century). Working class and minority youth used to be able to graduate from or drop out of high school and find stable, long-term, relatively well-paying employment in manufacturing, mining, and other resource extraction industries—as well as in what was, for many years, an expanding public sector. With the collapse of America's manufacturing base and the freeze or downsizing of public sector employment (brought about by fiscal crisis and the rise of neoliberal ideology), job opportunities for working class youth were altered almost beyond recognition (*The Forgotten Half* 1988; Weis 1990). Poverty rates for working youth close to doubled over the last two decades (Newman 1999: 42); while in inner-city neighborhoods across the country, unemployment rates for minority youth soared (Newman 1999; Wilson 1996).

Stable, well-paying jobs these days are increasingly available primarily for "knowledge workers" (i.e., professionals, administrators, technology workers) with advanced levels of training and education. High school graduates and dropouts now find themselves, upon leaving school, floundering in what *The Forgotten Half* (1988, 11), the influential report on work, youth and family from the William T. Grant Foundation, described as "a sea of part-time, low-paying, limited-future" service-sector jobs—that is, if they are lucky enough to get a job at all. Post-industrialism is creating a society increasingly polarized along the lines of education between the haves and the have-nots: between high wage knowledge workers who require high levels of education, and much larger numbers of low wage service workers, whose advanced educational accomplishments or potential are made largely irrelevant by the limited educational demands of their jobs (Harrison and Bluestone 1988; Herzenberg, Alic and Wial 1998; Reich 1992). New generations of working class youth, some worry, are at risk of being locked into a new "service proletariat" (Esping-Andersen 1993). Only those who are able to continue with further education will be able to use their post-secondary credentials to secure increased employment opportunities.

Getting more education, however, is precisely what more and more youth—working class and middle class alike—are spending more and more of their lives trying to do. In a society in which higher education is increasingly seen as being the *only* ticket to a middle class level of living, it is not surprising that the U.S. has seen a steady and continual increase in post-secondary education participation rates over the last century. Indeed, as sociologist David Livingstone (1999) argues, the United States is home to an escalating "educational arms race," as individuals from all social backgrounds invest in ever higher levels of education in the hope of winning entrance into that elite minority of the country's jobs that pay high wages, offer stable employment and require college degrees. "The popular demand for schooling is not diminishing," Livingstone (1999, 17) writes, "on the contrary, it is extending further and further into adulthood." The vast majority of youth in this country now spend the years following high school pursuing (occasionally in sporadic fashion) some kind of formal or non-formal education, whether in GED programs; private technology, arts, or media academies; trade or vocational institutes; or two-year or four-year colleges. Only a minority of U.S. youth ever obtain a bachelor's (or higher) degree: many youth (working class and minority, especially) drop out of higher education without earning any type of credential whatsoever; others are able to earn a credential below the bachelor degree level and enter into what Norton Grubb (1996) has identified as a vast "sub-baccalaureate labor market" in which wages and working conditions sometimes constitute only limited improvements over the entry-level service jobs in which youth are initially employed.

Educational expansion, spurred by the shift from an industrial to a post-industrial society, has had a tremendous impact on both the nature and scope of youth work. The very category of youth itself—

which historically has been closely associated with enrollment in formal education, exclusion from the full-time or primary labor market, and, consequently, an extended period of economic semi-dependence and legal and social semi-autonomy (Demos 1986; Fasick 1994; Griffin 1993)—has expanded upwards in its normative age range (Côté and Allahar 1994; Wallace and Kovatcheva 1998). Workers in their 20s and even early 30s, for example, who might have been identified in another era as clearly being "adult" workers, may now see themselves (and be seen by others) as being "youth" workers. A key factor in this shift has been the rise and proliferation of the social category of the "student worker." Whereas once it was usual that youth either went to school or they went into the workforce, nowadays in the United States, most youth, whether at the high school or post-high school level, combine both schooling and employment (Greenberger and Steinberg 1986; Horn 1998; U.S. Bureau of Labor Statistics 2001). An ever expanding segment of the nation's workforce, therefore, is made up of (young) individuals who work in the low-end service sector, who identify themselves primarily as students rather than as workers, and who orient to their current service jobs as being temporary (or "youth") places of employment that they hope will be left far behind once their programs of study have been completed (Tannock 2001; Tannock and Flocks 2002).

Educational expansion has also shaped where youth are working: in the low-end service sector. The reason is that students who want or need to work must find jobs that they can fit around their school schedules—they seek, typically, part-time, temporary, week-end, evening, or seasonal employment. As will be described in the following section, it is precisely these kinds of "irregular" or "nonstandard" jobs that have proliferated at an often breath-taking pace over the last few decades within the low-end service and retail industry sector. Youth, it is important to recognize, do not work in low-end service jobs just because of an absence of better employment opportunities in manufacturing or the public sector; they also work in these jobs because of their own presence within institutions of secondary and post-secondary education. This, in particular, is the irony of college student employment. College students, who work to cover rising costs of tuition, books, rent and personal living expenses, often find themselves having to look for employment in exactly the same kinds of low-status, low-wage service sector jobs that they have gone to college in the first place in order to escape (Tannock and Flocks 2002).

Transformations in the retail and service industries

In *Dishing it Out: Waitresses and their Unions in the Twentieth Century*, Dorothy Sue Cobble (1991) recalls an often forgotten history of restaurant work in the United States. Waitresses in the U.S. were once highly unionized. At their peak in the 1940s and 1950s, waitress unions represented one-quarter of restaurant waitstaff nationally, and as much as 70, 80 and even 90 per cent of waitresses in cities such as Seattle, San Francisco, Detroit, New York and Butte, Montana. Unionized waitresses saw themselves as skilled craftswomen, developed a strong occupational craft consciousness, and fought collectively to transform their work into a steady, respectable, rewarding, well-paid and career form of employment.

Despite considerable strength and success, however, the waitress unions, by the beginning of the 1980s, had all but disappeared. "Granny unionists" and full-time, career waitresses were increasingly being forced aside by waves upon waves of young, temporary, part-time, and often student workers:

> Part-time and temporary waitresses had always been a significant sector of the trade but definitely a minority faction. In the postwar era, the retail food industry became a primary employer of part-timers—teenagers, college students, married mothers, and multiple job-holders or "moonlighters" flooded into the new part-time job openings. In 1940, 21 percent of female servers were part-time; thirty years later the figure had skyrocketed to 63 percent. The rise of male part-timers was just as phenomenal: from roughly one in ten in 1940 to a majority of the trade by 1970.... By 1980, the Department of Labor estimated that only one-fifth of food service workers were employed year-round and full-time, the lowest of any occupational category except private household. The average age of food servers dropped as well as employers turned to teenage and student help. (Cobble 1991, 195)

The waitress unions, with their highly developed sense of craft consciousness and occupational solidarity, had a difficult time connecting with the new generations of workers who were spilling into the nation's restaurants. Few of these young workers, writes Cobble (1991, 196), "saw their primary commitment as being to the culinary workplace; their interests and identity resided elsewhere. They considered themselves actresses or students or some other label—but not food servers. Waiting, said one, 'is like the way station of life. You can't have your dream now, so you work in a restaurant.'"

The story of radical labor market transformation that Cobble tells is not unique to the restaurant industry. Similar accounts have been produced, for example, for the department store and retail clothing sector (Benson 1986; Bernhardt 1999; Noyelle 1987); and for the grocery trade (Hughes 1999; Mayo 1993; Walsh 1993). What happened to cause such transformations? In part, labor market shifts were the simple result of the rapid expansion of many service industries during the post-war period—an expansion brought about by increasing prosperity, rising consumerism, and a "self-fulfilling cycle" in which the mass entrance of women into the labor force led to the spreading commodification of services that had previously been provided by housewives within the home (Macdonald and Sirianni 1996, 2). Finding it difficult to fill burgeoning job openings, service employers turned to exploit a new, massive, cheap and largely untapped source of labor: teenagers and students (Marquardt 1998; Reiter 1991). The explosion of fastfood and other franchise industries in the 1960s and 1970s happened to coincide, fortuitously from employers' point of view, with the baby-boom expansion of the teenaged population in the United States, so that there were more teenagers in the country than there ever had been in history (Luxenberg 1985; Schlosser 2001).

Structural shifts within restaurant, retail and service industries facilitated the move from a workforce dominated by skilled, career craftsmen and craftswomen to one based upon young, temporary, minimally trained and minimum wage workers. Regional and national chains and franchises, building their empires on cheap, fast and no-frills service, swept through a sector that had once been made up largely of small, local and independent proprietorships (Luxenberg 1985). "In 1931," writes Cobble (1991, 193), "fewer than 3 percent of the nation's restaurants were chain-operated; in the 1980s, McDonald's alone accounted for 17 percent of all restaurant visits." In their search for greater efficiency and reduced production costs, the chains turned to increased automation and routinization (Leidner 1993; Ritzer 1996); to the mass employment of cheap teenaged labor (whose low wages could be subsidized by parental earnings); and to what Nona Glazer (1993) calls "work transfer," that is, the shift from a full-service to a self-service retail model. From grocery stores to gas stations, department stores to restaurants, customers were increasingly asked to help themselves, while the core tasks for which service workers were held responsible were whittled down to a mundane core of stocking, cleaning, machine-tending, script-following and cashiering.

Low end service industries moved geographically during the postwar era, from city centers to the suburbs where the bulk of the nation's white, middle-class consumers were now living (Luxenberg 1985). This suburbanization of service work had a considerable impact on one of the more widely noted characteristics of youth (specifically teenage) employment in the United States: unlike in many other countries, in the U.S., middle class teenagers are more likely to work than poor teenagers (Greenberger and Steinberg 1986). One direct cause of this is differential access to employment (Boyden, Ling and Myers 1998). Middle class teenagers work in the low end service sector in part because low end service jobs have come to them. The restaurants, retail outlets, supermarkets and movie theaters in which these youth find employment are close to their homes, in their neighborhoods, and adjacent to their high school and college campuses.

Expanded work hours also had a pivotal effect on the service sector workforce. Whereas retail had once been organized as a Monday to Friday (or Saturday) and 9 to 5 business, consumer demand and the large-scale entrance of women into the workforce (that made day shopping more inaccessible for many women) pushed the industry increasingly toward a seven day a week, round the clock schedule (Macdonald and Sirianni 1996; Walsh 1993). Expanded work hours led employers to turn to teenagers and students to fill irregular evening and weekend work shifts. Expanded work hours were also one of the critical wedges that initially sparked the growth of part-time jobs in the retail sector (Tilly 1996). Once employers began using part-timers en masse to staff irregular work shifts, they quickly became aware that switching entirely from a full-time to a part-time workforce could bring considerable cost savings—both through reduced wage and benefit packages, and through new "lean and mean" just-in-time scheduling practices that minimized shift lengths and staggered shift starting points throughout the day in an effort to squeeze out every last minute of "excess" staffing time (Tilly 1996). The ensuing part-time revolution transformed working conditions for all workers in the low end service industry; it also shifted the very make-up of the service workforce, by favoring the employment of youth (and other groups) who were willing and able to work only part-time hours.

That service sector employers were able to make such dramatic changes in their labor process—changes which led to the steady deterioration of working conditions for their employees—was a product of several broader factors. The collapse of high wage manufacturing in the U.S. meant that service employers faced little competition in securing their workforce. Educational expansion created a ballooning population of secondary and post-secondary students who were willing and eager to take on part-time jobs and see themselves as only temporary service workers. The long history of assigning youth to menial service tasks—in other words, the pre-existing ageist, patriarchal or seniority-based structure of work discussed earlier—provided service employers with a widely accepted set of practices and ideologies with which they could expand and entrench a ghettoized youth labor market.

By the start of the twenty-first century, many low end service employers were deliberately constructing all of the jobs they offered as being explicitly youth jobs—even when these jobs were being held by individuals who were no longer teenagers and no longer in school (Klein 1999). When a group of Borders Books and Music Store employees, most of whom were in their 20s, tried to unionize with the UFCW during the late 1990's, for example, their employer sent out the following response in its monthly newsletter:

> We have highly educated employees who consider themselves 'professionals,' but who are in reality working at an early level retail job. Ultimately, each person must make a choice within the modalities of the possible. If you desire an enjoyable job while you figure out what to do with your life, this is a good place to be. But if you try to make a career path out of something which can never be a well-paying job, you will be up against an impossible task because of all of the economic constraints in the retail industry. (quoted in Slaughter 1997, 3)

As Naomi Klein (1999, 232–233) writes, service sector workers are increasingly being treated as if they are not "real" workers and as if the jobs they hold are no more than "hobby" jobs: "Most of the large employers in the service sector manage their workforce as if their clerks didn't depend on their paychecks for anything essential, such as rent or child support. Instead, retail and service employers tend to view their employees as children: students looking for summer jobs, spending money or a quick stopover on the road to a more fulfilling and better-paying career.... Never mind that the service sector is now filled with workers who have multiple university degrees, immigrants unable to find manufacturing jobs, laid-off nurses and teachers, and downsized middle managers. Never mind, too, that the students who do work in retail and fast food—as many of them do—are facing higher tuition costs, less financial assistance from parents and government and more years in school."

Consumerism and the Commodification of Youth

The Kinko's, Starbucks and Blockbuster clerks buy their uniforms of khakis and white or blue shirts at the Gap; the "Hi! Welcome to the Gap!" greeting cheer is fueled by Starbucks double espressos; the résumés that got them the jobs were designed at Kinko's on friendly Macs, in 12-point Helvetica on Microsoft Word. The troops show up for work smelling of CK One (except at Starbucks, where colognes and perfumes are thought to compete with the "romance of coffee" aroma), their faces freshly scrubbed with Body Shop Blue Corn Mask, before leaving apartments furnished with Ikea self-assembled bookcases and coffee tables.
— Naomi Klein (1999) No Logo

There is a strong sense of circularity in much youth employment, particularly in the retail sector. Youth often seem to work where they shop and shop where they work. Their paltry wages seem to cycle back inescapably to their employers through their endless purchase of overpriced consumer goods that they themselves are hired to market and move. Dressed in the same types of clothing they are selling, and eating the same kinds of food they are serving, the lines between consumer and worker in the lives of contemporary youth frequently seem to blur.

Such circularity in youth employment, of course, is anything but accidental. The spread of mass consumerism in post-war America and the rampant fetishization and commodification of youth in mass advertising has created an apparently endless demand for and supply of young service sector workers. Service sector employers hire young workers because youth is what sells their product—indeed, youth often *is* the real product that is being sold, whether a business is ostensibly hawking jeans or t-shirts, sneakers or snowboards, soft drinks or CDs (Giroux 1997; Klein 1999). Retail and food service companies routinely exploit the sexuality of young workers (women especially) in order to attract customers and increase sales. More generally, employers staff their stores by hiring young workers who have the right "look"—they screen, in their recruitment and hiring process, for an appearance, attitude and demeanor that is strongly age, gender, race and class based.

As the distinction for service sector employers vanishes between advertising youth and hiring youth, young workers find themselves literally becoming walking, talking billboards (Klein 1994). Abercrombie and Fitch, a national clothing chain that is heavily oriented to the youth consumer market, represents an extreme example of the general trend. The company no longer hires cashiers or clerks but instead refers to its young employees as "brand representatives":

> Exhibiting the "A&F Look" is a tremendously important part of the overall experience at the Abercrombie & Fitch Stores. We are selling an experience for our customer; an energized store environment creates an atmosphere that people want to experience again and again. The combination of our **Brand Representatives**' style and our Stores' Visual Presentation has brought brand recognition across the country. Our people in the store are an inspiration to the customer. The customer sees the natural Abercrombie style and wants to be like the **Brand Representative. Brand Representatives** will do just what the title suggests: represent the Abercrombie brand to the customer. Our Brand is natural, classic and current, with an emphasis on style. This is what a **Brand Representative** must be; this is what a **Brand Representative** must present in order to fulfill the conditions of employment. (*Abercrombie Look Book: Guidelines for Brand Representatives of Abercrombie & Fitch*, boldface in original)

Abercrombie & Fitch, writes a young college student (White 1997), "entices us into their store with employees who are our peers. In fact, our peers have been scouted—probably on campus—and chosen to sell an image back to us. College students are the featured models in the huge posters adorning the walls of the shop, and we flock to Abercrombie in large numbers to get a piece of the look for ourselves." Another college student—and Abercrombie & Fitch employee—describes the outlet where he works: "Every Brand Rep is between the age of 18 and 23, attractive, slender and always dressed well. Abercrombie imposes extremely strict rules concerning the physical appearance of their Brand Reps. Although nowhere is it written on paper, few will disagree that 'good looks' are an essential attribute to possess in order to be employed. In fact, there are countless rumors of managers being confronted by people higher in management because their store employees are not 'adequately attractive'" (Cavenay 2000).

If service sector employers hire young workers because it helps them build a preferred image and sell their particular product, young workers, likewise, often seek out certain retail and service jobs over others because of their desire to be associated with an idealized company image (or logo) and, more materially, because of their interest in obtaining price reductions and give-aways on much sought after brands of clothing and other heavily marketed commodities. While preferences vary by time, place and peer group, youth in any neighborhood in the country can tell you what are "cool" and "uncool" places for local youth to work—working at Starbucks and Banana Republic may be "in" for the moment, while jobs at McDonald's and Target may be decidedly "out" (Johnson 2001; Newman 1999). Employers such as The Gap commonly find that they are able to attract young workers even in a tight labor market, and even without raising wage offers much above the legal minimum, by holding out the seemingly irresistible lure of promised clothing discounts (Reuters/CBS 2000).

The link between youth consumerism and youth employment has sometimes been singled out for censure as a telling indictment of the state of youth in the contemporary U.S. Young people work, some worry, for no better reason than to feed their ravenous appetites for expensive, luxury consumer items that they don't really need; youth employment, some fear, has become, by the start of the twenty-first century, closely linked with growing materialism, self-indulgence and frivolity among the nation's younger generations (see, for example, Greenberger and Steinberg 1986). It is critically important to put concerns about youth consumerism in proper perspective—for otherwise, these kinds of sentiments lead all too easily to youth bashing and the production of inaccurate and unjust youth stereotypes. As Mike Males (1999) points out, consumerism is by no means a specifically youth phenomenon. It is all too common for social commentators to sound the alarm over growing youth consumerism while completely ignoring an even larger growth in adult consumerism. As Males (1999, 274) reminds us:

> Adults, including parents and teachers, spend $5 trillion per year on personal consumption, including $100 billion on alcohol and tobacco, $40 billion on jewelry, $45 billion on sports supplies, and $90 billion on video and audio products (including 600 million "adult movie" rentals). American adults spend three times more ($300 billion per year) on clothes and accessories than on their own education. American adults gamble half a trillion dollars per year, an amount equal to the total national, state, and local spending on all primary, secondary, and higher education. Where's the liberal tongue-clucking on that "moral barometer"?

Youth consumerism, furthermore, is deliberately manufactured and manipulated by an enormous, adult-led, round-the-clock army of advertisers, marketing consultants and youth researchers (Klein 1999; PBS Frontline 2001). "Teens are exploited," as Cynthia Peters (2001) puts it succinctly, "from both directions in the retail world—as cheap labor and as a demographic to be analyzed, probed and minutely nurtured as consumers. When they're not working the cash register as an employee, we seem to expect them to be working it from the other end—purchasing a steady flow of brand name goods that keep marketers drooling over the current teen baby boom."

The stereotype of the youth worker in discussions of youth employment and consumerism, finally, tends to be an image of a middle-class fifteen or sixteen year old, still living at home, getting his or her first experience in the workforce, earning some extra pocket money, and having no "real" financial needs (Tannock and Flocks 2002). As I have written elsewhere, this "stereotype of the affluent, middle-class teenage worker obscures the fact that, in the United States, there is a sizable group of teenage workers from working-class and poor family backgrounds whose minimum wage earnings constitute critical financial supplements to the well-being of their parental families and households" (Tannock 2001, 2–3). The stereotype of the middle-class, fifteen or sixteen year old worker also obscures the fact that most of the workers who we would think of today as being "youth" workers are actually in their late teens and twenties. These youth are often working to pay rent, cover college tuition, meet personal expenses, help out their parents and support their children (Tannock and Flocks 2002). In other words, while they may be drowning in consumerism like the rest of us, most young workers undeniably have serious financial concerns that drive them to seek employment under the limited circumstances available to youth and young adults in the contemporary U.S.

Conclusion

Improving the generally poor working conditions of young workers in the low end service sector is critically important—not just for the interests of youth, but for adult workers as well. Employers have a long history of exploiting divisions within the workforce, along the lines of race, ethnicity, gender, as well as age. When service sector employers decide that they prefer to hire youth because they feel that they can pay them less, work them harder or exploit their youthful appearance, adult and youth workers alike suffer: indeed, adult workers may find themselves being displaced and put out of work by an exploited teen and youth workforce. The easy access of low end service employers to large, cheap and disposable pools of student workers exerts industry-wide downward pressure on wages and working conditions.

Improving working conditions for working youth—and by extension, for all workers throughout the low end service sector—requires, however, a robust understanding of why working youth work where they do. Too often we seek answers to this question in narrow, unidimensional and localized fashion—at worst, we hear social commentators invoke internalized, psychologistic factors that reproduce prejudicial stereotypes of youth and function to hold youth responsible for their own workplace and labor market difficulties (Tannock 2001). What I have sought to demonstrate in this brief discussion is that addressing the position of youth in the workforce requires an approach that is at once historical and global. Issues that need to considered by educators, policy makers, youth and labor activists when thinking about working youth include: the changing conditions within the service sector workplace itself; the struggles and transformations that are occurring within the manufacturing sector; the besieged and constricted state of public sector employment; the explosive growth of educational participation rates across the U.S. population; the spread of mass consumerism and advertising; as well as the age-old phenomenon of age-based discrimination in the workplace.

References

Ben-Amos, Ilana. 1995. Adolescence as a Cultural Invention: Phillippe Ariès and the Sociology of Youth. *History of the Human Sciences* 8 (2): 69–89.

Benson, Susan Porter. 1986. *Counter Cultures: Saleswomen, Managers and Customers in American Department Stores, 1890–1940*. Urbana: University of Illinois Press.

Bernhardt, Annette. 1999. *The Future of Low-Wage Jobs: Case Studies in the Retail Industry*. Institute on Education and the Economy (IEE) Working Paper No. 10. New York: Teachers College, Columbia University.

Boyden, Jo, Birgitta Ling, and William Myers. 1998. *What Works for Working Children*. Sweden: UNICEF/Rädda Barnen.

Cavenay, Jeff. 2000. *Saturday Morning, Time to Blow Through Friday's Paycheck at the Mall* [online]. Available from World Wide Wed: (http://www.oakland.edu/~jjcavene/ rht150/essay2.html).

Cobble, Dorothy Sue. 1991. *Dishing it Out: Waitresses and their Unions in the Twentieth Century*. Urbana: University of Illinois Press.

Cohen, Phil. 1999. *Rethinking the Youth Question: Education, Labour, and Cultural Studies*. Durham: Duke University Press.

Côté, James, and Anton Allahar. 1994. *Generation on Hold: Coming of Age in the Late Twentieth Century*. Toronto: Stoddart Publishing.

Demos, John. 1986. *Past, Present, and Personal: The Family and the Life Course in American History*. New York: Oxford University Press.

Elson, Diane. 1982. The Differentiation of Children's Labour in the Capitalist Labour Market. *Development and Change* 13: 479–497.

Esping-Anderson, Gosta, ed. 1993. *Changing Classes: Stratification and Mobility in Post-Industrial Societies*. London: Sage.

Fasick, Frank. 1994. On the 'Invention' of Adolescence. *Journal of Early Adolescence* 14 (1): 6–23.

The Forgotten Half: Non-College Youth in America. 1988. Washington, D.C.: William T. Grant Foundation Commission on Work, Family and Citizenship.

Giroux, Henry. 1997. *Channel Surfing: Race Talk and the Destruction of Today's Youth*. Toronto: Canadian Scholars' Press.

Glazer, Nona. 1993. *Women's Paid and Unpaid Labor: The Work Transfer in Health Care and Retailing*. Philadelphia: Temple University Press.

Glenn, Evelyn Nakano. 1992. From Servitude to Service Work: Historical Continuities in the Racial Division of Paid Reproductive Labor. *Signs* 18: 1–43.

Greenberger, Ellen, and Laurence Steinberg. 1986. *When Teenagers Work: The Psychological and Social Costs of Adolescent Employment*. New York: Basic Books.

Griffin, Christine. 1993. *Representations of Youth: The Study of Youth and Adolescence in Britain and America*. Cambridge: Polity Press.

Grubb, Norton. 1996. *Working in the Middle: Strengthening Education and Training for the Mid-Skilled Labor Force*. San Francisco: Jossey-Bass.

Harrison, Bennett, and Barry Bluestone. 1988. *The Great U-Turn: Corporate Restructuring and the Polarizing of America*. New York: Basic Books.

Herzenberg, Stephen, John Alic, and Howard Wial. 1998. *New Rules for a New Economy: Employment and Opportunity in Post-Industrial America*. Ithaca: ILR Press.

Hine, Thomas. 1999. *The Rise and Fall of the American Teenager*. New York: Avon Books.

Hollingshead, A. B. 1961 [1949]. *Elmtown's Youth*. New York: Science Editions.

Horn, Laura. 1998. *Undergraduates Who Work: National Post-Secondary Student Aid Study, 1996*. Washington, D.C.: National Center for Educational Statistics.

Hughes, Katherine. 1999. *Supermarket Employment: Good Jobs at Good Wages?* Institute on Education and the Economy (IEE) Working Paper No. 11. New York: Teachers College, Columbia University.

Johnson, Dirk. 2001. For Teenagers, Fast Food is a Snack, Not a Job. *New York Times*, 8 January.

Kett, Joseph. 1977. *Rites of Passage: Adolescence in America 1790 to the Present*. New York: Basic Books.

Klein, Naomi. 1994. Salesgirl Solidarity. *This Magazine*, February, 12–19.

———. 1999. *No Logo: Taking Aim at the Brand Bullies*. New York: Picador.

Leidner, Robin. 1993. *Fast Food, Fast Talk: Service Work and the Routinization of Everyday Life*. Berkeley: University of California Press.

Livingstone, David. 1999. *The Education-Jobs Gap: Underemployment or Economic Democracy*. Toronto: Garamond Press.

Luxenberg, Stan. 1985. *Roadside Empires: How the Chains Franchised America*. New York: Viking.

Macdonald, Cameron, and Carmen Sirianni. 1996. The Service Society and the Changing Experience of Work. *Working in the Service Society*. Ed. Cameron Macdonald and Carmen Sirianni. Philadelphia: Temple University Press: 1–26.

Males, Mike. 1999. *Framing Youth: 10 Myths About the Next Generation*. Monroe: Common Courage Press.

Marquardt, Richard. 1998. *Enter at Your Own Risk: Canadian Youth and the Labour Market*. Toronto: Between the Lines.

Mayo, James. 1993. *The American Grocery Store: The Business Evolution of an Architectural Space*. Westport: Greenwood Press.

Nardinelli, Clark. 1990. *Child Labor and the Industrial Revolution*. Bloomington: Indiana University Press.

Nasaw, David. 1985. *Children of the City: At Work & At Play*. New York: Oxford University Press.
National Research Council. 1998. *Protecting Youth at Work*. Washington, D.C.: National Academy Press.
Newman, Katherine. 1999. *No Shame in My Game: The Working Poor in the Inner City*. New York: Alfred Knopf.
Nieuwenhuys, Olga. 1996. The Paradox of Child Labor and Anthropology. *Annual Review of Anthropology* 25: 237–251.
Noyelle, Thierry. 1987. *Beyond Industrial Dualism: Market and Job Segmentation in the New Economy*. Boulder: Westview Press.
Osterman, Paul. 1980. *Getting Started: The Youth Labor Market*. Cambridge: MIT Press.
PBS Frontline. 2001. *The Merchants of Cool*. Video documentary. First aired February 27.
Peters, Cynthia. 2001. Treating Teens Contemptuously: The Retail Squeeze. *Znet Daily Commentaries*, 4 August.
Reich, Robert. 1991. *The Work of Nations*. New York: Vintage.
Reiter, Esther. 1991. *Making Fast Food: From the Frying Pan into the Fryer*. Montreal: McGill-Queen's University Press.
Reuters/CBS. 2000. Summer Job Prospects Sizzle. *CBS Evening News*, 31 July.
Ritzer, George. 1996. *The McDonaldization of Society: An Investigation into the Changing Character of Contemporary Social Life*. Rev. ed. Thousand Oaks: Pine Forge Press.
Schlosser, Eric. 2001. *Fast Food Nation*. Boston: Houghton Mifflin.
Slaughter, Jane. 1997. Can Selling Books Ever Be a 'Good Job'? *Labor Notes*, November, 3.
Tannock, Stuart. 2001. *Youth at Work: The Unionized Fast-food and Grocery Workplace*. Philadelphia: Temple University Press.
Tannock, Stuart, and Sara Flocks. 2002. 'I Know What It's Like to Struggle': The Working Lives of Young Students in an Urban Community College. Center for Labor Research and Education (CLRE) Working Paper. Berkeley: University of California.
Tilly, Chris. 1996. *Half a Job: Bad and Good Jobs in a Changing Labor Market*. Philadelphia: Temple University Press.
U.S. Bureau of Labor Statistics. 2001. *College Enrollment and Work Activity of Year 2000 High School Graduates*. Washington, D.C.: U.S. Department of Labor.
Wallace, Claire, and Sijka Kovatcheva. 1998. *Youth in Society: The Construction and Deconstruction of Youth in East and West Europe*. New York: St Martin's Press.
Walsh, John. 1993. *Supermarkets Transformed: Understanding Organizational and Technological Innovations*. New Brunswick: Rutgers University Press.
Weis, Lois. 1990. *Working Class Without Work: High School Students in a De-Industrializing Economy*. New York: Routledge.
White, Kate. 1997. Image's Steep Pricetag. *The Cavalier Daily*, 21 October.
Wilson, William Julius. 1996. *When Work Disappears: The World of the New Urban Poor*. New York: Vintage Books.
Zelizer, Viviana. 1985. *Pricing the Priceless Child: The Changing Social Value of Children*. New York: Basic Books.

DO YOUNG PEOPLE HAVE A SPECIFIC RELATIONSHIP TO WORK?

Robert Castel*

On the face of it, the question: "Do young people have a specific relationship to work?" should elicit a positive response. Firstly, the profound changes in work and work organisation that have occurred over the past 25 years, and which have been reflected mainly in mass unemployment and the spread of precarious employment relations, affect young people in particular, whether they are in their first jobs or looking for employment. Secondly, young people's socialisation into the world of work is still incomplete, and it is perfectly understandable that their attitudes to work should be different from those of earlier generations, whose lives have for several decades been organised around and socialised through work. This difference seems to apply both to those in employment and to those without a job. For example, it is reasonable to assume that enforced inactivity will be experienced differently by a worker who finds himself unemployed after 25 years' continuous work in a factory and a young person who has never worked or who has only ever done a few menial jobs.

However, such statements and assumptions provide little in the way of hard evidence, and the interpretation that should be put on them is by no means self-evident. Many see them as a strong indication of an increasing detachment from work. From this point of view, young people's attitude to work is the most obvious expression of the cultural transformation we are all experiencing and which marks the end of the central role played by work in our daily lives. The majority of young people who are refusing to settle down in permanent jobs are said to be anticipating the advent of new forms of activity and of new reasons for living other than work. This is the argument advanced by Douglas Coupland, for example, which has met with great success in North America[1] and been taken up

---

* This paper was yet edited in Roulleau-Berger, L., Gauthier, M. (2001), *Les jeunes et l'emploi dans les villes d'Europe et d'Amérique du Nord*, Editions de l'Aube, La Tour d'Aigues.

[1] Douglas Coupland, *Generation X, Tales for an Accelerated Culture*, New York, St. Martin Press, 1991.

by André Gorz in his latest book.[2] In this respect, young people are said to represent the future of humanity, presaging as it were that "disengagement from work" that Gorz advocates and which will, it is said, increasingly affect everybody.

I would like to suggest that things are not as simple as this. It is undeniable that young people are the ones most affected by the radical changes currently taking place in the world of work, the most striking feature of which is undoubtedly the development of *increasingly uncertain relationships* to work. However, can it be concluded from this that these more uncertain relationships necessarily bring with them *more distanced relationships* to work? It is this common assumption that *more problematic* relationships to work necessarily involve *greater detachment* from work that I would like to question here.

The questioning will be conducted in two stages. I will begin by attempting to summarise the objective interpretation that might be made of the (equally objective) changes that have taken place in employment relationships and in employment relationships as they affect young people in particular. I will then discuss the "ideological" interpretations to which these data are generally subjected in the course of the debate on the position, importance and future of work in contemporary culture. If all the factors currently restructuring the world of work and employment are taken into account, then the greatest possible caution should be exercised.[3] The content and significance of work have certainly undergone profound changes, but those changes have taken so many different and sometimes even contradictory paths that the complexity of the situations in which social actors now negotiate their relationship to work requires serious sociological research that bears little relation to the much-touted prophecies of a major cultural shift that will lead—so it is alleged—to a generalised and irreversible decline in the value attached to work.

I. *Young people and the changing labour market*

a) *"Young people" or new entrants?*

The difference in attitude among young people compared with earlier generations has to be viewed against the background of the gen-

---

[2] André Gorz, *Misères du présent, richesse du possible*, Paris, Galilée, 1997.
[3] For a survey of the wide diversity of situations, cf. Jacques Kergoat et al. *Le monde du travail*, Paris, La Découverte, 1998.

eral process of change that has been affecting work and relationships to work for a quarter of a century. In general terms, this change is characterised by increasing precariousness, which means that for young people *as well*—but not *only* for young people and not for *all* young people—career paths, and even the possibility of having a career at all, often bear the stamp of uncertainty. It is not possible to instance here the innumerable empirical data that might be used to justify this general diagnosis, and it is scarcely necessary to do so since it is now generally accepted.[4]

In 1997–98, the Centre Etudes et Recherches sur les Qualifications (CEREQ) carried out a survey of 27,000 young people who left the initial education and training system in 1992 with qualifications and specialisms of all kinds and levels. The survey confirms the well-known fact that precarious employment conditions and long-term unemployment are a particular problem for young people leaving the education system with the lowest levels of qualification. Thus some members of the "class of 92" who were questioned had had as many as 15 different jobs in five years, while the length of the average unemployment spell was 22 months for those with the lowest levels of qualification (CAP-BEP), compared with a maximum of 12 months for those with higher qualifications. However, one of the findings of this survey deserves special attention. Almost 15% of the young people with the lowest qualifications had never held a job in five years. Thus approximately 10,000 young people a year, almost 1.5% of their age cohort, seem to be completely excluded from the labour market.[5] What seems to be discernible here is a process leading to the establishment of *structural poverty* or *exclusion* that permanently affects a whole category of young people. In the past, this structural poverty particularly affected older people who had become incapable of working, but it was largely overcome by the establishment of employment-related social protection that provided cover for those periods when people were unable to work, and particularly, through the introduction of pension schemes, for old age. One of the specific characteristics of the erosion of the wage-earning society is perhaps the emergence and possible development of an irreversible process of invalidation affecting a category of inadequately

---

[4] I attempted to summarise these changes in Robert Castel, *Les metamorphoses de la question sociale. Une chronique du salariat*, Paris, Fayard, 1995, particularly in chapters 7 and 8.

[5] CEREQ, *Bref*, no. 149, January 1999.

qualified young people, who seem condemned to a future with no prospects at all even before they have started their working lives.

Another recent finding that helps to update the problematic of young people's relationships to work is derived from a special analysis of the ANPE (the French national employment office) data file that examined the way in which young people and adults have entered and left unemployment since 1993.[6] Overall, young people experience more frequent spells of unemployment, but their periods out of work are shorter (four and a half months on average for 18–19 year-olds), while adults experience fewer spells of unemployment but remain out of work for longer periods (10 months on average for 44–45 year-olds). Thus young people are likely to leave unemployment more rapidly, but for more precarious jobs. However, the vital factor in explaining this disparity is not so much the age variable as such but rather the fact that young people account for the majority of *new entrants* into the labour market. It is in fact the change in the employment regime arising out of the policies adopted by employers seeking increasing flexibility that has given rise to this new dynamic. Thus the age variable conceals a more deep-seated process of determination linked to structural changes in the labour market: because they form the bulk of new entrants into this market, young people are bearing the brunt of the new labour force management policies being adopted by firms. Of course, those with the lowest qualificational levels are the ones most adversely affected by these changes. For this group in particular, the mere fact of being young, a generational fact, may well be reflected in the misfortune of becoming socially unemployable. Being a new entrant into the labour market is the real handicap here, rather than being a young person, although these two characteristics are in reality very frequently associated.[7] However, what is at stake here essentially is the greater or

---

[6] Marie-Odile Lebeau, Alain Degenne, *Etude sur les sorties du chômage, comparaisons jeunes et adultes*, a study conducted by LASMAS at the request of the Commissariat Général du Plan with the assistance of the ANPE, unpublished document of the Commissariat Général du Plan, 1999.

[7] It should be noted that, counted in terms of stocks, permanent employment contracts still account for the highest share of all such contracts (of the order of 60%), but that in terms of flows approximately 70% of new hires take the form of so-called "atypical" jobs. Thus it seems "natural", but is in fact socially determined, that the new flexibility policies adopted by firms have been implemented largely at the expense of young people, since they account for the majority of new entrants into the new system.

lesser objective probability of occupying the weakest and most exposed segments of the labour market, and it is mainly because it determines this probability to a large extent that age comes into play here.

b) *The "biographical pattern"*

Thus young people undoubtedly find themselves in a specific position relative to work, but this specificity cannot be understood without taking account of the general changes in the organisation of work. The overall direction of these changes can be summarised by drawing on the vocabulary used by Ulrich Beck.[8] Beck uses the term "destandardisation of labour" to denote the erosion of the full employment model, whose significance was so great that it was capable of structuring and unifying the career paths of the vast majority of employees throughout the whole of their working lives. One of the major effects of the shock wave now coursing through broad swathes of the employment system is the development of what Beck calls a "biographical pattern": careers frequently take on a chaotic aspect, with individuals usually being abandoned to their own devices, since their place in the world of work is no longer structured by objective and permanent regulations. They have to deal with unexpected situations, change tack and branch out into new areas, frequently recombining the various elements of their lives in more or less risky ways and seeking to establish new, more or less uncertain balances. As a result of the waves of deregulation impinging on the employment system, individuals are being forced to move centre stage and to take charge of their own destinies. They are firstly disaffiliated and then have to seek to reaffiliate themselves in ways that are not always mapped out in advance and for which individuals do not always have the resources required to enable them to land on their feet. Thus these uncertain, confused situations—and this is a point I would stress more than Beck does—increase the disparities between individuals. It is not difficult to understand that some individuals will feel themselves "liberated" from oppressive regulations or even protective arrangements and be able to develop their spirit of enterprise and maximise their opportunities, in short to espouse their roles as winners. However, it is often forgotten, even if we entertain an a

---

[8] Ulrich Beck, *Risk Society*, (1986), English translation, London, SAGE Publications, 1992.

historical and substantialist concept of the individual endowed, a priori, with full powers, that not everybody is capable of reacting in this way. This is a reminder of the influence of the basic sociological determinants of culture, education, social inheritance, qualification level—the various types of "capital" in Bourdieu's sense of the term, in the absence of which the notion of the individual is merely an empty shell, or the daydream of a naïve ideologue. For individuals who lack the objective aids required to exist positively as individuals, the "biographical pattern" may well turn into the biographical nightmare. For them, there can be no stable planning for nor long-term investment in the future. It is not difficult to imagine that this situation may be particularly uncomfortable for young people who, to quote a phrase, "have their lives in front of them". But what lives? Under these circumstances, to be an individual is to pay for the privilege in blood, sweat and tears, to be constantly in the front time without reserves or any chance of having a breather, living from day to day without knowing what the next day will bring.

Thus while it is true that young people are less well integrated into the regulatory and protective frameworks of the standard employment relationship and are therefore more likely to find themselves in those sectors in which the most radical changes are taking place and in which the most innovative experiments are being conducted, it is not wrong to infer from this that certain categories of young people (not all young people of course occupy such a position in the labour market) constitute the advance guard in a process of transformation affecting society as a whole. We should not for all that consider this process out of context nor celebrate unreservedly the opportunities it opens up to emancipate ourselves from the old constraints. If young people are more "individualistic", it is also because they are often the ones most profoundly affected by the objective processes of deregulation and decollectivisation affecting work organisation in general. Thus account has to be taken both of the newness and importance of the "biographical pattern" and of the permanence of the structural determinants driving the development of such a model. Thus to note the increasing individualisation of career paths is an invitation to take equally seriously the new systems of constraints to which work organisation is being subjected.[9]

---

[9] Cf. also A. Furlong, F. Cartmel, *Young People and Social Change: Individualisation and Risk in Late Modernity*, Buckingham, Open University Press, 1997. Following on

As for the consequences of these transformations on attitudes to work, it can readily be understood that work has lost much of its *consistency* since the 1970s. Thus relationships to work are likely to be more problematic than when there was every possibility of finding employment and pursuing a career without interruptions. However, can it justifiably be inferred from this that work has lost its *importance*? This is the conclusion now being drawn by those who speak of a shift in the relationship to work: young people in particular are said to be on the way to abandoning work and to be anticipating alternative forms of organising their existence in society. For example, the attitude of the young unemployed is said to exemplify an emerging alternative concept of unemployment, which is no longer to be interpreted principally as the misfortune of being deprived of work but rather as an opportunity to take part in the construction of new "social worlds" that have been emancipated from work.[10]

It is this shift that has to be questioned, not in order to downplay the importance of the changes currently taking place but in an attempt to assess their exact significance by also taking account of the constant factors that still structure young people's relationship to work. The only way of doing this is to draw on the objective data currently available that takes into account the full range of young people's attitudes to work. To the best of my knowledge, such data are relatively scarce, since few serious surveys have been conducted in this area, their place being taken by inferences pointing to the ineluctable erosion of the value of work. I will have to confine myself here to referring to two types of data which, in my view, refute these all-embracing pronouncements. The first is based on opinion polls, the second on some of the few sociological surveys that have taken the trouble to analyse, with some degree of rigour, changes in attitudes towards work from a generational perspective.

---

from K. Roberts (*Young People and Employment in Modern Britain*, Oxford, Oxford University Press, 1995), these authors speak of "structured individualisation" to denote both the fragmentation effects that shatter the coherence of biographies and the permanence of the objective determining factors of which this individualistic fragmentation is one of the consequences.

[10] For an illustration of this stance, with its claims of liberation from an attachment to the value of work now said to be old-fashioned, cf. Sebastien Schehr, *La vie quotidienne des jeunes chômeurs*, Paris, PUF, 1991, and the encomium penned by André Gorz by way of a preface to the book.

II. *The diversity of young people's attitudes to work*

a) *The constancy of the preoccupation with work*

A number of surveys and opinion polls have been conducted in recent years on the changing attitude of the French to work. Contrary to what is often said, it cannot be concluded from these surveys and polls that there has been a decisive change in the importance that French people attach to work. In other words, the vast majority of them continue to regard work as one of their central preoccupations, and there do not seem to be any significant differences in this respect between young people and adults.

Thus the double survey conducted in 1981 and in 1991 on the changes affecting "French people's values" shows that work still occupies a central position in people's value systems and that this central position is maintained over the long term for all age groups and for all income brackets, irrespective of whether the individuals surveyed are in work or not.[11] If there were any difference at all to be noted between the early 1980s and early 1990s, it would be that there has been an *increase* in the importance attached to work, since a higher share of the people surveyed, *particularly among the young*, thought that a reduction in the importance of work in their lives would be a *"bad thing"*.[12]

The special issue of the magazine *Autrement* published in October 1997 devoted to the question "What is work?" echoes these findings.[13] Despite the "post-modern" stance of this publication and its concern to reflect the most recent changes, it agrees, apparently with a certain degree of vexation, that "the values around work remain robust".[14] This finding would seem to be confirmed by opinion polls, the most recent of which at this present writing was published in *Le Monde* in November 1999. In this poll, young people were asked to judge the value of the main contemporary institutions.[15] While these judgments are generally very critical, the discredit does not extend to work, which is ranked very highly in young people's value systems, just after family but before love and more hedonistic values such as

---

[11] Hélène Riffant (ed.) Les valeurs des Français, Paris, PUF, 1994.
[12] Ibid., pp. 97–98.
[13] *C'est quoi le travail? Autrement*, no. 174, October 1997.
[14] Ibid., p. 15.
[15] *Le Monde*, 15 November 1999.

money or sexuality. The fear of unemployment is also a major preoccupation of the young. For most young people, furthermore, job security is more important than the intrinsic interest of any job as a source of fulfilment. Thus it would certainly seem to be the case that the need to work continues to be perceived as essential by young people, even though the relationship to work is frequently experienced in terms of its negative aspects: fear of unemployment, and an awareness of the uninteresting nature of many jobs. Surveys and opinion polls should not of course be overestimated. Nevertheless, the information they provide can be regarded as an expression, albeit at the most superficial level, of the views of those surveyed as to the importance they attach to work. On this level, and contrary to what is frequently said and repeated, there is no evidence to support the argument that work is "a value on its way out", either among young people or among adults.

b) *Young people and work: detachment, or a problematic area of investment?*

Some sociological surveys allow us to go further, although apparently in the same direction. What is more, they enable us to dispel a misunderstanding, already alluded to above, that is inherent in many of the critiques of the value attached to work: the mere fact that work is becoming increasingly problematic for many people does not mean that it will necessarily cease to occupy a central position in their lives. It is true that mass unemployment and the increasingly precarious nature of jobs frequently give rise to an unhappy relationship to work (which should not make us forget that certain forms of full employment and stable occupations, as in the Taylorist division of labour, were far from giving rise in all cases to a happy relationship to work). However, it is wrong to conclude from this that, as a rule, these difficulties emancipate people from work. In some respects, the opposite is true.

The surveys conducted by Stéphane Beaud and Michel Pialoux are some of the few French studies that have explicitly looked at the relationship to work from an inter-generational perspective. They are based, moreover, on a considerable volume of empirical data gathered over a period of almost ten years in the employment zone of the Peugeot factories at Sochaux-Montbéliard. These authors analyse the differences in the relationship to work between generations both in the work situation and outside work, focusing in particular on the transmission of the notion of work within families from the parents' generation to that the children.[16]

What we are dealing with here, in the first instance, is the intergenerational difference in the relationship to work apprehended within the factory itself. In the pursuit of flexibility, the Peugeot factories have recruited many young temporary agency workers, who work on the shop floor alongside the "old" semi-skilled manual workers who still embody the old traditions of the working classes. The survey describes the relationships between the two groups, which are generally bad and based on a mutual lack of regard: the "young" workers tend to despise the "old" semi-skilled workers who seek to preserve a shop-floor culture based on group solidarity, hostility to self-important supervisor and managers and "crawlers", resourcefulness and the little bit of "cheating" required to give workers some respite from the relentless pace of the production line. What most of the temporary agency workers want, on the other hand, is to show an interest in their work in the hope of being taken on permanently. Paradoxically, they frequently exaggerate the extent of their investment in work, even in comparison with Taylorist workers, who are generally considered to be a paradigm of alienation in the workplace. Thus the experience of being a temporary agency worker, that is to have experienced complicated life histories, to have known hard times and to have often found oneself left alone and isolated to face an uncertain future, has not led to a more casual relationship to work. In certain respects, the contrary is the case. Their past difficulties encourage them to mobilise all their resources in an attempt to seize the opportunity they glimpse of becoming permanent workers; to that end, they make every effort to prove that they are capable of being modern and efficient, always available, serious, co-operative etc. Thus they distance themselves clearly from the generation of "old" manual workers. For all that, however, their relationship to work is no more distanced than that of older workers. In the argot of the factory, it is they who are the "crawlers", the ones who do everything possible to submit to the new constraints of work and to the new managerial rules, while the older generation of manual workers struggled and continue to struggle under

---

[16] In addition to numerous articles, cf. a synthesis of these studies in Stéphane Beaud, Michel Pialoux, *Retour sur la condition ouvrière*, Paris, Fayard, 1999.

increasingly difficult conditions to retain a minimal level of independence from work.[17]

This generational difference in attitude is even more revealing if we turn to an earlier phase in the life cycle in order to analyse the way in which young people begin to develop their ideas about work in the family and at school. Stéphane Beaud and Michel Pialoux show that, among the working classes at least, the change of attitude towards work is produced firstly through a breakdown in the process of inter-generational transmission within the family. Working-class families, particularly the fathers, often feel distressed that they are no longer able to transmit their work culture, which has been devalued by the technological changes that have radically changed work organisation and the socio-political changes that have affected perceptions of the historical role of the working class. Thus their children's decision to extend their education is, firstly, the result of a certain cultural distancing from the previous generation. This choice in fact leads them to stay at school in order to escape the factory.[18] However, this decision to stay at school does not necessarily mean that the conditions required for success in the education system are fulfilled. Young people from working-class backgrounds frequently find themselves cut off from their original cultures without having at their disposal sufficient means to integrate themselves into a new culture shaped by the values and behaviour of the middle classes. They no longer wish to follow in their parents' footsteps, since the jobs they did now have negative connotations, but they lack the capacities required to gain the qualifications that would give them access to new occupations. Hence the confusion of these adolescents caught up in a headlong flight whose parameters they are unable to control. They have committed a sort of cultural parricide for which they may pay dearly by becoming entrapped in lengthy courses of study without any real prospects.

It is easy to imagine why it might be difficult for such young people to establish a positive relationship to work. But does this mean that they are emancipated from work? It would seem that this question can no longer be answered in general terms. Such circumstances may induce some people to cease to invest in the world of work in

---

[17] Ibid., particularly pp. 355–367.
[18] Ibid., pp. 205–278.

order to try to live or to survive. There is certainly a grey area in social life, still ill-defined, in which what might be called a culture of precariousness or culture of uncertainty is developing and which is inhabited by large numbers of young people whose existence is no longer structured around stable employment and who no longer organise their lives around the need to gain access to such employment.[19] However, the difficulty of gaining a foothold in the labour market may also go hand in hand with a considerable level of investment in work. As we have already seen, this was the case with the temporary agency workers at Peugeot. However, it may also be the attitude of many school-leavers from working-class backgrounds who are no longer able or willing to adopt their parents' relationship to work, who are confused about work while at the same time being *highly motivated by work*. This is what is shown by a survey of young people on a housing development close to Paris, many of them the sons or daughters of immigrants, who have obtained the *baccalauréat*.[20] Like the young people studied by Beaud and Pialoux, they reject the system of constraints in which their parents were trapped. However, they also expressed a strong desire for success at work, display a healthy sense of independence and initiative in putting together credible plans and sometimes even develop a work ethic bordering on the ascetic. "I'm someone," said one of them, "even in my work; when I work I work, I mean I don't mess around. That's how I am; when I'm working, I'm totally involved in what I'm doing."

This survey suggests that there are very contrasting attitudes to work among young people from the most disadvantaged sections of

---

[19] For a description of these activities, cf. for example Laurence Roulleau-Berger, *La Ville Intervalle*, Paris, Méridiens-Klincksieck, 1991, and *Le travail en friche, les mondes de la petite production urbaine*, Editions de l'Aube, 1999. For an analysis of exchange networks in a parallel economy characteristic of certain suburban areas, cf. M. Joubert, J. Fr. Laë, A. Madec, N. Murard, "Economie et banlieue", *Réseaux productifs et territoires urbains*, Toulouse, P.U.M., 1996. It is difficult to estimate with any accuracy the number of young people involved in these activities, which some commentators describe, with excessive optimism no doubt, as alternatives to standard employment. However, the 1990 census showed that 10% of young people in the 18–25 age group are not listed anywhere: they are not in work, in education, in the Armed Forces or undergoing training of any kind. It might reasonably be assumed that a high proportion of them are engaged in these "informal" activities.

[20] Laurence Ould Ferhat, "N'avoir que le bac mais avoir quand même le bac: l'école, le travail et les transmission intergénérationnelles chez les jeunes de niveau IV", an as yet unpublished paper of the "Précarité, trajectoires, projet de vie" network of the Mission Interministérielle Recherche-Expérimentation (MIRE), Paris, survey conducted in 1998–99.

the working class. Those who are most at sea, who have failed in the school system, have indeed lost that positive attitude to work; this is readily understandable, since their chances of finding a job with any interest in it at all are extremely slim. It is this group in particular that becomes involved in various forms of informal economic activities, legal or otherwise, which may be interpreted as a search for alternatives to work. However, those who go through this "exile from work" pay a heavy price, and it is debatable whether it can really provide the basis for a positive model of emancipation from work for the future. On the other hand, young people from the same sort of background who have performed better in the school system and who are aware that they bring with them certain "baggage" that will help them confront the future often retain a very positive relationship to work.

These are not indisputable findings but rather inferences based on partial data of possibly limited scope. However, this is precisely what I want to suggest. We need more precise data and serious surveys before giving a definitive response to a complex question that may have apparently contradictory aspects.

Thus, by way of a provisional conclusion, we can say that before we have more information, and in order to gather that information, we will have to be more sensitive to the diversity of attitudes among young people and not to allow ourselves to be locked into an all-embracing, culturalist discourse, in which it is claimed that "young people" are the frontrunners in a generalised change in our relationship to work. We have noted that attitudes can indeed be very contrasting, even among young people from disadvantaged backgrounds. However, they are also very different from those that might be observed in other social categories that seem able to develop much more effective strategies for gaining access to jobs and sustaining and passing on more positive attitudes in respect of work. For example, if the upper middle classes have generally succeeded in bringing themselves up to date, it is because they have understood that work is at least as necessary as rent in order to occupy and retain dominant positions in society. Not just any work, of course, but those "top-of-the-range" jobs for which advanced qualifications acquired in elite educational establishments are required. In these particularly advantaged circles, there does not seem to be any "work crisis", and the heirs of these families do not generally seem to have many qualms either about the value of work: they retain these positions because they have acquired high-status qualifications and adhere to an ethic of success at work. The argument that there has been a massive, unilateral change in our attitudes to work is based largely, but without always making it explicit, on the experience of young people whose socialisation within the family has been most problematic and who have the slimmest objective chances of finding good-quality jobs. Of course, these analyses must be further refined, and they would undoubtedly show that there are even more disparities in attitudes to work among and within the various social categories. Thus certain sections of the middle classes also seem to have been left behind by the changes now taking place and to be incapable of passing on to their children positive attitudes to work and the means required to find it. However, their confusion is probably very different from that experienced by the working classes, and particularly the most disadvantaged among them. However, in order to be justified, these observations need to be investigated more thoroughly.

Thus the position I have advanced here is not intended to underestimate the importance of the changes that have taken place in young people's attitudes to work. Rather, it is an attempt to interpret them by taking full account of the social determinants that continue to control access to work and the more or less positive or negative relationships that people might have to it. If it is indeed the increasingly precarious nature of employment relationships and mass unemployment that have undermined confidence in work as a privileged means of gaining access to a stable position in society, we have to ask who is mainly affected by these changes, to what extent and how. It is not young people in general and in an undifferentiated way. And yet young people are indeed more affected than the representatives of the previous generation because it is they who are now coming onto the labour market and are most directly affected by the most recent changes that have taken place there. Nevertheless not all young people are helpless in the face of these new situations. We have noted that the importance of the "biographical pattern" that is becoming increasingly dominant, whether one is looking for work or seeking to manage the uncertainties of working life, does not preclude us from taking account of the social rootedness of individuals, but indeed demands that we should do so. Indeed, it is by drawing on socially distributed resources that we are able to exist more or less positively as individuals in the face of the new set of problems posed by work.

The hypothesis advanced here is that young people's attitude work depends largely—though to an extent that has itself to be specified—on the nature and quality of the social resources of this type that they are able to mobilise. An exhaustive list of these resources, and of their differential distribution, needs to be drawn up. Thus it is a question that remains open to sociological analysis, whereas merely affirming that there has been an overall change in young people's attitude to work simply serves to mask the problem.

YOUNG PEOPLE AND WORK IN QUEBEC: TAKING STOCK*

Jacques Hamel

Young people in Quebec as elsewhere are giving work a new complexion. This continues a long-standing tradition, for owing to their age, young people form the social group first affected by changing patterns of work, jobs and the labour market. For this same reason, they are the ones who have the greatest hand in crafting those changes (Nicole-Drancourt and Roulleau-Berger 2001).

Current sociological propositions on this subject would suggest that work is far from coming first in the lives of young people and indeed does not rank high in their present or future plans. It is argued that few of them make the effort to acquire the attitudes and skills that would make work the cornerstone of their life and identity. The model employee, dedicated to work and company, is fading from view. This is shown by surveys and interviews of American, British, German and Dutch youth (Cannon 1994; Baethge 1994), which make it clear that work is losing momentum as both an activity and a value. Recreation, family, the couple relationship and community activities seem to be winning out over work and becoming the implements likely to shape young people's values, identity and lives. André Gorz, a commentator on those surveys, writes that "the majority of those under 30 have never experienced identity through 'work' and job security. They have never lost that kind of identity for the simple reason that they have never been able to find it" (Gorz 1999: 3). This proposition is quite fashionable, suggesting that "young people thus represent the future of humankind and foretell, as it were, the coming of this *exile from work*" (Castel 2001: 287–288).

Strangely enough, the surveys also indicate that young people come in contact with work at an early age when they combine it with study, at the cost of school success. They experience the study-work tandem to earn money needed to break free of dependence on their

---

* This article grew out of research funded by the Science Research Council of Canada. I gratefully acknowledge the comments and constructive criticism received from colleagues and students.

parents and also to build peer relations. Through menial work, or "McJobs" as the latest jargon goes, they confront the demands and requirements of employment and the labour market so as to give direction to their studies, lives and plans. Furthermore, the new technologies enable them to test their skills and fashion personal competencies which school could not draw forth and fully develop and which young people apply with élan in the work world. To use the stock phrase, the "relationship to work" of young people is far from straightforward under these conditions.

Brief review of the "relationship to work" concept

"Relationship to work" was a subject of choice of traditional and contemporary sociological theory before becoming the concept constantly put forward in the name of sociology. Indeed, sociologists of all stripes have contemplated work, the action meant to produce all manner of "goods" and thus account for society. From that perspective, work is the cornerstone of social life.

The "relationship to work" concept then came to designate that productive action broadened to encompass the values, representations, statutes and rights which it mobilizes and engenders and which form the basis for ontological security, perceived by Anthony Giddens as "the trust of human beings in the continuity of their own identity and in the consistency of the environments where social and material action is played out" [unofficial translation] (Giddens 1994: 98). Work thus represents "the door to social as well as personal identity," being in other words a unique opportunity for self-definition and for building meaning into one's path in life" (Sainsaulieu 1995: 188).

From the sociological vantage, the "relationship to work" is therefore contemplated in light of the emphasis put on the means and ends of the action per se or else on the ensuing social interaction. This means that it is construed from two angles that usage has set at odds with one another. On the one hand, work is the instrumental action intended to fulfil needs; on the other, it is an "expressive action" through which work becomes a channel for expression of the worker's personal qualities and sense of belonging to a whole, whether a company, a community or society as a whole.

Jürgen Habermas, more than any other author, has sought to unpack these opposing perspectives. He sees the instrumental action as a "rational activity relating to an end" (Habermas 1973: 21). The expressive action is based on "symbol-mediated interaction" (Ibid. 22). According to Habermas, salaried employment as the hard and fast rule in capitalist societies has pushed the instrumental action to "colonize" (his expression) all interaction governed by values and norms geared towards reciprocity and expectations of shared behaviour. Work in this case is emptied of all its normative and integrating characteristics, ultimately becoming an activity centred on the relationship of means to end, one clear illustration being technology.

Through a sort of pendulum effect, reciprocity based on shared expectations seems to have spread to other hearths of social integration—the family and the community, for instance—that are threatened, however, by the relationship of means to end, which is the *raison d'être* for work. Habermas observes in this regard that "the markets dealing in goods, capital and labour currently have a logic all their own, apart from the players' intentions ... Integration (through work) competes with social integration, which occurs through the values, norms and mutual understanding of the players, and thus their conscience" (Habermas 1998: 78). In his view, work is far from being an expressive action inseparable in theory from rational activity relating to an end. Instead, it has become the basis for a purely instrumental action whose implementation flies in the face of any mutual understanding based on shared values and norms.

According to many authors (e.g. Grell 1998; Schehr 1999; Schor 1992; Zoll 2001), these are the grounds for young people's relationship to work. Indeed, it is widely held that the misfires of salaried employment, evidenced by job insecurity and flextime, render the integrating function of work obsolete. Salaried employment thus becomes no more than a means of earning a living and creates no attendant expectations. Studies on this subject eagerly conclude that "the relationship to work is losing muscle because life takes place elsewhere," especially in "unpaid activities regarded as socially useful" (Lebaube 1992). Companies no longer resemble "one big happy family," as employers once boasted. Young people feel no sense of importance faced with companies that are more inclined to offer them fixed-term contracts than to hire them on a regular basis. Work embodied in its highest form of salaried employment becomes solely the means of earning a living and thus takes on a purely instrumental hue" (Zoll 2001: 264).

These propositions, raised to the rank of theory, seem to be contradicted, or at least qualified, by the portraits of Quebec youth sketched from empirical labour data.

Early entrance into the work world

Starting in adolescence, Quebec youth share their studies with work in the form of menial jobs (McJobs). They enter the work world early on, in other words. According to official statistics, this is a growing trend that has now spread to over 60% of Secondary V students. This figure matches comparable figures from the U.S. Bureau of Labour Statistics, but breaks rank with the percentage of French college students who also work (20%). Adolescents work mainly in stores and fast food establishments, mostly on weekends. A vast range of motivations are given for the propensity to work at that age. Adolescents from underprivileged families work to meet their recreational and consumer needs. Preferences in clothes and recreation developed through associating with school mates motivate them to hold down a regular job involving longer hours, i.e. eight to twelve hours a week (Gauthier et al. 1997: 89–113). For middle-class adolescents, the McJob is less about satisfying needs and more a bid to break free of their parents' tastes and consumer habits, while at the same time offsetting parental authority.

So strong is the tendency to work among Quebec adolescents than parent-teacher associations publicly demanded legislative measures to restrict their working hours. That call on legislation was not without reservations, however. Many businesses, the fast-food chains in particular, hire hordes of adolescents, who often see that work not only as a source of income but also the place for socialization that is lacking at school. Furthermore, the strict regulation of youth employment infringes on the rights and freedoms enacted for them in the charters. The parent-teacher associations backed off and, with government support, settled for a warning to employers to limit the working hours of adolescents and schedule them for time slots that in no way jeopardize their education or school success.

The McJobs favoured by adolescents reflect a new relationship to work. The household chores that were once their lot rarely extended beyond the home or immediate vicinity. In rural areas, farming enlisted their services under the watchful eye of parents wishing to pass on that inheritance in exchange for a show of dedication that could certainly not be regarded as "work." Adolescents today opt for paid employment early on, discovering its mechanisms and rules and often experiencing a concomitant socialization, with the result that work pulls out ahead of school, family and neighbourhood. Menial jobs provide competition on this score and in many ways turn out to be the setting in which individual and social identities crystallize.

In working, adolescents also discover firsthand the constraints involved, if not the exploitation that work conceals at their expense. Quebec takes pride in being the arena for the first attempt to unionize the young workers of the McDonald's chain in a bid to fight the job insecurity and mobility they face. To everyone's surprise, those young employees united to demand rights and benefits from a company that did everything it could to block those demands. From an analytical standpoint, that spectacular development showed that work is far from being a purely "instrumental action" at that age. At the same time, it is a form of interaction mediated by values and norms that bind adolescents among themselves and with others.

Youth work and extended studies

The period of formal schooling has grown longer in Quebec since the time of the "Quiet Revolution."[1] Young people tend to extend their studies over a longer period. Consequently, more of them are climbing the rungs of the education ladder, and increasing numbers of them are earning college and university diplomas.[2] The figures speak volumes.

---

[1] The Quiet Revolution refers to the time in which Quebec society was modernized after a long political regime marked by conservatism, the pre-eminence of the Church and subordination to Anglo-American capitalism. Numerous commentators state that the revolution was indeed quiet, without clashes or violence, although it was the fastest industrial, social, educational and religious revolution in the history of the Western world.

[2] The Quebec school system has four levels: i) primary school (grades 1 through 6), ii) secondary school (grades I through V, with students able to learn a trade in the final two years), iii) college, or CEGEP (collège d'enseignement général et professionnel: which provides three years for vocational training or two years of preparation for university), and iv) university, which awards the bachelor's degree after three years of study, as well as further studies and degrees.

Number of graduates by level of schooling, type of training and gender

	COLLEGE				UNIVERSITY					
	University track		Technical		Undergraduate		Graduate		Postgraduate	
Year	Male	Female	Male	Female	Male	Female	Male	Female	Male	Female
1983–84	—	—	—	—	11 021	10 716	2 241	1 480	306	114
1984–85	11 206	12 957	8 918	10 624	11 085	11 136	2 361	1 664	365	134
1985–86	—	—	—	—	11 615	12 010	2 626	1 918	373	143
1986–87	—	—	—	—	11 465	12 395	2 516	2 037	429	164
1987–88	—	—	—	—	11 663	13 394	2 555	2 053	424	177
1988–89	10 833	13 970	6 090	8 966	—	—	—	—	—	—
1989–90	10 779	14 127	6 302	9 059	—	—	—	—	—	—
1990–91	10 684	14 200	6 141	8 827	11 872	14 938	2 866	2 570	583	244
1991–92	10 441	14 708	6 758	9 519	12 038	15 740	3 020	2 805	647	268
1992–93	10 247	14 466	7 722	10 133	12 083	16 321	3 105	2 977	611	280

Source: Secrétariat à la jeunesse, *Indicateurs jeunesse. La jeunesse québécoise en chiffres (15–29 ans)*, Québec, MRCI, 1999, p. 64.

School dropout is becoming confined to youth with learning difficulties, youth for whom "dropping out of school and paid employment are means of escaping a demoralizing school experience" (Hirmech and Théorêt 1997: 371). But more and more students are staying the course, with crowds of them knocking on college and university doors, either willingly or forced by circumstances. In fact, it is very difficult to know whether the trend to continue studies reflects a thirst for higher education or the inability to gain a solid toehold in the labour market.

Schooling affects young people in different ways, however. The rise in academic attainment and the earning of diplomas and degrees strongly reflect the rise of women to the circles of higher education and their academic persistence. The gender gap is definitely greater in Quebec than elsewhere. Women are gaining ground across the board, invading, for example, what were once the private bastions of their male colleagues—medicine, engineering and law. Furthermore, an equal balance of the sexes among the student population in specialized medicine was recently attained in Quebec's French-language universities.

The extension of studies is accompanied by trends specific to today's youth. Part-time study is much in favour and even becoming necessary for post-secondary students. Rarely are students enrolling full-time in college or university. The part-time formula is gaining in popularity as it makes its way into their college curriculum and at the time of university enrolment as well.

Students who complete their program of study within the prescribed time are in the minority, practically speaking. By way of example, 41.9%[3] of college students earn their diploma within the normal time. As one can imagine, balancing studies and work is once more given as the reason for this deviation from the rule, although other reasons are alleged, mostly the switch from one discipline or field to another or "sabbatical" time for taking stock.

The colleges, concerned about the delay in completing their curricula, recently instituted a "failure tax" for failure due to repeated absence from class. But they soon realized that students tended to enrol in fewer courses so as to complete them and still have the option of spending more time working and thereby boosting their spending level, which in turn makes it all the more necessary to work. Students carefully calculate the time and energy they can devote to studies before study encroaches on work or, for a minority among them, before work encroaches on study.

For young people, the choice of a field of study is dictated less and less by personal interests, but rather by the needs and expectations of companies. Early entrance into the labour market provides students with basic information that motivates those choices. The trend is clear from the two-way traffic in and out of school. Legions of young people who have earned their first diploma are giving the labour market a try, in hopes of joining it. But having bit the dust, they decide to return to school and, based on that first foray, channel their studies towards the field or training that employers apparently prize. This would make the first job a way of testing the waters, assessing and weighing business needs and expectations to determine which factors are useful for winning the prize of stable employment.

Entering the labour market, a real obstacle course

In terms of numbers, unemployment hits harder at young people, who are at the starting line owing to their age and are for that same reason directly exposed to the vicissitudes of the economy. They are

---
[3] This percentage is the highest achieved only in 1998-1999.

automatically the first victims of economic recession or fluctuation. In times of economic recovery, however, they benefit from newly created jobs. As regards Quebec, the economic recovery following on the heels of the 1993 recession did not entail the hoped-for turnaround in the job situation, and the rate of youth unemployment rose steadily. On the other hand, those aged 25–64 have experienced a downtrend in unemployment since 1994, despite a slight jump in 1996. Still, unemployment for the 15–24 bracket has remained below the rate recorded during the 1981 recession, with 23% of those young people actively seeking work in 1982.

As one can imagine, the unemployment rate varies with age. Youth in the 15–19 age bracket, sorely exposed to the fits and starts of the economy, post the highest unemployment, which was 27.4% in 1997, practically in sync with the 28.2% posted in 1982 during the worst of the economic slowdown. The trend in unemployment for the 20–24 age bracket compares with that for the older group in many respects: the gap was 7.1% in 1975, then jumped to 9.4% in 1982 and subsequently dropped to 5.7% in 1997. Unemployment for 20–24 year olds hovered around 15.7% at the time, or barely more than half the rate for the younger age bracket.

The official statistics also reveal the trends taking shape in the background, i.e. 15–19 year olds are more vulnerable to unemployment than are those in the next bracket (20–24 years old) and males are more vulnerable than females, who are making their way nicely in the labour force. The obstacle of unemployment facing young people points up the changing forms that are giving work its new complexion.

Flextime and mobility are law in the Quebec labour market as in others. Contract employment with its many permutations and self-employment are gaining the upper hand. According to the statistics, half of the jobs created since 1976 fall into these categories. Roughly 7% of those age 25 and over worked part time back then, and that figure doubled in the space of twenty years to 13.4% in 1996. The trend was especially vigorous among young people, whose share of part-time jobs jumped from 14.6% to 44.4%.

This picture needs to be qualified in the circumstances. Part-time work is practically all there is for 15–19 year olds since that employment is largely shared with studies at that age. This was in fact the reason given by 58% of the members of that age bracket in 1976 and by 61% of them in 1995. Furthermore, young people in that bracket cannot find full-time employment. In 1976, 17% of those working part time cited that reason, by comparison with 28% in 1995. The 15–24 year olds do better in this respect than those aged 25 and over, since that was the reason which 43% of them gave for working part time in 1995, whereas that figure was 12% in 1976.

Being necessarily at the starting gate, young people are hit hard by job insecurity, to use the stock phrase. Massive company layoffs in step with economic recessions, government finance crises with their procession of cuts in social services and public administration, and the emergence of new technologies have been instrumental in creating flextime, occasional work and mobility. This is gradually leading to the obsolescence of salaried employment, which grew out of the Glorious Thirties, a time of post-war prosperity. Its form of choice, imposed by the worker struggles waged since the Industrial Revolution, is being stripped of the characteristics ascribed to paid employment, i.e. steady, full time and protected by mutual agreement between those involved.

Contract work of fixed duration has been mushrooming in all sectors of the economy since the 1981 recession. The turnaround in government finance through absorption of the chronic national deficit momentarily suggested that the doors of the civil service would swing open for young people, with the backing of official commitments.[4] To date, however, government departments and services have not resumed hiring young people to any significant extent. Those newly recruited into the government bureaucracy still contend with contract work. Even after years of service, very few of them enjoy the benefits of employment as set out by civil service rules.

On the other hand, the labour market is struggling with a shortage of workers in the trades governed by guilds and professional orders, one example being the construction trade. The large-scale retirement of tradesmen within a short space of time, a phenomenon tied to demographic reasons, is shrinking this particular workforce, whose replenishment is threatened by the scarcity of young people opting

---

[4] The Government of Quebec took a bold initiative by staging the Quebec and Youth Summit on the eve of the year 2000. That forum provided public policy makers, management, unions and youth advocacy representatives with an opportunity to put their cards on the table and draw up an intervention program so that young people could find their place in the labour market, in the halls of power and in society. It concluded with the drafting of an action plan containing specific commitments. Those commitments were formalized two years ago; the promises are long in coming.

for vocational training. The trades have lost their "sex appeal" for young people, who are encouraged from every side to join ranks with the knowledge-based society, driven by the new technologies. The vocational training streams, especially in secondary school, have long been perceived as second-rate options recommended for the least gifted students or those inclined to drop out of school early on.

In view of this sudden labour shortage, vocational training is earning its stripes and looking like a gold mine for young people seeking a smooth entry into the labour market. The demand is so strong, in fact, that employers are hiring young people before they have received their credentials, diplomas or qualification certificates. In fact, entering the workforce without a diploma is shaping up as a trend even in the sectors focused on the new economy.

Young people, the new economy and their paradoxes

The "new economy" is a well-known expression that grew out of the U.S. economic boom of 1992–93, which was spurred by stock-market capitalization, market globalization and the Internet revolution. The qualifier "new" is justified by the fact that, unlike previous economic cycles, that particular cycle of growth did not usher in a return to inflation. More specifically, the new economy designates the sector comprising new information and communication technologies, familiarly known as NICT. This sector is said to be the engine powering the economic growth and social change born of the Internet and online services tied to e-commerce, which is embodied in the Nasdaq and new companies such as Yahoo!, Microsoft and Amazon. Not to be outdone, Quebec has its own key players, such as SoftImage and De M@rque, which were the initiatives of entrepreneurs under age 30.

In the present context, young people form the group of society immediately affected by the new economy in its literal meaning, i.e. the economy born in the early 1990s and centred on what are generally termed "the new technologies." Indeed, more than any other group in society, many young people must take up those technologies for their livelihood and will have to rely on them in future as well. Consequently, they must be sufficiently knowledgeable to wield them properly. This is why many authors dub them "the digital generation," for they must cope with the demands and constraints associated with the new information and communication technologies, the acquisition and upgrading of knowledge required by those rapidly changing NICT, and ceaseless changes in corporate requirements stemming from the fast flow of capital, knowledge and labour on a world scale.

Nevertheless, the present situation is strongly tempering the new economy, or at least the image one has of it. Many of the conglomerates listed on the Nasdaq are in free fall, including Nortel, the jewel of Quebec enterprise. They are putting legions of highly skilled new technology workers on unemployment. Young people are first among those workers, needless to say. Based on statistics from the Centre d'étude sur l'emploi et la technologie (CETECH), the massive numbers of jobs created from 1992 to 2000 are not tied to computer science, databases or the Internet. Jobs created in those fields number 65,000 by comparison with 280,000 newly created public service jobs in health and education (CETECH 2001: 9). Projections for the period 2000–2005 bear out this trend: of the 25 vocations and professions that lead in job creation, eight require college or university qualifications, whereas only three require specialization in NICT (IMT 2001).

The early economic and sociological portraits of the multimedia industry are especially revealing on this score. It is said that the young people working in multimedia, either within a company or from home, are about 25 years old, and a large percentage of them terminated their studies without earning a college or university diploma (CRIM 1999; Masi 2000). Thus, the young new-technology enthusiasts opt for learning by using (or doing). They are trained through using computer technologies on the job and can therefore forge individual aptitudes, although they have no credentials the likes of diplomas or formal certification.

Salaries and working conditions, especially the number of hours spent working, in no way reflect the highly skilled jobs that discourse on the new economy paints in such radiant colours. Actually, they are more akin to jobs at the bottom of the ladder. Young people lacking formal certification have a difficult time selling their skills or capitalizing financially on them except through learning by using, a practice being eroded by rapid, ever changing technological development.

Learning by doing further underscores the individualism of young people when, based on the skills learned by doing, they find an outlet for their resourcefulness and entrepreneurial drive. This would apparently explain their opposition to unions and, more broadly, to any type of regulated work or collective rights, including norms governing labour and job security.

In fact, union coverage applies to a meagre 13% of working youth aged 15–19 and barely 22% of those aged 20–24, i.e. half the percentage of workers over 25 years subject to the same standards. In the eyes of young people, the unions are temples of corporatism associated with defending rights and benefits which were gained by previous generations and for which they are footing the bill in a context where flextime is the rule in their "new" economy. At grips with "flexploitation" (Bourdieu 1998: 99), young people are nevertheless closing ranks around various guardians that are sometimes on the same wavelength as the long-standing unions. This is seen in the struggle waged by adolescents working in McDonald restaurants, although the initiative attracts young people still enrolled in studies that provide the amount of schooling needed to arouse their political awareness and militant commitment, in addition to tempering the essential character of their work.

Clearly, then, young people do not readily rally to unions as champions of their common interest, blurred by the pervading individualism that they are the first to craft. In theory, that individualism inclines them towards flextime, which may possibly turn into job insecurity to their detriment, as evidenced by the experiences of business ownership and self-employment that young people were encouraged, if not compelled, to undertake.

Quebec was the paramount stage for the ascendancy of young people encouraged to create their own jobs and even their own businesses. During its darkest hours, the 1991 economic recession prompted the Quebec government to set up workforce integration programs christened "Create Your Own Job," which soon became a kind of battle cry. Government support took the form of financing or tax credits for companies willing to meet the specific demands of young people, i.e., to accept them on a work-study basis, with the promise of tailoring a job for them or hiring them for their first job upon completion of their studies. Companies jumped on the bandwagon, recruiting large numbers of young people to reap the benefits of cheap labour—momentarily, that is, precisely the time prescribed for obtaining government funding earmarked for job creation.

Business start-ups were also on the agenda for the most adventurous young people. The State generously supported those start-ups by offering services designed to put them on the road to profit and success, in other words, the seed money and guarantees required by financial institutions, as well as basic capitalization. As it turned out, companies headed by young people fell far short of being the expected gold mines, with the exception of a few brilliant success stories that made the headlines and thus created a mirage. The table below profiles the status of most of those businesses.

Characteristics of young entrepreneurs	
Proportion of males	59%
Proportion of females	41%
Age	27 years
Has entrepreneur among close relations	44%
Schooling	14 years on average
Most common training	Technical and trade (44%)
Work experience	5.5 years on average
Seed money	CAN$40,000 on average
Principal source of financing	Government programs (34%)
Most common sector of activity	Services
Most common legal status	Single owner (50%)
Number of employees	None in 68% of cases
Owner's income	CAN$15,000 a year on average
Length of work week	53 hours on average

Source: Madeleine Gauthier, "Les jeunes et le travail: un terrain mouvant", dans Jean-Pierre Dupuis et André Kuzminski (Ed.), *Sociologie de l'économie, du travail et de l'entreprise*, Montréal, Gaëtan Morin éditeur, 1998, p. 256.

Based on this table, today's unrelenting decline in entrepreneurship among young people comes as no surprise, as they were pushed in that direction by government agencies seeking a way out of a dead-end situation. Entrepreneurial drive suddenly collapsed under the prevailing conditions and now tends to move in step with the rest of the workforce. The plug was eventually pulled on businesses that sprang from the impetus which young people received from the lairs of power. As undeniable as they are, the economic successes that occurred in the multimedia, Internet and biotechnology sectors cannot conceal the failures of businesses headed by young entrepreneurs who sought with blind faith to succeed in business, but ultimately failed miserably.

If we go by the Labour Force Survey, the pitfalls of the labour market provide precious little encouragement for young people to turn to self-employment in droves. The option of self-employment, without benefit of a corporate name, was taken up in 1997 by 10% of young people aged 25 and over, as compared with 9% ten years earlier. For 20–24 years olds, that figure remained unchanged at 4%. But unlike for the population as a whole, self-employment made a forward leap among women, whereas it fell off significantly among men.

By way of conclusion
Need for longitudinal vision of young people and work
so as to qualify theory

Going by the picture of their relationship to work, young Quebecers belie the fashionable propositions contending that work now takes a back seat (cf. Trottier 2000) and is less important than other "value-mediated activities," to quote Jürgen Habermas. As we have just seen, work enters their lives in adolescence and consists at that early age of paid employment, as opposed to the household chores formerly performed within the immediate family and vicinity. Young people are thus initiated into salaried work very early on. Their socialization plays out largely within the workplace and is consequently modelled on the relationship of means to end, from which springs their individualism in any case.

The perimeters of work are extending onto the terrain of school and recreation and bringing the rules of flextime and entrepreneurship into those spaces. Job insecurity follows this same trend and is becoming the norm, to young people's way of thinking. For them, field surveys reveal, an insecure job is no longer a value-less job that creates a "negative relationship to work" (Baudelot and Gollac 1997: 2).

The surveys have consistently shown that young people are growing accustomed to this situation and even tend to valorize it. More than any other age bracket, they find that it is good not to take root in a company and thus fall into a rut. These findings should nevertheless be entertained with some caution and should be scrutinized. While at first glance, insecurity seems to be prized, it is because young *women* want the *choice* of combining work, motherhood and family. From this standpoint, flextime suits their purposes. Young adults who still enjoy the parental support—by living at home, for instance—can cope with the ups and down of flexploitation without having their back to the wall. Lastly, young people can declare themselves "satisfied" with insecure jobs and the resulting wage (MEQ

2001, Paugam 2000) simply because they are just beginning their career and think, or hope, they can adjust their sights soon enough.

Quebec is like other places in this respect, lacking a longitudinal view of young people through which one could observe their changing relationship to work at various stages of their lives. Makeshift efforts to address university graduates from this viewpoint (Dufour, Fortin and Hamel 1994; Hamel 2001a and b) reveal what can only be described as resounding reversals. In 1990, students fresh out of university, at grips with job insecurity, flextime and mobility upon entering the labour market, were not inclined as a rule to view work as a means of social integration but disclaimed the value of the rights and benefits that work provides in the way of ontological security. When interviewed on the same subject ten years later, their comments were punctuated with opposing views and values: work is now a keystone, even in the minds of graduates still coping with job insecurity, flextime or mobility, which are experienced as challenges. "Insecure work unrelated to insecurity" (Nicole-Drancourt and Roulleau-Berger 1995: 75–76), which is starting to incarnate the relationship of today's young people to work, may engender stability, which cannot however translate into new values apt to weaken, or even underline, the norms based on salaried employment.

The theory needs to be qualified. There is an argument opposing the proposition of Jürgen Habermas, for whom salaried work, reinforced by technological development, has eliminated from its orbit symbol-mediated interaction, and even any expressive action capable of revealing individuality and community one in the other and, simultaneously, generating the "socially useful activities" which elicit the citizen values recognized in young people by André Gorz (1997) and many other authors (cf. Saint-Pierre 2001). That argument is that work is still the principal lever for entering society and enjoying ontological security on an individual scale.

In theory, work should therefore be regarded as an instrumental action *and* an expressive action, even though the former action takes the form of the relationship of means to end, which Habermas refuses to see as "symbols that mediate interaction." In Quebec at any rate, young people's relationship to work shows, on the contrary, that in the wake of the associated instrumental action, that relationship forms values and norms that definitely shape their expectations of shared behaviour, even when salaried work disappoints them. Thus, work reveals its "dual truth," to use the title of an article on the subject by Pierre Bourdieu, who takes pains to point out that it "provides of itself a benefit relating to the very investment in work or work relations, as exemplified by the symbolic mutilation that takes place among the unemployed (or the vulnerable) and can be attributed not just to loss of salary, but equally to loss of the *raisons d'être associated* with work and the world of work" (Bourdieu 1996: 89).

Bibliography

Baethge, Martin (1994), "Le rapport au travail des jeunes" in Gérard Mauger, René Bendit et Christian Von Wolffersdorff (dir.), *Jeunesses et société. Perspectives de la recherche en France et en Allemagne*, Paris, Armand Colin: 151–166.
Baudelot Christian et M. Gollac (1997), "Faut-il travailler pour être heureux", *INSEE Première*, n° 560.
Bourdieu, Pierre (1998), "La précarité est aujourd'hui partout", dans *Contre-feux*, Paris, Liber: 95–101.
Bourdieu, Pierre (1996), "La double vérité du travail", *Actes de la recherche en sciences sociales*, n° 114: 89–90.
Cannon, David (1994), *Generation X and the New Work Ethic*, London, Demos.
Castel, Robert (2001), "Les jeunes ont-ils un rapport spécifique au travail?", dans Laurence Roulleau-Berger et Madeleine Gauthier (dir.), *Les jeunes et l'emploi dans les villes d'Europe et d'Amérique du Nord*, Paris, Éditions de l'Aube: 287–298.
Cetech (Centre d'étude sur l'emploi et la technologie) (2001), *Les indicateurs du CETECH. Revue du nouveau marché du travail*, Québec, Emploi-Québec.
Crim (Centre de recherche informatique de Montréal) (1999), *La maison des hautes technologies de Montréal*, (www.hht.qc.ca).
Dufour, Stéphane, Dominic Fortin et Jacques Hamel (1994), "La génération du *baby boom* et les *baby busters*: une étude", *Cahiers internationaux de sociologie*, vol. XLVII: 277–300.
IMT (Information sur le marché du travail) (2001), *Le marché du travail au Québec. Perspectives professionnelles 2000–2004 pour l'ensemble des métiers et professions*, Québec, Emploi-Québec.
Gauthier, Madeleine et Léon Bernier (dir.) (1997), *Les 15–19 ans. Quel présent? Vers quel avenir*, Québec, IQRC.
Giddens, Anthony (1994), *Les conséquences de la modernité*, Paris, L'Harmattan.
Gorz, André (1999), "Préface", dans Sébastien Schehr, *La vie quotidienne des jeunes chômeurs*, Paris, Presses Universitaires de France: 1–6.
Gorz, André (1997), *Misères du présent. Richesse du possible*, Paris, Galilée.
Grell, Paul (1998), "L'État providence", dans Louise Boivin et Mark Fortier (dir.), *L'économie sociale. L'avenir d'une illusion*, Montréal, Fidès: 187–214.
Habermas, Jürgen (1998), "Citoyenneté et identité nationale", dans *L'intégration républicaine*, Paris, Fayard: 67–94.
Habermas, Jürgen (1973), *La technique et la science comme « idéologie »*, Paris, Gallimard.
Hamel, Jacques (2001a), "Brèves remarques sur le travail comme vecteur de la citoyenneté", *Revue canadienne de sociologie et d'anthropologie*, vol. 38, n° 1: 1–17.
Hamel, Jacques (2001b), "Sur les notions de travail et de citoyenneté à l'heure de la précarité chez les jeunes", *Le Travail*, n° 48: 1–16.
Hirmech, Mohamed et Manon Théorêt (1997), "L'abandon scolaire au secondaire: une comparaison entre les élèves montréalais nés au Canada et ceux nés de l'étranger", *Revue canadienne de l'éducation*, vol. 22, n° 3: 268–282.
Lebaube, Alain (1992), "Premier travail", *Le Monde Initiatives*, 22 janvier 1992: 14.

Masi, Marie (2000), "Montréal au palmarès des capitales nord-américaines de l'emploi high-tech", *Multimédium* (Les données s'appuient sur l'étude de Price Waterhouse *Technopole Montréal*).
Ministère de l'Éducation du Québec (MEQ) (2001), *Indicateurs de l'Éducation*, Québec, ministère de l'Éducation du Québec.
Nicole-Drancourt, Chantal et Laurence Roulleau-Berger (2001), *Les jeunes et le travail, 1950-2000*, Paris, Presses Universitaires de France.
Nicole-Drancourt, Chantal et Laurence Roulleau-Berger (1995), *L'insertion des jeunes en France*, coll. Que sais-je?, Paris, Presses Universitaires de France.
Palmade, Jacqueline et Réjean Dorval (2000), "L'évolution du rapport au travail en vingt ans. La fragilisation de l'ancrage identitaire", dans Isabelle Billiard, Danièle Debordeaux et Martine Lurol (dir.), *Vivre la précarité. Trajectoires et projets de vie*, Paris, Éditions de l'Aube: 61-108.
Paugam, Serge (2000), *Le salarié de la précarité*, Paris, Presses Universitaires de France.
Sainsaulieu, Renaud (1995), "Quel avenir pour le travail?", *Esprit*, décembre 1995: 185-191.
Saint-Pierre, Céline (2001), "L'insertion professionnelle et citoyenne des jeunes au Québec", dans Laurence Roulleau-Berger et Madeleine Gauthier (dir.), *Les jeunes et l'emploi dans les villes d'Europe et d'Amérique du Nord*, Paris, Éditions de l'Aube: 57-70.
Schehr, Sébastien (1999), *La vie quotidienne des jeunes chômeurs*, Paris, Presses Universitaires de France.
Schor, Julier B. (1992), *The Overworked American*, New York, Basic Books.
Trottier, Claude (2000), "Le rapport au travail et l'accès à l'emploi stable, à temps plein, lié à la formation: vers l'émergence de nouvelles normes?", dans Geneviève Fournier et Bruno Bourassa (dir.), *Les 18 à 30 ans et le marché du travail*, Québec, Presses de l'Université Laval: 35-57.
Zoll, Rainer (2001), "Jeunes, sens du travail et nouvel individualisme en Allemagne", dans Laurence Roulleau-Berger et Madeleine Gauthier (dir.), *Les jeunes et l'emploi dans les villes d'Europe et d'Amérique du Nord*, Paris, Éditions de l'Aube: 261-271.

ECONOMIC DISQUALIFICATION AND SOCIAL DIFFERENCIATION IN THE POST-INDUSTRIAL CITY: YOUTH, WORK AND MARGINALIZATION IN FRANCE

Laurence Roulleau-Berger

Engagement with the issue of young people and work in French towns and cities raises broader questions about fragmentation, marginalization and polarization in our societies and the dynamics of their restructuring. Indeed we might ask, like Beck (1992), whether we are living in a 'world risk society'. If the process of risk distribution is following the lines of the social, ethnic and sexual divides between the skilled and flexible workers operating in the new information societies and the young under-qualified workers, then the notion of the risk society expresses very clearly the fragmentation of identities associated with the precariousness and indeed the discrimination experienced by certain groups of young people. However, if we are to examine the dynamics of restructuring at work in risk societies, we have to theorize young people living with precariousness both as the objects of economic and social disqualification and of ethnic discrimination and as endowed with competences that enable them to bring into being urban economies, some more formal, more visible and more legitimate than others and embedded to varying degrees in the mainstream economies of global cities.

Access to jobs in France today

During the thirty years of economic growth that followed the Second World War, a standard employment relationship emerged based on the permanent employment contract. At that time, the likelihood of an economically active person obtaining stable employment was high. In the mid-1970s, the French economy entered a crisis. This 'crisis' found expression in a series of ruptures affecting job opportunities, growth and job creation and in a climate of permanent uncertainty concerning annual growth rates, the development of employment, investment and so on. This crisis was both national and international. The Taylorist mode of work organization was to be called into question, to be replaced by the then emerging 'network firm', which exports the labour-intensive parts of the production process. The intensification of competition, the emergence of mass unemployment and of new employment relationships and increasing precariousness in the labour market were to shatter workers' employment conditions. Two consequences of the French socio-economic choice were subsequently to become apparent. Only a single generation, that aged between 24 and 50, is in work at any one time, to the detriment of the under-25s and the over-50s.[1] In other words, the markets reserve their 'best' jobs for a few, adult men in the first instance, and then adult women; young people are assigned to very specific areas of employment characterized by the use of 'special employment forms', which frequently alternate with periods of unemployment. Young people seem to be increasingly vulnerable to unemployment: they find it difficult to enter the labour market in the first place and subsequently experience repeated spells of unemployment (Verdier, 1995). Forty years ago, young workers aged between 15 and 25 accounted for a good half of all young people; today, they are in the process of disappearing from the labour market. On the other hand, those young people in that age group who are available in the labour market seem to be increasingly 'deskilled' relative to the average for young entrants to the labour market (Nicole-Drancourt, Roulleau-Berger, 2002).

The labour market has become gradually fragmented over the last thirty years with the spread of subcontracting, temporary jobs, various measures for labour market entrants, homeworking and so on, with the result that jobs are now divided between the primary and secondary sectors. There are in fact several different labour markets: that for executive staff, who combine the advantages of salaried work with the functions of an employer, that for ordinary employees on full-time, permanent contracts, who in theory enjoy all the advantages of being a salary or wage earner, that for precarious jobs (fixed-term or temporary contracts), many of which, whether in law or in reality, do not give workers the rights associated with permanent jobs (training, representation and so on) and, finally, that for subsidized jobs (the entrants' market) (Supiot, 1994). This plurality of labour markets reflects the fragmentation and intersection of the various

---

[1] Participation rates in 1996 were: 15–24 age group: 29%; 25–49 age group: 87%; 50–60 age group: 71%. *Enquête Emploi*, 1996.

spheres of production: at one end of the spectrum are the highly legitimated spheres with their stable, skilled workforces earning relatively high salaries, while at the other end are those with little legitimation and unstable, unskilled and low-paid workers employed in small firms and enjoying little in the way of social protection (Berger, Piore, 1980). This process has exacerbated the social differentiations based on gender, age, education and ethnic origin. Unskilled workers, young people with few educational qualifications, particularly those of foreign origin, foreign workers without residence or work permits, are particularly affected by unemployment and job insecurity.

This process leading to increasing precariousness in employment is above all selective, excluding as it does the least 'adaptable', the least competent and the weakest, socially, physically and psychologically. It has developed through an accumulation of changes and shifts: mass redundancies, the downgrading of skilled jobs into much less advantageous ones (particularly by subcontracting to developing countries), the circumvention of labour law and training courses in which individuals are put to the test and selected on the basis of their ability to commit themselves to work situations requiring a high degree of flexibility and availability. However, other measures, linked in part to educational level, relational and communication skills and to personal qualities such as the ability to interact with others, availability, flexibility, commitment and emotional involvement and adaptability, have also helped to exclude the 'less mobile', the 'less adaptable', the 'less well qualified', those who are too young and young people of North African or Black African origin (Chiapello, Boltanski, 1999). Young people in precarious situations, with little in the way of educational qualifications and living in working-class suburbs have been particularly hard hit and are becoming increasingly desperate.

The plural and differentiated careers of young people living in precariousness

So various European studies (Roulleau-Berger, Gauthier, 2001) have shown that a process of differentiation and individualisation is helping to produce a plurality and diversity of complex trajectories that are now replacing life histories built on continuity and stability. Young people living in precariousness find themselves forced to change jobs, to adapt to a diversity of new, constantly overlapping work situations that are difficult to hierarachise (Michon, Ségrestin, 1990) and to move from one activity to another; as a result, they are having to adopt a succession of different identities. Under these circumstances, the term 'transitional socialisation' might be used to describe a process informed by the most diverse and contradictory risks affecting both individuals and the wider society (Beck, 1999).

While the objective dimension of the careers[2] of young people living in precariousness is put together in a variety of different ways depending on the family, educational, social, economic and cultural resources available to them, those careers can also be distinguished from each other by virtue of the fact that they are made up of various forms of work and other activities that alternate with and overlay each other in a number of different ways. Thus young people might rely on various combinations of agency work, part-time, menial jobs and fixed-term contracts, subsidised jobs of different kinds, programmes combining work and training, state benefits funded on the solidarity principle, such as the guaranteed minimum income, casual work in the entertainment industry, moonlighting and work in informal, 'neighbourhood' economies. Moreover, such arrangements might be combined with various associative, cultural or sporting activities that play a more central role during the periods of unemployment interpolated between the subsidised employment contracts, the series of menial jobs and the periods of temporary work.

Three organisational principles contribute actively to the differenciation and the individualisation of the careers of young people living in precariousness: the alternation principle, the superimposition principle and the reversibility principle.

The alternation principle denotes the succession and linking of various forms of work and other activities that take a diversity of forms depending on level of educational attainment, gender and ethnic origin. The higher the level of educational attainment, the more

---

[2] Our approach to careers is that defined by E. C. Hughes (1994): "Career, in the most generic sense, refers to the fate of a man running his life-cycle in a particular society at a particular time. The limitations put upon his choice of occupation by his own peculiarities (sex, race, abilities, class, wealth, access to and motivation for education, and access to knowledge of the system itself) in interaction with the 'times' have been the object of many studies . . . The career includes not only the processes and sequences of learning the techniques of the occupation but also the progressive perception of the whole system and of possible places in it and the accompanying changes in conception of the work and of one's self in relation to it".

dominant the alternation principle becomes; it is particularly strong among young men of European origin. The lower the level of educational attainment, the less dominant the alternation principle becomes, particularly among young men of Maghrebi-an origin, although it is stronger among young women of Maghrebi-an origin.

The superimposition or overlaying principle denotes the 'stacking up' of various forms of work and other activities at any given moment in time; as with the alternation principle, this superimposition may take a range of different forms. Approaches to the careers of young people living in precariousness do not generally take account of the superimposition principle. In cases where two or more forms of work coexist simultaneously, that is when the young people in question are not involved solely in a single form of employment, only one of those forms of work is perceived, generally the one that seems closest to wage work. In reality, the image of a socially integrated individual is mediated through the idea that he is involved in only one form of work; this being the case, that individual cannot be perceived as being involved in a multiplicity of different work spaces. Taking account of the superimposition principle amounts to an invitation to stop defining work simply as a homogeneous whole and to apprehend it in the full diversity of its content and in conjunction with other forms of activity. In this way, work can be liberated from the original, reified conception of it as a single category consisting solely of wage work and productive organisations as the sole form and locus of the creation of value (Haicault, 1993).

The reversibility principle denotes the repetition of changements of situations from precarious work into unemployment and a situation of unemployment into a pracrious employment. The lower the level of educational attainment, the more dominant the reversiblity principle becomes; it is particularly strong among young men of Maghrebi origin. The higher the level of educational attainment, the less dominant the reversibility principle becomes, particularly among young men of European origin.

Reversibility and uncertainty are the principal characteristics of these non-standardised, non-linear, non-continuous and non-progressive careers, which clearly reflect a trend towards individualisation in which the lifestyles that characterised industrial societies are being 'dis-embedded' and then 're-embedded' on an individual basis (Beck in Beck, Giddens and Lash, 1995).

Between shame and self-esteem

The experience of precariousness includes situations characterised by what might be called 'social distortion', in which a considerable gap opens up between individuals' subjective feelings about themselves and their real identities (Goffman, 1975). This in turn gives rise to cleavages, conflicts and reversals of identity that young people have to manage: their self-esteem is continuously being undermined[3] and may gradually give way to shame (Bourgois, 1995; Stack, 1997; Newmann, 1999). Faced with situations in which their social status is being constantly downgraded, the identities of young people living with precariousness are damaged (Tannock, 2001). Socially and publicly disqualified and deprived of a place in the world of wage work, they are unable to draw up a rational life plan (Furlong, Cartmel, 1997) and experience difficulties in gaining public recognition for themselves. The main issue in this respect seems to be that the need for public recognition takes precedence over that for social recognition (Ion, Péroni, 1997). They oscillate continuously between feelings of shame and self-esteem (Roulleau-Berger, 1999). An individual's sense of his own worth is put to the test each time he or she changes job, and particularly during periods of unemployment.

Self-esteem seems to be linked to self-worth, to the ideas we have about what others think of us and to our power to influence our self-esteem. Thus it depends on young people's educational, social and cultural resources as well as on the social interactions through which those resources are mobilised and transformed. The nature of forms of work and activities to which young people have access affects the way in which self-esteem is strengthened or weakened; degrading situations, for example, may weaken self-esteem. The more the principles of alternation and superimposition come into play in young people's careers, the more self-esteem tends to prevail over feelings of shame. Indeed, among the diversity of precarious employment situations and activities in which young people are involved,

---

[3] According to Bruno Bettelheim's theory, in which description and prescription are indissolubly linked, the subject acquires the status of a person in his own right after a period during which the essentially spiritual capacities likely to create 'self-esteem' through the autonomous and independent definition of the place he occupies in the social world are formed and reach maturity. This self-esteem is, according to Bettelheim, the basis of an assured identity, in other words of an individual's capacity to remain the 'same' despite changes in his social environment (Pollak, 1990).

some have 'positive' effects on self-esteem; the more the principle of reversibility come into play in young people's careers, the more shame tends to prevail over self-esteem.

However, self-esteem may quickly develop into shame and, conversely, shame may turn into self-esteem. When potentially enabling employment situations present themselves to young people after a series of disabling situations, self-esteem is reinforced as a result of the attention others have directed towards thim. And conversely, in humiliating work situations, shame wins out over self-esteem. Self-esteem and shame seem to be aspects of identity that are reversible and dynamic. However, there are saturation thresholds beyond which they no longer seem to be reversible when young people lose the capacity for reflexive analysis and cannot access to a "culture de soi" (Foucault, 1984). For example, the repetition and duplication of degrading situations, such as precarious employment and racism, may make the feeling of shame irreversible among some young people at certain times in their careers.

Commitment to and disengagement from work, or the double bind effect

The superimposition and reversibility principles inherent in the construction of young people's careers give rise to a multiplicity of paradoxical socialisation processes that in turn create a double-bind situation in which the exhortation to work conflicts irresolvably with the impossibility of working within the prescribed forms (Castel, 1995). This double bind equates to a social or interpersonal situation characterised by inequality and domination that does not become established until the same experience has been repeated on several occasions (Barel, 1979). Young people who, on several occasions, have experienced unemployment or precariousness when they were expecting stable employment oscillate between a commitment to work and the rejection of all precarious or disabling work. However, several forms of double bind emerge out of the various types of careers pursued by young people; they range in severity from the ineluctable, in which the "victim" is preventing from leaving the double-bind system, to those from which exit is possible. The more the superimposition principle comes into play in young people's careers, that is the more they stack various forms of work and other activities on top of each other, the less pronounced the double bind seems to be.

Conversely, the more the reversibility principle comes into play in young people's careers, that is the fewer socialisation spaces they have at their disposal, the more the double bind manifests itself in conflicts of identity.

When the double bind equates to a situation of great inequality and domination that has its roots in the impossibility of gaining access to employment and the repetition of disabling, negatively perceived experiences, a double bind of such severity can accurately be described as ineluctable. Self-esteem sustains considerable damage and young people become trapped in the double bind: they lose their capacity to act, paralysed as they are by their inability to obtain public or social recognition. The double bind makes it impossible to draw up plans likely to provide access to fulfilling work and creates a disjuncture between objective and subjective identities.[4] This disjuncture contributes to the fragmentation of the various aspects of work, with the result that the instrumental, social and symbolic aspects cease to function in harmony with each other. Work seems to lose its meaning because it is no longer clear where young people locate their social commitment.

Young people oscillate between choices and their opposites but manage to commit themselves to certain forms of work, provided that work situations that are experienced positively coexist with situations that are experienced negatively. We can see here how young people caught between the exhortation to work and the impossibility of working in the prescribed forms attempt to manage this double bind situation by committing themselves only half-heartedly to precarious employment forms but much more strongly to other activities. A gap opens up between the selves, between the objective and subjective identities. Indeed, while the instrumental and social aspects of work are present in the forms of precarious work the young people do, the symbolic aspects of work can be seen in the other activities in which they are involved.

When young people concerned escape from or invert the domination relationship by distancing themselves as much as possible from precarious work and channelling their energies into non-wage work or other activities, although the various aspects of work are fragmented here too, they are at the same time controlled by individuals

---

[4] Goffman, E.: *Stigmates*, Paris, Minuit, 1975.

who concentrate their investments in those areas in which they feel recognised publicly and/or socially.

When the young people's commitment to work is a crucial one, particularly since it appears to be reversible and protean, fluctuating from moment to moment, from situation to situation and from place to place. While wage work remains a fundamental factor in the construction of young people's social identities, young people's relationship to wage work is damaged by the effects of social disqualification and racial discrimination. The erosion of the wage work norm by the development of precarious or low-skill work damages self-esteem and creates disjunctures, conflicts and reversals of identity.

Double bind, loss and production of competences

Precarious situations linked to the development of flexible capitalism generate losses when young people find themselves obliged to take a succession of jobs, each one of which is different from the previous one. When careers are not constructed around the principle of accumulation, experience and knowledge can be lost. Depending on the educational, family and cultural resources on which they can draw, young people are going to accumulate a series of retrospective losses (Sennett, 2000), albeit of varying magnitudes. The lower their level of educational attainment, the greater the losses seem to be; the higher their level of educational attainment, the more experiences linked to precariousness seem to accrue.

However, the superimposition principle also gives rise to the production of competences that are not widely recognised when the alternation principle comes into operation and generates a succession of precarious employment situations to which young people usually gain access solely on the basis of their educational competences. Although young people living in precariousness suffer acts of real structural violence (Bourdieu, 1993) and experience losses, they also acquire symbolic goods. When self-esteem acquires a dynamism of its own, it creates a feeling of competence, that is a capacity for self-reflection, self-management, action, mobilisation and invention: young people then begin to acquire different competences to place alongside their educational competences. Now the notion that, out of the experience of precariousness, there emerges a diversity of competences that young people construct for themselves and then circulate among their peers, is not yet widely accepted. Young people living with precariousness are labelled primarily in terms of their formal educational competences, with too much attention being paid to their "inadequacies" in this respect. The principle of dividing those who 'are in work' from those who are not seems to be based on their 'educationally validated competences' (Bourdieu, 1998; Eymard-Duvernay, 1998) and conceals this plurality of competences that develop as young people become involved in precarious work and other activities. Indeed, out of these diverse and overlapping forms of work and activities, young people construct knowledge and competences of varying degrees of visibility that make up their experience of precariousness.

The losses and symbolic goods are produced unequally in the various career types. The stronger the principle of reversibility, the more violent the double bind becomes, the young people concerned lose the feeling of competence. In other words, their ability to exert control over events, to motivate themselves and to deploy their cognitive resources in order to manage precarious situations declines considerably. As a result, the competences become invisible. The stronger the principle of alternance, the less violent the double-bind becomes and the feeling of competence is maintained; young people's capacity for self-reflection and self-management enables them to conserve but not to draw simultaneously on the benefits of previous experiences. The competences become partially visible.

When the principle of superimposition is really strong, young people appear able to manage positively the situations of double-bind, the feeling of competence seems to be strong and young people's competences may then become visible, although this does not mean that they are legitimated in the labour market.

These competences are constantly evolving and being redefined in the course of the experiences the young people undergo. The more the alternation and superimposition principles come into play, the less pronounced the double bind is, the more young people seem to be endowed with competences. The more the reversibility principle comes into play, the less young people are recognised as socially competent and labelled 'employable'.

Struggle for recognition in the "worlds of small-scale, urban production"

So the urban economies on French cities are characterised by widespread insecurity and precarious employment relationships (Wacquant, 1996, 2000). As a result, a hierarchy emerges, dividing the economy into worlds of legitimate production and worlds that have less legitimacy. The worlds of legitimate production equate to the inter-personal, the market, the industrial and the intangible worlds (Salais, Storper, 1993). These worlds of legitimate production conceal those that have less legitimacy by rendering invisible. These worlds of "small-scale urban production" are never perceived as worlds in themselves but rather as marginal zones that are supplanted by the mainstream economy at those points where they impinge on the worlds of legitimate production (Sassen, 1998). Thus it is their mode of organisation which appears to produce marginality, rather than the activites and goods produced within these worlds (Sassen, 1994). These worlds are made up of groups of young people living in precarious situations who cooperate in order to produce a diverse range of activities that are difficult to categorise but may trigger a dynamic of economic and social recomposition, what we have termed *intermediate spaces* (Roulleau-Berger, 1991, 1993, 1997).

Within these spaces, young people mobilise in order to develop economic survival strategies and to put together and bring into circulation resources of various kinds. The worlds of small-scale, urban production are a locus for the development of a polymorphous economy based on the coming together of "semi-formal neighbourhood economies" (Sassen, 1998), symbolic economies and 'coping' economies. Semi-formal neighbourhood economies are structured around activities intended to inject new life into local areas. These activities may be cultural, extracurricular or sporting in nature; they may include activities such as IT programmes, small-scale catering and hairdressing services, as well as integration programmes aimed at the inhabitants of working-class housing estates. Symbolic economies are based on the production of cultural goods such as artistic productions, symbolic goods such as hospitality and moral goods such as self-esteem. 'Coping' economies are structured around bartering and moonlighting; illegal activities (Kokoreff, 1997; Joubert, 1998) also play an obvious part in the worlds of small-scale, urban production.

These intermediate spaces are also a locus for the development of collective learning processes which give rise in turn to small-scale urban production and activate and transform individual knowledge and competences. They are constructed around a distribution of roles likely to create the conditions for this small-scale urban production and develop through the management of situations characterised by uncertainty, instability and urgency. These intermediate spaces give rise to *cultures of uncertainty* that define themselves through unobtrusive inversions of a regime of precariousness that ends up being subverted by individuals who metaphorize it, making it operate in a different register without leaving it. These cultures are born out of a style of social exchanges that is constructed from the experience of precariousness, of economic invention, of a style of moral resistance and an ethic of tenacity expressed through different ways of rejecting disqualification, humiliation and discrimination in precarious work. Of course, these cultures of uncertainty are constructed against a background of social, urban, economic and cultural capital: individuals draw on their previous social experiences in order to be able to navigate their ways through the floating networks that make up the cultures of uncertainty. These cultures may be the points of embarkation for careers based on integration into the world of wage work or, conversely, for careers marked by social disaffiliation. The decisive factor is the process of translation that may or may not take place at the boundaries of the various worlds of small-scale production at local, societal or global level.

The worlds of small-scale urban production cannot be thought of as disassociated or separate from the more legitimate worlds, even though certain urban structures at times encourage such dissocation, thereby giving rise to partial, localised enclaves. The process of ghettoisation certainly helps to shape the worlds of small-scale urban production, although in France it never fully permeates them. The worlds of legitimate production and those of small-scale urban production are closely linked, even though at certain points they seem to be separate. The main issue at stake then becomes the question of the porosity or impermeability of the boundaries between these worlds and their fluctuation rather than the characteristics of the activities specific to these different worlds (Roulleau-Berger, 2000).

*From the worlds of "small-scale production" to the
worlds of legitimate production*

The transition from the worlds of small-scale production to those of legitimate production emerges out of a dynamic process of accommodation between young people's abilities to transfer their competences into the worlds of production governed by social, economic and cultural conventions. This process of translation is dependent on individual and collective capabilities and on the effects of the political and economic contexts in which it takes place. However, to translate is to transfer (Callon, 1986). Here, the act of translation involves the de-contextualisation of young people's competences constructed in the worlds of small-scale production and their recontextualisation in the worlds of legitimate production, that is the transfer of resources from a space with little legitimacy to one with greater legitimacy.

In order for this process of translation to take place, the young people in question have to be able to identify the competences to be transferred. This task is made all the more difficult by the fact that, in the course of their experience of precariousness, their aspirations have become blurred by their involvement in numerous different forms of work and other activities, many of them overlapping with each other. In such a situation, the task of translation requires young people to order and hierarachise their experiences in order to make themselves look competent in a professional role. Their aim must be to highlight the role in which they feel competent: for example, a young musician with a vocational qualification in plumbing who has set up an extracurricular association in his neighbourhood will have to be able to hierarachise these different roles in accordance with the kind of employment to which he aspires. The ways in which experiences and competences are ordered and hierarachised vary in accordance with young people's trajectories and the educational, family and cultural resources available to them. The more young people seem to be well qualified educationally and the closer they come to entering the world of wage work, the more rapidly they are able to hierarchieze their repertoire of roles and activities; the more distant they are from the formal labour market, the less easy it seems to be for them to arrange their roles in some kind of order of priority. Once young people have put their repertoire of resources in some kind of order, they have to appear competent in a particular trade or occupation. However, in order to enter the worlds of "large-scale" production, they have to be recognised as such before they can gain access to a job.

The transition from one world to another is effected through a process of translation, which may be "good", "bad" translation or partial.

A "good" translation is produced by the combined efforts of young people able to arrange and hierarachise their repertoire of resources in accordance with what is expected in the worlds of legitimate production and of employers willing to recognise and legitimate their competences. The "ferrymen", together with entrepreneurs and translators, may also play a role in helping young people to hierarachise their experiences and to make their plans and aspirations capable of legitimation in the worlds of large-scale production.

When the young people's competences are transferred into the worlds of large-scale production by being diverted away from the framework in which they were constructed and legitimated as such in the intermediate spaces, then the translation is a "bad" one. It emerges out of the combined actions of young people capable of arranging and hierarachising their repertoire of resources and of employers who do not recognise their competences. In this case, the figure of the ferryman is absent. For example, community leaders of North African origin may be called on to mediate between those engaged in the informal economy and public transport users fearful for their safety while at the same time being requested to conceal their bilingualism.

When young people's competences are transferred in part to the worlds of large-scale production, then the translation is a partial one. Such a translation is produced by the combined actions of young people able partially to arrange and hierarachise their repertoire of resources and of mediators and employers who grant partial recognition to their competences. For example, the technical competences of a former graphic designer from Marseille were legitimated when he found employment as a housepainter, but his artistic competences were ignored.

In this case, those involved in the translation process can be said to have "almost" succeeded in their attempts to make different social worlds cohere with each other. However, the boundaries between these different worlds are porous when competences and experiences are "well" translated but become more difficult to cross when the translation process is partial or inaccurate.

From city to partial enclaves

When the process of translation does not take place, that is when competences and knowledge are not decontextualised and when resources cannot be mobilised, then we speak of discrimination and relegation (Dubet, 1994; Dubet, Lapeyronnie, 1995). These terms reflect the scale of the processes of relegation and racism which, at the local level, prevent population living in precariousness from gaining access to the worlds of legitimate production.

When the links between the different worlds of production no longer function, the boundaries between those worlds become impassable at certain points, social conflicts and risks intensify, young people's horizons fragment (Taylor, 1998) and social fears and violence are given expression, both individually and collectively. The worlds of small-scale production give rise to what might be termed "partial enclaves" around situations of great poverty and exclusion (Sassen 1995; Laé, 1996).[5] It is these enclaves that give the urban fabric its archipelago-like structure (Viard, 1994). These partial enclaves constitute a break in the continuity of the urban fabric in which social, economic and symbolic resources are frozen, the dynamics of the city have come to a halt and young people's competences are unable to circulate freely. In such enclaves, the dynamics of withdrawal win out temporarily over those of social, economic and cultural linkages.

The partial enclaves that may form at any time indicate that the city is producing inhospitality. French society as a whole is becoming inhospitable since it is inhibiting access to certain productive networks by creating discrimination and segregation. These partial enclaves, which are linked to the process of impoverishment, show that urban societies, faced with the limitations of mechanisms based on mutual support and collective action, are coping increasingly unsuccessfully with the task of integrating all its members, whether they be young migrants, the young homeless or the young "jobless".

---

[5] "An enclave is the experience of precariousness, which is characterised by minor incidents of disorientation and feelings of resignation in the face of diminishing prospects and the ever-present fear of expulsion associated with legal proceedings, distraint or indebtedness. To produce a history of enclaves, where mobility is prohibited, is to examine occupational and familial discontinuities, modes of adjustment to precariousness and resentment of institutions, disputes with landlords and neighbourhood quarrels" (Laé, 1996).

Conclusion

An analysis couched in terms of careers and worlds of small-scale, urban production marks a shift away from the dominant social and economic categorisations and opens up the possibility of investigating both the conjunctions and disjunctions of the social space. By recognising social worlds in which work is constructed other than on the basis of productivity and economic rationality, by establishing equivalencies between these hierarachised worlds and by investigating the zones of conflict and convergence, it becomes possible to reject all reductive and static approaches to the social sphere. The sociology of translation and discrimination makes it possible to identify the areas of porosity and impermeability on the boundaries between the various economic and social worlds. At the heart of this approach, however, lies the notion of intermediate spaces which allows us to examine that mix of continuity and discontinuity that characterises the various social worlds.

As wage work becomes increasingly precarious and the effects of globalisation make themselves felt, the urban economies in which we live seem increasingly to be informed by various forms of insecurity, uncertainty and reversibility. As the pace of technical and social change in Western societies becomes ever quicker, systems of meaning and significance are being uprooted: individuals are losing their bearings, periods of crisis are becoming ever more acute and individuals' relationship with the world and with other people are becoming ever harsher (Le Breton, 2000). However, even though individuals seem to be disoriented and socially bereft, they are developing forms of creativity which, though unevenly distributed, reflect an attitude of resistance that finds expression in their ability to take responsibility for their lives and to organise collectively. Thus individual and collective responses develop within a multiplicity of different spaces and time domains against a background of individuals' creative resources; however, they do not entirely dispel the fears, the sufferings, the unease and the sheer difficulty of existing, of "finding one's place". The plural and paradoxical processes of socialisation that emerge out of young people's experience of precariousness clearly reveal one of the essential elements of modernity in global cities (Sassen, 1991): the multiplicities of economies, new social and racial inequalities and new moorings and unmoorings of identities (Sassen, 2000).

Bibliography

Barel, Y. (1979), *Le paradoxe et le système*, PUG, Grenoble.
Beck, U. (1992), *Risk Society. Toward a new modernity*. London/Sage.
—— (1999), World Risk Society. Toward a new modernity, Cambridge, Polity Press.
Beck, U., Giddens, A., Lash, S. (1994), *Reflexive modernization: politics, tradition and aesthetics in the modern social order*, Cambridge: Polity.
Berger, S., Piore, M. (1980), *Dualism and discontinuity in industrial societies*, New York, Cambridge University Press.
Bourdieu, P. (1993), *La misère du monde*, Seuil, Paris.
—— (1998), *Contre-feux*, Liber, Paris.
Bourgois, P. (1995), *In Search of respect: selling crack in el barrio*, Cambridge University Press, New York.
Callon, M. (1986), Elements pour une sociologie de la traduction, *l'Année sociologique*, 36.
Castel, R. (1995), *Les métaporphoses de la question sociale*, Fayard, Paris.
Chiapello, E., Boltanski, L. (1999), *Le Nouvel Esprit du capitalisme*, Paris, Gallimard.
Dubet, F. (1994), *Pour une sociologie de l'expérience*, Seuil, Paris.
Dubet, F., Lapeyronnie, D. (1995), *Quartiers d'exil*, Seuil, Paris.
Eymard-Duvernay, F., Marchal E. (1997), *Façons de recruter*, Métailié, Paris.
Foucault, M. (1984), *Histoire de la sexualité III: le souci de soi*, Gallimard, Paris.
Furlong, A., Cartmel, F. (1997), *Young people and social change: individualisation and risk in the Age of High Modernity*, Open University Press, Buckingham.
Goffman, E., (1975), *Stigmates*, Minuit, Paris.
Haicault (M), (1993), *Plasticité des rapports sociaux de sexe et processus de transformation: complexification et accélération*, Rapport LEST, Aix-en-provence.
Hughes, E. C. (1994), edited and with an introduction by L. A. Coser, *On work, race, and the sociological imagination*, The University of Chicago Press, Chicago.
Ian, J., Peroni, R.: Engagement public et exposition de la personne, La Tour d'Aigues, Editions de l'Aube.
Joubert, M. (1998), *Le trafic de drogues comme mode d'inscription urbaine et spatiale*, Annales marocaines d'économie, N° 22–23, Printemps-Eté 1998.
Kokoreff, M. (1997), *De la défonce à l'économie informelle*, Rapport de recherche Clersé/Ifesi.
Lae, J. F., Madec A., Joubert, M., Murard, N. (1996), Economie et banlieue in Péraldi, M., Perrin, E.: *Réseaux productifs et territoires urbains*, PUM, Toulouse.
Lebreton, D. (2000), *Passions du risque*, Métailié, Paris.
Michon, F., Segrestin, D. (1990), Histoire d'une rencontre in *L'emploi, l'entreprise et la société* sous la direction de F. Michon et D. Ségrestin, Paris, Economica.
Newman, K. S. (1999), *No shame in my game*, The Russell Sage Edition, New York.
Nicole-Drancourt, C., Roulleau-Berger, L. (2002), Vresiemè édition musè á jour, *L'insertion sociale des jeunes en France*, Paris, PUF.
Pollak, M. (1990), *L'expérience concentationnaire. Essai sur le maintien de l'identité sociale*, Métailié, Paris.
Roulleau-Berger, L. (1991), réédité en (1993): *La Ville-Intervalle. Jeunes entre centre et banlieue*, Paris, Méridiens Klincksieck.
—— (1993), La construction sociale des espaces intermédiaires: jeunes en emploi précaire face aux politiques sociales, *Sociétés contemporaines*, n° 14/15.
—— (1997), L'expérience de la précarité juvénile, *Formation/Emploi*, janv.-mars 1997.
—— (1999), *Le travail en friche. Les mondes de la petite production urbaine*, Editions de l'Aube, La Tour D'aigues.
—— (2000), Traductions et discriminations dans les mondes de la petite production urbaine, in Ion, J., Péroni, M. (dir): *Ce qui nous relie*, Editions de l'Aube, La Tour d'Aigues.

Roulleau-Berger, L., Gauthier, M. (eds) (2001), *Les jeunes et l'emploi dans les villes d'Amérique du Nord et d'Europe*, Editions de l'Aube, La Tour d'Aigues.
Salais, R., Storper, M. (1993), *Les mondes de production: enquête sur l'identité économique de la France*, Editions EHESS, Paris.
Sassen, S. (1991), *The global city: New York, London, Tokyo*, Princeton, N.J.: Princeton University Press.
―――― (1995), L'identité de la ville globale. Enclaves économiques et culturelles in Péraldi, M., Perrin, E.: *Réseaux productifs et territoires urbains*, PUM, Toulouse.
―――― (1994), *Cities in a world economy*, Pine Forge Press, California.
―――― (1998), *Globalization and its discontents*, The new press, New York, 1998.
―――― (2001), Ancrages transversaux: les jeunes et le monde du travail, in Roulleau-Berger, L., Gauthier, M. (eds) (2001): *Les jeunes et l'emploi dans les villes d'Amérique du Nord et d'Europe*, Editions de l'Aube, La Tour d'Aigues.
Sennett, R. (2000), *Le travail sans qualités*, Albin Michel, Paris.
Stack, C. B. (1997), *Beyond what are given as givens: ethnography and critical policy studies*, American Anthropology Association.
Supiot, A. (1994), *Critique du droit du travail*, Paris, PUF.
Tannock, S. (2001), *Youth at work. The Unionized Fast-food and Grocery Workplace*, Temple University Press, Philadelphia.
Taylor, C. (1998), *Les sources du moi*, Seuil, Paris.
Verdier, E. (1995), Politiques de formation des jeunes et marché du travail. La France des années 80, *Formation Emploi* nº 50.
Viard, J. (1994), *La société d'archipel*, La Tour d'Aigues, Editions de l'Aube.
Wacquant, J. D., Loïc, (1996), La généralisation de l'insécurité salariale en Amérique, *Actes de la recherche en sciences sociales*, nº 115.
―――― (2000), *Les prisons de la misère*, Liber, Paris.

PART SIX

YOUTH AND MARGINALIZATION IN THE
POST-INDUSTRIAL CITY

THE LAW OF NETWORKS:
CASE HISTORIES OF SECOND-GENERATION
IMMIGRANTS IN THE WORLDS OF TRADE

Michel Peraldi

In Western societies it seems taken for granted that such phenomena as chronic youth unemployment, the precariousness of labour markets and widespread poverty are not simply signs of a temporary crisis. Rather, they are endemic, part of the new economic and social order which has established itself in the aftermath of the former industrial worlds.

These phenomena no longer are a matter of dealing with a few residual pockets of large-scale poverty. They are part of a more extreme and enigmatic problem, that of "the apparently increasingly insistent presence of individuals who seem to be drifting within the social structure, and who fill the interstices without finding a definite place" (Castel 1995). The problem is even more acute in that we are now in a second period of this cycle of overall change. Since the end of the 1980s, a phase of rising employment in certain economic sectors followed the breakdown of industrial economies in the preceeding decade. This movement is, of course, quite the opposite of the return to full employment which public opinion hoped for. Everything suggests that it is a matter rather of very selective readjustments characterized by a great precariousness in the creation of jobs, an expansion of the informal sector within the context of a reduction in the overall volume of fixed work contracts.

Thus, it seems less relevant to analyse the effects and the conditions of exclusion and idleness—what at one time was called in France a "galère"—"drudgery" (Dubet 1987)—than to observe, who finds what place in the new economic effervescence and under what conditions ("who gets what sort of job?", cf. Waldinger 1996). This implies knowing that economic integration under conditions of precariousness and flexibility, that is into the informal sector, is no longer a sufficient condition for social integration; and it means knowing, as well, that it is unlikely that one enters this economy from the top of the ladder and benefits from the professional and social conditions of the "pacte salarial"—the "salary agreement". The new economy is clearly not only about "start ups" and "yuppies". It is also more silently and yet more regularly an economy of hybrid forms of entrepreneurship in which the former protected worker becomes "his own entrepreneur" (Lazzarato 1996); it is an economy of "ethnic enclaves" (Waldinger 1993) in which the rules of the community replace salary agreements; and, finally, it is an economy of extreme disorder and of movement towards the informal of entire productive sectors (Portes, Castells, Benton 1989).

With these questions in mind, I want to examine those conditions and circumstances which "excluded" young people—prisoners of stigmatised residential situations, those ousted very early in their lives from the educational system, the offspring of Algerian immigrants—encounter in the course of their careers. What meanings do they attach to the increasing inflexibility of their social destiny and to the ways in which they take up places in a social and economic world for which it seems they are totally unprepared? To answer these questions I have tried to draw upon some situations and persons encountered in the course of different periods of research during recent years in Marseille and Toulouse, in urban settings of economic confusion (Peraldi 1997).

Indeed, it is in the commercial sectors and the "worlds of merchants", in the theoretical sense given to these terms by Salais and Storper (1993), that not only the labour market but, more fundamentally, something like a positive model of social status, that of a VSE ("very small enterprise", has developed. This model ascribes to the entrepreneurs a creative competence and savoir faire. The national press features the "start up" saga, but the local or specialised press is more willing to focus on the success of an unemployed person who sets up an enterprise in the service sector, often supported by public subsidies or institutional aid. On the dark side of the media's emphasis on commerce, the profiles of a drug dealer, or of a criminal, or fraudulent enterprises of "family mafias", with their power rooted in underprivileged neighbourhoods of cities, serve as negative counterpoints to the exaltation of the VSE. These all come together to present "the return to employment" as the result of a personal adventure and a virtuous commitment within the fold of "the new spirit of capitalism" (Boltanski and Chiapello 1999). It is a spectacular reversal of our understanding and representation of salaried work. The commitment to work was perceived throughout the long industrial phase as the outcome of a social destiny which was consented to, chosen, or submitted to. Now it tends to become the consequence of a way of facing the world, one among other rituals of civil commitment, a form of acting out rather than a fatality.

These "careers" and histories of the young people who I studied are good illustrations of the model. Nevertheless, it is the opposite of the commonly held view that represents their commitment to the world of trade as a continuation and perpetuation of some kind of fated exclusion from which they ought to escape. There is no doubt that the new economic order is not simply a conjuncture of an ethic of commitment and of new technical skills. It calls for intricate social ties behind the scenes which, like economic action, strengthen the construction of new statuses. The new generations, thanks to their emancipation and their cultural conformity to the spirit of the times, think that these positions are accessible because they find them desirable. But something comes between them and their aspirations. It is what I call the law of networks. It tends gradually to replace corporations and institutions, and the paradigm of labour unions and the state which still to some extent organise companies according to "the salary agreement".

'Bizniss' stories

Moussa is 29 years old; he never actually exercised in the time of triumphant Fordism what might be called a "profession". When he was younger he worked on several bricklaying sites with his father and brother. The experience left him with the disagreeable memory of an exhausting, dirty and poorly paid job. The only pay slips which he could produce were several years old. They dated from when he was recruited by an enterprise for job creation in his neighbourhood, a three month trainee job in clearing away weeds. It was after his release from prison. He is the third of twelve children, has lived in shanty towns and then emergency housing, and quit school after a stormy history of schooling as soon as he turned 16. Since then, Moussa is what the press, the media, social workers and neighbourhood gossip call a "dealer"; he earns most of his income from selling and trafficking in drugs—exclusively "from 'shit' ('hash'—cannabis resin)", he declares.

Like many of his friends, he began by simply smoking hash and selling some to pay for his consumption. Then, several years ago, he became thanks to his savings a "semi-wholesaler", working with relatively large quantities, bundles of 40 to 50 kilos. Two years ago, he was arrested for dealing in narcotics and spent a period of three months in Beaumettes Prison. Moussa's trade secured for him a comfortable income and style of life which he tried to maintain; it was somewhere between ostentation and discretion: the discretion fit in with his activities and the ostentation in his view suited his status and respectability. That behaviour, often highlighted by the press when it reports on "drug dealing in the high-rise slums of the suburbs", aside, what Moussa has to say about his trade has little in common with the general descriptions of this kind of activity. Articles in the press, as well as police reports or some of the studies done by research workers (Bouhnik 1996), give accounts of well organised and structured arrangements under the control of family clans, a veritable division of labour among wholesalers, dealers, "chouffeurs" (from the Arabic word *chouf*—"look", i.e., those who keep a lookout for the possible arrival on the scene of the deal by the police), "laundry-men", etc. There is none of that in this case. Moussa speaks rather of a very segmented economy in which independent entrepreneurs at each level individually handle the transit and exchange of goods.

In the long chain of transmission which carries the goods from Morocco via Spain to Marseilles, Moussa moves no further than the few kilometres necessary to reach those bars in the city centre which he frequents. It is there that most of his activities take place. The trade is simple: cash is collected "among friends", each one promising an amount; the drug is ordered by telephone by the person who is the main operator and the only one who knows the Spanish and Moroccan suppliers. The product is delivered a few days later. Each one receives the merchandise that he has ordered, sells it within his own circuit and without taking into account the others. Rarely do the orders bring together in an ongoing manner the same individuals. The "purchasing groups" vary according to circumstances, to the financial capacities of each individual, to passing situations. Moussa has direct contact with the merchandise only when it is delivered, and it is then that he risks getting caught. Therefore, deliveries often take place in the "quiet" neighbourhoods in the south of the city, in apartments that have been rented for the occasion to persons who make them available for drug traffic during the period of the transaction. There, by appointment, the exchanges with buyers take place. According to Moussa, they fit into two categories—young men from the housing estates, including one of Moussa's brothers, and buyers from the Cote d'Azur who sell in night clubs. Each of them buys his goods and pays cash. Moussa assured me that each buyer is independent and manages his own business as he sees fit; he prepares the balls of hash, mixes in various additives if he chooses to do so, and determines his own prices. Moussa puts his money into different bank accounts under various names of friends or relatives to whom he pays interest. "At the age of 19", he tells me, "I had put aside a hundred grand ($15,000)".

Thus, there is no structured organisation. Rather, there is a segmented set-up for a product that is more an object of speculation than one of industry. The heart of this activity takes place in bars that Moussa frequents, in that universe where on the basis of experience a sense of circumstantial confidence exists. Its value never goes beyond the last arrangement. There is no credit. The confidence is rooted in weak ties woven in bars and on dance floors among people who know almost nothing of each other's lives except what happens within the walls of those places where they spend time together (Granovetter 1973). It is here that Moussa knew both "how to make himself respected" and how to charm—to be available and "in step", to do favours and "to be a big spender". Although he no longer lives in the housing estate, preferring a more discrete apartment in a poor neighbourhood in the city centre, it is unlikely that anyone in the estate is unaware of his activities. But this tolerance towards dealers, as well as those who smoke drugs, is not the same thing as complicity. It does not mean necessarily that the dealer is "protected" by the housing estate. Even his parents, Moussa says, "pretend not to know".

Moussa has plans for the future. He intends to continue his business for a few years and then buy a bar or restaurant. But this is more difficult than it appears. He must either bring his capital into the open and thereby risk getting caught by the police, who have kept an eye on him since his prison term, or find an associate sufficiently trustworthy to transact things in the open under his own name. However, Moussa has failed to find such a person within the world of his relations. The members of his own family, he says, could make him lose everything. His business relations, for whom he has only a confidence of circumstances or who, like him, live in semi-hiding, are not considered as possible partners. All this is proof, if it were necessary, of the weakness of the ties within which he operates. When we met, Moussa was looking for a radical solution—

"a little job" that would allow him "to resurface" and be forgotten by the police. He hoped thereby that one day he could claim his capital as "personal savings".

Soufiane thinks that at his age of 26 it is time to turn a new leaf. Up until now he was "a business man" (*"un homme d'affaires"*). The term does not have its usual sense; rather, it refers to people "on the lookout for a deal" (*une affaire*). It is an almost exclusively masculine world of those men who spend their time in the business district searching for deals which they can enter into. They are not recognised traders, but they often buy merchandise in transit, putting into contact buyers and sellers and especially, as they put it, "doing favours". When we first met, Soufiane was preparing for his next voyage to Tunisia. He was also looking for an "associate" who had more capital than him in order to buy a consignment of pinball machines which he hoped to sell in Algeria. "A friend is selling them for 1500 francs each; they can easily be re-sold for 3000 each in Algeria. In other words, at least three grand only by sweet talking. Since he was a kid he has been selling job lots of perfume and watches, fake ten franc coins, job lots of socks and other sewn goods. He has often delivered cars to Algeria, especially since Algerian law forbade the importation of unaccompanied used cars, and most of all his speciality has been to have jewellery brought in. In fact, Soufiane had worked several years for someone in the neighbourhood. who made false jewellery, from whom, as he put it, he "had learned the trade". He no longer practises that trade, claiming that he is allergic to products used in the jewellery business. Nonetheless, he has remained on good terms with his former boss who often gives him job lots of jewellery to move, sends him to Tunisia to look for gems and sometimes gives him jewelry to sell "under the table".

Soufiane was born to Algerian parents in the city centre of Marseilles, quite near to the port. He knows many people in the commercial district and combines three networks of relations. There is dispersed kinship which seems as if it is pulverised in the constellation of local social groups as a result of marriages, divorces, remarriages, departures and returns between France and Algeria. Thus, he could benefit from the help of an uncle, the brother of his father's second wife, in meeting a local politician for whom the uncle worked as a chauffeur. He was able as a result to work for a few months in an association for the creation of jobs, just long enough to get himself a work contract. This brief passage into the world of local politics allowed him to get onto an electoral list for the last municipal elections. To be sure, it was a minor place from which there was no hope of gaining access to power, but it did bring to Soufiane a bit more notability in the neighbourhood. His ex-wife, who is of Algerian origin, works for an airline company. She provides him with a very useful means of short-cutting the long waiting lines to get a ticket for trips to Algeria. Soufiane knows how to help his friends by these shortcuts. Another very useful network of relations which Soufiane inherited from his period with the jeweller is the quite closed world of bourgeois Jewish merchants. He is attracted to this bourgeoisie and keeps in touch with them regularly in order "to do favours". The owner of the apartment he occupies in the city centre belongs to this world, and he often turns to Soufiane for minor repairs of his apartments. Soufiane is also very proud of the access that he has thanks to his relations with the most prestigious night spots of Marseilles—access to night clubs, restaurants, bars or very closed gambling circles. Finally, he participates in a more diffuse network of "business relations" which he maintains between Marseilles and Algeria. These days Soufiane travels frequently to Tunisia where he recently has remarried, a good marriage, in fact, inasmuch as his wife belongs to a rich family of merchants living in Nabeul. Thus, he goes to Tunisia once a month, and to Nabeul, as well, where he has begun some trade in items brought from Marseilles. At the moment, he has to pick up a job lot of mobile phones which he chanced upon "by accident" while looking for a mobile phone to offer to his brother-in-law.

Thus, Soufiane seems to be well integrated in a constellation of networks that have an international dimension and which shape the commercial life of Marseilles. (This "colonial comptoir" at the heart of the city centre which organises trade with the countries of the Maghreb will be discussed below.) Nonetheless, he has experienced regularly periods of difficulty. Like Moussa, he sometimes was "led into" illegal operations. These put him in danger of being radically excluded by the most respectable of his relations. Moreover, Soufiane was subject to very irregular payments of money and thus also suffered financial difficulties periodically. A good portion of his activities, in fact, consisted of doing favours which often brought no financial benefit.

Like the "street guys" whose activities in Boston of the 1950s have been described by W. F. White (1996), Soufiane is a "broker" who maintains connections between the worlds of respectability and legality and those of the more hidden informal economy. Doing favours is a way of doing things in the open for people who cannot show themselves without incurring danger. At the same time, it is a way of doing things in the shadows which could compromise the reputations of established traders. Finally, Soufiane is certainly a hypochondriac, obsessed by the idea of a long illness. He dreams of maximal health insurance which he does not have from his irregular and limited work in above-the-board employment. He is integrated in terms of his relations, but his ties are also weak. He moves about from the periphery of worlds to the interiors, unable to take control of a stable position. Undoubtedly he will never have enough capital to open a shop in Marseilles, nor enough presence and integration in the "client" countries which he visits to establish a business. He also has not enough "educational capital" and technical competence to hope to conquer by means of the political sphere of his relations anything other than an unqualified and precarious job—as a storekeeper, a maintenance man, etc. In short, he possesses no card with which he might win the social advancement that would put him at a distance from his parents' world of labourers, a world from which, nonetheless, he is far removed.

Hassen is older than the others mentioned above, and he can make claim to a more successful educational history. He is at present 32 years old. At the beginning of the 1980s he completed a school for technical training with the diploma of an electrician. This allowed him quite rapidly to get a job in a local business. After a few years as a salaried worker, he decided to establish his own business. But he left the world of his initial profession and joined up with his brother, a young fellow with a license to drive heavy-duty lorries, and they bought themselves a truck. Hassen also passed his driving test for heavy-duty lorries, and with his brother started up a delivery service as subcontractors for large transport companies. He very soon became one of the subcontractors licensed by an important company which controlled a significant part of delivery transport in the region of Marseilles. In this way Hassen became introduced into the world of trade, that of wholesalers and merchants who deal in clothing, sporting goods and electrical supplies in the industrial districts of Spain, Italy or Belgium. Serious about his work, devoted, honest, ready to take on responsibilities or do favours beyond the norms of work, Hassen won the confidence of his clients and began to undertake trips on his own for them. In this way, he learned the nature of relations of wholesale commerce, the places of trade and the ways in which it was carried out.

In 1990, the transport company that was his principle source of work went resoundingly bankrupt. For a while Hassen continued his delivery service at his own expense. Then he decided to sell his truck in order to go into business for himself. He rented a locale in the industrial warehouses of the northern part of the city and established a second-hand tyre business there. He knew from his former profession the favourable conditions which made this kind of business possible: that in Switzerland and Germany the norms for tyre treads are more severe than in France, while they are non-existent in the Maghreb and in Africa. There are wholesalers who specialise in tyres in Switzerland, Germany, and in Bordeaux. Hassen had already gone to these places on behalf of traders who had their businesses in Marseilles. Afterwards he would go to buy them in Switzerland and then take them to sell in Algeria in the native village of his parents where he has family ties. A cousin of his would buy the whole of the lot and order others from him. When Hassen had established his business, he hired a worker, and used forwarding agents to handle the transfer of merchandise. These steps were undoubtedly premature for an item whose profitability is conditioned first of all by doing away with intermediaries. His business prospered as long as he could himself furnish and deliver the goods. Two unhappy experiences with an African country, of merchandise delivered but not paid for, undermined his business. Hassen tried to diversify. Along with two other forwarder friends, he bought job lots of goods that had been confiscated by the douanes, for example tea and small electrical items. However, the small and out-of-the-way depot where he stocked and sold his tyres proved quite unsuited for the sale of other goods. With another friend from his neighbourhood, a maintenance man in the housing estate where they were born and both still live, Hassen set up a Sunday business with his modest stock. He did this in the housing estate itself and he sells from "door to door" like an itinerant salesman. It has been a success, but it is a business that has moved into the zone of the illegal. Then Hassen tried to negotiate the rental of a ground floor site in the housing estate, but was refused by the office in charge of rentals. These kinds of street sales continued. Indeed, Hassen had to continue to buy job lots if he wanted, as he put it, "to maintain a presence in the marketplace". He shut down his tyre business and continued door-to-door selling.

When I met him, he was negotiating by phone for a job lot of sportswear and considering going back to work as a salaried driver.

In order to understand these histories and to put them into a wider framework, it is first of all necessary to place them in their context, that is the very specific place of Marseilles' commerce and its international ramifications.

The world of business

A commercial area established on the edge of the city centre, bound to the north by the railway station and to the south by the commercial port, was established nearby the ethnic-based businesses that had existed there since the beginning of the century. It constitutes one of the main points of provision for Maghrebi communities, and more recently Africans, who live on one side of the Mediterranean or the other. Between 1980 and 1988, about 400 shops there had a turnover of an estimated three billion French Francs. This resulted from a stream of over 400,000 persons coming by ship for the weekend from the Maghreb, plus local and regional customers (Tarrius 1995). This area does not only bring together foodstuffs that cannot be found in Europe, such as meat slaughtered according to religious injunctions (halal), herbs and other special foods; it also offers manufactured goods that are difficult to find in the those countries: textile fabrics, automotive parts, electrical goods, new or second-hand cars, etc.

The commercial facade was opened by Algerian traders who came to Marseilles in the years 1970–75. Since then Tunisians, Senegalese and Moroccan traders have joined them. But the area also draws support from a wide commercial network, some of whom have set up businesses in the neighbourhood—from Sephardic Jewish garment wholesalers from Morocco and Algeria who moved to Marseilles after decolonisation, from suppliers and wholesalers from Belgium for carpets, Germany for cars, Italy for leather goods and shoes, from forwarders for Asian electrical goods, and from Turkey for jewellery and garments. This "colonial comptoir" (Tarrius 1995) is therefore not a circumscribed area. It is above all a place of redistribution by trade routes which connect producers of the north with the consumers of the south, routes on which merchandise, people, capital and information circulate. The particularity of this commerce essentially stems from the fact that most of this circulation is handled largely without the usual logistics of transport, either by the traders themselves, or by networks of "ants" and itinerant salesmen. The district of Belsunce is, to be sure, a place of neighbourhood businesses and of direct commercial exchange. But it is also a place of trade which creates economic and social conditions on a Mediterranean scale for all those goods subject to social prohibitions or political embargoes: unauthorised gold which comes from Istanbul or Naples on its way to the Maghreb and Africa; German cars on their way to Libya at the time that it is under an embargo; but,as well, low-priced, unsold and end-of-series goods, American basketball shoes, imitations of luxury items. These few examples are meant to show that Belsunce is primarily a place of trade where on the basis of actors' initiatives, oral agreements and reciprocal promises, the circulation and profitability of merchandise otherwise cut-off by social and political blockages can take place.

The commercial district of Belsunce has chananged continually: there are fluctuations because of political relations between Europe and the countries of the Maghreb, often that much more fragile because of the political crises that have shaken Algeria, in particular; the district is subject to the pressures of urban development by local institutions and by its "evil" image chronically maintained by local public opinion; and yet it is constantly made dynamic through the initiatives of entrepreneurs. Indeed, the different waves of immigration in this central neighbourhood have taken place in a relation of succession/co-operation. It is both a place of residence and a centre of business and exchanges. The co-operation among "old-timers" and "newcomers" make it possible to renew continually the areas of supply, trade routes and even the provision of available labour. Algerian traders of the 1970–1980s followed the Armenian and Italian craftsmen who occupied the neighbourhood in the years 1930–1950. At the same time, they found new outlets for the goods produced by those craftsmen who remained in the neighbourhood. The same Algerians were introduced and "protected" in their settling in by Sephardic wholesalers who had arrived at the end of the 1950s. In this way the wholesalers were enabled to re-open the commercial routes of the Maghreb which had been closed for a while by decolonisation. At the end of the 1980s, these same Algerians brought African and Tunisian traders into the marketplace, once again on the basis of new trade agreements. Perpetually evolving, the commercial existence of Belsunce gives a concrete and rare example of the intercultural ordering of commercial functions. Rather than ethnic relations, it is the flux of the migrants themselves and their differences that have served as economic resources that could be mobilised.

The most significant trait of this evolution is the opening up of new markets and the creation of new spaces in the city. Some of these are in the immediate periphery of the historical area of Belsunce; others, that is the case notably of the Flea Market, have spread into the warehouses at the heart of the former industrial sites of the northern neighbourhoods (cf. Peraldi 1995). These new commercial areas, often opened on the initiative of prosperous traders coming from the original area, mark a clear change of direction in regard to commercial strategies: without necessarily losing their direct attachment to customers coming from the Maghreb, these new markets are also more systematically oriented towards local consumption, especially the sale of foodstuffs, clothing, and cheap household goods; theses strategies are calculated on the model of "hard discounters". Businesses conceived in this way become more widely available to local populations, to those who live in the worlds of poverty and exclusion, as well as to those along the edges of the middle classes who are uncontaminated by the cultural differences and symbolic signs that mark the social distance from the lower classes.

This "commercial comptoir" was at first mainly turned towards the Maghreb. It was reserved for "the fathers", that is both the transmigrants and tourist buyers coming from the Maghreb, as well as the first generation of immigrants who maintained their ties and attachments in their mother countries. Until the beginning of the 1990s, a very clear cultural and social border kept the young children of immigrants born in France at a distance. They only very gradually became integrated as customers or directly involved in trade. That only happened when the market became open to other logics of goods and commercial channels. It is striking to note, for example, that most young traders who set themselves up in the heart of the marketplace during these years of prosperity are entirely first generation migrants. They came directly from Algeria or Tunisia, taking advantage of kinship ties in the district itself, or re-investing in Marseilles their capital or know-how acquired in other places or commercial centres in the Maghreb. Young people born in France only appeared later on. They became integrated either through new commercial slots—notably outlets for sport shoes and "fashionable" clothes, or through new commercial spots with mixed clientele—that was the case in the Flea Market, or in those areas which were normalised and integrated into an industrial rationality. That is the case notably for the forwarding agents and the maritime companies. They developed the container business to Algeria, hired young Algerians born in France but lacking diplomas and technical skills, especially in regard to international commercial law.

However astonishing it may appear, a marketplace which seems dominated by the informal can only be penetrated by following one of two royal paths: that of birth or inheritance and that of technical specialisation ratified by a diploma. The interest of the cases presented above stems from the fact that they concretely describe the overgrown paths taken by those who appear on the commercial scene. But they also show how difficult it is to attain stability in those positions which are most profitable and most valued socially.

Byways

In addition to the royal paths of inheritance and the acquisition of technical skills defined and validated by a diploma, there are a few byways which illustrate the "bizness stories" presented above. One such way, apparently easy because it seems banal and rational in regard to the evolution of new forms of becoming employable, is that of converting the knowledge that workers gain in industry. That was the way taken by Hassen and numerous others who I encountered in the course of my fieldwork (Peraldi 1997, 1999). For example, in the Provençal region more than 30,000 VSEs were created in 1998. Of these, 80% had no more than one salaried worker and had not used the banking system to constitute their initial capital. Most of them had been created by entrepreneurs who had been professional workers (cf. INSEE, December 1999). Most of these VSEs had been created in the sector service. Very few of them actually gain access to a market which might be a possible stepping-stone for the industrial development of the business, or which might provide international openings or at least go beyond the narrow circle of the local market. The example of Hassen makes that quite clear: the "conversion" of a worker's know-how into an individual business is a false analogy. It should be said that, on the one hand, a business rarely, if ever, is established on the basis of the initial occupation of a worker and, on the other hand, that the formation and extension of a clientele group supposes less of a technical competency than the ability to mobilise "acquaintances" and networks of relations.

Idri, for example, a young Algerian and former worker in the BTP (Batiment et Travaux Publique, Construction and Public Works), recently opened a garage where he sold used cars in a northern neighbourhood, not far from the housing estate in which he lives. Discretely and above all informally, he had been given a hand by a salesman who works for an important car dealer. He was able to profit from vehicles used as trade-ins by people buying new cars from the dealer, as well as from a network of friends from Lyon to Marseilles, mobilised by the salesman.

His first "index of clients" was simply made up of 1000 persons who he had invited to his marriage, all of them connected somehow to the immense Algerian kinship network to which he belongs, and most of whom now live in Marseilles or in the region. Idri specialised in a range of low-priced cars, selling at between 10,000 and 30,000 francs ($1,300–$3,900), which are pegged at the working classes of the housing estates. But this set-up, including the spatial dimension—his garage was in the midst of high-rise buildings in the neighbourhoods of the north—cut him off from the marketplace of used cars which can be exported to the Maghreb or Africa. That market demands cars from the upper range or utility vehicles. When I met Idri, he was getting ready to sell his garage after liquidating his stock. In fact, he had just been convicted for receiving and concealing stolen goods. It is a complicated affair: he was accused of having sold a stolen car, a car which he bought from one of his cousins. In fact, the car belonged to the cousin's sister-in-law who had entrusted him with its sale. But the cousin had kept the money from the sale for himself, and his sister-in-law had brought an action against him. The judiciary machine went into action and came down upon Idri. At last word, after a trial in which he had received a suspended sentence, he resumed his former occupation as a house painter....

Thus, family networks play an essential and strategic role not only in the creating of a personal engagement in one's commercial career, but also in defining commercial channels and openings. That has been seen in following the career of Soufiane. This would deserve only a brief mention if it were simply a matter of demonstrating the familial nature of the commercial enterprise. The strategic dimension only assumes importance insofar as crosscutting ties are mobilised, that is among those closely related within a narrowly defined family circle. Those ties allow one "to travel" within a social space without needing to acknowledge anything other than a cultural identity. That is so because the social space of kinship networks, ethnic networks, and networks of friendship is marked, traversed and even maintained by relations of exchange. Their everyday nature in some ways makes the "fluctuation" in commercial careers natural. In the world of immigrants in particular, merchandise is the logical prolongation, the natural extension, of a gift or a favour. In the everyday nature of relations of exchange in the marketplace, gifts, favours and merchandise continue to interact to weave, to bind and to loosen ties.

Victor, who comes from Nigeria, now sells a car a month by means of small ads, or on Sundays in the parking lots of supermarkets in one of the occasional markets which have become widespread in recent years. He goes to look these days for cars (only big models from the 1980s) in Germany—in the large markets organised from time to time in Dusseldorf, Cologne or Fribourg; previously he would go to Belgium to the famous Abattoirs market, or to Holland. His trade is prospering, his ability to spot good deals and his trustworthiness are by now recognised in the marketplace. Yet in no way was he predisposed to this choice of "career". He had a scholarship from the Nigerian state and came to France to complete his university studies, which he did. But very quickly, requests asking him to bring European goods back home began to arrive. Initially, he brought back a Mercedes for his brother-in-law. Then other relatives and relatives of his brother-in-law also began making requests to Victor who discovered, thereby, a way of financing his way home during university vacations. As a result of his numerous trips to markets in Europe, he accumulated know-how and relations. Today it seems to him logical and financially sound to sell his cars in Marseilles rather than mobilise the complicated logistics necessary to ship them to Africa.

Much of the merchandise taken back by migrants simply pays for their return trip. They secure their reputations through gifts offered to their circles of friends and relatives, and they give tangible signs thereby of the higher status that they have achieved. Inversely, the uncertainty, the lack of clarity in regard to the status of the objects— goods or gifts?—is an efficient way of protecting a beginner at trade when he goes through customs or through the marketplace. The wife of Anouar, a young Algerian teacher whose status allows her to be in Europe frequently, does not do business in perfumes and lingerie that her husband brings: she allows her friends, as it happens, "to profit" from the gifts that her husband brings her at prices based on friendship.

Thus, involvement in commerce can be born from the density of exchanges which mark social networks. These exchanges maintain ties inside the dispersed worlds of migration. The involvement may also be related to the apparent plasticity of the social status of objects that can sometimes be a gift, at others a favour, at yet others merchandise. All depends on the relations that tie those who exchange the object at that particular moment. But the looser the ties, the more infrequent the exchanges and the less familiarity in business. The "law of networks" in this case gives superiority to the first immigrants over their children, to fathers over sons. Finally, involvement in commerce does not mean ipso facto passage to the recognized status of a trader. To acquire that supposes conditions other than the sole fact of being "in business". The case of Soufiane presented above illustrates this clearly.

"To become a trader it's necessary to be honest and well known". Pronounced by an Algerian trader in the marketplace of Marseilles, this rule of ethics is considered a maxim in the worlds of commerce. To be honest is to deserve a confidence that is less a moral value than it is a value based on experience: every transaction "puts the meter back to zero". One is given confidence until next time, as an experienced trader put it. Thus, it is the duration in trade which establishes the certainty and reputation of someone in a milieu in which one is as good as one's word. To be known then is to construct an unsullied reputation over time and through tests. That is the sole condition by which an apprentice, a youngster working in a cafe, an employee or a driver can slowly climb the steps that lead to the status of an associate and from there have access to the knowledge of channels which open directly onto the marketplace. The metaphor of a hierarchy in this case fits poorly. One does not become a trader like one becomes a foreman, by climbing the rungs of a ladder of merit or ability. One becomes a trader by building up a portefolio of privileged relations along the pathway of a product. These relations make it possible to obtain credit from suppliers or exclusive rights to a product, the reliability of a clientele or commercial agreements with one or another provider of services. Parallel to this "royal" path, the way of virtue of a trader properly speaking, there is another which is more risky; it ties together the same sorts of relations, but no longer by means of daily tests of one's respectability. Rather, it takes place in bars, restauraunts, night clubs, in hidden underworld places, or gambling dens.

Like sport, artistic creation, or religious practice, commercial activity may be lived as "an intense experience" (Simmel 1971). It is a form of experience which supposes a surrender of self, a total implication of the individual, the incarnation of a self in an activity and the social relations that accompany it, moments spent together among the initiated. One hears repeated from shop to shop, sayings like the following: trade is a passion that one is born with; a trader cares about neither his time nor his fatigue, sacrifices family and leisure; like a sports activity, trade alternates between long hours of waiting and routine and moments of great dramatic intensity in which, like in the performance of a sport, it is a matter of outdoing oneself. There are two types which construct the space of the imaginary in which the activity of commerce achieves its meaning: on the one hand, there is the ascetic workalcoholic, a model of honesty, of scrupulousness and as demanding of himself as he is of others; on the other hand, there is the "flame thrower" who is always in a critical position and who goes from one audacious action to another with a playful attitude to money, to merchandise and to life, in general. These two types are antithetical from the point of view of ethics. Yet, given the economic realities, they mark out quite well the ground of economic constraints on which commercial activity takes place, that is between a speculative dynamism and a logic of savings. The places of sociability, the backstages of commercial activity, combine and superimpose at times these two cardinal types. The "moral regions" (Park 1979) of commercial activities, the closed places of intimacy and complicity among the initiated, thus combine virtue and debauchery. First of all, these are cafes, restaurants, places of meeting where current business affairs are discussed, where matters of the day are commented upon, but also where agreements and contracts are negotiated, at least those that call for the presence of a third party. Often near mosques attended by the Muslim population, these places and the forms of sociability that develop in them bring together other virtues which reach there by way of religious practice. Religious institutions are necessary supports for activities that take place elsewhere, alongside or even in opposition to the areas of competence of the state. As one tradesman put it, God goes where the state will not. It follows that regular religious practice, constant attendance at prayer and continual presence in places of religion may be a good introduction into the worlds of commerce. At the same time, these virtues are transferable from religion to culture, and it is socially legitimate to make that transfer.

Yet in the same way, commerce is in the waiting-room of those places where "big spending" and "winning" are possible. It is the excessive and ostentatious spending, however illusory, which gives the impression of a tradesman's prosperity. (One who spends a lot is considered to have as much capital as one who has savings.) His virility is demonstrated by taking on bets, through gambling, at poker as well as in the stadiums. These are always ways of measuring courage and self-control, as well as solidarity and reciprocal commitment. A constellation of night clubs, restaurants open at night (often the difference between places open during the day and those open during the night make for the distinction between "virtue" and "vice"), gaming circles and clandestine gambling-dens go along with and encompass the lives of traders. These shady places where the worlds of night life come together for a moment of "common passion" (Park 1979) bring together established traders, thieves, gangsters, businessmen, but also young men caught up in the conviviality and good-will which characterise the worlds of parties and music, concerts and artistic life. Here, too, in the continual frequentation of these places, in the regular participation in dice or card games, in the buying rounds of drinks, in these manufactured "ambiances" (Macgaffey, Bazenguissa 1995), careers and involvement in the world of business can take root.

A lost generation?

The fragments of biographies that appear here and support my presentation are not only singular because they were produced in the interaction of the research situation. The account of one's life is singular by its very nature; that is its object. But in the context these biographies trace the processes of the emergence of individuals. These are in some ways inherent to the activities that are described in the accounts. Entering into the world of trade is for young second-generation immigrants, if not an act of bravery, at least one of bravado and an ostentatious affirmation of one's self. To be sure, the urban economic environment makes this inclination, which certain individuals lend to their personal destiny, more or less possible, legitimate or desirable. These "adventurers" are more numerous in Marseilles—a distinctly commercial place, a port city and, as such, a frontier marketplace with great traditions of commerce and of immigration—than they are, for example, in Toulouse—a university and technological centre that is far away from commercial routes. However familiar with the world of commercial exchange the young of Marseilles may be, their long-term involvement in this world is an acting out, and implies a transgression and a distancing of oneself from the general fate of their generation. At best, one can point out that there is an increase in practises that are partially commercial.

The involvement of young people of immigrant origin in the world of trade does not stem automatically from their belonging to this or that ethnic group which, owing to the force of circumstances, leads them to enter into worlds that are constructed like enclaves. Nor does this involvement stem from the ease with which, rejected by the normal labour markets and seemingly out of hopelessness, they become delinquent. The theme of "easy money", which is widespread today in much of the representations by social workers in rundown neighbourhoods, does not stand up to the facts. The familiarity that young people have with mind-altering drugs, even the positive image that is sometimes associated with "dealers" is to a large extent a provocation and the desire to set themselves apart. Like all commercial careers, those that touch the world of crime imply at times a long series of tests rather than a familiarity or a "skill".

The social destiny of these young sons and daughters of Algerian immigrants, born and brought up in the large housing estates of high-rises during the 1960s, was sealed in the 1980s by a double blind alley and a confrontation. With the breakdown of the French industrial structure and the end of Fordism, it soon became apparent that it would no longer be possible for them to continue, prolong or follow the professional paths of their fathers. Most of their fathers had been workers in the industries destroyed by the economic changes of the time. Many of the young of this generation participated in the great campaign of denouncing the conditions of workers in order to demonstrate their radical distance from that universe which had made their fathers into invalids after having humiliated them. This did not stop the great majority of them, forced to a large extent by the system of education, from pursuing technical studies which then led them towards trades which in fact no longer exist in the local industrial structure. Quite logically, they aspired to a social betterment identical to that which the young French of the same generation and from the same class position could realise or desire. That is by extending their education to the university, they might attain professional careers oriented, on the whole, towards the status of a salaried employee or a bureaucrat, more often in government employment than in private enterprises.

They tended all the more to aim for these places in society because their residential and social situation placed them on, a daily basis and often exclusively face-to-face, just opposite those middle classes. It was especially such people—from school teachers to professors and from social workers to employees of housing estate organisms—who had benefited in earlier days from social mobility. These were the secular and republican "priests" (Ion 1991) whose cultural codes and moral values they often adopted. Nonetheless, only a tiny minority amongst them have managed to reach these positions. They have been limited by the weakness of their educational capital, as well as by the complexity of their legal and civic status which denies them access to professions in the public sector. No doubt, a minority get there after long years of university studies and the acquisition of French citizenship. But all too often they occupy an inferior and particularly a more precarious place than their French elders in the apparatuses of social action (Duport 2000). They are behind and lack social position, even that elite who have created a political career and moved into spheres of power, especially on the local level (Geisser 1997).

The young children of immigrants are caught in what Waldinger (1996) defines in regard to Afro-Americans as a kind of "mismatch". They are excluded at one and the same time from the dying industrial world and from a possible social betterment to which they aspire. They are shaped, it needs repeating, in an institutional, political and social environment which is dominated by their being face-to-face with the middle classes. They watch the economic recovery, as it were, pass under their noses and leave them stranded. Some of them, parts of whose lives I have attempted to follow, try the pathways of smuggling to escape from the destiny that awaits them. But they do so notwithstanding and in opposition to the rules, norms and codes of their social universe. They are marginal and alone.

Bibliography

Boltanski, L., Chiapello, E. 1999, *Le nouvel esprit du capitalisme*, Paris, Gallimard.
Bouhnik, P. 1994, "Le monde social des usagers de drogues dures en milieu urbain défavorisé," Thèse 3° cycle, Université Paris 8.
Castel, R. 1996, *Les métamorphoses de la question sociale*, Paris, Fayard
Dubet, F. 1987, *La galère: jeunes en survie*, Fayard, Paris.
Duport, C. 2000, "A l'école de l'indignation", in Metral, J. (ed.), *Cultures en ville*, Paris, Ed. de l'Aube.
Geisser, V. 1997, *Ethnicité républicaine, les élites d'origine maghrébine dans le système politique français*, Paris, Presses de Sciences Po.
Granovetter, M. 1973, "The strength of weak ties," in *American Journal of Sociology*, vol. 78, n° 6.
INSEE, décembre 1999, "Les très petites entreprises en région Provence Alpes Côte d'Azur", in *Sud infos économiques*.
Ion, J. 1991, "La fin des petits clercs", in Donzelot, J. (dir.) *Face à l'exclusion. Le modèle français*, Paris Editions Esprit.
Lazzarato, M. 1996, "Les concepts de travail immatériel et de bassin immatériel", in M. Peraldi, E. Perrin (ed.), *Réseaux productifs et territoires urbains*, Presses Universitaires du Mirail, Toulouse.
Macgaffey, J., Bazenguissa, G. R., 1995, "Ostentation in a clandestine setting: young congolese and Zaïrian migrants in Nganda bars in Paris," in *Mondes en développement*, n° 91, tome XXIII.
Park, R., 1979, "La ville," in Joseph, I., Grafmeyer, Y. (ed.) *L'école de Chicago*, Champ Urbain/Aubier, Paris.
Peraldi, M., Foughali, N., Spinouza, N. 1995, "L'abondance des pauvres; le marché aux Puces à Marseille," in *Revue Européenne des Migrations Internationales*, vol. 1/95.
Peraldi, M. 1997, "Portraits d'entrepreneurs," in (Collectif) *En marge de la ville, au cœur de la société: ces quartiers dont on parle*, Ed. De l'Aube, La tour d'Aigues.
———, "Migrant's careers and commercial expertise in Marseilles," in S. Body-Gendrot, M. Martinitello, *Minorities in European cities*, New York, St. Martin's Press.
Portes, A., Castells, M., Benton, L. A. 1989, *The informal economy*, Baltimore, The Johns Hopkins University Press.
Salais, R., Storper, M. 1993, *Les mondes de production*, ED. de l'EHESS, Paris.
Simmel, G., "The adventurer, 1911," in Levine, D. N. (ed.), 1971, *On individuality and social form*, Chicago, The University of Chicago Press.
Tarrius, A. 1995, *Arabes de France dans le commerce international*, Ed. de l'Aube, Marseille.
Waldinger, R., 1993, "Le débat sur l'enclave ethnique: revue critique," in *Revue Européenne des migrations internationales*, vol. 9, n° 2.
———, 1995, "The other side of embeddedness: a case-study of the interplace of economy and ethnicity," in *Ethnic and racial studies*, vol. 18, n° 3.
———, 1996, *Still the promised city?: African-americans and new immigrants in postindustrial New York*, Cambridge, Harvard University Press.
White, W. F. 1996, *Street corner society; la structure sociale d'un quartier italo-américain*, Paris, La Découverte.

RUSSIAN YOUTH AND WORK: SOCIAL INTEGRATION AND EXCLUSION UNDER CONDITIONS OF RISK

Vladimir I. Chuprov and Julia A. Zubok

Entering social structure young people search for a desirable place in society, and are aware of the certain positions occupied in different spheres of society (education, labour, policy, etc.). Orientations towards different social niches are maintained by one's personal abilities and interests that refer to young people's self-actualization. This is decisive for their *social integration* that is generally understood to mean the character of relations between a society as a whole, on the one hand, and the youth as one of its constituent parts, on the other. The process of social integration is not limited simply to the mechanistic inclusion in a social community, type of activity or a structure but the feeling of being an integral part of them. A combination of these two processes of physical involvement and identification makes youth integration sustainable and *organic* in character.

Social integration of youth as a key issue

In the course of this empirical research the level of a young person's integration into society is defined as a degree of his or her involvement in various social structures (professional, political, marital etc.) and the degree of self-identification with them. Self-identification presuppose internalisation of all the values and the norms shared by other members of the community or the society. It is determined by both the social integration mechanisms and the degree to which young people are ready to become involved in social life. Desire to be a part of society is mainly maintained by opportunities open to everyone to get the social status of referent groups. Hence, integration of young people is objective in nature, a continuous, non-stop process that is impossible without the young people's successful mobility and self-expression.

The direction and the results of youth integration depend both on the young people themselves, i.e. their aspirations and abilities, and on the opportunities provided by society. Since the principles of social

Darwinism in social policy has been left behind, social institutions are expected to carry all responsibility for integration of youth into society. Obviously the better indicators of economic and social development the less problematic social integration is. However, more or less dynamic changes typical for the modern global world mainly break this ideal model.

Firstly, these rapid changes themselves do not give time to social groups including young people for adaptation to new situation or to use the experience of the older generation. In an extremely changeable world the younger generation has to be ready for individual decision—made in order to keep pace with new social reality. Moreover on the level of personal consciousness such a situation makes a strong impression of existing instability and uncertainty inevitably going alongside any social changes. Besides, liberal doctrine, basic for social policy in many countries across the world presumes not just personal freedom but personal responsibility for individual choice as well.

Thus, a combination of "developmental" and "political" factors determines individualisation among contemporary youth and affects it's social integration. Consequently as sociological surveys undertaken in the West prove, the majority of young people make a stronger connection between successful mobility and one's individual efforts than with social institutions' assistance. Young people continue to plan their career and their biographies in correspondence with personal interests in different spheres of social life and demonstrate by the way readiness for better activity in achieving personal goals.

However, life planning may take place in a society differed by sufficient level of certainty and predictability. Only youth reflexivity concerning individual life is sensible. However certainty is not any more characteristic of modern societies, where it is replaced by opposed trends of uncertainty and unpredictability. Dialectically it has inverse consequences. From one, positive side, young people find themselves in front of a rich choice when they can experiment with different models of self-expression, activity and identities. This kind of freedom is particularly supported by young Russians. Liberalization in Russia has broken the former unification of young people's biographies when every one's life was mainly predicted by the dominant ideology and its collapse is seen by youth as one of the great achievements of reforms.

From the other, negative side, along with ideological determination of one's life course security of social integration was also lost.

So that, open opportunities remain among the most important values but young people can hardly enjoy them in reality. Ascribed social inequality is not more diminished by social institutions. Russian and Western sociologists draw the rather pessimistic conclusions that real determinants of youth integration lie somewhere outside of their control. In highly stratified society young people are again dependent on the old social factors such as social background, gender, ethnicity (Chuprov and Zubok, 2000; Machacek and Roberts, 1997; Machacek, 1998; Nagel and Wallace, 1997; Furlong and Cartmel, 1997; Furlong, Stadler and Azzopardi, 2000; Roberts, 1995; Wallace and Kovatcheva, 1998). Besides, in the case of Russia with it's social polarization the list of stratification factors is extended by regional factors and the type of property of the enterprise in which young people are employed. Both of them define the level of living standards among Russian youth whose social integration has appeared to be under the pressure of all these factors.

Contradictions of social integration under pressure of uncertainty and risk

Most of the difficulties arising on the way of integration are caused by gradually increasing uncertainty and unpredictability in contemporary societies. Absolutely identical societies do not exist; however uncertainty has become a distinctive feature of the stage of late modernity.

Uncertainty of societal goals, uncertainty of norms and values, uncertainty in functioning of social mechanisms produce the whole range of risks: risk of false starts, risks of downward mobility, risks of social disorientation and anomie, risks of breaking with social institutions, risks of delinquent identity. Turning to the particular atmosphere in which young people are making their transitions, risk has become the main factor of its social integration and its social and individual development.

Thus, risk is the common trend and the basis for similarities that manifest themselves in very different societies now described as "risk societies". In very general terms risk society is seen as the peculiar stage that modern and postmodern societies eventually entered on the way of their successful development. This stage is defined as a crisis of modernity when production of goods is being at least accompanied and even replaced by production of risks. Hence, risk was produced by modernization itself (Beck, 1992; Giddens, 1991).

Different types of risks among which are the consequences of nature disasters, ecological catastrophes, over-use of the modern technologies, economic recessions, management mistakes, political crisis and terrorist actions across the world concern men and women, rich and poor. It is particularly painful for the younger generation whose integration into societies is fundamentally dependent on the social, economic and political climate but now not only that in their countries but in remote places in the world due to globalization.

In fact, the very basis of many of societies is threatened by uncertainty and risk. As soon as risk is becoming a more or less general characteristic of modernity it determines similar spectra of specific social problems faced by youth. Within every risk society young people constantly face many risks: receiving no education, having no jobs, starting no family, failing in surviving social competition and finding no proper place in society.

However, societies have passed different stages of modernisation before they entered state of risk. That is why risks could also be different in their degree or in prerequisites. Moreover in relatively sustainable societies going through broad social changes without shock the scale of existing risks are not the same as of those in the society surviving long-term crisis on the societal level. These and other risks are more pronounced in highly unstable societies, such as Russia, the former USSR and many East-Central European countries, where a larger proportion of young people suffer from the economic and political crisis, which has varied in its intensity during the last decade, has been extremely prolonged and shows no signs of ending.

Such conditions have a crucial influence on youth integration into society. Any attempts to overcome this uncertainty inevitably involve risk: in risky environment all career steps that young people might take involve risk.

At the same time, risk is one of the essential characteristics of youth as a socio-demographic group. Despite negative aspects of risk, there is always someone's chance to win. Strong desire for innovations, for something previously unknown is more common for youth in comparison with older generation. Facing risk young people are less reflexive on possible negative results and believe to be potentially among winners and fearlessly take risk. One can conclude that risk is a normal and common trend in youth behaviour. It is not surprising that western youth integration strategies described by British sociologists K. Evans and A. Furlong include the model called the "taking chance" model (Evans and Furlong, 1997).

It is youth's response to the situation typical for risk society: young people's awareness of unpredictability in professional and other spheres of life goes hand by hand with their efforts driven in the direction of personal social ambitions and interests. In risk society such opportunities undergo dramatic changes. Young people are obliged to go through the whole range of risky situations. In the individual perspective risk expresses itself in uncertainty, unpredictability and incalculability of professional lives. Young people are hardly able to follow life plans in accordance with their inclinations and wishes, to express themselves via interesting work, to enjoy professional growth. In extended meaning it may lead to deformation of youth integration and young people's growing dependence on circumstances when *risk of social exclusion* is on the increase.

In this context *risk* is a special attribute of one's activity i.e. risk-taking, and particular conditions of society, group or a personal position as well. Thus, on the one hand, risk is a characteristic of social conditions in which young people are to undertake integration into society. On the other hand, risk is a part of the integration process and an essential youth activity.

Social exclusion versus integration in risk society

There are two ways for social integration to be achieved. Firstly, by conformism, which refers to the acceptance of the values and norms of community or society *and* the measures needed to achieve this goal. And secondly, via innovation, namely innovative activity on the part of the younger generation grounded on common agreement on social goals but search for new ways for these goals to be reached. Both these routes might lead to the sustainable development of young generation and society. However, not all forms of conformism in a certain context may have favourable consequences.

Every society faces major issues here. *What structures* should the young generation integrate into? *Whom* and *what* does youth identify with in a society? *What directions* of youth integration are to be encouraged by society and which of them should be slowed down by social policy? *What balance* between conformism and innovation is appropriate under particular social conditions? And, finally *which criteria* should be used here?

In Russia that is surviving a systemic crisis for the last fifteen years and where the most painful outcome of this crisis is criminalisation of society these questions are of particular importance. For example, conformism is classically seen as being the basis for stabilisation of crisis-ridden society in structural functionalism, but in reality conforming orientations of youth towards a criminal environment is not healthy for both younger generation and society in the long-term. Innovations are more desirable in this context.

However, if honest productive labour, high professional ethics and achievements in education less and less assist social mobility of young people, as it is in Russia, different sorts of illegal activity promise better promotion; and it is also very difficult to block deviation. Accepting the goal of personal enrichment proclaimed by society and having no institutionalised ways to achieve this goal via civilised business (due to ineffective economic, investment and tax policies and bureaucracy corruption) it is not surprising that young entrepreneurs are looking to avoid all these obstacles and choose any kinds of swindle and fraud (not paying taxes, racketeering, etc.).

Ironically, from the sociological point of view, this is nothing else but innovation: young people share social goals but just propose other methods and means for them to be reached, especially if those supposed by society do not really bring about desirable results. One can witness such *negative* innovation as well as time-serving conformism do not contribute to the solidarity of society as a whole and its development. Nevertheless, the socio-economic climate in Russian society itself pushes the younger generation in the direction of illegal forms of employment that is paradoxly a more attractive prospect in terms of better living standards. One can say this is a basis not for youth integration, but rather for differentiation.

Generally speaking situation of social differentiation is corresponding to *bifurcation* in which general emphasize is made in the first turn on the problem of choice itself. There is a whole range of crucial turning points which society or a group are to step over. These points are the borders between the phases of society's or group's development. Moreover, due to the big number of alternatives in the situation of bifurcation, the trajectory of development may change direction radically. Speaking figuratively, in this situation the social system is like a knight standing at the crossroads choosing it's way. From time to time every society, not to speak of individuals, stands in front of the necessity of making different kinds of choice. Purposive individual action is supposed to be the main factor of choice and generally of the further character of social integration and development.

Obviously a decisive role in working out and determining strategies of social integration belongs to society. Society creates the most acceptable models of socialization and places certain demands on youth that are usually determined by historical, social and other kinds of traditions and norms, as well as by the nature of the society in which they live. Using mechanisms of social policy society stimulates or brings to a stop different social processes among youth.

At the same time, being to a notable extent guided by social factors such choices and actions are naturally based on individual orientations of young people themselves. One can hardly hope that a young person perceive him/herself as such a social actor who is thinking not by individual but societal priorities. It is natural that the young generation is inclined to accept these particular structures and relations that open successful social promotion and reject the opposed ones. Thus, making particular choice in education, career, etc. young people rather choose these professional areas that give them wider opportunities for social mobility, better living standards, career promotion and self-expression.

Principally, awareness of the very fact of risk situations by young individuals is the first step in direction to it's overcoming choosing one of the alternatives, i.e. by risk-taking. Meanwhile, this is possible if the area of opportunities is known. Information on opportunities increases reliability of risk-estimations and calculation of corresponding gain and loss. This refers to *motivated* risk.

However one specific of uncertainty is that neither the rules of the game, nor direct and indirect results are predictable. Situation of uncertainty when probability, i.e. degree to what different events may come into being produces *non-motivated* risks. Thus, risk is transformed into the fabric of social environment, concerns entire societies and groups, is less and less calculated and determines spontaneous individual choices. Unpredictable behaviour neither assists in overcoming uncertainty nor in decreasing individual risks. This is a reproduction mechanism of uncertainty and risk.

Another problem is that youth orientations cannot always go alongside the commonly accepted means and this is becoming by the way the vitally important prologue for social innovations. In this sense a positive effect of differentiation gives rise to new structures and new relations, and leads to social creativity and progress. In the case of youth, differentiation manifests itself in newly formed subcultures, associations, unions and movements.

The nature of youth actions together with society's reaction to them determine their further destiny. Coming into existence as a single phenomenon youth innovations in the sphere of work is eventually being accepted and institutionalised by society and becoming a part of its everyday practise.

However, on this way young people again face obstacles and difficulties built up by a crisis-ridden social structure. Structurally disintegrated society is not ready to react adequately to youth entering social relations. Crisis of the number of industrial branches and unemployment, commercialization of education and decreasing living standards, regional differences and defects in labour market and material and legal constraints of moving across the country—all of that is leading to inequality among youth, goal displacement and fragmentation. Hence society resists youth innovations either because of it's conservatism and situation of crisis or because of the negative nature of these innovations.

When destructive trends prevail, differentiation is accompanied instead of the higher level of integration by the exactly opposite process of *social exclusion*, and this leads to disintegration in society. What are the empirical evidences for social exclusion of youth? There are different types of *discrimination* against young people which are predominantly based on their age, the *alienation* from education, labour, participation and *marginalization* of young people as breaking identification with the formal society. All these process have specific expression and lead to exclusion on the practical level determining *tearing* some sections of young people away: a) from *means of life-support systems*, i.e. labour market, certain types of work, living conditions of a civilized being; and b) from *political and social rights* via breaking with socialization agencies, social protection system, opportunities for representing of one's political interests.

As a chain of social events the process of exclusion of young people has produced social groups with particular status as a result of their natural development. (Table 1).

Table 1. Social exclusion forms.

Social exclusion as process	Way of expressing	Social exclusion as Status
Social discrimination	Downward occupation and social mobility, based on violations of youth rights in labour, education, etc. and absence of meritocratic (based on ability) factors of promotion	Low status, unprivileged, deprived groups
Social alienation	Deformation of the role in social reproduction, when young generation is gradually losing it's intellectual, professional and social potential	Outcast and untypical social groups (homeless, vagrants, disabled)
Marginalisation	Break of social ties and identity deformation	Youth subcultures, counterculture (risky groups)

Existing general backgrounds for reproduction of risk on the societal level involve the following: unemployment, under-employment and semi-employment in the sphere of work; inequality in access to different levels of education by different categories of young people based on the poor living standards of Russian families; low possibilities for successful competition in business value crisis, anomie and wild forms of aggressive individualization as opposed to the sense of solidarity and responsibility to others in youth consciousness. These factors cause the exclusion of many young people from the process of civilized social relations.

Russian risk society: particular features

According to these trends some western concepts of risk can be applied to the Russian case. However, very notable particular circumstances have come into being and distinguish Russian risk society from European risk society's finished process of modernisation. In transitional societies such as Russia the situation is characterised on the one hand by negation of the old socio-economic relations and non-effective mechanisms of social reproduction. On the other hand, there is a new system with no new established mechanisms. In the interim increasing social, economic and political contradictions bring uncertainty and risk into existence. Obviously a risk society drifts towards uncertainty. However it is true of opposed direction as well when attempt to make situation clear are not necessary successful. Thus, risk is essential for any kind of motion and this embraces the whole society.

Meanwhile the degree of risk is dependent on the scale and acuteness of tension and contradictions taking place in the society. In societies surviving evolution without shock well functioning integration mechanisms maintain relatively sustainable levels of social solidarity. This allows to keep risks in latent forms. On the contrary, long-term, protracted instability, intensification of social conflicts and unclear values and goals of societal transformation provoke escalation of risk. The whole society turns into risk society in which exit from one risky situation does not lead to it's elimination but to emergence of new ones.

What kind of particular trends have produced risks and allowed to define Russia as risk society?

The character of transformation in Russia includes complex uncertainties. Uncertainty of goals for societal and social development and spontaneous and chaotic reforms without clear program of social, economic and political measures as a consequence remain in Russia. Principles of social-economic functioning are predominantly built up not on gradual development production, but on degradation, ruin and plundering of what was accumulated by previous generations. The whole system is becoming "oriented on safeguarding, but not on progress; sources for production degrade; social institutions are becoming archaic" (Yanitskiy, 2000), seamy and criminal structures are being institutionalized. Alienated from society the state is turning into a permanent source for crisis and the evolution of Russian society is accompanied by "growing emission of risk energy" (Yanitskiy, 2000) that is the energy of disintegration. The latter is the "direct result of the collapse of the social order". Political battles, social and legal vulnerability, anomie and erosion of identities have led to the upset of social cohesion.

Thus, there are at least three distinctive features of Russian risk society. *Firstly*, reproduction of crisis, but not production of wealth is the basis of risk in Russia. Hence, fatal and unavoidable hyper risks reinforce each other. *Secondly*, produced risks are not the result of modernisation but of opposed processes of de-modernisation going alongside destructive economic trends. *Thirdly*, social aspects of risks aggregate consequences of all other risks. Thus, Russia as well as other modern societies survive conditions of uncertainty, but due to these numerous factors Russian risk society has gained it's specific character.

Broad societal consequences of uncertainty and risk for young peoples' self-realisation in the sphere of work can be observed in the changes which affect youth's social position, its social mobility and social differentiation in Russian unstable and risk society.

Youth integration and exclusion trends in the sphere of work

Although one's integration is not limited by just professional achievements there is a strong connection between these different aspects (Nagel and Wallace, 1997; Coles, 1995). Delayed professional integration as well as accelerated entry to the labour market may be determined by differences in social backgrounds of young individuals, in the status of their families or challenged by personal bad luck. Such deformation in youth integration in it's turn leads to unavoidable youth dependency and eventually to the conflicts with social institutions, intergenerational tensions, postponed marriage and household and frustration.

Since the beginning of social-economic reforms the first signs of it's destructive direction expressed themselves. Comparative analysis of sociological data* proves that this trend particularly exists in the sphere of material production. Youth employment in this sphere was constantly decreasing from 80% in 1990 to 42% by the end of the decade. In 1999–2000 more than half young Russians instead of 38% in 1996–7 are forced to work outside of their professional area and two thirds do not have opportunities for professional growth. Just one in ten young persons gives high estimation to his/her occupational status, skill, salary and satisfaction with work. The crucial

---

* An analysis is based on the on-going project concerning "Youth Integration and Social Exclusion". This project covers 12 regions of the Russian Federation and includes a sample of young people aged 15 to 29 years. Comparable methods were used between 1990–99. The sample sizes of the research using in the paper were as follows: 1994 (N = 2,612), 1997 (N = 2,500), 1999 (N = 2,004).

fall of all these indicators happened by 1997 and then some positive trends were discovered. Finally more than 80% could not reach economic autonomy until they are thirty years old. (Table 2)

Table 2. Youth estimations of opportunities for increasing qualification and living standards in material production. (Means in accordance with seven rank scale)

Opportunities to increase	1990	1994	1997	1999
qualification	4,46	3,43	2,35	4,54
salary	3,29	2,70	1,81	3,66

Motivation of work is an important factor of youth integration into the labour market. Meanwhile the notable damage was done to motivation of work among young Russians. It is necessary to stress that this trend began much earlier than reforms started in the so called period of socio-economic stagnation (1970–80s) when social origins provided better career promotion. This trend was continuing during the period of "*perestroyka*" that also failed to encourage the young generation for diligent work. The trend reached it's apogee under conditions of market reforms with the new ideology of militant individualism and devaluation of honest work.

Instrumental orientations towards work when it is just the means of achieving other goals is one of the main trends among the majority of Russian youth. After the period of socialism with work as one of the basic proclaimed values such an orientation looked like a dramatic change. Generally such instrumentalisation is more relevant for conditions of market competition. However it is accompanied by erosion of legal foundation of most spheres of social life including labour relations. In the situation of unsatisfied basic needs and normative uncertainty youth consciousness does not resist any illegal means to reach desirable living standards. Hence, prerequisites for exclusion of some young people from the institutionalized economic relations developed.

Data clearly show that social sustainability and uncertainty affect value orientations towards work among youth. As can be seen from Table 3, terminal value of work dominates among those young people living to their estimation under sustainable conditions and instrumental ones are faster spreading among young people whose situation seems to them to be uncertain and risky.

Table 3. Comparison of youth value orientations in the sphere of work in accordance with different conditions. (In %)

Life conditions	Terminal	Instrumental
Sustainable	51,2	48,8
Uncertain	44,3	55,7

Revolutionary changes in the social and economic spheres clearly expressed itself in contradictory youth attitudes to such undoubtedly basic notions of the market relations as skill and qualification, honest work and responsibility for its result. They lost their meaning rapidly as soon as youth's well being stopped to be dependent on their work, education and qualifications and more on types of property—state or private. The majority of youth entering the labour market in Russia fail for lack of necessary qualification. And despite some positive reverses concerning skill, qualification (moved from the 6th rank to the 1st in 1999) and diligence and industry (moved from the 9th position to the 5th) conscientiousness and honesty have fallen from the 5th position to 8th. Money left 9th position and occupied the 3rd. However, despite their importance for social and economic development of youth these social needs such as skill, professionalism and sensible wages remain unsatisfied by the collapsed economic system.

Some of these changes naturally correspond to a complex of values, particularly in money importance and the later changes in professionalism as a value. Comparison with European youth shows similar trends towards industrial materialistic values which are spread predominantly in those countries in the south of the continent with relatively slow economic growth. On the contrary in economically advanced countries of the Center and North Europe values of higher material standards give way to post-industrial and post-materialistic values of self-development and quality of life among young people (Helve, H. 1996; Lagree, J. Ch., 1996) that refer to the *sustainable development* paradigm.

Indifference of the society to youth's needs leads to the reproduction of irrational consciousness among youth. Some groups do not demonstrate desire to work even being poor: prefer not to work at all than to earn. Some groups do not want to study even entering education and paying for it: it is better to spend time nicely or to buy a diploma than to waste time in the institute. Some groups prefer not to refuse any pleasures, leading a hedonistic life: it is better to squander money than lose it pretty soon investing in uncertain and unpredictable Russian businesses. Such expressions are discovered either in the labour goals or in the ways they are to be achieved and have nothing in common with integration into the civilized market economy.

Youth exclusion from the sphere of work is evident as every fourth young person is not oriented towards work at all. If in 1990 only 21,5% of young Russians would keep working even if they were better off, ten years later this group lost a half of it's members. Today 14,3% would never work if they had everything for a comfortable life and 9,4% had not defined their position. Since vocational education and well-qualified jobs no longer guarantee a good living standard young people have in fact excluded work ethic from the list of supported values. This type of orientations is equally spreading in different groups of young Russians in reference with age, gender, living standards and place of settlement. This points to the existence of a particular socio-cultural group of youth that does not see work as a factor of their integration into society. This group is growing in size and will so due to the number of those young people hesitating in their positive view of work. These trends together with popularization of non-labour ways of enrichment in Russian society support the process of exclusion of youth from productive labour. Thus, the causes of exclusion have economic aspects and also ethical ones.

Youth integration and exclusion is different in the state and in the non-state sector of the economy. During the whole period of reforms the main trend was that of growing proportion of youth employed in non-state enterprises and a gradual outflow of labour force from the state factories and enterprises. Defect in development of the state economy was determined by a number of causes among which unemployment and underemployment as a consequence of investment lack, staff reduction and scanty earnings.

Youth salary in this sphere stays on the poverty line during the whole period of reforms. A better situation differentiates those employed in transport, sales and building. The proportion of low-paid young people continues increasing. Since the year 1997 it has risen by 1,3 times and reached 44,4%. The lowest incomes remain among workers of agriculture and light industry. At the same time, the number of better paid young people has also become bigger by 1,7 times and constituted 7,2% at the end of 90s. Most of the better paid work is in non-state sector where incomes are slightly higher. However, financial crisis and permanent inflation have devoured their incomes and once again reduced living standards to the level of basic needs.

The leading factor of youth exclusion from the sphere of work is unemployment. Although the proportion of young people registered as unemployed is changing it still stands somewhere in-between 38,1% in 1992 and 32% in 1998. About 15% are not temporary working or studying. Taking into consideration uncertain opportunities to fined new job, realised by 16,7% of young respondents, most of them would keep any work. In Russian society youth unemployment goes along with stagnation and degradation of the economy. Unlike the West where social exclusion is a sword of Damocles for the non-qualified manual workers in Russian society it has become a problem for highly educated young people.

In the competition between the state and non-state sectors the latter definitely wins. However, youth integration into the private sector is more uncertain and risky and often turns into exclusion of youth. Among youth involved in non-state economy only 2,3% are employers having property in the means of labour, 8,2% are self-employed and the rest of them work for a wage.

Young people confess opportunities for their sustainable integration into sphere of business and self-realisation leave much to be desired. During the course of reform, youth was the least protected part of the labour force and has suffered from all forms of social discrimination especially in questions of salary and career. Youth's aspirations for freedom in the sphere of work have not been converted into practice. Young people are highly dependent on employers and shareholders, whose activity is not restrained by an undeveloped social protection system. Unlawful dismissals, penalty sanctions, arbitrary regulation of working time by employers, exploitation for the test period without any guarantee of a permanent job and adequate remuneration are being practised on a large scale.

Whether or not young people are successful in their jobs largely depends upon their relations with their boss and colleagues. As a result, in our surveys, amicable colleagues and friendly bosses were ranked in second and third place of importance after salary. This situation strongly influences the occupational mobility of youth, which is determined by subjective factors and not based on ability, is mainly horizontal and causes later exclusion. In general, youth suffers from downward occupation and social mobility. In the private enterprises predominantly oriented towards quick profits by any means for the boss youth destiny does not go further than a second or third role without real chance to display initiative and knowledge. As a result 43,8% of youth showed low opportunities to make career; 36,3% are unable to protect their rights; 70,8% abandoned the idea of setting up their own business. (Table 4)

Table 4. Youth estimation of self-realization opportunities in dependence with particular life conditions. (Means in accordance with seven-rank scale)

Life conditions	Estimations					
	To find job	To improve qualification	To increase salary	To make career	To protect rights	To protect business
Sustainability and certainty	4,15	4,63	3,97	3,57	4,09	2,45
Uncertainty and risk	4,05	4,49	3,74	3,78	4,07	2,77

The table shows that under sustainable conditions young people see prospects of successful search for a job, gaining qualification and even earnings as more favorable. However they have better chances for promotion and free enterprise. Ambivalence of risk is becoming obvious in this context. Naturally desire for innovation and recognition presupposes risk as an immanent element of activity. Namely risk-taking opens social potential of this socio-demographic group. The problem is that those young people who see the positive effect of risk are likely to try their innovations outside institutional channels. It is to a big extent caused by the system crisis and break in integration mechanisms when youth social energy is not being used by a degraded economic structure.

Thus, despite some positive trends in youth work its general situation remains difficult. Due to this two thirds of young people in Russian risk society feel uncertainty and vulnerability in the sphere of work. Risk of professional failure is a leading factor of the sense of alarm (21,1%), despair (3,4%) or indifference (13,8). Every fifth young respondent is afraid to lose his job and a half of youth is frightened of not surviving poverty.

Escalation of these and other risks and uncertainty in youth integration are inherent elements of particular Russian risk society. It is resulting in low socio-economic status of youth, different forms of protest and confrontation, alienation from the society and escapism.

All of that indicates exclusion of the new generation from the process of economic modernisation and deterioration of the natural role in both types of social reproduction: simple reproduction and especially extended reproduction.

BIBLIOGRAPHY

Beck, U. *Risk Society: Towards a New Modernity*. Sage, London, 1992.
Evans, K. and Furlong A. "Metaphors of youth transitions: niches, pathways, trajectories or navigations" // J. Bynner, L. Chisholm and A. Furlong (eds.), *Youth, Citizenship and Social Change in a European Context*. Ashgate, Aldershot and Brookfield, USA, 1997, p. 36.
Furlong, A. and Cartmel, F. *Young People and Social Change. Individualization and Risk in Late Modernity*, Open University Press, 1997.
Furlong, A., B. Stadler and A. Azzopardi *Vulnerable Youth. European Youth Trends 2000*, Council of Europe Publishing, 2000.
Giddens, A. *The Consequences of Modernity*. Polity Press, Cambridge, 1991.
Helve, H. *Values, World Views and Gender Differences among Young People* //.
H. Helve and J. Bynner (eds.) *Youth and Life Management. Research Perspectives*. Helsinki University Press, Helsinki, 1996, pp. 171–188.
——— (eds.) *Youth and Life Management. Research Perspectives*, ?. 165–169.
Lagree, J. Ch. *Youth in Europe* //.
Machacek, L. 1998, *Youth in the Processes of Transition and Modernisation in Slovakia*. Bratislava: SAS.
Machacek, L. and K. Roberts (eds.) *Youth Unemployment and Self-employment in East-Central Europe*, Bratislava: SAS, 1997.
Nagel, U. and Wallace, C. *Participation and Identification in Risk Societies: European Perspectives*. ?. 45.
———. *Participation and Identification in Risk Societies: European Perspectives*, p. 48; Coles, B. *Youth and Social Policy*. University College London Press, London, 1995.
Roberts, K. *Youth and Employment in Modern Britain*. Oxford University Press, 1995, p. 117.
Wallace C. and S. Kovatcheva, *Youth in Society: The Construction and Deconstruction of Youth in East and West Europe*, Macmillan, London 1998.
Yanitskiy O. N. "Russia as Risk Society." In *Sociology and Society. The I National Sociological Congress "Society and Sociology: the New Reality and New Ideas"*, Saint-Petersburg, Skiphiya, 2000, p. 4 (in Russian).

YOUTH HOMELESSNESS: THE STREET AND WORK—FROM EXCLUSION TO INTEGRATION

Roch Hurtubise, Shirley Roy and Céline Bellot

Introduction

In Quebec as elsewhere, urban homelessness is not a new issue. What is new is the place this issue now occupies in the public debate, in view of the emerging social transformations and the questions being asked about the future of our societies. Are the new forms of poverty, marginality, and homelessness the result of increasingly selective and fragmented societies which render individual integration and adaptation to a changing world difficult or impossible? Can youth homelessness provide us with an illustration of exclusion and non-work?

In this text, we will argue that youth homelessness can be accounted for by a complex framework of explanations that links structural and individual determining factors. We propose two interpretations of youth homelessness in the North American context. The first considers the phenomenon as a specific form of homelessness resulting from social transformations in post-industrial societies. The second presents youth homelessness as a particular mode of the youth experience and a response to the ongoing social transformations. Moreover, we will assert that the work environment and youth homelessness cannot be seen as mutually exclusive, closed spheres. Rather, the life of homeless youth involves the implementation of diverse practices and types of expertise which are generally underestimated or qualified as exclusion strategies. We will illustrate three forms of relationship between work and youth homelessness: the street as a space of exclusion and non-work, integration into a world of marginal and parallel work, and the transfer of abilities acquired on the street to regular work activities.

Before describing these forms, their analytical perspectives, and the specific realities that characterize them, let us examine the findings of studies on urban homelessness in North American societies and specifically in Quebec.

1. *Homelessness:*[1] *A complex phenomenon*

In recent years, the homelessness phenomenon has been marked by a quantitative increase, an accelerated diversification in the characteristics of homeless people, and a worsening of the associated problems (Laberge, 2000). The last census (in 1998) recorded 28,214 homeless people in Montreal, of whom 12,666 had no fixed address (NFA) for the preceding year (Fournier et al., 1998). In Toronto, users of shelter facilities were estimated at 26,000 different individuals in 1996 (Mayor's Homelessness Action Task Force, 1999). Diversification in the characteristics of those affected by homelessness appears mainly in the age and sex of the population; the proportion of women has increased considerably (Laberge, Morin, and Roy, 2000). With regard to the age structure, certain studies show that nearly one-third of the homeless population are between the ages of 18 and 30, which constitutes an increase in this group over the last ten years (Fournier et al., 1998). Studies conducted on street youth (Roy, 1998) demonstrate the difficulties and risks faced by this group; this is particularly apparent in their death rate, which is fourteen times higher than the rate for youth of the same age (Roy et al., 1996).

The worsening of the problems associated with homelessness constitutes the third facet of the transformation this phenomenon has undergone. The known problems associated with homelessness (severe deterioration in physical and mental health, alcoholism, drug addiction, and referral to the courts) are now being joined by new ones, such as HIV/AIDS, hepatitis, multiple drug addictions, tuberculosis, intellectual deficiency, violence, and suicide (Fournier, 2001; Calloway and Morrisey, 1998; Hassin, 1998; Greer, 1990–1991). These new problems simply lengthen the list of difficulties homeless people may face. By virtue of their intrinsic severity and the multiple combinations in which they occur, these difficulties alter the life dynamic, capacity for social interaction, and resourcefulness of the homeless.

---

[1] In 1992, the Quebec government's Politique de la santé et du bien-être (Health and Welfare Policy) listed homelessness as one of the most important social problems in Quebec. Referring back to the definition used by the City of Montreal's committee on homelessness, homeless people are defined by the following characteristics: lack of a fixed address or of stable, secure, salubrious housing for the next 60 days; low income; discrimination in access to services; mental or physical health problems or problems of alcoholism, drug addiction, or social disorganization; and lack of a stable membership group.

Homelessness is thus neither an inevitable historical outcome nor a "normal" form of marginality. It cannot be analyzed using a simple, linear, and progressive model but rather as the resultant of a combination of social and individual factors (Laberge and Roy, 2002). Explaining homelessness is complex. It has not one cause, but many causes; not one form, but multiple forms; not one trajectory, but a diversity of trajectories.

2. *Different Theoretical Constructs*

The homelessness phenomenon in the street youth population can be understood and theoretically modelled in a number of ways. We have grouped these explanations under two distinct trends which, while they do not account for the diversity of the theses put forward, suggest two different points of view. One way of explaining youth homelessness is to situate it as a specific case of homelessness. The other way is to suggest that youth homelessness is a particular form of the youth experience, one that constitutes a response to social transformations.

2.1 *Homeless youth: as a specific case of homelessness*

Homelessness is a growing social phenomenon in many societies which seems to have developed considerably in the youth population over the last ten years. Different studies emphasize the role of structural and individual factors in the genesis of this phenomenon (Castel, 1995; Roy, 1995). At issue are multiple factors that interact and combine in personal trajectories. Arising out of current social transformations, youth homelessness would presumably constitute a specific form of homelessness.

Among the structural explanations, there are some on which there is consensus: disinvestment by the State, transformations in the form of work, increasing poverty, the affordable housing crisis[2] (Campeau, 2000; Fournier and Mercier, 1996; Koegel et al., 1996). The backdrop is the impoverishment process which has been intensifying for

---

[2] Very prosaically, this means that a single person receiving the regular benefit from the income security program today (i.e., $510/month) should be able to find housing for $153/month or less. To look at the situation from a different angle, a single person receiving income security benefits who spends $280/month to rent a single room is spending more than 50% of his or her budget on housing.

the last twenty years, due to changes in public policy and in the job market. This poverty, which affects an increasing number of young people, would be directly responsible for their vulnerability and their insecurity regarding the different components of life.

As a direct result of the budget cuts in the United States and Canada, the social policies adopted have either eliminated or decreased the allowances for people under 30 years of age, thus inflating the number of poor people.[3] The modifications made to income security benefit programs show how the fight against youth poverty has become a fight against poor young people, notably by way of a tightening of control measures that introduces a distinction between worthy and unworthy poor (Mayor's Homelessness Action Task Force, 1999; Katz, 1989).

At the institutional level, homelessness can be explained by increasing court prosecution and criminalization of certain social acts (Laberge and Landreville, 2000), deinstitutionalization of psychiatric patients, and changes in the family structure. In North American societies, there are more and more taboos regulating social behaviours in public spaces; control measures are increasing and forms of repression are proliferating.[4] Some of the young people caught in these situations are taken into custody by the penal authorities, which is often the first step in the process leading to the street. As for psychiatric deinstitutionalization as an explanation for homelessness, consensus has yet to be reached regarding its causal role. The main point to remember is that some of those who were formerly taken in charge by institutions because of serious mental health problems are no longer institutionalized. Due to a lack of adequate measures and programs,[5] these people do not have at their disposal the care or the support they need to function. As a last factor, let us mention the profound change in family structures, whose consequence has been to weaken or break down mutual aid and solidarity movements. In

---

[3] Numerous authors have examined this issue, among others Fontan (1997), Leduc Browne (1997), Ulysse and Lesemann (1997), Villeneuve (1996), and Katz (1989).

[4] For example, there are prohibitions against fighting, loitering in parks, sleeping there, or taking drugs there; drunk driving is repressed, soliciting for purposes of prostitution is criminalized, drug use is forbidden, squeegeeing is not tolerated, and bicycle helmets are compulsory.

[5] Studies on the issue of homelessness and mental health state that close to 30% of homeless people have major mental health problems.

difficult situations, some people may find themselves isolated, without support, and, eventually, on the street.

With regard to the individual explanations, we can cite accumulated relational problems (Laberge, Poirier and Charest, 1998) and social and affective learning deficiencies resulting from dysfunction (Poirier et al., 1999; Poirier, 1996; Stefanidis et al., 1992; Dennis et al., 1991; D'Ercole and Struening, 1990; Lamontagne et al., 1987; Susser et al., 1987). Loss of or abandonment by a parent, situations of sexual violence or abuse, and repeated placement in foster families or homes have been the lot of many young homeless people. Often, their stories have been played out against the background of uprooted or split families, without acceptance from the environment, or in the framework of numerous migrations: from neighbourhood to neighbourhood, city to city, or country to country. They express gaps in "compensatory support." No one covers for the inadequacies of the family: not grandparents, uncles and aunts, social workers, or neighbours. In such situations, young people are thus detached from a meaningful social network (Lussier and Poirier, 2000).

Youth homelessness is specifically and markedly characterized by certain problems. This is the group most affected by social policies of the "workfare" type, by cuts to certain assistance programs, and by the absence of housing measures. Furthermore, they are particularly vulnerable to problems related to drug use, such as HIV/AIDS and Hepatitis. Finally, those young people who have been subjected to family transformations and different types of institutional management have suffered serious consequences in terms of their construction of self and identity.

2.2 *Analyzing youth homelessness to understand youth*

Certain studies, inspired by sociological analyses of youth and marginal subcultures, propose a comprehensive analysis of youth homelessness to shed light on certain youth-specific issues. The street offers unique opportunities to observe alternative forms of identity construction, participation, and social integration. Difficulties accompanying the passage to adulthood, both within the family and in the work world, can be expected to play out in particular ways on the street. Life on the street does not appear solely as a negative consequence of social transformations, but also as a transition space in which young people move away from family constraints, school, and work to explore a marginal world. Far from being a symptom of lost youth, it would constitute a particular adaptation to a social context in which the possibilities for integration are experienced as restrictive or incomplete.

These studies distance themselves from readings of the street in terms of risks, problems, crime, or pathologies. The challenge is to convey forms of life in society that are more than merely homelessness in anomic spaces characterized by deficiencies, lack of resources, and isolation. On the street, young people experiment with new activities and new relationships and integrate themselves into a diversified cultural universe marked by specific styles and practices.

In an ethnographic perspective, the objective is to describe the world of street youth by identifying its referents (cultural, political, economic, and psychological) as a social world with its own particular rules of operation. For example, the subcultures of marginal existence allow us to understand the principles of meaning and action around which this experience is organized. Linked to musical styles, political movements, or original cultural amalgams, these subcultures can be privileged means of asserting a difference that is sometimes expressed in body markings (tattoos, piercing, make-up). The street represents a form of no-man's-land where homelessness can become a way of life (Côté, 1988). In this context, the life cycles and transitions of youth are formulated as initiation rites fostering the passage to another stage of existence (Sheriff, 1999).

For street youth, the collective appropriation of certain places (parks, subway stations, the corridors of the underground city) constitutes a way of drawing borders between an alternative social space that is theirs and an institutional social space which belongs to others. Issues of identity, which link the social and individual dimensions of the phenomenon, are the focus of a number of studies. Original processes of identity construction (transitional space) among youth who have broken with traditional forms of socialization would presumably be observable (Parazelli, 2002). This quest for identity is structured around several paradoxes: the pursuit of freedom vs. the risk of being confined to a marginal existence, the desire for autonomy vs. dependence on drugs and alcohol, etc. (Bellot, 2001).

The collective dimensions of the street youth experience are addressed in several ways. The young people are also portrayed as the agents of their own existence, notably through description of the strategies, skills, forms of solidarity, and abilities deployed to live and survive on the street. Be it via the image of the tribe, group, or network, the figure of the street youth is presented first and foremost in connection with a social network formed of peers and others. While the usual interpretation is in terms of youth gangs with links to the criminal world, interest needs to be taken in the supple, flexible mode of operation by networking, which performs functions of protection, socialization, and social participation in the same way an institution would (Hurtubise et Vatz-Laaroussi, 2000).

3. Urban youth homelessness and the world of work

The experience of youth living an urban vagrant existence can be interpreted in several ways, depending which of the trends presented earlier is adopted. This experience can be seen in terms of individual or collective actions, skills or deficiencies; as being produced or endured; as falling within the specific space of marginality or a more global social space. The examples that we have constructed, based on our knowledge of the diversity of young people's experience, illustrate three ways in which the street and work universes interact.

3.1 The street as a space of exclusion and non-work

The most widespread image of life on the street depicts homelessness as the outcome of an exclusion process. This invokes a set of accumulated structural, institutional, and individual deficits and difficulties which in some sense paralyze the individual. Changes in the organization of work, training deficiencies, weak personal abilities, deficiencies (intellectual and physical), and mental health or addiction problems are so many obstacles to stable integration into the work world. Activities of everyday living are reduced to survival practices. In this case, exclusion from work or non-integration into the work setting is bound to be observed and simply adds to the difficulties encountered. Considering integration into the workplace means solving a certain number of personal problems, envisaging programs and measures that will continue over a long period, and devising suitable forms of training and work organization that take into account the difficulties and potential of these individuals.

We know, for instance, that the longer the time spent on the street or out of the workplace, the more problematic integration or reintegration becomes. We know that certain groups grappling with serious mental health problems will need an adapted workplace; we know that young people without adequate education have little chance of being integrated into motivating, remunerated, stable work.

Here, the worlds of homelessness and the workplace are on parallel tracks or, worse still, in opposition. In a way, the difficulties encountered, singly and in combination, result in the individual's taking a path where the obstacles become insurmountable and reintegration is severely jeopardized. The social measures addressed to these young people take two different forms. On the one hand, there are those formulated with the goal of assisting individuals so that they can meet certain fundamental needs. On the other hand, certain actions seek to adapt the work world to the reality of these individuals, by considerably modifying profitability and efficiency objectives. In the first situation, the young person is still out of work; in the second, he or she is in a form of supervised work that can allow certain young people to redeploy the necessary abilities for eventual integration into the workplace.

3.2 *Integration into a marginal and parallel work world*

A second illustration of the relationship between the work world and the street is the one that evokes practices linked to a marginal, underground, or even delinquent economy. Often associated with street youth or street gangs, it allows us to observe diverse situations and activities that can be related to forms of work, even if the relationship is not obvious: prostitution, drug dealing, theft and possession of stolen goods, squeegeeing, panhandling, black market work, etc. Because these activities mobilize their potential, abilities, and resources, individuals acquire a degree of autonomy relative to state programs and aid resources. They thus become partially capable of supporting themselves.

The street is a physical and symbolic space where marginal, delinquent, and atypical activities presuppose more or less permanent forms of work organization. This means that there are cooperative networks, procedures for supervision and production control, means of surveillance, exchanges of necessary skills, training and recruitment mechanisms, etc.

The case of the squeegee[6] is an interesting illustration of the struc-

---

[6] "Squeegee" is the brand name of the tool used to clean car windshields. The

tures within the parallel economy that allow many young people to make a living. This activity involves locating the place where the young people will practise their trade, based on traffic patterns and public tolerance. The young people plan and discuss how they will occupy the space in a rational way, to avoid being concentrated in one place. Moreover, the activity requires certain abilities having to do with contacts with "customers." Certain ways of doing things have been changed following complaints from drivers who felt they were being attacked. The young people have developed a convivial approach centred on customer satisfaction, often built around courtesy and humour. For instance, they negotiate with storekeepers for supplies of water and soap, in exchange for limits on the time spent at their stores and acceptable behaviour towards other customers.

The abilities thus developed may enable and aid young people to move from the street to the workplace. Nevertheless, it is important not to underestimate the obstacle the criminalization of these activities represents. Because of a municipal by-law, squeegeeing is prohibited and punishable by fines that can lead to arrest and imprisonment. One consequence of this criminalization is to push youth back into marginal zones or more serious forms of criminal activities.

Public morality and security and measures, which tend to refer to the courts certain acts whose criminal nature is debatable, promote the passage from marginality into crime, resulting in the near-permanent exclusion of the young people thus affected from the regular work world. The forms of work organization observed here are linked to the difficult objective conditions that mark street life, both from a personal standpoint (violence, addiction, problems of criminal behaviour, etc.) and as regards the social reading assigned to it.

3.3 *From street to workplace: the transfer and acknowledgement of acquired skills*

Can the abilities and skills developed on the street be acknowledged in the work world? The third image we present is that of the young person who, in his or her work strategies, utilizes abilities and knowledge developed on the street. This model allows us to revisit the

---

meaning of the term has changed and it is now used to designate the activity of young people who offer their services to car drivers. We can read this activity as a form of protest against traditional work, an expression of entrepreneurship, a lucrative activity, or a marginal activity allowing survival on the street.

usual opposition between the street and work worlds to grasp continuities and processes of expertise transfer. The skills concerned are of several types. They include transactional skills such as conflict and tension management and the identification of issues and divergences that allow for the development of relationships between people and groups; operational skills linked to work planning, resource mobilization, and project development; artistic skills, through the creation and diffusion of cultural products (tags, music, interaction with the public); and, finally, experiential skills such as comprehension of others, listening and empathy, and problem resolution.

We will use three examples to illustrate these diverse skills and their transfer from one world to the other. The first case is that of the street worker, often recruited for his or her concrete experience of street life. These individuals thus have a legitimacy that allows them proximity to youth and the problems they experience. Their work is done essentially in the marginal world, but it is a professional type of work whose objectives are support, reintegration, and rehabilitation. What led to their hiring is their own story, the fact that they constitute a living memory of this reality, their listening skills, their knowledge of the environment, and their contact with key players, both marginal and institutional. These assets are important features of this example of a way out of the street.

The second example concerns the training given by circus professionals to street youth to promote the development of their artistic abilities and stage performance skills. The young people may then be able to use these skills in lucrative activities, either by giving performances on the street or by joining a company of clowns and street performers. The activity put forward is coherent with the world of the street: nomads, gypsies, and wanderers have played a preponderant role in the history of the circus and the street arts occupations. The training, which requires regular attendance, physical fitness, group work, perseverance, and self-confidence, allows youth to develop and discover previously unexplored abilities. Some young people who have completed the training can now make a living and acquire an expertise that would otherwise have been inaccessible. To receive this type of training, one must have access to the great schools, which are both very selective and very expensive. While street youth do not have the aptitudes and the means to attend these schools, they may still possess genuine talent that could be fulfilled through the street.

The third example is that of youth with a talent for drawing who put this talent to work in the form of tags on the walls of the city. These young people see their skills recognized and utilized by employers in the new multimedia occupations, where originality and non-conventional forms are the trademark. In this case, the transfer of skills occurs in a more direct way since no updating of the skills is required.

In this last example, there is a certain continuity between street and work. The skills developed in a marginal experience can be used directly or serve as a lever for the acquisition of other skills. The examples put forward do not exhaust the diversity of what we observed. They open up new avenues to explore in pondering skill transfer and acknowledgement processes.

Conclusion

The objective of this text was to propose a different way of looking at youth homelessness and the relationship of homeless youth with work. All too often, we tend to see only one side of the issue, the confinement to the street and the impossibility of finding a way out. We can now look on the street as a positive experience, representing a form of protest, an alternative mode of life, and a parallel path to job training. That being said, it is important not to idealize the street, obscuring the experiences of these young people that could bar their access to any work world. Not all skills can be transferred; certain situations may prevent them from being put into practice or slow the process. The journey away from the street cannot be made at a steady pace. It involves a series of round trips, corresponding to failed attempts to have one's skills acknowledged and gain recognition of one's worth. In this context, the place of work in these young people's lives assumes its full importance.

REFERENCES

Bellot, Céline. "Le monde social de la rue: Expériences des jeunes et pratiques d'intervention à Montréal". Doctoral Thesis in Criminology. Université de Montréal, 2001.
Calloway, Michael O., and Joseph P. Morrissey. "Overcoming Service Barriers for Homeless Persons With Serious Psychiatric Disorders". *Psychiatric Services* 49, no. 12: 1568–72, 1998.
Campeau, Paule. "La place des facteurs structurels dans la production de l'itinérance".

In *L'Errance urbaine*, sous la dir. de Danielle Laberge, 49–69:439. Sainte-Foy: Éditions MultiMondes, 2000.
Castel, Robert. *Les métamorphoses de la question sociale. Une chronique du salariat.* Paris: Fayard, 1995.
Côté, M.-M. "Les jeunes de la rue à Montréal. Une étude d'éthonologie urbaine". Université de Montréal. Doctoral Thesis in anthropology, 1988.
D'ercole, A., and E. Struening. "Victimization Among Homeless Women: Implications for Service Delivery". *Journal of Community Psychology* 18: 141–52, 1990.
Dennis, Deborah L., John C. Buckner, Frank R. Lipton, and Irene S. Levine. "A Decade of Research and Services for Homeless Mentally Ill Persons". *American Psychologist* 46, no. 11: 1129–38, 1991.
Fontan, Jean-Marc. "La pauvreté en mutation". *Cahiers de recherche sociologique*, no. 29, 1997.
Fournier, Louise. *Enquête auprès de la clientèle des ressources pour personnes itinérantes des régions de Montréal-Centre et de Québec, 1998–1999*, Québec: Institut de la statistique du Québec, 2001.
Fournier, Louise, Serge Chevalier, Micheline Ostoj, Malijaï Caulet, Robert Courtemanche et Nathalie Plante. *Dénombrement de la clientèle itinérante dans les centres d'hébergement, les soupes populaires et les centres de jour des villes de Montréal et de Québec, 1996–97*, Santé Québec, Montréal, 1998.
Fournier, Louise et Céline Mercier, sous la dir. de *Sans Domicile Fixe: au-delà du stéréotype*, 341. Montréal: Éditions du Méridien, 1996.
Greer, Pedro J. Jr. "Medical Problems of the Homeless: Consequences of Lack of Social Policy—A Local Approach". *University of Miami Law Review* 45, nos. 2–3: 407–16, 1990–1991.
Hassin, Jacques. "État de santé et prise en charge des populations Sans Domicile Fixe à Paris". In *Précarité et santé*, sous la dir. de Jacques Lebas et Pierre Chauvin, 107–118. Paris: Flammarion, 1998.
Hurtubise, Roch et Michèle Vatz-Laaroussi. "Jeunes dans/de la rue et stratégies de réseaux". In *L'Errance urbaine*, sous la dir. de Danielle Laberge, 179–192. Sainte-Foy: Éditions MutliMondes, 2000.
Hurtubise, Roch. "Réseaux, stratégies et compétences: pour une analyse des dynamiques sociales à l'œuvre chez les jeunes de la rue". *Revue Homme et société* (spring, 2002).
Katz, Michael B. *The Undeserving Poor. From the War on Poverty to the War on Welfare.* New-York: Pantheon Books, 1989.
Koegel, Paul, Audrey M. Burman, and Baumohl Jim. "The Causes of Homelessness". In *Homelessness in America*, Ed. Jim Baumohl, 24–33. Phoenix: Oryx Press, 1996.
Laberge, Danielle et Shirley Roy. "Pour être, il faut être quelque part: la domiciliation comme condition d'accès à l'espace public". *Sociologie et sociétés* (spring 2002).
Laberge, Danielle. *L'Errance Urbaine*, sous la dir. de Sainte-Foy: Éditions MultiMondes, 2000.
Laberge, Danielle et Pierre Landreville. "De l'événement à l'infraction. du sans-abri au délinquant. réflexions sur le processus de catégorisation dans le champ pénal". In *L'Errance urbaine*, sous la dir. de Danielle Laberge, 121–136. Ste-Foy: Éditions MultiMondes, 2000.
Laberge, Danielle, Pierre Landreville et Daphné Morin. "The Criminalization of Mental Illness: A Complex Process of Interpretation". In *New Perspective on Deviance. The Construction of Deviance in Everyday Life.* Scarborough: Prentice Hall Allyn and Bacon Canada, 85–108, 2000.
Laberge, Danielle, Daphné Morin, et Shirley Roy. "L'itinérance des femmes: les effets convergents de transformations sociétales". In *L'Errance urbaine*, sous la dir. de Danielle Laberge, 83–99. Sainte-Foy: Éditions MultiMondes, 2000.

Laberge, Danielle, Mario Poirier et René Charest. "Un étranger dans la cité: la présence de l'itinérant et la représentation de l'itinérance". *Nouvelles Pratiques Sociales* 11, no. 1: 19–24, 1998.

Lamontagne, Yves, Yvette Garceau-Durand, Suzanne Blais et Robert Élie. *La jeunesse québécoise et le phénomène des sans-abri*. Montréal: Presses de l'Université du Québec, 1987.

Leduc Browne, Paul. "Les sources de la pauvreté, les moyens de la combattre". *Cahiers de recherche sociologique*, no. 29: 119–35, 1997.

Lussier, Véronique et Mario Poirier. "Parcours de rupture ou quête de reconnaissance et d'identité? L'impact des représentations parentales sur l'itinéraire de jeunes itinérants et itinérantes de Montréal". In *L'Errance urbaine*, sous la dir. de Danielle Laberge, 161–178. Sainte-Foy: Éditions MultiMondes, 2000.

Mayor's Homelessness Action Task Force. *Taking Responsibility for Homelessness. An Action Plan for Toronto*, Ville de Toronto, Toronto, 1999.

Parazelli, Michel, *La rue attractive. Parcours et pratiques identitaires des jeunes de la rue*. Sainte-Foy: Les Presses de l'Université du Québec, 2002.

Poirier, Mario, Véronique Lussier, Robert Letendre, P. Michaud, Monique Morval, Sophie Gilbert et A. Pelletier. *Relations et représentations interpersonnelles de jeunes adultes itinérants*, Rapport de recherche soumis au Conseil québécois de la recherche sociale (CQRS) par le Groupe de recherche sur l'itinérance des jeunes adultes, Montréal, 1999.

Poirier, Mario. "La relation d'aide avec les jeunes adultes itinérants". *Cahiers de recherche sociologique*, no. 27: 87–97, 1996.

Roy, Elise "Étude de cohorte sur l'infection au VIH chez les jeunes de la rue de Montréal". Montréal: Direction de la santé publique, Montréal-Centre, 1998.

Roy, Élise, Nancy Haley, Jean-François Boivin, Jean-Yves Frappier et Christiane Claessens. *Les jeunes de la rue de montréal et l'infection au VIH. Étude de prévalence, rapport final, version revisée.*, Unité de santé publique, RRSSSM-C, Montréal, 1996.

Roy, Shirley. "L'itinérance, forme exemplaire d'exclusion sociale?". *Lien social et politiques RIAC* 34: 73–80, 1995.

Shériff, T. *Le trip de la rue. parcours initiatique des jeunes de la rue*, Centre Jeunesse de Québec, Beauport, 1999.

Stefanidis, Nikolaos, Julia Pennbridge, Richard G. Mackenzie, and Karl Pottharst. "Runaway and Homeless Youth: The Effects of Attachment History on Stabilization". *American Journal of Orthopsychiatry* 62, no. 3: 442–446, 1992.

Susser, E., E. L. Struening, and J. Conover. "Childhood Experiences of Homeless Men". *American Journal of Psychiatry*, 144: 1599–1601, 1987.

Ulysse, Pierre-Joseph et Frédéric Lesemann. "Pauvreté, citoyenneté et marché aux États-Unis". *Cahiers de recherche sociologique*, no. 29: 137–52, 1997.

Villeneuve, Patrick. "La réforme de l'aide sociale de 1996: le pari de Bill Clinton". *Lien social et politiques-RIAC*, no 36: 55–59, 1996.

LABOR MARKET INSECURITY AND THE CRIMINALIZATION OF POVERTY

Loïc Wacquant

The criminalization to which militants from many social movements battling joblessness, homelessness and xenophobia across Europe are currently being subjected—as represented in extreme form by the wanton police assaults on anti-globalization demonstrators in Genoa during the G-8 meeting in the summer of 2001—cannot be understood outside of a broader pattern of *penalisation of poverty* designed to manage the effects of neo-liberal policies at the lower end of the social structure of advanced societies. The harsh police practices and prison measures adopted today throughout the continent are indeed part and parcel of a wider transformation of the state, a transformation which is itself called for by the mutation of wage labor and precipitated by the overturning of the inherited balance of power between the classes and groups fighting over control of both employment and the state. In this struggle, transnational business and the 'modernizing' fractions of the bourgeoisie and state nobility, allied under the banner of neoliberalism, have gained the upper hand and engaged a vast campaign aimed at reconstructing public authority. Social deregulation, the rise of precarious wage work (against a backdrop of continued mass unemployment in Europe and steadily rising 'working poverty' in the United States) and the return of an old-style punitive state go hand in hand: the 'invisible hand' of the casualized labor market finds its institutional complement and counterpart in the 'iron fist' of the state which is being redeployed so as *to check the disorders generated by the diffusion of social insecurity* (Wacquant 1999a).

The regulation of the working classes by what Pierre Bourdieu calls "the left hand" of the State, symbolised by education, public health care, social security and social housing (Bourdieu 1998) is being *superseded*—in the United States—or *supplemented*—in Western Europe—by regulation through its 'right hand', i.e., the police, courts and prison system, which are becoming increasingly active and intrusive in the lower regions of social space. The sudden and obsessive reaffirmation of the 'right to security' by leading politicians of both right and left, concurrent with the quiet dereliction of the 'right to employment' in its traditional form (that is, to full-time work, with a full entitlement package, for an indeterminate term and a livable wage), and the growing interest in and increased means devoted to law enforcement also come in handy to compensate the *deficit in legitimacy* suffered by political leaders, owing to the very fact that they have renounced the established missions of the state on the economic and social front.

Everywhere in Europe governments are thus trying to undermine the new legitimacy of militants and 'active minorities' within emerging social movements, acquired in and through daily struggles, so as to prevent further increases in collective mobilisation. More than mere repressive measures, the criminalisation of the advocates of social and economic rights partakes of a broader political agenda leading to the creation of a new regime that can be characterized as 'liberal-paternalist': it is *liberal* at the top, towards business and the privileged classes, at the level of the causes of rising social inequality and marginality; and it is *paternalistic* and punitive at the bottom, towards those destabilized by the conjoint restructuring of employment and withering away of welfare state protection or their reconversion into instrument of surveillance of the poor.

Three species of imprisonment and their meaning in the neo-liberal project

To put in perspective the unexpected resurgence of prisons at the forefront of the institutional horizon in advanced societies over the past two decades (King and Maguire 1998, Christie 2000), it is helpful to recall that putting people being bars to punish them is a recent historical invention. This fact comes as a surprise to many since we are have grown so accustomed to seeing people locked up that it seems perfectly natural to us: prison presents itself as an indispensable and immutable organization, operating since times immemorial. In reality, up until the end of the eighteenth century, places of confinement served mainly to detain those suspected or found guilty of crimes to await the administration of their sentence, which consisted then in various corporeal punishments (whipping, pillorying, burial, branding or mutilation, being put to death with or without torture), supplemented by banishment and condemnation to forced labour or to the galleys (Spierenburg 1995). Depriving people of freedom became itself a punishment, and the criminal sentence par excellence (to the point that it has become difficult to conceive or implement other penal sanctions without them appearing insufficiently severe) only with the advent of the modern individual presumed to enjoy personal freedom, imbued with a natural right to bodily integrity that could be removed by neither family nor state, except for the most serious motives. Reminding ourselves that *the prison is a very young institution* on the scale of the history of humankind is to stress that its growth and permanence are not a foregone conclusion.

Secondly, once it becomes the normative form of criminal sanction, imprisonment can *fulfil several functions at the same time*, successively or simultaneously. Sociologist Claude Faugeron (1995) establishes a fruitful distinction between what she calls "imprisonment of safety," aimed at preventing individuals considered dangerous from causing harm; "imprisonment of differentiation," designed to exclude social categories deemed undesirable; and "imprisonment of authority," whose purpose is primarily to reaffirm the prerogatives and powers of the state. One perceives immediately that these three forms of imprisonment do not target the same populations—e.g., pedophiles, illegal migrants and violent 'trouble-makers' at demonstrations—and do not communicate the same message to society.

This plurality of functions fulfilled by the prison does not prevent such or such particular mission from predominating at a given time. Thus in European countries today, imprisonment for purposes of differentiation is currently applied with growing frequency to non-European foreigners (i.e., immigrants from the former colonies of the old continent), particularly young people, who are thus designated as not being part of the 'social body' of the emerging Europe (Palidda 2000: 219–240). In America prison has taken over the function of the black ghettos as an instrument of control and containment of a population considered as a lower caste with which one should not mix. And there it is African-Americans who 'benefit' from a *de facto* policy of *carceral affirmative action* resulting in their massive overrepresentation in the country's jails and prisons: black men make up 6% of the national population but have accounted for over half of new admissions in state and federal prison every year since 1989 (see Wacquant 2000a and 2001).

Nonetheless, the signal fact of the end of century is without doubt the tremendous inflation of prison populations in all the advanced societies (Stern 1997, Tonry and Petersilia 1999, Garland 2001) due to the increasingly frequent, indeed routine, use of imprisonment as an instrument for managing social insecurity. This is what I argue in my book *Prisons of Poverty*: in all the countries where the neoliberal ideology of submission to the "free market" has spread, we observe a spectacular rise in the number of people put being bars as the state relies increasingly on the police and penal institutions to contain the disorders produced by mass unemployment, the imposition of precarious wage work and the shrinking of social protection. And poor urban youths are the first concerned on all fronts: they are massively overrepresented among holders of jobs in the secondary sectors of the employment market and they furnish the brunt of the prison population in all the major countries.

How neoliberal penality is spreading and mutating

Erasing of the economic state, dismantling of the social state, strengthening of the penal state: these three transformations are intimately linked to one another and all three result essentially from the conversion of the ruling classes to neoliberal ideology. In point of fact, those who are glorifying the penal state today, in America as in Europe, are the same ones who, yesterday, were demanding the end of "Big government" on the social and economic front, and who did indeed succeed in curtailing the prerogatives, expectations, and exigencies of the collectivity in the face of the market—that is, in the face of the dictatorship of large corporations. This may seem like a contradiction, but in reality these are the two components of the new institutional machinery for managing poverty that is being put in place in the era of mass joblessness and precarious employment. This new "government" of social insecurity—to speak like Michel Foucault—rests, on the one hand, on the disciplining of the deskilled and deregulated labor market and, on the other, on an intrusive and omnipresent penal apparatus. *The invisible hand of the market and the iron fist of the state combine* and complement each other to make the lower classes accept desocialized wage labor and the social instability it brings in its wake. After a long eclipse, the prison thus returns to the frontline of institutions entrusted with maintaining the social order.

The overpowering ascent of the theme of "urban violence" and crime in the discourse and policies of European governments, and especially in France since the return to power of the so-called "*Gauche*

Plurielle" [plural left, composed of the Socialist, Communist and Green parties], does not have much to do with the evolution of "youth" delinquency (one should always add: youths *of working-class and foreign origin*, since it is squarely they who are meant; besides, in many countries, such as Italy and Germany, politicians feel no discomfort in coming straight out and saying "immigrant crime"). Instead, its aim is to foster the redefinition of the perimeter and modalities of state action: the Keynesian state that was the historic vehicle of *solidarity*, and whose mission was to counter the cycles and damaging effects of the market, to ensure the collective "well-fare" and to reduce inequalities, is succeeded by a Darwinian state that makes a fetish of *competition* and celebrates individual responsibility (whose counterpart is collective irresponsibility), and which withdraws into its kingly functions of "law and order," themselves hypertrophied.

The usefulness of the penal apparatus in the post-Keynesian era of *employment of insecurity* is therefore threefold: it serves to discipline the fractions of the working class that buck at the new, precarious service jobs; it neutralizes and warehouses its most disruptive elements, or those considered superfluous in regard to the transformations of the demand for labor; and it reaffirms the authority of the state in the limited domain that is henceforth assigned to it.

One can distinguish three stages in the worldwide diffusion of the new "*made-in-the-U.S.A.*" ideologies and policies of law and order, and in particular the so-called "zero tolerance" measures—which, interestingly, are called "quality of life" measures in New York (see Wacquant 1999b, for a more detailed examination). The first is the phase of *gestation, implementation, and showcasing in American cities*, and especially in New York, which was elevated to the rank of Mecca of security by a systematic propaganda campaign. During this phase, the neoconservative think tanks, such as the Manhattan Institute, the Heritage Foundation, the American Enterprise Institute and a few others, play a pivotal role, for it is they who manufacture these notions before disseminating them within the American ruling classes in the course of the war against the welfare state, which has been raging in the wake of the social and racial backlash experienced by America since the mid-70's.

The second stage is that of *import-export*, facilitated by the links forged with the kindred "think tanks" that have mushroomed throughout Europe over the past decade, and especially in England. Just as in matters of employment and social policy, England serves as the

Trojan horse and "acclimation chamber" for the new, neoliberal penality with a view to its propagation across the European continent (a major influence here is the Institute for Economic Affairs, which brings to the U.K., first Charles Murray to advocate cutting welfare, then Lawrence Mead to urge workfare, and finally William Bratton to proselytize on "zero tolerance"). But if the export of the new American law-and-order products is having stunning success, it is because it meets the demand of the state rulers of the importing countries: in the intervening years, the latter have converted to the dogmas of the so-called "free" market and to the imperative of "less government"—in social and economic affairs, that is.

A third and final stage consists in applying a thin *scholarly whitewash* to these measures, and then the trick is pulled: a conservative pig is sold in a criminological poke. In each country one finds local intellectuals who spontaneously take up the part of "smuggler" (*passeur*) or relay by vouchsafing with their university authority the adaptation of U.S. policies and methods for enforcing law and order to their own societies. In France, for instance, there are a number of academics who live solely off of the second-hand resale of American security ideologies (one of them is about to publish a book entitled *Is There a French "Broken Window"?* when the so-called "broken windows" theory has been discredited among serious U.S. criminologists). These are the ideologies that one encounters afterwards in the form of pseudo-concepts in the seminars of the Institute for Advanced Studies in Domestic Security (IHESI), in a "Que Sais-Je" on *Urban Violences and Insecurity*, in the documents handed to mayors when they negotiate their "Local Contracts for Security" with the central state, and then in the newspapers and in everyday conversations.[1]

This is not to say that Europe is importing US-style police and penal policies wholesale, blindly imitating the politicians from across the Atlantic. European countries with a strong state tradition, either Catholic or social-democratic, are not headed towards a slavish dupli-

---

[1] The IHESI is a state institute which conducts training seminars and "studies" on security and law-and-order issues and policies; it is placed under the aegis not of the Ministry of Research but of the Minister of the Interior, who is in charge of the police, and its works pertain more to bureaucratic propaganda than to scholarly research. "Que Sais-Je" is a high-prestige book series published by Presses Universitaires de France consisting of short volumes reputed to provide the best, up-to-date scientific information on a given topic. Local Contracts for Security (*Contrats locaux de sécurité*) are compacts signed with the central state through which municipalities plan, promote, and implement proactive anti-crime measures.

cation of the American model, that is to say, a sharp and brutal substitution of the social-welfare treatment of poverty by penal treatment backed by all-out "carceralization." Rather, they are groping towards the invention of a "European" (French, Italian, German, etc.) road to the penal state, suited to the different European political and cultural traditions, and characterized by a *conjoint, twofold accentuation* of *both* the social regulation *and* the penal regulation of social insecurity.

Thus the French state is simultaneously increasing its social intervention and its penal intervention. On the one hand, it has multiplied youth jobs and government-sponsored work contracts for the unemployed that include training (CES, or *Contrats Emploi-Solidarité*); it has raised the level of various public aid packages (however little) and significantly extended the reach of the guaranteed minimum income plan (RMI); it has instituted truly universal health coverage, and so on. But, on the other hand, it is also stationing riot police squads in so-called "sensitive neighborhoods" and it has set up special surveillance units for detecting and repressing delinquency there; it is substituting judges for social workers and educators when "at-risk" youth need to be warned to not run afoul of the law; cities are passing and enforcing utterly illegal anti-begging ordinances that serve to sweep the homeless and the derelict off the streets; the government has refused to align the norms for provisional detention for "*comparution immédiate*" (live arrests and fast-track prosecution) with the norms for "*affaires à instruction*" (investigative cases following a police complaint), on the grounds that one must fight "urban violence" (thus granting the youths of declining public housing estates a form of "carceral affirmative action"); penalties for recidivism are made harsher; the deportation of foreigners subjected to "double sanction"[2] are speeded up, release on parole has been practically eliminated . . .

A second difference between the United States and France (and the countries of continental Europe more generally): the penalization of poverty *à la française* is mainly effected by means of the police and the courts, rather than through prison. It obeys a logic that is more

---

[2] [Translator's note] The "*double peine*" refers to the fact that most foreigners sentenced to prison in France first serve the detention term to which the court sentenced them and then are expelled from the national territory following an administrative decree of banishment. Its primary target is young men of foreign nationality who, in many cases, have lived most of their lives in France and have few social and cultural connections with their country of origin.

panoptic than retributive or segregative, with the significant exception of foreigners (Wacquant 1999c). Correspondingly, the social service bureaucracies are called on to take an active part in it, since they possess the informational and human means to exercise a close surveillance of "problem populations"—this is what I call *social panopticism*.

The whole question is whether this European road is a genuine alternative to American-style carceralization, or whether it is simply a stage on the way to mass imprisonment, particularly youths of working class and foreign origin. If one saturates neighborhoods of social exclusion with police officers without improving the life chances and employment options of its residents, one is sure to increase arrests and penal sentences and thus, in the end, the incarcerated population. In what proportions? The future will tell. The same question arises, in much more dramatic and urgent terms, in Latin America, where U.S.-style police and penal policies are being imported *wholesale*. Two decades after the "Chicago Boys" reshaped the economies of that continent, the "New York Boys" of William Bratton, Rudolph Giuliani and the Manhattan Institute are spreading their law-and-order gospel there, with devastating consequences due to much higher levels of poverty, the embryonic nature of social welfare programs, and the corrupt and violent behavior of the crime and justice bureaucracies. In the formerly authoritarian societies of the Second World such as Argentina and Brazil, the application of neoliberal penality amounts to reestablishing a dictatorship over the poor (see Wacquant 2000b and 2001b on Argentina and Brazil, respectively).

France's 'plural left' joins the 'Washington consensus' on law and order

But it is at the heart of Europe that the worldwide battle for setting the transnational goals and norms of the penal institution in the era of hegemonic neoliberalism and, through them, for shaping the visage of the postkeynesian state, is being waged. And here the new crime and security orientations of France play a pivotal role. In the 1980's, the successive Mitterrand governments contributed powerfully to legitimating neoliberal economic ideology by capitulating under the pressure from the financial markets and monetary speculation to adopt policies of budgetary austerity and privatization policies. Today Jospin finds himself in much the same position on the penal front as a result of being perceived—rightly or wrongly—as the last truly Left leader in Europe and even in the world. He could anchor a breakwater of resistance to *"la pensée unique"* [consensual thinking] in matters of criminal justice. Instead, he rallies the "Washington consensus" on law-and-order dictated by the U.S. neoconservative think tanks. When he denigrates the social causes of delinquency as so many "sociological excuses" (in a high-visibility interview published in *Le Monde* at the beginning of 1999 under the unwittingly ironic title, "Against 'one-way thinking'"), Jospin renounces sociological thought, even though the latter is organically linked to socialist thought, and he legitimates the neoliberal vision of the world in its most retrograde aspects. More generally, one might have hoped that the Left, back in power, would launch a bold policy of decriminalization and decarceration, that it would increase the perimeter and prerogatives of the social state, and diminish those of the penal state. And it is the opposite that is happening (Sainatti and Bonelli 2000). The same pedagogy of retreat and renunciation that has guided economic policy is now being applied in the area of criminal justice.

The emergence in France of a so-called 'Republican left' which rues the days when minors received severe disciplining is a worrying trend in this respect, a teratological form of Republicanism fed by nostalgia for a 'golden age' that never existed. This old-fashioned education, some people seem to have forgotten, rested on fundamentally inegalitarian and violent social relations, especially between age groups and between the sexes. It is society as a whole that educates, and one cannot restore an old-fashioned system of discipline when everywhere else such a form of rigid authority has been questioned and overturned. When Mr. Chevènement was Minister of Education in the 80s under Mitterrand, his ambition was to sprinkle France with universities. When he took up the Ministry of the Interior [which oversees the national police] in the late 90s, his plan was to line the neighborhoods laid to waste by the government's economic policy with police stations, while waiting perhaps to open up jails in them...

In both scenarios, the presence of the state is being reinforced, but with diametrically opposed means and consequences: the first scenario translates into an expansion of life chances, the second into their amputation; the one reinforces the legitimacy of public authority, the other undermines it. Hardly caricaturing, one could sum up this duality by this formula: for the children of the middle and upper classes, universities and professional-managerial jobs; for the offspring of the working class confined in declining housing estates, precarious service jobs, or positions as police adjuncts, surveilling the outcasts and refuse of the new labor market—under threat of being locked up. Thus fully ten percent of the government-sponsored "youth jobs" are "*adjoints de sécurité*," police officer's aides recruited in low-income areas and entrusted with facilitating and expanding the reach of the forces of order in these neighborhoods.

Coda: resisting the coming of the penal state

Unlike in the United States, where the criminalization of poverty has entered into custom and habit and is henceforth inscribed in the very structure of the state as well as in public culture, in Europe the dice is not yet cast, far from it. No more than precarious employment, which some try to present to us as a sort of natural necessity (it too comes from America), carceral inflation is not an inevitability. Recourse to the prison apparatus is not destiny in advanced societies but a matter of political choices, and these choices must be made in full knowledge of the fact and of their consequences.

To oppose the penalization of social precariousness, a threefold battle must be waged. First of all, on the level of *words and discourses*, one must put the brakes on the semantic drifts that lead, on the one hand, to compressing the space of debate (e.g., by limiting the notion of "insecurity" to *physical* or criminal insecurity, to the exclusion of social and economic insecurity) and, on the other, to the banalization of the penal treatment of the tensions linked to the deepening of social inequalities (through the use of such vague and incoherent notions as "urban violences"). It is imperative to keep close track of the pseudo-theories concocted by the American think tanks and assorted law-and-order ideologists, and to submit them to strict customs checks in the form of a rigorous logical and empirical critique.

Next, on the front of *judicial policies and practices*, one must thwart the multiplication of measures tending to "widen" the penal dragnet and propose a social, health, or educational alternative whenever feasible. We must stress the fact that, far from being a solution, police surveillance and imprisonment typically aggravate and amplify the problems they are supposed to resolve. We know that, in addition to hitting mostly the destitute strata of the working class—the unemployed, the precariously employed, recent immigrants—incarceration is itself a powerful engine for impoverishment. It is useful, in this connection, to recall relentlessly what are the deleterious conditions and effects of detention today, not only upon the inmates themselves but also on their families and their neighborhoods.

Finally, much is to be gained from forging links between activists and researchers who work on the penal front and those who battle on the social front, and this *at the European level* so as to optimize the intellectual and practical resources to be invested in this struggle. There is a tremendous mine of scientific and political knowledge to be exploited and shared on the scale of the continent—and beyond: American scholars and activists have a wealth of experiences to offer that demonstrate the colossal social and human costs of mass imprisonment. For the true alternative to the drift towards the penalization, soft or hard, of poverty is the construction of a European social state worthy of the name. The best means of making prison recede is, again and always, to strengthen and expand social and economic rights.

References

Bourdieu, P., *Contre-feux*. Paris: Raisons d'agir, 1998 (translation in English: *Acts of Resistance: Against the Tyranny of the Market*, Cambridge, Polity Press, 1999).

Christie, Nils, 2000, *Crime Control as Industry: Towards Gulags, Western Style*. London: Routledge, new enlarged ed.

Faugeron, Claude. "La dérive pénale," *Esprit* 215 (October 1995), pp. 132–144.

Garland, David (ed.), 2001, *Mass Imprisonment: Social Causes and Consequences*. London: Sage.

King, Roy D. and Mike Maguire (eds.), 1998, *Prisons in Context*. New York: Oxford University Press.

Palidda, Salvatore, 2000, *Polizia Postmoderna. Etnografia del nuovo controllo sociale*. Milano: Feltrenelli.

Sainatti, Gilles and Laurent Bonelli (eds.), 2000, *La Machine à punir. Pratique et discours sécuritaires*. Paris: Dagorno.

Spierenburg, Peter, 1995, "The Body and the State: Early Modern Europe." Pp. 49–78 in *The Oxford History of the Prison: The Practice of Punishment in Modern Society*. Edited by Norval Morris and David J. Rothman. Oxford: Oxford University Press.

Stern, Vivian, 1997, *A Sin Against the Future: Imprisonment in the World*. Boston: Northeastern University Press.

Tonry, Michael and Joan Petersilia, 1999, *Prisons*. Chicago: The University of Chicago Press.

Wacquant, L., *Les Prisons de la Misère*. Paris: Raisons d'agir Edition, 1999a. (Translation in German: *Elend hinter Gittern*, Konstanz, UVK, 2000; Italian: *Parola d'ordine*, Milano, Feltrinelli, 2000; Portuguese: *As Prisões da miséria*, Oeiras, Celta, 2000; Spanish: *Las Cárceles de la miseria*, Madrid, Alianza, 2001; Swedish: Brutus Ostlings, 2001; Greek: Patakis, 2001; Hungarian: Helikon, 2001; English: *Prisons of Poverty*, University of Minnesota Press, 2002).

———, "How Penal Common Sense Comes to Europeans: Notes on the Transatlantic Diffusion of Neoliberal Doxa," *European Societies*, 1–3, Fall 1999b, pp. 319–352.

———, "'Suitable Enemies': Foreigners and Immigrants in Europe's Prisons," *Punishment and Society*, 1–2, Fall 1999c, pp. 215–223.

———, 2000a, "The New 'Peculiar Institution': On the Prison as Surrogate Ghetto." *Theoretical Criminology*, 4–3, Special issue on "New Social Studies of the Prison": 377–389.

———, "Mister Bratton Goes to Buenos Aires. Prefacio à la edición para América latina," in *Cárceles de la miseria*, Buenos Aires, Ediciones Manantial, 2000b, pp. 11–17.

———, 2001a, "Deadly Symbiosis: When Ghetto and Prison Meet and Mesh." *Punishment & Society*, 3–1 (Winter): 95–134.

———, 2001b, "Rumo a uma ditadura sobre os pobres? Nota aos leitores brasileiros." Preface to *As Prisões da miséria*, Rio de Janeiro, Zahar Editor, pp. 7–15.

EPILOGUE: TRANSVERSAL ANCHORINGS AMONG YOUTH TODAY

Saskia Sassen

The focus on youth in this book gives us a very particular empirical specification of a broader dynamic evident in today's advanced urban economies mostly studied through the experience of adults. This focus on today's situation of youth brings to the fore the conditioning of future trajectories: the current options of these young people spell the limitations of their possible future worklives. But this focus also makes wider the emergence of new trajectories that relocate to the world of peers and the imaginary what in the past or among adults is centrally located in the world of work.

Two subjects stand out and are discussed in this brief epilogue. One is that as the world of employment is increasingly fragile for a growing number of young people, though by no means for all, other social spheres begin to replace employment as anchors. Analytically this expands the terrain within which to situate the condition of youth in the transition from school to work usually understood as self-reliant adulthood. A second major theme that comes out of some of these chapters is the fact that the current constraints on youth and their consequent re-anchoring in non-work worlds can bring with it a different sense of the political and of citizenship. This is not a fully developed theme in the book, but it is present in some of the chapters.

Economic moorings and unmoorings

Reading these chapters makes it quite clear that overall, poverty and economic insecurity are not simply functions of an individual's failings or of young age. The young people described mostly find themselves in strongly determined situations that produce their poverty, economic insecurity, and precarious employment. This raises a question about the extent to which employment-based economic insecurity and poverty are features of advanced economies. Major changes in the organization of economic activity over the last fifteen years have emerged as a source of general economic insecurity, of low-wage jobs, and of new forms of employment-centered poverty.

This is a broad subject. Because the world of employment is increasingly precarious for a growing number of young people, though by no means for all, other social spheres begin to replace employment as anchors. Several of the chapters describe the ascendant role of peer groups, gangs, diasporic networks (Roulleau-Berger; Dubet; Hurtubise, Roy, Bellot; see also Roulleau-Berger 1999).[1] An examination of the question of youth and employment or the transition from school to jobs can no longer be centered in the world of work if we are to understand these young people as emerging subjects (see Furlong and Cartmel; Anisef and Axelrod; Gauthier). This holds both for youth as economic actors striving for survival and for the processes whereby their subjectivity is being constituted in this particular domain of survival: in either case the non-economic is ascendant.

Further, given the nature of the jobs when these are available, the non-economic spheres of their lives are the ones more likely to give them satisfaction and a sense of worth and identity than the world of work. Analytically this expands the terrain within which to situate the condition of youth in the transition from school to self-reliant adulthood: clearly, the world of work no longer functions as the institutional major realm within which adulthood is forged. It never was for all youth, but the evidence suggests that today it is for fewer and fewer young people, including those with jobs.

There are multiple qualifiers that need to be brought to this conceptualization. Castel reminds us that for many young people the transition from school to work is just that. One can interpret this transition as an event embedded in the features of each of these institutional domains which function as bridges into adulthood but also produce new social inequalities and reinforce racializing dynamics (see Verdier, Braun, Noguera, Payet). Secondly, for many young people the new economy has produced unexpected opportunities for quick economic advancement. Third, for second generation immigrants, the transition from school to work can function as an enabling mechanism that can give them the advantage in the world of work that their parents lacked, as the evidence presented by Zhou and Schiff shows us so clearly.

---

[1] Roulleau-Berger, L. (1999): *Le Travail En Friche*. La Tour d'Aigues: Editions de l'Aube.

There is another major theme that comes out of some of these chapters, most particularly Wacquant's, and that could be interpreted as one more qualifying condition beyond those already discussed. The current constraints on youth when it comes to the world of work and their re-anchoring in non-work worlds can bring with them a different sense of the political and of citizenship. These constraints create a strategic context for redefinitions of one's sense of the political and the civic.

New employment regimes

We can identify at least three processes in the current economic phase that produce an institutional setting for the outcomes described in this book (Munger 2002, Sassen 2001: chapters 8 and 9[2]).[3] These three processes either produce or contribute to new, or merely accentuating older, forms of inequality/distance between firms and workers at the bottom of the economic system and those who prosper. While these processes are not necessarily mutually exclusive, it is helpful to distinguish them analytically. They are: a) the growing inequality in i) the profit-making capacities of different economic sectors and types of firms and ii) the growing inequality in the earnings capacities of different types of workers and households; b) socio-economic polarization tendencies resulting from the organization of service industries and from the casualization of the employment relation; and c) the production of urban marginality (see Chuprov and Zubok; Péraldi) particularly as a result of new structural processes of economic growth rather than those producing marginality through abandonment, even though the latter is a continuing factor as well.

The new employment regimes that have emerged out of these structural trends in highly developed countries have reconfigured the job supply and employment relations. Much analysis of post-industrial society and advanced economies generally posits a massive growth in the need for highly educated workers and little need for the types of jobs that a majority of the people described in the chapters of this book are likely to hold (see Trottier, Vultur, Gauthier; Hamel). This suggests sharply reduced employment opportunities for these

---

[3] Sassen, S., Munger, F. (ed.) *Laboring below the line*, New York: Russel Sage Foundation, 2002: *The Global City*, New Updated Edition, Princeton, University Press, 2001.

workers. Yet detailed empirical studies, especially of major cities in highly developed countries, show ongoing demand for low-wage workers and a significant supply of old and new jobs requiring little education and paying low wages (see Tannock, Hamel). Wages in these jobs are often below minimum subsistence standards. Several of the chapters in this book show us how this works in the case of young people (see Ortega; Tremblay; Cammarota).

What much of the general available evidence fails to provide is information about the interaction effects between workers and jobs, or workers and workplace, and how these interaction effects shape not only employment outcomes but also the role played by the world of work in shaping workers' subjectivities. An important contribution by several chapters in this book is the evidence they provide about these interaction effects. One kind of interaction effect several authors (see Cammarota; Ortega; Roulleau-Berger; Tobio) examine is what the workers bring to these jobs. They want or expect more from these jobs than they can get: an interesting, engaging environment, from which they can learn and where they can advance. When such conditions are absent, these young workers re-situate themselves in other social spheres where they can find at least some of what they aspire to. One way of conceptualizing these subjective operations is as a creation of cultures.

Another interaction effect captured in some of these chapters is that because of the weaker capacity for the world of work to define the subject, unemployed youth can more easily find the conditions for producing themselves as subjects in other realms. Indeed, in today's large cities especially, there are a whole range of rituals of transition that are located outside the world of work.

A third interaction effect is that the growth of informal economies re-introduces the community and the household as an important economic space. Informalization in major cities of highly developed countries—whether New York, London, Paris or Toronto—can be seen as a downgrading of a variety of activities that produce goods or deliver services for which there is an effective demand in these cities. But notwithstanding effective demand, there is also a devaluing of these activities and enormous competition given low entry costs and few alternative forms of employment. Hence the profits are low and mostly marginal. Going informal is one way of producing and distributing goods and services at a lower cost and with greater flexibility. This further devalues these types of activities. Immigrants and women are important actors in the new informal economies of these cities but increasingly so are youth in large and small cities.

Work, youth and immigration

The case of immigrants allows us to see that notwithstanding vast distances, workers may actually be moving in a very restricted job search. Much of the data suggest the act of migrating involves a move pattern from one particular community in the country of origin to another particular community in country of destination. We can interpret this as representing movement from one particular local labor market to another. This specific job search pattern has the effect of altering the geographic dimension often implied by job search models, especially among low-wage workers i.e. short distance. It also qualifies an important proposition in the economics literature that analyzes immigration in terms of standard neoclassical labor market dynamics—to wit, that immigrants move in response to the better relative returns on skill they expect in the country of destination compared with the relative returns in their country of origin. It would seem rather that the immigrant's decision and evaluation operate in terms of very specific local labor markets.[4]

The fact of a highly restricted institutional environment for job searcher appears to continue to operate once they are in the area of destination. But its restrictive character operates rather differently from what seems to be the case among native workers (particularly, in the case of the US, African-Americans) of analogous skill levels, and from what standard models suggest. In both of these cases distance—willingness to leave one's neighborhood, to travel a considerable distance, to move to another city—signals upward mobility. Thus, the evidence about the willingness of immigrants to move and cover long commuting distances to get a job, is easily interpreted as showing that immigrants are willing to try for far more outlying markets than natives. But in fact, it is that their networks have a different spatial patterning, one that often involves long commuting distances. Notwithstanding a far ranging area within which many search for jobs, they

---

[4] Sassen, S. (1996): "Immigration and Local Labor Markets." In A. Portes (ed.) *The Economic Sociology of Immigration*. New York: Russell Sage Foundation, 1996.

are actually largely moving within a very confined institutional setting, even when they travel long distances and improvise informal transportation systems. In some ways the findings about youth and migration or mobility (Simard) signal similar patterns of confinement to limited circuits notwithstanding geographic distances travelled.

Conclusion

There is a sub-text present in some of these trends which signals that a culture of desire is operative even under these adverse conditions. The broader social environment with its possibilities for enormously interesting and rewarding and well-paid jobs is a factor that needs to be intermediated in the case of disadvantaged youths with few objective opportunities to achieve this. What these chapters show us is that it gets intermediated by a re-situating of their subjectivity into a variety of social groupings that function outside the world of work yet become presences in this world of work for those youth who have jobs: their subjectivity is constructed in terms of these other spheres, and less and less in terms of their actual job situation. This dynamic can also intermediate the fact that some youths are enormously successful in terms of jobs and salaries and even amass large fortunes at a very young age: the star system in sports and in the world of media and music produces highly visible "success" stories. Re-situating one's subjectivity away from dead-end, low-wage and often precarious jobs is one exit strategy from a dismal economic condition.

NOTES ON CONTRIBUTORS

Paul Anisef, Professor in Sociology at York University, and Associate Director of the Joint Centre of Excellence on Immigration and Settlement, Toronto has conducted extensive research on the topics of accessibility to Canadian higher education, the transition from school to work at the secondary and postsecondary levels of education and careers for Canadian youth and the experiences of immigrant youth. He is co-author of *Opportunity and Uncertainty: Life Course Experiences of the Class of '73* (2000). His other publications include: *Transitions: Schooling and Employment in Canada* (1993) and *Learning and Sociological Profiles of Canadian High School Students* (1994).

Paul Axelrod, Dean of the Faculty of Education at York University in Toronto, is a historian who specializes in the study of schooling and higher education. He is co-author of *Opportunity and Uncertainty: Life Course Experiences of the Class of '73* (2000). His other publications include *Values in Conflict: the University, the Marketplace, and the Trials of Liberal Education* (2002); *The Promise of Schooling: Education in Canada, 1800–1914* (1997); and *Making a Middle Class: Student Life in English Canada during the Thirties* (1990).

Céline Bellot, a postdoctoral candidate at Université du Québec à Montréal, earned her doctorate in 2001 from the School of Criminology at Université de Montréal. Her thesis is an examination of the trajectories of Montreal street youth, grounded in ethnographic interpretation and biographical analysis. She is now developing an assessment approach for services and practices that takes the experience of street youth into account.

Frank Braun (M. Ed., Pittsburgh, USA, Ph.D., University of Bremen, Germany) is Head of the Research Unit "Transition to Work" of the German Youth Institute in Munich, Germany. His research background includes contributions to a Max-Planck-Institute of Educational Research comparative study on the development of secondary education in several European countries. He was member of a European research team that studied the relationships between youth unemployment, delinquency and urban settings in Belgium, Germany,

Great Britain and France. Some recent publications: Frank Braun: Übergangshilfen: Sackgassen, Umleitungen, Überholspuren. In: Pohl/Schneider (eds.): *Sackgassen, Umleitungen, Überholspuren—Ausgrenzungsrisiken und neue Perspektiven im Übergang in die Arbeit.* Tübingen: Neuling 200, pp. 35–48—Frank Braun/Tilly Lex/Hermann Rademacker (eds.): *Jugend in Arbeit: Neue Wege des Übergangs Jugendlicher in die Arbeitswelt.* Opladen: Leske & Budrich 2001.

Julio Cammarota is a research associate in the Bureau of Applied Research in Anthropology at the University of Arizona. He recently completed a dissertation that focuses on the perceptions and experiences of work among Latino youth from Oakland, California. The Center for Working Families at UC Berkeley has published two of Dr Cammarota's working papers on labor, family, and Latino youth. He also published a paper entitled, "Latino Immigrants and Labor Control: Language Barriers and The Social Devaluation of Skills in Fast Food Work" in *Les Jeunes et l'emploi dans les villes d'Europe et d'Amérique du Nord*, Eds. Laurence Roulleau-Berger and Madeleine Gauthier, L'Aube, 2001.

Fred Cartmel, Research Associate in the Youth, Education and Employment Research Unit at the University of Glasgow, Scotland. He has written extensively on youth transitions, education and the youth labour market and is author of *Young People and Social Change* (Open University Press, 1997—with Andy Furlong).

Robert Castel is Directeur d'études at the EHESS (Ecole des Hautes Etudes en Sciences Sociales) in Paris. His recent researches are focused on relationships between the transformations of regulations of work and social protection, the new forms of sociability and the status of the modern individuals. She has published numerous articles and books; his recent books are: *Les métamorphoses de la question sociale. Une chronique du salariat*, Fayard, 1995; *Chômage: le cas français*, la Documentation française, 1997; *Propriété privée, propriété sociale, propriété de soi. Entretiens sur la construction de l'individu moderne*, avec C. Haroche, Fayard, 2001.

Vladimir I. Chuprov is Professor of Sociology, Head of the Centre for Sociology of Youth in the Institute of Socio-Political Research of the Russian Academy of Sciences. He currently works on the problems of social development of young people under conditions of risk. Recent publications: *Russian Society in Transition (co-editor), 1996; Youth in Social reproduction: Problems and perspectives, 2000.*

François Dubet is Professor of sociology at the Université Victor Segalen in Bordeaux and Directeur d'études at the EHESS (Ecole des Hautes Etudes en Sciences Sociales) in Paris. He is a member of the Institut Universitaire de France. He is the author of many articles and books on youth, marginality, education, work, social movements and sociological theory, in particular: *La galère: jeunes en survie*, Paris, Fayard, 1987 (édition de poche en 1993 et 1995); *Les lycéens*, Paris, Seuil, 1991 (édition de poche en 1992, 1996 et 1998); *Sociologie de l'expérience*, Paris, Seuil, 1994; *A l'école* (avec Danilo Martuccelli), Paris, Seuil, 1996; *Le déclin de l'institution*, Paris, Seuil, 2002.

Andy Furlong is Professor of sociology and head of the department of sociology and anthropology at the University of Glasgow, Scotland. He has written extensively on youth transitions, education and the youth labour market and is author of *Young People and Social Change* (Open University Press, 1997—with Fred Cartmel) and editor of *the Journal of Youth Studies* (Taylor and Francis).

Madeleine Gauthier is Professor at INRS-Urbanisation, Culture et Société, Québec, Canada. She is the director of the Observatoire Jeunes et Société, of the Group of Research on Youth Migration an of another on the professional integration of the drop-out. She is also the director of the Group of Sociology of Youth at the International Association of French-speaking sociologists. Amongst her publications: *Une société sans les jeunes?* (1994); with Léon Bernier, ed., *Les 15–19 ans. Quel présent? Vers quel avenir?* (1997); editor of *Pourquoi partir? La migration des jeunes d'hier et d'aujourd'hui?* (1997); with Jean-François Guillaume, ed., *Définir la jeunesse? D'un bout à l'autre du monde* (1999); with Laurence Roulleau-Berger, ed., *Les jeunes et l'emploi dans les villes d'Europe et d'Amérique du Nord* (2001); with Diane Pacom, ed., *Spotlight on Canadian Youth Research* (2001).

Jacques Hamel is Professor titulaire in the Département de sociologie at the Université de Montréal. He is associated with the Observatoire Jeunes et Société at the Institut national de la recherche scientifique (Urbanisation, Culture et Société). His research interests include youth and work, epistemology, qualitative methodology and cultural theory. He is the author of *Précis d'épistémologie de la sociologie* and *La production du social*.

Roch Hurtubise is a Professor in the Department of Social Work at Université de Sherbrooke and joint coordinator of the Collective for Research on Homelessness, Poverty, and Social Exclusion at Université du Québec, Montréal. He is interested in representations of homeless people's health and the analysis of professional practices and action principles employed with marginalized groups. His recent papers: "Réseaux, stratégies et compétences: pour une analyse des dynamiques sociales à l'œuvre chez les jeunes de la rue" avec M. Vatz Laaroussi in *L'Homme et la Société*, n° 143–144 2002/1–2; "Jeunes dans/de larue et stratégies de réseaux in *L'errance urbaine*, D. Laberge (ed.), Ed. Multimondes, Ste-Foy, 2000.

Antonio Santos Ortega is Professor of Sociology at the University of Valencia, Spain. His present research priorities deal with the study of long term unemployment, labour precariousness low wages and junk jobs in youth employment. His research has been published in Sociología del Trabajo, Sociologia del Lavoro or in the International Review of Sociology. His books include *El reparto del trabajo* (Germania, 1998) *and Trabajo, Empleo y Cambio Social* (Tirant lo Blanch, 2001).

Pedro Noguera is Professor of of Communities and Schools in the Graduate School of Education at Harvard University. Noguera's research focuses on the ways in which schools respond to social and economic forces within the urban environment. Noguera has also done extensive research on the role of education in political and social change in the Caribbean. His recent publications: Noguera, P. A. (2002) *"The Role of Schools of Education in Transforming Inner-City School in Transforming Urban Education: Community, Equity and Access*. Buffalo, N.Y.: SUNY Press. Noguera, P. A. (2002) Beyond Size: The Challenge of School reform" in *Educational Leadership*, Volume 59, No. 5, February; Noguera, P. A. (2001). "The Role of Research in Challenging Racial Inequality in Education." In L. Roulleau-Berger and M. Gauthier (eds.) *"Les jeunes et l'emploi dans les villes d'Europe et d'Amérique du Nord."* Editions de l'Aube.

Jean-Paul Payet, Professor of Sociology, University Lyon 2, researcher of Groupe de Recherche sur la Socialisation. Author of numerous articles and several books on migrants children in schools, scholar violence, ethnicity and segregation in urban schools as: *L'école dans la ville* (with A. Henriot-van Zanten and L. Roulleau-Berger), L'Harmattan, 1994, *Collèges de banlieue. Ethnographie d'un monde scolaire*, Colin, 1995. His principal articles are published in *Revue Française de Pédagogie* and *Les Annales de la Recherche urbaine*.

Michel Peraldi is researcher at the Laboratory of Sociological Mediterranean Studies (LAMES), unit of the CNRS. He has written numerous articles and books about maghrebian migrations in Europe, urban ethnic districts in Marseilles, informal economies and transnational migrant's networks in mediterranean cities, among which: L. Mozere, H. Rey, M. Peraldi, *L'intelligence des banlieues*, Ed. de l'Aube, 2000; La métropole déchue in A. Donzel (ed.): *Gouvernance et citoyenneté dans la région urbaine marseillaise*, Paris, Maisonneuve et Larose, 2001; *Cabas et containers, activités marchandes informelles et réseaux migrants transfrontaliers*, ed. Péraldi, Maisonneuve et Larose, Paris, 2001; Marseille, pop culture, in *Mediterraneans*, N° 13, Spring 2002.

Laurence Roulleau-Berger, is Chargée de recherches at CNRS in the Laboratory of Sociological Studies on Socialization (GRS) habilitée à dirigen les recherche. She has published numerous articles and books about the process of marginalization in cities, youth and employment in France and in Europe, intermediate spaces and urban economies, among with. Her main books are *La Ville-Intervalle: jeunes entre centre et banlieue*, Klincksieck, 1991, rééd en 1993, *L'insertion des jeunes en France* avec C. Nicole-Drancourt, PUF, 1995, rééd en 1998 et 2002, *Le travail en friche.*, L'Aube, 1999, *Les jeunes et le travail en France 1950–2000* avec C. Nicole-Drancourt, PUF, 2001, *Les jeunes et l'emploi dans les villes d'Amérique du Nord et d'Europe*, L. Roulleau-Berger, M. Gauthier (eds.), L'Aube, 2001.

Shirley Roy is a Professor in the Department of Sociology at Université du Québec à Montréal and joint coordinator of the Collectif de recherche sur l'itinérance, la pauvreté et l'exclusion sociale (CRI) at Université du Québec à Montréal. Her areas of specialization are marginality and social exclusion. In recent years, her research has focused on homelessness among women, community intervention, and street youth. She is currently directing research projects on the trajectories of the homeless and the organizational forms of services that address HIV-related problems. She is the author of *Seuls dans la rue* (Alone on the Street), a study of Montreal's homeless men, published in 1988 by Éditions Saint-Martin.

Claire Schiff teaches sociology and anthropology at the Université Victor Segalen in Bordeaux, France and is a member of CADIS. Her main areas of study are minority and immigrant adaptation to French society and interethnic relations, particularly among recent immigrant and post-colonial minority youth. She has published a variety of articles in French sociological journals on this topic. She also participated in one of the first wide range research project on racial discrimination in the workplace with Philippe Bataille, (*Le racisme au travail*, La Découverte, Paris, 1995). Her doctoral thesis on the schooling and employment of new immigrant youth in France is soon to be published and she is presently involved in reseach on the obstacles to the acces of such youth to primary and secondary level education within the French school system.

Saskia Sassen is the Ralph Lewis Professor of Sociology, The University of Chicago and Centennial Visiting Professor, London School of Economics. Her most recent books are *Global Networks, Linked Cities* (New York and London: Routledge) and *Guests and Aliens* (New York: New Press 1999). The *Global City* has come out in a fully updated edition in 2001. Her books have been translated into twelve languages. She is completing her research project on "Governance and Accountability in a Global Economy," to be published as *Denationalization: Territory, Authority and Rights in a Global Digital Age* (Under contract with Princeton University Press).

Myriam Simard is a professor-researcher at the Institut national de la recherche scientifique of the Université du Québec (INRS-Urbanisation, Culture et Société). An anthropologist and sociologist by training, her work and publications focus primarily on the regionalization of immigration and the immigrant integration process outside metropolitan areas, as seen from a diachronic and intergenerational perspective. She is particularly interested in the factors that attract and retain immigrants in non-metropolitan and rural areas. She has published numerous articles and books, including the following: "La politique québécoise de régionalisation de l'immigration: enjeux et paradoxes," *Recherches sociographiques*, Vol. XXXVII, No. 3, 1996;

"Identité des jeunes régionaux de parents immigrés au Québec: métissage et ouverture sur le monde," *Cahiers de recherche sociologique*, 2001 (with I. Mimeault and J. Le Gall).

Stuart Tannock is a lecturer in Social and Cultural Studies in the School of Education at the University of California, Berkeley. He received his Ph.D. in the Program in Modern Thought at Stanford University in 2000. Tannock is the author of "*Youth at Work: The Unionized Fast-food and Grocery Workplace.*" His research interests focus on the sociology of youth, labor, work and education.

Constanza Tobío graduated in Political Science and Sociology at the Universidad Complutense de Madrid. She is currently Profesora Titular at the Universidad Carlos III de Madrid and Vice-Dean in charge of the degree in Sociology. She has been visiting professor at the universities of Bilbao, Granada, Bath, Siena and at the Centre d'Etudes de l'Emploi in Paris. Her main areas of research are urban sociology, social structure and the family-employment relationship. She has recently a published a book and several articles in international journals on one-parent families in Spain, as well as on Spanish working mothers' strategies to make family and employment compatible. Her recent publications: 2001, "Women's Strategies and the Family-Employment Relationship in Spain" in Mazur, A. G. (ed.), *State Feminism, Women's Movements and Job Training. Making Democracies Work in a Global Economy*, Routledge, New York and London, 49–64; 2001, "Marriage, Cohabitation and Youth Residential Independence in Spain", *International Journal of Law, Policy and the Family*, 15, 68–87.

Diane-Gabrielle Tremblay, Ph.D. in Econcomics is Professor of labour economics and Director of Research at the Télé-université (Distance learning component) of the University of Québec, Canada; she has just been appointed codirector of the Bell Canada-Teluq-Enap Research Chair on Technology and work organisation. She has published many articles and books, amongst which *a Labour Economics textbook*, *a Sociology of Work textbook*, two books on Working time issues, and a book on *Local Economic Development*. She is president of the Political Economy Association of Québec, and member of the executive of the Society for the advancement of Socio-Economics. Her research interests are related localized employment systems and networks and community local economic development, to work-family balancing, working time, employment policies, work organization, teamwork, to work-family balancing, working time, employment policies, work organization, teamwork and communities of practice.

Claude Trottier (Ph.D. in sociology) is a Professor in the Department of Educational Foundations and Practices of the Faculty of Education at Laval University. He teaches sociology of education and education policy analysis. His research focuses on the transition from school to work. He has co-authored "Vocational Integration of University Graduates, Typology and Multivariate Analysis" in *International Sociology* vol. 11, no. 1, 1996), co-edited *Les cheminements scolaires et l'insertion professionnelle des étudiants de l'université* (Presses de l'Université Laval, 1995) and was coordinator of the thematic issue *Entre éducation et travail: les acteurs de l'insertion* (2001, 1) of the journal *Éducation et sociétés*.

Eric Verdier is Economist, Senior Researcher (Directeur de recherche) at the National Center for Scientific Research (CNRS), Director of the Laboratoire d'Economie et de Sociologie du Travail, Aix en Provence. His present studies deal with the Education and Training Policies, the relationships between Industrial Innovation and Higher Education Systems and the Evaluation of Public Policies. Selected publications: "Sources of resilience in the computer and software industries in France" (with H. Nohara), *Industry and Innovation*, Vol. 8, 2001—"Reintroducing public action into societal analysis" in Maurice M. and Sorge A. (eds.), *Embedding Organizations, Societal analysis of actors, organizations and socio-economic contexts*, Benjamins, Amsterdam and Philadelphia. 2000, 325–338 "Education and Training Regimes: Macro-Institutional Evidence" (with C. Buechtemann), *Revue d'économie politique*, vol. 108 n° 3/1998, pp. 291–320.

Mircea Vultur is a professor at INRS-Urbanisation, Culture et Société and sits on the Science Committee of Observatoire Jeunes et Société. An alumnus of the Doctoral School of Central Europe, he also holds a Ph.D. in sociology from Université Laval. Vultur's main interest is the study of democratic transitions and the new work dynamics in Western societies. He is currently pursuing research on the relationship to work of young school leavers, the role of educational streams in vocational integration and integration of the "digital generation" into the New Economy. Mircea Vultur has authored book sections and papers for trade journals. In fall 2002, Université

Laval Press will publish his book on the transformation of identity and work ethics within the East European transition to democracy in its *Sociologie contemporaine* series.

Loïc Wacquant is Professor of Sociology at the University of California, Berkeley, and Researcher at the Centre de Sociologie européenne du Collège de France. His work deals with comparative urban inequality, racial domination, imprisonment, violence and the body, and social theory. A MacArthur Prize Fellow, he has been a visiting professor in Rio de Janeiro, Paris, Los Angeles and New York. His books include *An Invitation to Reflexive Sociology* (with Pierre Bourdieu) Seuil, 1992, *Prisons of Poverty* Raison d'Agir, 2000 (translated into twelve languages), *Punir Os Pobres, Corps et âme. Carnets ethnographiques dun apprenti-boxeur*, Agues, 2000 and Simbiosi mortale. He is a regular contributor to *Le Monde diplomatique* and editor of the international journal Ethnography.

Min Zhou is Professor of Sociology and Chair of Asian Amer-ican Studies Interdepartmental Degree Program at the University of California, Los Angeles. Her main areas of research are immigration and immigrant adaptation; ethnic and racial relations; Asian Americans; ethnic entrepreneurship; the community; and urban sociology. She is author of *Chinatown: The Socioeconomic Potential of an Urban Enclave* (Temple University Press, 1992); co-author of *Growing up American: How Vietnamese Children Adapt to Life in the United States* (Russell Sage Foundation Press, 1998); and co-editor of *Contemporary Asian America* (New York University Press, 2000).

Julia A. Zubok, Ph.D. in Sociology, Senior Researcher in the Centre for Sociology of Youth in the Institute of Socio-Political Research of the Russian Academy of Sciences. Her main interest is the dialectic of social integration and exclusion of young people in risk society. Her last publication was "*Youth in Risk Society*" (2001 in Russian).

INTERNATIONAL COMPARATIVE SOCIAL STUDIES

ISSN 1568-4474

1. H.T. WILSON, *Bureaucratic Representation*. Civil Servants and the Future of Capitalist Democracies. 2001. ISBN 90 04 12194 3
2. J. RATH, *Western Europe and its Islam*. 2001. ISBN 90 04 12192 7
3. S. INAYATULLAH, *Understanding Sarkar*. The Indian Episteme, Macrohistory and Transformative Knowledge. 2002. ISBN 90 04 12193 5 (hardcover) ISBN 90 04 12842 5 (paperback)
4. J. GELISSEN, *Worlds of Welfare, Worlds of Consent?* Public Opinion on the Welfare State. 2002. ISBN 9004 12457 8
5. H.T. WILSON, *Capitalism after Postmodernism*. Neo-Conservatism, Legitimacy, and the Theory of Public Capital. 2002. ISBN 9004 12458 6
6. L. ROULLEAU-BERGER, *Youth and Work in the Post-Industrial City of North America and Europe*. With an Epilogue by Saskia Sassen. 2003. ISBN 9004 12533 7